Samson Raphael Hirsch's Religious Universalism *and the* German-Jewish Quest *for* Emancipation

---

Moshe Y. Miller

The University of Alabama Press
Tuscaloosa

The University of Alabama Press
Tuscaloosa, Alabama 35487-0380
uapress.ua.edu

Typeface: Adobe Caslon

Cover image: Samson Raphael Hirsch, undated;
the National Library of Israel.
Cover design: Lori Lynch

Cataloging-in-Publication data is available from the
Library of Congress.
ISBN: 978-0-8173-2183-3 (cloth)
ISBN: 978-0-8173-6129-7 (paper)
E-ISBN: 978-0-8173-9485-1

Samson Raphael Hirsch's Religious Universalism *and the* German-Jewish Quest *for* Emancipation

For my dear wife, Aviva

> A woman of valor, who can find?
> Far beyond pearls is her value.
> —Proverbs 31:10

This does not mean that it is impossible to find her [the woman of valor], but that few are those who do find her . . .
He who *does* merit to find her, how fortunate is he and his lot [in life]!
—Commentary of Rabbi Menahem ha-Meiri to Proverbs 31:10

Contents

Acknowledgments

The present work benefited enormously from the guidance of mentors at the Bernard Revel Graduate School of Yeshiva University; they helped make this book a reality. I would therefore like to thank (in alphabetical order) Professors David Berger, Judith Bleich, and Jess Olson. Dr. Berger, formerly the dean of the Bernard Revel Graduate School of Yeshiva University, got me started in the field of Jewish Studies many years ago and provided guidance every step of the way. Thankfully, I have achieved a degree of success that has exceeded my early expectations. Dr. Berger's commitment to rigorous interrogation of primary sources and meticulous examination of secondary sources has served as a model for my own research. Likewise, his commitment to a sensitive reading of rabbinic sources that may present ethical challenges has informed the central thesis of this book.

Dr. Bleich, a professor of Jewish history at Touro University, was my first teacher in the field of Jewish studies and remains my primary mentor in the field to the present day. She has also been enormously supportive of this project as well as my entire career in academia. Her dedication to my success exceeds that expected of any academic mentor. Dr. Olson, whose knowledge of the field I was researching serves as an example to which I aspire, was extremely helpful in getting me to structure this book in a manner that is in keeping with current academic monographs in this field. He also pointed out strengths and weaknesses of my arguments that helped me formulate them more persuasively. His support and encouragement of this project have helped me reach this point.

I am grateful to Professor David Ellenson for his support of my research. It was his 1990 book, *Rabbi Esriel Hildesheimer and the Creation of a Modern Jewish Orthodoxy*, published by the University of Alabama Press, that inspired me to pursue a career in Jewish studies. Dr. Ellenson's fastidious scholarship and integrated interdisciplinary methodology in the study of history and religion remain a model for my own scholarship.

I would like to take this opportunity to thank Professor Ross Zucker, my undergraduate academic mentor in the field of political science, who has never ceased to be a source of support and inspiration in of all of my academic endeavors, despite our often-vigorous disagreements. Discussions with Professors Gershon Bacon, Alan Brill, Joshua Karlip, Shnayer Z. Leiman, and David Shatz, as well as with my colleague Tania Tulcin, have been very helpful. Exchanges with students in my classes The Life and Works of Rabbi Samson Raphael Hirsch and Readings in Rav Hirsch—both at Lander College for Women—have helped me sharpen some of my arguments, and I thank them for their thoughtful remarks. It goes without saying that none of these parties are responsible for any of this work's errors or shortcomings, for which I take sole responsibility.

Librarians at the Mendel Gottesman Library of Yeshiva University, particularly Zvi Erenyi and Carla Hanauer, have been crucial to this project. I would also like to single out the library's former interlibrary loan specialist, Mary Ann Linahan, for her help in obtaining items for me that would have otherwise involved extensive trips. The librarians of two campuses of Touro University, Irene Cherry, Tova Friedman, and David B. Levy, deserve notable mention due to their help in obtaining various books for me. Dr. Levy's encyclopedic knowledge and warm friendship have enriched this book immeasurably.

I would like to thank Daniel Waterman, editor-in-chief of the University of Alabama Press, for the unwavering support he has given to this project. I would also like to thank the assistant managing editor, Joanna Jacobs, and my copyeditor, Irina du Quenoy, for their dedication to my manuscript and for the patience they have shown me during the editing process.

A project of this nature could not have been completed without the constant support of family. I thank my in-laws, Jay and Lorraine Hill, for their support. I thank my parents, Reuven and Chava Miller, for all they have done for me: their dedication to our family has been far beyond the call of duty, and it is no exaggeration to say that this book could not have been written without their help. My sister, Sara, has always been there to help, especially with readying this book for publication, and I thank her for her dedication. I wish to thank my children, Chana Serka, Naomi, Yael, Zevi, and Dina, for putting up with my "being so busy with work."

Finally, I thank my dear wife, Aviva, without whose constant support this book would still be on page one. The saying of Rabbi Akiva, "What's mine is hers," really applies here in its fullest sense. It is to her that I dedicate this book.

Please note that in this book, the first time a rabbi's name is mentioned, the title "Rabbi" is employed. In subsequent references to that individual, this title may be dropped. No disrespect is intended.

Introduction

The French Revolution had drastic consequences for the course of European Jewish life. Jewish communities, which had previously been self-governing autonomous units, entered into the civic life of the countries in which they were situated.[1] There have been numerous studies about the impact these changes had on the emergence of new forms of Jewish identity and modern Jewish religious movements, such as Reform Judaism, the Positive-Historical school (which later developed into Conservative Judaism), Neo-Orthodoxy, and Ultra-Orthodoxy.[2] One area that is largely overlooked in these studies is the change in how Jews who belonged to the Neo-Orthodox movement began to view their non-Jewish neighbors. This change in particular is worthy of further examination as the Neo-Orthodox was the only group that consciously regarded itself as a vanguard in the defense of tradition against the movements situated to its religious left that advocated reforms to Jewish practice and belief that the Neo-Orthodox considered an unpardonable departure from classical Judaism, and yet simultaneously consciously embraced those aspects of modernity that it regarded as desirable and not interfering with the preservation of tradition. By contrast, the Ultra-Orthodox, although sharing with the Neo-Orthodox a self-perception as standing in the breach against reforms to Judaism, opposed most forms of adaptation to the changed historical circumstances and cultural climate. Thus, there are no substantial revisions in the image of the non-Jew fostered by the Ultra-Orthodox that could be distinguished from what is found in premodern traditional Jewish society. Both traditionalist groups did, however, grapple with how to relate to non-Orthodox Jews, and this issue has been the subject of several studies.[3] There is thus a lacuna in existing scholarship with respect to the Neo-Orthodox camp's perception of non-Jews and, particularly, the religion most European gentiles practiced, Christianity.

This book will demonstrate that the views of Christianity that developed in this school during the nineteenth century were a direct outgrowth of the developing views of German rabbis concerning the worth and value of non-Jews.

It further argues and that these views were influenced by the desire to demonstrate that Judaism's humanistic values were in no way inferior to Enlightenment and post-Enlightenment European values. The Reform movement consciously adopted the values of Enlightenment, as well as those of Romanticism, and advocated doctrinal and ritual changes on the basis of these values. By contrast, the Neo-Orthodox resisted attempts at ritual or doctrinal changes and countenanced only those changes its leaders regarded as falling outside the domain of halacha (Jewish law), such as matters relating to decorum and aesthetics. Of all the leaders in this camp, Samson Raphael Hirsch was the staunchest advocate for making one's ideological posture a litmus test for acceptance as a rabbi. The best-known case of this is his attack on the Breslau Theological Seminary, founded by Zechariah Frankel in 1854. Hirsch demanded a formal declaration from Frankel that he believed—and therefore taught his students—that not only the Written Law but the Oral Law was revealed in its entirety on Mount Sinai.[4] When Frankel ignored this call, Hirsch declared the Breslau Seminary off limits to Orthodox Jews.[5] Yet, the same Hirsch incorporated a deeply humanistic attitude toward non-Jews that cannot be seen as merely a reformulation of the views found in rabbinic texts on this issue. Consonant with his opposition to the Breslau seminary, Hirsch opposed any form of Wissenschaft employed in the elucidation of rabbinic texts, even when such an endeavor was carried out by the strictly Orthodox rabbi David Zvi Hoffmann.[6] Therefore, Hirsch would not have been open—or so it would appear—to the historical contextualization of anti-gentile rabbinic texts. A different understanding of his religious humanism must therefore be sought.

There has long been a debate about the extent to which Hirsch was indebted to the Haskalah, the modernizing Jewish movement that began in Berlin in the mid-eighteenth century. Noah Rosenbloom developed one of the most extreme formulations of the Hirsch-as-maskil thesis. According to Rosenbloom, Hirsch's family were maskilim (meaning "adherents of the Haskalah"), he was given a maskilic education, and his own worldview is remarkably similar to that of eighteenth-century maskilim. Like them, Hirsch was a weak talmudist but a superior biblical scholar and, like them, he wished to reform Jewish life in keeping with Haskalah ideals. If we accept this thesis, the present study is superfluous. Hirsch's "progressive" views concerning non-Jews is not a problem waiting for a solution. Hirsch, according to this view, developed his views because he was enamored of German culture and found traditional Jewish society lacking in comparison to European society. He preached universalism not because the canonical rabbinic texts—such as the Talmud and halachic codes—preached universalism but because universalism was a Haskalah ideal and Hirsch was a maskil.

Leading scholars of German Orthodoxy, such as Mordechai Breuer, Shnayer Leiman, and Matthias Morgenstern, have rejected Rosenbloom's thesis. However, one of the great Hirsch scholars of our time, Michah Gottlieb, argues in a recent book for a modified version of the Rosenbloom thesis. Many of the flaws of Rosenbloom's methodology do not apply to Gottlieb's arguments. Yet, several assertions proposed by Gottlieb may be challenged. Further analysis will provide more opportunity to discuss the views of Rosenbloom and Gottlieb. (These matters are examined in chapter 8.) Once the issues with their positions have been presented, the reader will understand why accounting for Hirsch's universalism requires a new approach, one that has not previously been presented systematically.

The other leaders of Neo-Orthodoxy, such as Hirsch's teacher Rabbi Jacob Ettlinger (1798–1871) and his colleague Rabbi Esriel Hildesheimer (1820–1899), continued to employ traditional rabbinic language when referring to gentiles in their Hebrew writings but nevertheless incorporated into their worldview the more liberal view of non-Jews that was shared by all sectors of nineteenth-century German Jewry. For these rabbis, to whom the very notion that Judaism preaches an inferior morality to that of Christianity or of Western civilization more generally was unthinkable, rabbinic texts that do seem to advocate certain forms of discrimination against non-Jews were understood to be inapplicable in modern times.

The quest for emancipation and the battle for the religious allegiances of German Jews served to ensure that the anti-gentile discrimination accepted by most medieval authorities would be rejected as irrelevant by the religious leaders of nineteenth-century German Orthodoxy. As German Orthodox leaders directed their attention to the struggle with Reform, the "enemy" of the Torah could no longer be, as it had been for many centuries of Diaspora life, the gentile nations. As "heretical" Jews were openly identified as "the opposition" to the traditional Jewish way of life, an opening developed for a reappraisal of the value and worth of non-Jews. Adam Ferziger's pioneering study of hierarchical models of German Orthodoxy's relationship to the non-Orthodox is thus an essential corollary to the present study.[7]

Another essential consideration for the proper understanding of the views of Orthodox rabbis examined here is the German critique of Jewish morality. Nineteenth-century German Jews faced an onslaught of attacks alleging Judaism's various deficiencies. Even opponents of anti-Jewish prejudice, such as Friedrich Schleiermacher, expressed critiques of Judaism's alleged tribal morality. German-Jewish religious leaders responded by affirming that Judaism preaches a genuinely universalist ethic and that the welfare of all of mankind falls under its purview.

While Reform leaders were comfortable asserting that seemingly exclusionary biblical or rabbinic passages are mere relics of the ancient times in which they were written, the German Orthodox had no such option. For them, the entirety of the Torah—the Scriptures and their rabbinic interpretation—was divinely revealed and thus not subject to historical contextualization. However, harsh statements about gentiles found in rabbinic literature were not directly referred to, with the implicit assumption that these texts were inapplicable to Christians since their original context was anti-pagan, not anti-gentile qua gentile.[8] Thus, for example, the German Orthodox do not cite the anti-gentile passages in places where we would expect their citation, such as where earlier authorities do cite them.[9] Still, this point about the original context of these passages and their contemporary inapplicability is not stated explicitly by these rabbis.[10]

It must be stressed that the tolerant views regarding other religions (specifically Christianity) expressed by the German Orthodox rabbis generally fall into the category of what some contemporary scholars of religious thought call the "inclusivist" approach, not the "pluralist" approach.[11] That is, none of these rabbis affirmed the view that all religions are equally true as no one religion can claim that it has access to more than partial truth, which is the view of twenty-first-century religious pluralists (as described by Alan Brill). Rather, they affirmed the view that the monotheistic religions that sprang from Judaism (Christianity and Islam) contain many fundamental Jewish truths and that they offer their adherents a path toward salvation. It is true that this view used to be known as "pluralism," since it advocated for followers of each faith to follow their own traditions and for one group to not denigrate the other; today, however, some scholars have labeled it as "inclusivism," a view I share, interpreting it as less liberal than both universalism (which affirms a universal truth equally accessible to all of mankind and is not focused on divine revelation as the key to Truth) and pluralism.

The inclusivist tradition has ample precedent in rabbinic writings, from the Talmudic period through the Middle Ages and the Early Modern period. Eugene Korn has recently clarified the tolerant, inclusivist position that he believes should serve as a model for contemporary Jewish thinkers. Korn notes that religions that preach a universal theological Truth, the acceptance of which provides salvation, have the potential to become rather intolerant because they can insist that all humans subscribe to their teachings; at worst, they may persecute those who refuse to accept their faith. On the other hand, religions that preach doctrines relevant only to their own adherents may display indifference or even hostility to those outside their faith community, whom, the particularists allege, God deems to be inferior beings whose lives are meaningless, or possibly even enemies of God's "chosen ones." Judaism is not a universal religion in the sense outlined by Korn, since it does not expect all humans to become Jewish, nor does it limit salvation to those who do so. However, Judaism *can* be particularist, to the point of fostering hostility to "the goyim," whose fate is of no particular interest to the Chosen People, whose Torah's primary purpose is to foster a close relationship between God and Jews. Korn argues that this latter vision must be rejected by contemporary Jews and demonstrates how a more inclusivist and humanistic interpretation of Judaism can be developed strictly on the basis of classical Jewish texts.[12] The present book examines Orthodox rabbis who did just this.

Yet, the previously outlined particularist view was the perception of Judaism that non-Jewish critics of alleged Jewish tribalism imputed to all Jews. Hirsch and his colleagues insisted that Judaism does *not* demand that all humans accept its doctrines or rituals, as other religions can offer paths to salvation. Further, they stressed that Judaism is deeply concerned about the welfare of all humanity; the raison d'être of Judaism is to be a source of blessing to all humanity. Jews and non-Jews are to work concomitantly to advance the spiritual development of the world, together making it a suitable dwelling for the divine presence. The Jewish people, as the "priestly nation," is to live by a universalistic ethic and to display deep sensitivity to the physical and spiritual welfare of all humans, whom God values equally.

It should thus be clear at the outset that the rabbis examined in this book did not say or write anything that was truly revolutionary. Rather, they highlighted and emphasized currents of religious tolerance that had previously been either neglected or marginalized.[13] In so doing, they articulated a vision of Judaism and Jewish self-identity that, though traditionalist, bore the unmistakable imprint of modernity.

"Modernity," here, means—to quote David Ellenson's assessment of Jacob Katz's seminal treatment of the issue—the emergence of a mindset that led to "the creation of a Jew who turned to the non-Jewish world for his intellectual values," and who then reformulated his own values as part of a process of internalizing the norms of broader Western society.[14] "Traditionalist," here, refers to a mindset that regards itself as deriving moral and ethical values exclusively from what classical religious texts say and is thus disinterested in norms considered extraneous to the Jewish tradition. One can, of course, be simultaneously influenced by both modernity and traditionalism—as the primary subjects of this book were. But the Neo-Orthodox were still more traditional than modern in that they regarded the divinely revealed Torah as the only authoritative source of values, even as their interpretation of the Torah displayed a sensitivity to the sensibilities of post-Enlightenment Europeans.

The spirit of modernity evinced by the rabbis studied here is one of the most "modern" features of German Neo-Orthodoxy, and properly understanding it will prove to be critical to understanding the development of Orthodox Judaism in the modern world and, more generally, how religious groups utilize canonical texts to selectively endorse certain features of modernity while shunning others. This book will show that post-Enlightenment humanism was not only not shunned; it was embraced, at least in Hirsch's writings, as a key component of classical Judaism. Though perhaps somewhat dormant, this humanism is nevertheless to be regarded as *having been created by Judaism*. The Torah—so argued Hirsch—taught the Western world to value human dignity and to do so from the perspective of a universal ethic. What could have been denounced as an alien system of values was instead co-opted as a *Jewish* contribution to human progress.

This study of the views of German Orthodox rabbinical leaders sheds light not only on the local context of nineteenth century Christian-Jewish relations in Germany but also on broader issues of religious tolerance. The question of what Judaism says about non-Jews and their religion(s) is just as relevant now as it was one hundred and fifty years ago. Anti-Semites now have full recourse to many unpleasant remarks about non-Jews and Christianity that are found in certain Jewish texts, and many of these remarks have been posted on the internet. A study of the way in which rabbis who were wholeheartedly devoted to Jewish tradition grappled with these texts and how they formulated inclusivist positions is long overdue.[15] Hopefully, this study will encourage others to examine other facets of this important issue that are not treated here.

Finally, a word on objectivity. William Kolbrener has recently observed that "all scholarship is personal—that academic inquiry is never strictly 'objective.'" The insistence on objectivity, he avers, is "a fussy remnant of an older scholarship."[16] This observation applies to the present work as well. Although I have endeavored to present the figures herein examined dispassionately and in their historical context, the project grew out of an existential need. The acceptance of the eternally binding character of the rabbinic tradition, combined with the conviction—engendered by the ethos with which my pious and compassionate parents imbued me—of the intrinsic worth of every single human being regardless of race, nationality, or religion, turned me to the writings of S. R. Hirsch at a young age. The attempt to understand how he reconciled his humanistic convictions with the rabbinic tradition—to whose defense he devoted his entire career—served as a model for my own quest to properly interrogate the sources pertaining to this issue. It is my hope that my effort has been at least partially successful.

1

The Narrative of German-Jewish Cultural Engagement

Gershom Scholem (1897–1982), the pioneering historian of Jewish mysticism, was born in Germany at the end of the nineteenth century. Though his work on Kabbalah was hailed for its dispassionate treatment of a previously taboo subject, Scholem's writings about the "one-sided love affair" of German Jews with Germany were marked by a polemical style uncharacteristic of his other work. For example, Scholem wrote that "the Jews spoke to themselves, not to say that they outshouted themselves."[1] In a 1966 essay, Scholem used terms like "self-deception," "ecstatic illusion of being at home," and "wish fulfillment" and insisted that "the love affair of the Jews and the Germans remained one-sided and unreciprocated." In his view, the German Jews of the generations preceding the Holocaust were possessed of a naïveté that "taints almost everything they wrote about the position of the Jews in the German world of ideas."[2] This line of argument fundamentally asserts that the notion of a "German-Jewish symbiosis" is a flagrant deception without any connection to reality, a view shared by some contemporary writers such as David Aberbach and Enzo Traverso.

Scholem's charge was not new. The view that the German-Jewish attempt to integrate into German society was an exercise in futility had already been promulgated by a traditionalist Orthodox rabbi in Lithuania in the early twentieth century. A well-known passage penned by Rabbi Meir Simcha of Dvinsk (1843–1926), a leading rabbinic figure of East European Orthodoxy, stated that German-Jewish Reformers were deluding themselves into thinking that they would achieve tranquility. On the contrary, he predicted that they would never find comfort in Germany but instead would be uprooted from the very place they naively considered the new Jerusalem. To be sure, Rabbi Simcha's point was not that the anticipation felt by German Jews for reciprocation on the part of German Christians to their attempts at gaining acceptance was an illusion. Rather, he was asserting that divine providence would never allow for such a project to be successful. God does not want Jews to assimilate, so He will send a stormy wind from the very center of Jewish assimilation to uproot those Jews and place them in a land where they know well that they are foreigners.[3]

But this assertion was not as far from Scholem's as one might think. Although Scholem was focused specifically on Germany, underlying his thesis was the Zionist school of Jewish historiography, to which he fully belonged.[4] This school held that Jews could never truly be comfortable in a "foreign" land; Germany was the case study, as it were, that "proved" Scholem's preconceived view. Yet this view, that German Jews were participants in an unrequited love affair with (Christian) Germans that unsurprisingly ended in catastrophe, is both overly simplistic and fails to account for the unique niche of German Orthodoxy.

Other writers, less overtly partisan, have made arguments reminiscent of Scholem's. Amos Elon's book, *The Pity of It All: A History of Jews in Germany, 1743–1933*, carries a title that betrays the author's view concerning this question. Indeed, the much-debated *Sonderweg* thesis regarding Germany's unique path to modernity is inextricably linked with the question of Jewish attempts to be accepted in Germany.[5] If Germany was uniquely hospitable to antidemocratic and antihumanitarian forces for many years prior to World War II, then it ought not surprise us that the most visible minority group's attempts to be treated equitably would ultimately be met with rejection, of whatever magnitude.

What the present book attempts to do is provide a corrective to many of the assumptions underlying these studies. The argument is here presented that German Jews, of whatever denomination, who attempted to gain civic equality—emancipation—were not seeking assimilation and that their relationship with German culture was not one-sided. More than three decades ago, Mordechai Breuer authored a pathbreaking study of German-Jewish Orthodoxy, a sector of the population that engaged in a certain degree of integration but decidedly not assimilation. (Reform Jews did not desire total assimilation, but the degree to which they modified Jewish practice and beliefs in keeping with contemporary ethos and sensibilities far exceeded the "assimilatory" tendencies of their Orthodox co-religionists.) Breuer demonstrated the careful balance between the forces of tradition and assimilation that this community needed to maintain. The present study picks up where

Breuer left off in highlighting a hitherto underexplored facet of German Orthodoxy, one which demonstrates the existence of a reciprocal relationship with German society.

Although the quest for emancipation was ubiquitous among German Jewry, the Orthodox sector of the community was presented with a unique challenge. Orthodox Judaism accepted the binding authority of not only the Bible but of the rabbinic tradition, whose main repository is the Talmud. However, as noted by George Kohler, the charge that the Talmud was anti-gentile was "as old as the Talmud itself." The rabbinic tradition, as expressed in the Talmud, "seems to have caused suspicion among non-Jews . . . [thereby producing] a vast amount of anti-talmudic literature written by anti-Semites throughout the centuries."[6] If the charge was true, then German Orthodoxy was two-faced for insisting on civic equality while revering texts that deny human rights to non-Jews. It was unthinkable for this charge to remain unanswered and, thanks to Orthodoxy's leading spokesman, Rabbi Samson Raphael Hirsch (1808–88), it did not.

Hirsch's childhood coincided with the onset of the emancipation of German Jewry: the second decade of the nineteenth century. (The Prussian Emancipation Edict was issued by King Frederick William III on March 11, 1812.) But as that emancipation was not complete until the mature part of Hirsch's career, with the creation of the Second German Reich in 1871—well after he had already developed a coherent and thorough ideology of Orthodoxy in the modern world—his writings reflect the desire to see emancipation reach its completion and to demonstrate that its recipients were indeed worthy of it. He was fully conscious of the charges that had been leveled for centuries against rabbinic Judaism concerning its alleged tribalism, and his pronouncements pertaining to the universalism of Judaism must be read in that context. Nevertheless, as with everything else he wrote, Hirsch was thoroughly convinced that the views he advanced were identical to those of the talmudic rabbis themselves; there is no possibility of treating Hirsch's views as mere apologetics expressed for external consumption.

A stark illustration of this point is Hirsch's assertion, expressed with much certitude, that the talmudic rabbis would surely recite a blessing thanking God for granting wisdom to Friedrich von Schiller (1759–1805).[7] Such a claim would strike Hirsch's rabbinic predecessors, as well as his East European contemporaries and their successors in the following generations (until the present day!)—who demonstrated no interest in non-Jewish poetry, and who certainly saw no religious value in it—as odd, at the very least. But the hortatory and idealistic style of the speech leave little doubt that this was Hirsch's sincerely held view, as will be demonstrated.

It was not only Hirsch who evinced a universalistic ethos. Other Orthodox rabbis such as Isaac Bernays (1792–1849), Jacob Ettlinger (1798–1871), Esriel Hildesheimer (1820–99), Marcus Lehmann (1831–90), David Zvi Hoffmann (1843–1921), and Marcus Horovitz (1844–1910) similarly affirmed the universalism of Judaism's ethic and stressed that pious Christians are regarded as the spiritual fellows of Jews. With the exception of Lehmann, though, these rabbis authored classical rabbinic works, generally in the Hebrew language, which was not the ideal forum for the expression of such sentiments. Lehmann, who edited a newspaper intended for a wide readership, has been characterized as "Orthodoxy's propagandist," who, like Hirsch, offered programatic statements (in German) about Orthodoxy's position on contemporary issues. He too stressed the universalism of Judaism's ethic and its religious tolerance, and he enthusiastically welcomed emancipation.[8]

Orthodox rabbis such as Hirsch and Lehmann were not consciously striving to achieve the sort of symbiosis that Scholem would later characterize as one-sided. However, they believed that Jewish engagement with German culture would be enriching to the Judaism of its participants—and to broader German society. It was thus inevitable that some sort of cultural partnership would emerge from these endeavors. These rabbis were aware of the charges that Judaism preached a tribalistic ethos, and they were determined to disprove them. As champions of emancipation, they found the notion that Jews preach a dual system of ethics to be unconscionable. They thus subtly advanced the causes of Jewish rights and cultural engagement via their proclamations, often in the midst of a culture that, though not reciprocating their universalistic humanism, supported the cause of Jewish emancipation. The present study situates their views within this context.

It has sometimes been suggested that more important than ideological positions of the intelligentsia, who may not be representative of the common people, are the daily routines of the average person. Some of the most important scholarship on German Jewry, such as Marion Kaplan's pioneering studies of the daily lives of German Jews, certainly stress the social history of German Jewry more than their intellectual history.[9] This volume is predicated on the view that only by examining how rabbinic leaders steeped in talmudic culture and committed to preserving the authority of rabbinic Judaism—particularly in the face of strident detractors among their coreligionists—grappled with texts that were regarded rather differently in earlier centuries can the symbiotic nature of nineteenth-century Orthodox Judaism in Germany truly emerge. Day-to-day interactions with German Christians no doubt impacted the outlook of German-Orthodox Jews; however, the only way to quantify and analyze the unique response to modernity produced by this movement is to closely examine the legacy it bequeathed to the future—in the form of the views of its rabbinic leaders, particularly the greatest writer and thinker among them, Samson Raphael Hirsch. These views represent how *Orthodox Judaism* adapted to its environs via a reframing of the position of the non-Jew in the Jewish schema. (The twentieth century saw a similar adaptation within Orthodoxy with respect to the position of women.)

Hirsch was perfectly positioned to present Orthodoxy's case for emancipation. In his solitary foray outside of German lands, as chief rabbi of Moravia from 1847 to 1851, he expressly did so.[10] However, during his tenure in the German rabbinical positions that he held, Hirsch made the case for emancipation far more subtly. His writings are replete with humanistic interpretations of Judaism, and his universalistic ethic is consistent. In fact, there has probably not been another traditionalist rabbi with broad influence in the Jewish community, prior or subsequent to Hirsch, who has been as consistent in underscoring the universalistic ethos at the core of Judaism's Weltanschauung.[11]

The present study provides substantive evidentiary basis for this assertion and endeavors to contextualize Hirsch's views, as well as the precedents for them. However, it would be impossible to understand the innovative aspects of Hirsch's views without a proper understanding of rabbinic views of non-Jews and, particularly, of Christianity from the centuries preceding Hirsch's. While a thorough examination of rabbinic views of non-Jews is beyond the scope of the present work—though some salient points will emerge over the course of our analysis—the next chapter presents the trajectory of rabbinic views of Christianity in the medieval and early modern periods, the precedents that Hirsch would of necessity utilize, as an Orthodox rabbi committed to the integrity of Jewish tradition.

2

Rabbinic Views of Christianity from the Late Middle Ages until the Nineteenth Century

Discussions of Christianity in Rabbinic Literature

The Jewish tradition was not monolithic with respect to the value and role of Christianity in God's scheme for the world. Although the context of the Middle Ages was not conducive to a sober and objective assessment of the contribution made by Christianity to non-Jewish spirituality, some medieval rabbis did express views concerning this matter that were more fully developed in later centuries. The first hurdle to overcome was halachic: Christianity seemed to run afoul of the proscription against *avodah zarah*, often loosely but imprecisely translated as idolatry.[1]

Indeed, most medieval rabbinic authorities tended to classify Christianity as falling within the parameters of standard forms of avodah zarah in their discussions of the latter topic. *Avodah zarah*, lit., "foreign worship" (hereafter: AZ), has been more aptly defined by David Berger as "the formal recognition or worship as God of an entity that is in fact not God."[2] Such being the case, the Christian worship of Jesus of Nazareth as the Son of God and one of three persons that constitute the one God in the Trinitarian formulation, was regarded by most medieval authorities as—formally speaking—no different from the pre-Christian pagan worship of images that were seen as representing or, in some cases, constituting, the divinity. The fact that the pagans made no claim to a monotheistic worldview while medieval Christians consistently emphasized this claim was not seen as fundamentally altering the essence of Christian belief and worship, namely, that it involved the belief in, and worship of, a being (Jesus) as God who was not, in fact, God.

Although Maimonides is the only medieval authority who explicitly categorized Christians as *ovdei avodah zarah* (worshippers of AZ) whose halachic status is the same as that of all idolaters, the majority of medieval authorities implicitly concurred with the view that Christians were *ovdei avodah zarah*, although they tended to distinguish between Christians and the ancient pagans with respect to the degree to which the anti-idolatry legislation of the Talmud remained in effect concering Christians.[3] The evaluation of Christians as worshippers of AZ was not limited to halachic works but was found throughout medieval works of liturgical poetry (piyyut), polemical works, and other genres of writings.[4]

The only authority to explicitly deny that Christians were to be considered worshippers of AZ in any respect was the late thirteenth-century Provencal scholar Rabbi Menahem ha-Meiri (1249–1316).[5] Nevertheless, several other medieval Ashkenazic authorities formulated a statement that served as the "nucleus of a theory of religious tolerance."[6] This statement, first recorded in the glosses of twelfth-century Tosafists, later repeated by Rabbenu Asher (1250–1327) and Rabbenu Yeruham (1290–1350) (with a modified text), asserted that it would not be forbidden for a Jew to cause a *Christian* to make an oath on the occasion of some profitable business venture, despite the Talmudic proscription on any action taken by a Jew that might cause a *pagan* to make such an oath.[7] A Christian is not a pagan from the point of view of Jewish law.

The difference, asserted the Tosafists, was that Christians swear by their saints but do not attribute divinity to them. Furthermore, although they refer to "the name of Heaven" and have in mind "something else" (or "Jesus," in some versions of this passage), they do not explicitly cite the name of any pagan deity and, furthermore, their ultimate intention is directed toward "the Maker of heaven and earth." This passage notes that although these Christians are indeed "associating" the name of Heaven with something else, it is not forbidden to cause others to make such association, and there is no violation of "not placing a stumbling block before the blind" here because "non-Jews are not forbidden to do such an act."[8] (In Rabbi Yeruham's version the text reads: "Non-Jews are not commanded to avoid association" [*b'nei noah lo huzharu al ha-shittuf*]).[9]

This statement was sufficiently ambiguous as to give rise to an entire literature devoted to decoding its meaning. The medieval authorities who cited it did not necessarily draw the conclusion from it that Christians were entirely excluded from the category of worshippers of AZ, although this is precisely the interpretation of this statement that became popular among a number of prominent seventeenth- and eighteenth-century rabbis. Several authorities from this later period vigorously denied that such a meaning could possibly be read into the statement, which coaxed their more liberal colleagues to elaborate on the basis for how such a reading could be made and, more importantly, how such a view could be justified on legal grounds. As already noted, AZ, at least as far as Jews are concerned, was defined as the worship of any being other than God, and therefore the Christian view of Jesus as fully human and fully divine would, as a matter of course, be deemed AZ for Jews. On what basis, asked the opponents of the liberal reading of the Tosafist statement, could the parameters of AZ be defined differently for Jews and non-Jews? The question was all the more important since the prohibition of AZ is one of the Seven Noahide Laws that are incumbent upon all of mankind.[10] The advocates of the liberal reading of the statement were at pains to justify a distinction.

It may be suggested that in doing so, they were simultaneously, even if only subconsciously, engaged in the pursuit of religious tolerance. This is because a simple reading of the Talmudic sources gives no hint that the laws of AZ are different for Jews and for gentiles. This is precisely the point brought out by perhaps the most famous opponent of the liberal interpretation of the Tosafists' statement, Rabbi Samuel Landau (d. 1834) (son of the author of the responsa collection *Noda bi-Yehudah*), whose remarks are contained in that work:

> I have toiled but have not found this assertion [that *shittuf* is permissible for gentiles] in either of the Talmuds, the Babylonian and Jerusalemite, nor in the words of any of the medieval scholars. If it were true, Maimonides ought to have codified this in the Laws of Kings, namely, that gentiles are not proscribed from AZ of *shittuf*. Why did he omit this law? Furthermore, it is verifiable that there is no distinction in [the laws of] AZ worship between a Jew and a gentile, as it is an explicit *beraita* in Tractate *Sanhedrin* 56b: "when it comes to AZ, anything for which a Jewish court would administer the death penalty [to a Jew], a gentile is proscribed from," and so too has Maimonides codified . . .[11]

Those early modern authorities who read into the Tosafists' statement an assertion that Christianity was sufficiently monotheistic for gentiles were actively engaged in the promotion of religious tolerance by developing creative ways for Christian Trinitarian worship to be excluded from the category of AZ. To be sure, this does not mean that these authorities were purposively striving to work around the halachic sources solely in order to lend precedent to their view that Christians were not worshippers of AZ, out of some sense of calling to find leniency for Christianity in halacha. Rather, the preponderance of sources suggesting that Christianity is considered AZ, combined with the dearth of sources suggesting that this is not the case as far as non-Jews are concerned, meant that any halachist wishing to argue for the non-AZ status of Christianity had to do some far reaching.[12] That so many prominent halachists of the early modern period did just that is an indication of the value that religious tolerance played in their thinking, though there were arguably other considerations, such as economic concerns, at work as well.[13]

It must also be noted that those halachists who classified Christian Trinitarian worship as shittuf and therefore permissible for gentiles almost certainly had an imperfect understanding of the doctrine of the Trinity. The first halachist who *explicitly* classified Trinitarian worship as shittuf and thus permissible for non-Jews was Samuel ben Joseph, *dayan* of Cracow (d. 1699), in his *Olat Tamid*, first published in Amsterdam in 1681. In his glosses to *Shulhan Arukh Orah Hayyim* 156, which contains Rabbi Moses Isserles's codification of the principle that non-Jews are not proscribed from shittuf, Samuel comments, "This is [only] if they [gentiles] say that one [deity] is above the other, and do not detract from the unity of God. However, if they detract from the unity and say that there are two deities [equal in power], then it is considered *avodah zarah*, and even gentiles are proscribed from it."[14] Samuel clearly had the Trinity in mind when he referred to the view of one deity being "above the other," as in the concept of the Father and Son, with the understanding that the latter was subordinate to the former and therefore well within the confines of the shittuf that is permissible for gentiles.

Samuel's description does not match classical Christian doctrines regarding the Trinity, according to which the Godhead is conceived as being composed of three persons, of which the Son is the second. The Son was not created by the Father but was present at creation and constitutes the very essence of God as do the other two persons. The fact that halachists like Samuel found a way of categorizing Christian doctrine so that it fits within the confines of their understanding of the permissive shittuf category was a result of ignorance of classical Christian doctrine combined with a desire to find a way for Christians to be deemed monotheistic gentiles and thereby heirs to paradise.[15]

Two contemporaries of the author of *Olat Tamid* expressed similar views regarding Christianity, but they added positive attributes to Samuel's removal of the negative attribute of AZ. Rabbi Yair Hayyim Bacharach (1638–1702), author of the authoritative responsa collection *Havot Yair*, notes that contemporary gentiles (i.e., Christians) are not worshippers of AZ because gentiles are not proscribed from shittuf. Furthermore, Christians are excluded from all negative references to "goyim" in the Talmud and Codes since they believe in the Creator of heaven and earth and do not worship AZ.[16]

Rabbi Moses Rivkes of Vilna (1596–1671), in his glosses to the *Shulhan Arukh* known as *Be'er ha-Golah*, repeatedly stresses that the anti-gentile discrimination found in the Talmud and the Codes based on it was applicable only to ancient pagans but not to Christians, who shared many beliefs in common with Jews. Aside from the statement of the Tosafists that notes that Christian worship was directed, ultimately, to the Creator of heaven and earth, the primary text that Rivkes cites in support of his views is the work *Ma'asei Hashem* by Rabbi Eliezer Ashkenazi (1513–86). Ashkenazi had argued that the request made by Jews on Passover for God to pour out His wrath on "the nations that know Thee not" was meant to be taken literally, as a reference to ancient pagans who denied the One God.[17] Christians and Muslims, however, accept Him and are therefore not included in this Passover prayer.[18] While Ashkenazi was writing in a nonhalachic context, Rivkes took the idea one step further and used it to deny the applicability of Talmudic anti-gentile discrimination to his Christian contemporaries.

Rivkes's comments distinguishing between pagans and Christians with respect to discriminatory laws are found only in his glosses to the *Hoshen Mishpat* section of the *Shulhan Arukh*, which treats matters pertaining to monetary transactions. It would seem that there is a greater need for such a distinction in the *Yoreh Deah* section, which treats issues of idolatry directly, yet in that section Rivkes is silent about the contemporary applicability of the laws.

Rabbi David Zvi Hoffmann (1843–1921), suggests that this may have to do with the history of censorship in the different editions of the *Shulhan Arukh*. In Rivkes's hometown of Vilna, the editions of the *Yoreh Deah* section of the *Shulhan Arukh* in use around 1650 had not yet been altered by the Christian censors, and so the original terminological distinction between pagans ("ovdei elilim") and nonpagan gentiles ("goyim") remained intact, leaving no need to clarify to which sort of gentile the *Shulhan Arukh* referred. On the other hand, the edition of the *Hoshen Mishpat* section used in Vilna circa 1650 had been altered by the censors, which compelled Rivkes to clarify the intended "type" of non-Jew being discussed.[19] Whether or not one finds Hoffmann's explanation compelling, it is sufficient to stress here that Rivkes did indeed distinguish between pagans and Christians and that he may have had a sound basis for not doing so consistently.

Any overview of early modern halachists' attitudes toward Christianity would be remiss in not discussing the position of Rabbi Moses Isserles (1520–72), author of the glosses to the *Shulhan Arukh* presenting Ashkenazic practice, who is known as Rema, after his Hebrew initials. Rema codified the passage of the Tosafists that has been interpreted as permitting shittuf for gentiles and, following the text of Rabbi Yeruham, explicitly included the clause "non-Jews are not proscribed from shittuf."[20] Unlike the Tosafists, who issued their ruling in the context of making an oath, Rema (in his commentary to the *Tur* of Rabbi Jacob ben Asher) issued a halachic ruling that permits the sale of incense to Christians for religious worship on the same grounds that it is permissible to cause them to make an oath in the name of God with a Trinitarian understanding in mind, as Rema explained in his glosses to *Shulhan Arukh, Orah Hayyim* 156.[21]

Rema does not explain what these grounds are but Rabbi Shabetai ha-Kohen (known as Shakh [1621–62]) elaborates on this statement, explaining that just as acceptance of an oath was permitted due to the fact that contemporary gentiles only engage in shittuf but not outright AZ, so too selling them incense would be permitted for the same reason.[22] Thus, Rema clearly (though not explicitly) ruled that Christians are not to be considered worshippers of AZ and did not limit this ruling to the narrow case of accepting oaths. Had he done so, it could have been argued, as indeed it was by certain conservative halachists, that Christian Trinitarian worship was forbidden for gentiles and that only accepting oaths made in the name of the Trinity was allowed since no act of worship is performed when making an oath.

An important early nineteenth-century commentator to the *Shulhan Arukh* pointed out that although he agrees with those who interpret the Tosafists' words constrictively, this view cannot have been shared by Rema, who applied his principle to the allowance of the sale of incense to Christians.[23] The only question that remains is why Rema did not follow the lead of Meiri and apply his principle as to the nonidolatrous status of Christians across the board, thereby nullifying the relevance of most of the laws of idolatry that are found in the *Shulhan Arukh*.

Perhaps it was precisely Rema's concern for the possible unintended consequences of such a sweeping assertion—consequences that maskilic leaders in the late eighteenth and early nineteenth centuries explicitly drew, such as the view that Christians were to be excluded from rabbinic restrictions on social intercourse with gentiles—that inhibited him from applying his principle beyond the case of selling incense, a practice which was widely practiced despite the theoretical prohibition against it.

Although this concern did not deter Meiri from applying his theory of religious tolerance across the board, Rema, whose works were more widely circulated than Meiri's, had greater cause for concern about the unwarranted conclusions that some might draw from a sweeping ruling excluding Christians from the category of worshippers of AZ.[24] Nevertheless, the fact remains that Rema did clearly rule that Christian Trinitarian worship was a permissible act for non-Jews, which laid the groundwork for a broadening of this religious tolerance that would be found in the writings of later halachists who shared a commitment to a humanitarianism that included pious Christians within the orbit of those humans whose spiritual lives were meaningful and salvific.[25]

Although several important personalities in the development of a positive rabbinic assessment of Christianity have already been discussed, it should be noted that a disproportionate number of such authorities lived in the Germanic lands. Thus, Rabbi Bacharach lived in various Franco-Prussian lands throughout his life. Rabbi Jacob Emden, whose views will be analyzed shortly, also lived in Germany for most of his life, as did several other important rabbinic authorities who expressed a tolerant view of Christianity.

Yonah Emanuel has drawn attention to the fact that Samson Raphael Hirsch, when formulating his religious philosophy, was merely following in the footsteps of German rabbinic authorities from earlier generations.[26] Emanuel notes cases of other German rabbinic figures prior to Hirsch who expressed patriotism or, more generally, a tolerant attitude toward non-Jews.[27] Despite the pattern that Emanuel demonstrates, the precedents he notes are hardly sufficient basis for the liberal views regarding gentiles and their moral worth that are found in the writings of Hirsch, although it is possible that the views of Ettlinger and Hildesheimer were modeled on the precedents they found in earlier rabbinic sources. We must therefore find other explanations for the ideology that Hirsch espoused.

Indeed, there was ample precedent among Ashkenazic Jewry for a decidedly negative stance toward Christianity, aside from any halachic evaluations regarding its status with respect to AZ.[28] Most of the prominent European rabbis in the early modern period who expressed a more tolerant view of Christianity, based on their assessment of the moral virtues of contemporary Christians, stopped short of writing positively about the putative founder of Christianity, Jesus.[29] Instead, they praised the doctrines that Christians adhered to, such as the belief in the historicity of the biblical Exodus narrative, the veracity of the words of the Hebrew prophets, and the exemplary moral constraints to which Christians were bound. They did not reconsider the role that non-Jewish nations play in God's scheme for the world; nor did they regard Christians as fellows in any sense other than as human beings entitled to ethical treatment. Yet in the eighteenth century the early modern positive reappraisal of Christianity began to open the way for a more drastic reevaluation of Christianity and an appreciation for Jesus and the role of Christians in the divine scheme.

The first traditionalist Ashkenazic rabbi to move in this direction was

Rabbi Jacob Emden (1697–1776). According to Emden, Jesus did not intend to defect from Judaism but to spread the universal Noahide Laws among the gentiles. Although misunderstanding led to the creation of a new religion centered on him, Jesus nevertheless succeeded in spreading the divine moral code for all of humanity to millions of people around the world. Christian teachings, according to Emden, were to be admired for the strict moral compass that guides them and for successfully transforming barbarian peoples into enlightened moral beings knowledgeable in the Bible and its conception of human destiny. Some Christians have even become benefactors of the Jewish people as a result of the teachings of their religion, Emden asserted. The spread of Christianity thus represented for Emden a first step in the biblical promise that "the knowledge of the Lord will fill the world as the water covers the sea" (Isaiah 11:9).[30]

This "enlightened" view of Christianity was far from the dominant view among Jews of Emden's time, however. Emden himself noted how followers of his antagonist Rabbi Jonathan Eyebeschutz claimed Emden could not be trusted since he had such positive things to say about Christianity.[31] However, Eyebeschutz himself, while not going as far as Emden, also expressed positive sentiments about contemporary gentiles in his writings. Eyebeschutz's son, in his introduction to his father's *Kereti u-Peleti*, categorically removed Christians from any stigma that the Talmud attaches to goyim, asserting that such derogatory passages referred exclusively to ancient pagan nations.[32] Further, Eyebeschutz claims, those few comments about "Notserim" that are found in the Talmud refer to the Babylonian people who worshipped the sun, not Christians. Eyebeschutz was apparently unaware that this creative interpretation of *Notserim* had been given approximately five hundred years earlier by Rabbi Menahem ha-Meiri in his commentary to the tractate *Avodah Zarah*.[33]

Another prominent eighteenth-century rabbi who adopted the tolerant view with respect to Christian Trinitarian worship was Rabbi Isaiah Berlin-Pick (1725–99), who was the rabbi of Breslau in his later years. His views on shittuf are known from a citation of his correspondence with Rabbi Yosef ben Yaakov Yitzhak, author of *Sefer Mishnat Hakhamim*, in which Berlin "wrote at length in his strong hand" to prove that shittuf is entirely permissible for gentiles.[34] Further, Berlin also placed great emphasis on the need for Jews to conduct themselves with the highest ethical standards in their dealings with gentiles. He also highlighted the affirmation that righteous gentiles have a share in the World to Come and that they must be accorded the greatest honor in this world, which he cites in the name of Yehudah ben Samuel of Regensburg (known as "Yehudah he-Hasid" [1150–1217]). Berlin also cites other sources that emphasize the prohibition of dishonesty toward gentiles and even one rabbinic source that states that God "does not discriminate . . . and theft from a gentile is forbidden [like theft from a Jew]."[35] Although these comments do not relate directly to Christianity, when they are taken together with his remarks on the absolute permissibility of Christian Trinitarian worship, it paints a picture of a rabbi who regarded his Christian contemporaries as moral beings who observed the Noahide Commandments, would obtain salvation in the afterlife, and were deserving of the highest standards of ethical treatment.

Many prominent early nineteenth-century rabbis also voiced a positive evaluation of Christianity, but none of them expressed admiration for Jesus, as did Emden. Rabbi Wolf Boskowitz (1740–1818) devoted two essays to proving that Christian Trinitarian worship (shittuf) is permissible for gentiles.[36] Boskowitz supported this contention by arguing that strict monotheism was only imposed on those who were miraculously redeemed from Egypt by the direct hand of God. Non-Jews, who did not experience God's direct intervention in their history, are not required to adopt strict monotheism but are merely required to abstain from outright polytheism. It is noteworthy that Boskowitz emphasizes this point because his father, Rabbi Samuel Kolin (1720–1806), the author of the *Shulhan Arukh* commentary *Mahazit ha-Shekel*, takes the side of those authorities who forbid Trinitarian worship, allowing shittuf only in cases of making an oath.[37] Boskowitz does note that his father had disagreed with one fine point of argumentation found in the midst of an essay by one of the opponents of the lenient view concerning shittuf, but he does not refer to the fact that, fundamentally, his father's view was irreconcilable with his own.

Other early nineteenth-century rabbis took a liberal position on Christianity, notably Rabbi Jacob Zvi Mecklenburg (1785–1865) and Rabbi Zvi Hirsch Chajes (1805–55). Mecklenburg was the rabbi of Konigsberg from 1820 to his death in 1865 and is famous for his Pentateuch commentary called *Ha-Ketav ve-HaKabbalah*, which strives to demonstrate that the oral traditions of the Talmudic rabbis are based on the text of the Bible. In one lengthy passage, Mecklenburg takes Rabbi Samuel Landau to task for arguing that there is no difference between Jews and non-Jews with respect to the laws of idolatry. Quite the contrary, asserts Mecklenburg (echoing Boskowitz), there is a fundamental difference between the two groups regarding this issue because only the Jewish people experienced the revelation of God's omnipotence when they were redeemed from Egypt. As a result of that experience, they are expected to direct their worship solely to the one God who is the Master of the world. By contrast, non-Jewish nations, who have never experienced this direct divine intervention in their national lives, are permitted to worship other beings in addition to God.[38]

While it is clear that Mecklenburg had Christian Trinitarian worship in mind, his description of the manner in which gentiles worship beings besides God does not remotely approximate any form of Christian doctrine. Furthermore, Mecklenburg affixes a disclaimer to the end of his essay to the effect that all that was discussed therein only applied to the ancient pagans but not to contemporary nations, "in whose shade we dwell," who believe in the fundamentals of religion.[39] In addition to these comments, Mecklenburg also authored an approbation to a reprint of the book *Hesronot ha-Shas*, which contains all the passages in the Talmud and its major commentators that had been deleted by Christian censors based on the accusation that they contained anti-Christian blasphemy. In his approbation, Mecklenburg writes "every enlightened person [*kol ish maskil*] knows the great boon [afforded by this book so that] it [these texts] not be forgotten in the length of days, and it would be fitting to stand at the publisher's right side and help him bring his pure intention to fruition."[40] This may suggest that Mecklenburg is not to be counted among the leaders of Neo-Orthodoxy, despite his positive view of secular studies.[41]

Nevertheless, the passage in his commentary contending that shittuf is permissible for non-Jews relies on an argument that is based entirely on reason:

> In my view, the opinion of *Olat Tamid* [that shittuf is permissible for non-Jews] is correct, because the Jewish people whom God took out of Egypt, and did wondrous things for them, and took them as a people of inheritance who are not under the influence of the celestial spheres—upon them God decreed not to worship ought but Him alone, even in a shittuf manner [i.e., to worship no entities together with God Himself]. But for other nations, who are under the influence of the celestial spheres, if they recognize the existence of God and His omnipotence and nevertheless worship a created object—the celestial luminaries and the like—but concede that the said object is also under the dominion of God, *it is not within the bounds of just reason* [emphasis added] to forbid [such an act] for them, for their intention is not to remove themselves from the authority of the blessed Master of masters, but instead [they] believe that it is to the honor of the lofty God to praise and honor those who serve him . . .

This passage bears a striking resemblance to one authored by Moses Mendelssohn approximately fifty years prior to the composition of Mecklenburg's essay. In it, Mendelssohn stated that

> the judgment of the intellect does not require the forbidding of such worship to a Son of Noah [i.e., a non-Jew] if he does not intend to remove

> himself from the realm of God, for by what [obligation] must he offer service and prayer to God alone? And if he hopes for good and fears [that which is] bad from an entity besides Him, and acknowledges that also that entity is subject to God . . . and offers sacrifice, incense, libation and prayer to that entity, be it an angel, a demon, or an important person, a soldier, minister, or ruler—who has told us that all these forms of worship are to be directed solely to God, if not for God's injunction against this in His Torah? In truth, the Sages of blessed memory have stated that the Sons of Noah are not forbidden in shittuf, [that is to say] that such worship would not be considered an act of rebellion against the honor of God when it comes to them [non-Jews] . . . unless they intend thereby to exclude themselves from the authority of the God of gods and the Master of masters. However, we, His close nation, who were redeemed from Egypt, the house of slaves, for whom God performed all the wonders . . . [are bound to worship solely God without any intermediaries].[42]

Therefore, despite Mecklenburg's disclaimer at the end of his essay that all that he had written applies only to the ancient pagan nations, he expressed a view of religious tolerance—one that clearly included Christians—that closely approximated Moses Mendelssohn's. Furthermore, Mecklenburg is one of those traditional rabbinic authorities who consider the biblical command to "love thy neighbor as thyself" (Leviticus 19:18) to include love of non-Jews.[43] In fact, Mecklenburg sees the issue as noncontroversial and simply notes that the term *re'akha* (literally, "thy neighbor") used in the verse means "all humans." Interestingly, even Hirsch accepted the more widely held view that this biblical injunction requires love of fellow Jews only, although a Jew is indeed required to love non-Jews as well on the basis of other sources. Thus, Mecklenburg's views are a unique combination of premodern (his approbation to an anti-Christian source book) and modern (his tolerance of non-Jewish worship and inclusion of non-Jews in the biblical mandate of neighbor love).

Closer in spirit to the Neo-Orthodox rabbis was Rabbi Zvi Hirsch Chajes. Chajes has been characterized as a maskil and although that characterization is questionable, it is undoubtedly true that Chajes was acutely sensitive to the zeitgeist of the early nineteenth century and that he wished for Jews to participate in the world of European culture as much as possible.[44] Ephraim Chamiel, in his important study of Chajes's views, has argued that he should be seen as adopting the moderately conservative stance on modernity when compared to the reactions of Hirsch and especially of the Italian maskil, Samuel David Luzzatto (1800–65).[45]

Chajes displays remarkable sensitivity to the accusation that the Talmud has an anti-gentile bias and he is at pains throughout his writings to demonstrate that this is not the case. One notable example is Chajes's comment on the Talmudic statement (Yevamot 61a) that "[only] you [Jews] are called 'men' but the nations of the world are not called 'men.'" Chajes notes that it was not the intention of the Sages to exclude non-Jews from the category of humans but rather to state that whenever a command is addressed to a person, the reference is to Jews, just as in the holy books of any religion any reference to "a person" being obligated to do such and such must be understood as referring to adherents of that faith only.[46]

Chajes authored an entire essay devoted to refuting the blood libel charge in the wake of the Damascus Affair of 1840. In it Chajes states unequivocally that contemporary Christians and Muslims are, "without a doubt, to be classified as *gerei toshav*" since shittuf is permissible for gentiles and adherents of these faiths also scrupulously observe the other six Noahide Commandments.[47] It was only several years later, in response to a rabbi who had questioned Chajes's position on this matter that Chajes retracted his earlier assertion and stated that there were several insurmountable halachic impediments to classifying Christians as *gerei toshav*.[48] Thus, despite Chajes's sincere efforts to remove anti-gentile discrimination from the Talmudic literature, he was unable to uphold his formal liberal halachic position regarding the status of contemporary Christians, though he upheld his positive evaluation of Christians' moral virtues throughout his life.[49] (Thus, in his view, even if not formally classified as *gerei toshav*, Christians would still not be susceptible to anti-gentile discrimination in the ethical realm.)

Like other European Orthodox rabbis of the nineteenth century, Chajes was convinced that the purpose of the election of the Jewish people was to benefit all of mankind by spreading essential teachings about God, reward and punishment, and other Torah teachings. This has come to be known as the mission theory, and it is usually associated with German Reform Judaism. Yet, the view was ubiquitous among Jews of all denominations during the nineteenth century. Chajes draws attention to the providential role of Christianity and Islam in spreading Judaism's teachings to non-Jewish peoples. Despite obvious theological departures from Judaism, these religions have been successful in gaining adherents around the world specifically because they have borrowed the core teachings of the Torah.[50] (This echoed the view of Rabbi Jacob Emden from the previous century.) Chajes could not have been more explicit in his positive evaluation of these Abrahamitic religions, a view which was not shared by all of Chajes's European rabbinic contemporaries.

Perhaps the most direct precedent for a liberal attitude toward gentiles in early nineteenth-century Germany is the worldview of Rabbi Israel Lipschutz (1782–1860), rabbi of Danzig and author of the monumental Mishnah commentary *Tiferet Yisrael.* In several places in that work, Lipschutz expresses deeply humanistic and universalist sentiments. Perhaps the most important of these passages is his commentary to *Avot* 3:14, which declares "Beloved is man for he was created in the Divine Image." Although several earlier commentators grappled with the question of whether non-Jews were included in the term "man" [*adam*] since one Talmudic passage states that only Jews are called *adam*, Lipschutz is at pains to emphasize that the Mishnah definitely has in mind all of humanity in its declaration. After all, argued Lipschutz, a later clause in the same Mishnah states "Beloved are Israel . . . ," making it clear that the earlier reference to "man" refers to *all* human beings. This leads to a lengthy excursus in which Lipschutz develops an explanation of the Talmudic passage that excludes gentiles from the term *adam*, according to which no stigma whatsoever is attached to non-Jews by this exclusion. On the contrary, argues Lipschutz, such exclusion is actually a sign of certain superior qualities that gentiles possess but Jews do not. Non-Jews are not comparable to the first man, Adam, who was created directly by God and had no autonomously achieved worth. This is because non-Jews have, over the course of the centuries, escaped the pagan darkness that their ancestors walked in and have come to recognition of God on their own (through the development of Christianity and Islam, which Lipschutz does not refer to by name).

By contrast, what the Jewish people have achieved over the centuries has not been the result of their own efforts but rather came about through direct divine intervention in their national life. They are thus more comparable to Adam, who also became who he was solely through an act of God and not through any effort of his own.[51] In introducing this essay, Lipschutz notes that "for all my days I have been troubled by this statement of the Sages in *Yevamot* that 'You are called man but the nations of the world are not called man'—can one entertain the notion that the Sages would say about gentiles, who have the image of God, as we explained, that they are considered like mere animals?" The nineteenth-century ethos of the equality of all men seems to have impacted Lipschutz's thinking here, as I am not aware of any earlier sources that state that they were troubled by the Yevamot passage, although many sources do mitigate the harshness of that text in various ways.[52] The fact that Lipschutz was troubled by it suggests that he was not simply engaging in standard textual exegesis here but that a more substantive ethical issue lay behind this excursus. His conclusions, while not radical, are certainly novel and exceed any other evaluation of non-Jews that had previously been undertaken on the basis of the Talmudic passage from Yevamot.[53]

Even more striking is the role that Lipschutz assigns to human reason/ rationality in drawing his conclusions about the moral worth of gentiles and their chances for salvation. Referring to the rabbinic statement that the righteous of all nations have a share in the World to Come, Lipschutz states, "Even without the holy mouth of the Sages who have told us this, we would know this matter on the basis of [our] intellect, for God is righteous in all His ways and pious in all His actions." Lipschutz goes on to assert that there have been several prominent gentiles whose actions have greatly benefited mankind (and, in one case, the Jewish people specifically) and that it would be unthinkable for those people to be denied the reward due them by God.[54]

Thus, like the comments of Mecklenburg about gentiles worshipping celestial spheres in addition to God, Lipschutz's essay bears an unmistakable resemblance to the writings of Mendelssohn on this issue. Mendelssohn had also emphasized that a fundamental doctrine of reason is that all good people are rewarded for their deeds, in contradistinction to dogmatic Christianity, which insisted upon the acceptance of specific dogmas in order to attain salvation. There are thus grounds to question the extent to which Neo-Orthodoxy differed from earlier traditionalist Judaism in Germany with respect to the issue of religious tolerance. It would appear that several prominent leaders of the latter group (who possessed no formal secular education) had also imbibed the religious Enlightenment's axiom of the universality of salvation.[55]

This point is borne out even more clearly from a different passage in Lipschutz's Mishnah commentary. Commenting on the statement of the Mishnah that "without Torah, there can be no *derekh eretz* [civilization]," Lipschutz states that "Torah"

> does not mean the actual Torah, for many ignorant people have not studied it and many pious gentiles have not studied Torah, and nevertheless they are ethical and cultured people. Rather, it seems to me that every nation has a Divine religion that includes three principles, namely [the beliefs] that (1) the Torah is Divine (2) there is reward and punishment (3) there is immortality of the soul. (And the nations differ with one another only with respect to the explanations [of these matters].) And these three principles are what is here referred to as "Torah." Therefore, someone who denies these principles [thereby] regards man as [merely] an animal and he does not hold the soul in high regard to consider it necessary to conduct oneself with ethics and civilization like the cultures of each nation [do. Rather, such a person] regards all that occurs to be a result of determinism.[56]

Lipschutz here declares that all monotheistic religions are to be regarded as divinely inspired.[57] He thereby followed in the footsteps of Jacob Emden in creating a broad theory of religious tolerance for non-Jewish monotheistic religions. In many respects, the views of these rabbis can be seen as constituting further development of the theory of religious tolerance first espoused by Meiri in the thirteenth century. However, they arrived at their conclusions independently of Meiri, since Meiri's writings, particularly those passages which contain his positive assessments of Christianity, remained largely unpublished until the twentieth century.[58] These ideas served as rabbinic precedents for the views of nineteenth-century German rabbinic leaders, though the latter, particularly S. R. Hirsch, took them to a whole new level.

Disclaimers/Prefaces to Rabbinic Works in Early Modern Europe

One issue that deserves our attention at this point is the question of the sincerity of prefaces to rabbinic works that exclude Christians from anti-gentile legislation. As Jacob Katz has noted, it became commonplace in the eighteenth century for printed books on rabbinic and Talmudic topics to contain a disclaimer at the beginning or the end stating that all the references to goyim or *akum* contained therein refer only to ancient pagan nations and have no applicability to contemporary gentiles. This type of disclaimer emerged for the first time in the mid-sixteenth century.[59] One of the most famous examples comes from Rabbi Ezekiel Landau's (1713–93) responsa collection *Noda bi-Yehudah*, which states:

> It is already well-known in all the places that I have been to that I exhort and admonish in most of [my] public sermons to be extremely diligent about [preserving] the honor of the nations of our time. We dwell in their lands and countries, and we are obligated to pray for the wellbeing of the kings, ministers, and their aides, and to pray for the peace of the country and its inhabitants. It would be unthinkable for us to be ungrateful after they have done good for us and give us life and refuge in the land . . . [Landau then discusses the severity of the prohibitions against theft from, and dishonesty towards, gentiles.] It is thus clear that it is forbidden to rob or steal from a gentile and all the more so with respect to the nations of our times amongst whom we dwell, for they believe in the fundamentals of religion, and they believe in the creation of the world and in the prophecy of the prophets and in all the miracles and wonders that are written in the Pentateuch and the Books of the Prophets. If so, it is quite obvious that we are required to honor and respect them. Therefore

> I proclaim and make known: not only with respect to this book alone do I say this but [rather] in any place in any book in which a derogatory statement about *akum* or *goyim* or *kutim* and similar terms is to be found—do not err in interpreting [such statements] as referring to these nations of our times, for he who expresses such an interpretation is mistaken and is explaining against the religion of the Torah [*shelo kedat shel Torah*].[60] Rather, the intention is to the ancient nations who used to believe in [the divinity of] stars and constellations, such as the sect of the Sabians mentioned by Maimonides in the *Guide* [which states that] those nations were heretics and sectarians [*apikorsim u-minim*],[61] and they did not accept the creation of the world, and they denied all the wonders [mentioned in the Bible], and they denied prophecy. Therefore, let everyone be careful about these matters and place them upon one's heart as a remembrance.[62]

Landau's prefatory remarks are lengthier than those written by some of his contemporaries, whose similarly themed comments have a pro forma flavor. This raises the legitimate question of the sincerity of such comments.[63] Did rabbis like Landau make these statements either to evade the Christian censors—who might not allow for the publication of these books otherwise—or to avoid potential Christian animosity that the publication of anti-gentile comments might engender? (Or, at the very least—and this could have been regarded as the worse outcome by some rabbinic authorities—the references to gentiles in the books might have been removed.) Clearly, many people in the Haredi world today doubt the sincerity of these remarks since many of the newer printings of these books by Haredi publishing houses simply delete the pro-Christian disclaimers altogether.[64] But what did the rabbis who wrote these passages actually think?

One passage that may shed light on this question was penned by Rabbi Ezekiel Landau's most prominent disciple, Rabbi Eleazar Fleckeles (1754–1826). Fleckeles headed the Prague beth din and rabbinic council. His fame as a halachist results from his responsa collection, *Teshuvah me-Ahavah*.[65] In contrast to many works printed during this period that contain brief disclaimers about the terms for gentile that are employed in the text—and even in contrast to his teacher Landau's more lengthy disclaimer—Fleckeles penned a lengthy essay discussing the topic of non-Jews in a serious and authoritative fashion. Although there is an air of apologetics to his opening remarks—which is understandable given that he was effectively "setting the record straight" for anyone who might peruse his book—the remainder of the essay is clearly a sincere expression of the nonapplicability of Talmudic anti-gentile sentiments to contemporary Christians. His remarks go beyond the standard disclaimer-type notice that is found in many works from this period.

In the introduction to his responsa, Fleckeles writes:

> And know that a member of the nations who is cognizant of the commandments of God [a reference to the Noahide laws] is entitled to a portion in the World to Come and, furthermore, he is given the title *hasid* [pious one] . . . Therefore the matter is as clear as the sun [that] the nations of our time, who observe the Noahide laws, will receive a portion in the World to Come and are [entitled to be] called *hasidim* [pious ones]. . . .
>
> Behold, until now we have only seen and explained that with respect to monetary matters there is no distinction between Israel and the other nations. But if a Jewish enquirer would ask if it is permitted for a Jew to despise a member of the other nations or to hate him, so should you respond to him in accordance with the laws of the Torah. Not only have the sages of the Mishnah stated (Avot chapter 4 Mishnah 3), "Do not despise any man," [we must] infer from their words "any man" that [the reference is to someone] from whichever nation he may be. And they have further stated (infra, chapter 2 Mishnah 11), "R. Joshua says 'an evil eye, the evil inclination, and hatred of the beriyot remove a person from the world.'" And they carefully chose the term *beriyot*, which implies all creations [for] they are all the handiwork of God. And this is founded in rationality for do we not all have one father? How could it enter one's mind to treat lightly or to disrespect the honor of any human being on the earth, from whatever nation he may come? And this matter we have derived from the Torah of Moses. It states in the Torah (Deuteronomy 3:8), "Do not despise an Egyptian for you were a stranger in his land." Let us derive an *a fortiori* conclusion: the Egyptians who subjugated the Israelites bitterly and cast their male babies into the river—nevertheless, since Israel was hosted there, and the Torah proscribes us from despising an Egyptian and the Rabbis of the Talmud (Bava Kamma 92b) have derived from here that a flask from which one drank should not be rejected . . . the nations amongst whom we live in peace and tranquility, and permission is granted to us to perform all the words of the Torah and to engage in any form of commerce and to fill our hands with the pursuit of all occupations—who is foolish enough, lacking a heart and crazy [meshuga] to entertain the idea of despising and cursing these nations? This is naught but the evilness of the heart and it is against the Torah, fear [of Heaven], and wisdom . . .[66]

Fleckeles goes on to discuss the obligation to pray for the welfare of the government, the permissibility of entering into partnerships with non-Jews, the obligation to lend money and to give charity to non-Jews who are in need, and the obligation to pay all forms of taxes, even discriminatory taxes levied on Jews. After these discussions, Fleckeles makes the following statement:

> Let us now state: if these laws were stated with respect to idol worshippers who flout the will of God, then do they not apply in even greater force to those who fulfill His will, that is, those nations that observe the Noahide laws and who are deserving of the title *hasidim*? Whoever is fair-minded [will understand that] all the curses . . . [and the like] found in the Talmud and in all other Jewish books refer [solely] to the ancient nations who engaged in all of the abominable practices despised by God . . .
>
> Even with respect to those who do not know God . . . [it is best] to request [divine] compassion on them, that they may repent of their ways and [then] all residents of the earth will speak one language and have unity of purpose, to call in harmony upon the name of the living God, the King of the world, and to worship him in unity. On that day God will be one and His name will be one . . . [67]

It would seem that the disclaimers found in rabbinic works ought to be divided into two different categories: those that merely state the nonapplicability of anti-gentile sentiments to Christians and those that develop this view in a more substantive fashion. The first type will generally refer to the Jew's obligation to pray for the welfare of the government—something that applies whether the government is deemed to be guilty of theological errors or not. It was therefore easy to make this declaration regardless of the true views of the author about the legal status of Christianity and Christians because those questions are irrelevant. Further, declarations of the first type generally contained a reference to the idea that Judaism affirms that gentiles who observe the Noahide laws achieve immortality. Saying this allows the writer of such a declaration to remain agnostic about whether Christians actually fall into this category. More generally, the first type of disclaimer has an air of formality about it, indicating that it really is nothing more than a disclaimer.[68]

By contrast, disclaimers of the second type, which are better termed "clarifications," expressed the authentic sentiment of their authors as to the irrelevance of much of Talmudic anti-gentile sentiment and legislation in modern times (i.e., after the diffusion of Christianity). In these clarifications, the authors strove to demonstrate with prooftexts that it would be counter to the Torah to apply derogatory Talmudic comments about gentiles to Christians.

Their goal was not primarily to convince non-Jewish (or baptized Jewish) censors but to clarify—internally, to Jewish readers—the correct way to understand these texts.

It is quite evident that Fleckeles's lengthy introductory essay to his responsa collection was intended to do more than pacify the censor. That goal could have been achieved with a much shorter, and more formal, statement. Instead of writing such a statement, Fleckeles explicitly categorized contemporary Christians as among the "righteous of the nations." He argued passionately against the view that any of the anti-gentile statements could be applied to Christians, and he cited both biblical and rabbinic prooftexts in support of this position. There can be no doubt as to the sincerity of Fleckeles's essay.[69]

In fact, S. R. Hirsch clearly regarded both the disclaimers by Landau and Fleckeles to be sincere expressions of rabbinic Judaism's view of Christians. This is evidenced by Hirsch's lumping together these two rabbis' disclaimers with the much lengthier treatment of Christianity by Jacob Emden. Hirsch writes, "Toward the end of the eighteenth century, such noted Rabbinic authorities as R. Ezekiel Landau, R. Eleazar Fleckeles and R. Jacob Emden dealt extensively with this subject in their writings." The "subject" Hirsch refers to is the view of "the scholars of Jewish law" that emphasized the commonalities of faith between Jews and those gentiles who have "accepted the Jewish Bible of the Old Testament as a book of Divine revelation" (*doch auch die jüdische Bibel des alten Testaments als ein Buch göttlicher Offenbarung verehren*). Because they have accepted upon themselves to lead their lives in keeping with "the practical duties incumbent upon all men by the Will of God," these gentiles are considered "as the complete equals of the Jews and therefore entitled to our active charity and compassion in every respect."[70]

Another key that may help us to determine the sincerity of rabbinic disclaimers may be the examination of one such disclaimer written by an author who was absolutely certainly writing sincerely: the maskil Rabbi Naphtali Herz Wessely (1725–1805). At the end of his *Avot* commentary, *Yeyn Levanon*, he writes:

> Also to those who are wise, who will understand on their own [do I write that] the nations amongst whom we live are quite unlike those lived in the period of the Talmud, for they were idol worshippers and were attached to all abominations. They did not know the word of God and His holy word, whereas the nations of our time fear God and give honor to His Torah. They practice justice and righteousness in their land(s). And it is unthinkable to speak or write anything derogatory about them. And in any place

> where [Jewish] books mention *goy*, *nokhri*, or *umot ha-olam* and the like, the intention is to those idol worshippers who lived in the time of the Mishnah, as is evident from how I explained the Mishnaic statements "Beloved is man, who is created in the image" and "One should pray [for the welfare of the government]."[71]

In this case, there can be no doubt that Wessely genuinely wished to make it clear that derogatory statements about gentiles found in rabbinic writings do not apply to contemporary Christians. As he noted, there are several passages in his commentary to *Avot* where he stresses the distinctions between pagans and Christians. Yet, he felt compelled to write a disclaimer on the last page that reinforces the same point. Wessely probably did not want to seem remiss in failing to state, for the record, that *any* passage that might offend contemporary gentiles was not referring to them.[72] The very fact that Wessely included such a statement should call into question the presumption that disclaimers of this nature were written solely to placate the censor. Even those rabbis who authored pro forma disclaimers were not falsifying any aspects of Jewish law or thought since their assertions about the obligation to pray for the welfare of the government and their exhortations about dishonesty toward gentiles were not controversial positions. Thus, those rabbis who chose to write more substantive essays explaining the fundamental difference between the pagans of Talmudic times and contemporary Christians had obviously internalized that message.

While some of the rabbis in the latter category may not have intended to exclude Christians from the legal status of worshippers of AZ—many of these essays are cautiously worded formulations about contemporary gentiles believing in the fundamentals of faith and are careful not to declare that Christians are entirely excluded from the category of *ovdei avodah zarah* (although several rabbis do make this exclusion quite explicit)—they appear to have sincerely believed that Christians were to be regarded as occupying a different category than the pagans of Talmudic times.[73] That aspect of their declarations should be regarded as providing a solid precedent for the more overtly liberal positions on the status of Christians that are to be found in the writings of the German rabbis examined in this book.

The writings of the aforementioned rabbis, including the disclaimers about gentiles found in introductory and closing sections of books, have thus served as a basis for the views of the leaders of mid-nineteenth century German-Orthodoxy. By themselves, they are, at best, comparable to what Rabbis Ettlinger and Hildesheimer wrote on this subject. Hirsch's more extensive humanistic essays on these subjects cannot be characterized simply as an organic outgrowth of the rabbinic tradition that preceded him. Nevertheless, Hirsch himself referred to the views of some of his predecessors, especially Rabbi Emden, as a basis for the views which he espoused in his own writings. It will therefore be our task to develop an explanation that can account for the novelty of Hirsch's views.

3

East and Central European Rabbinic Views of Non-Jews and Christianity in the Nineteenth Century

The views of the leaders of nineteenth-century German Orthodoxy would hardly be worthy of special study if their contemporaries elsewhere in Europe shared fairly similar views.[1] It is precisely because rabbinic figures from elsewhere in Europe expressed a more exclusivist view of gentiles and a less tolerant approach toward Christianity that the views of German rabbis are noteworthy. I will endeavor to present a survey of the views of the rabbis of Eastern and Central Europe during the nineteenth century by citing passages from their responsa and sermons. Only those figures who had a significant impact on the intellectual orientation of East and Central European Orthodoxy will be discussed, as an in-depth examination of the views of all rabbis from this area would be beyond the scope of this book.

Perhaps the most famous nineteenth-century leader of Orthodoxy outside of Germany was Rabbi Moses Sofer (1762–1839), known as Hatam Sofer (the title of his responsa collection). Sofer is often characterized as the founder of Ultra-Orthodoxy, which is opposed to the more moderate Neo-Orthodoxy that Samson Raphael Hirsch is said to have founded.[2] Whatever the merits of this view are—and they are substantial—there can be no doubt that Sofer advocated a far more rigid and antimodern version of Orthodoxy than did Hirsch. It is therefore surprising that so little attention has been paid to his views of non-Jews and of Christianity in existing scholarship.[3]

What can be gleaned from Sofer's comments on these issues is that his attitude most closely resembles that of the premodern Ashkenazic halachists—specifically those who would not qualify for inclusion in the group that Jacob Katz has termed "the tolerant among traditionalists."[4] Of import to our discussion is Sofer's response to emancipation, which is often cited as evidence of his antimodern views but not as evidence of his anti-gentile stance. Sofer bewailed the advent of emancipation in his time, which he believed was a divine test to see if the Jewish people would abandon their heritage. He believed the gentiles were opening the gates to European culture to Jews in order to entice them to abandon their faith. He did not see the loosening of anti-Jewish restrictions as indicative of a milder attitude toward Jews on the part of gentiles; quite the contrary: "Their hatred [of Jews] increases daily."[5]

Sofer's halachic evaluation of contemporary gentiles was no less negative. In a responsum dated July 31, 1839 (just a few months before his death), which discusses the question of violating the Sabbath in order to save the life of a gentile, he classified his Christian contemporaries as worshippers of AZ, whose lives it is forbidden to save.[6] Although some authorities distinguished between the degree of the Christians' attachment to idolatry (and that of ancient pagans), Sofer writes, "it is obvious that their worship is outright AZ. [He then cites the uncensored texts of Maimonides's code, which so classifies Christians.] And it is obvious that we do not kill them but neither do we save them [even on weekdays] and it is forbidden to multiply the seed of Amalek . . . [So on the Sabbath the Jew] can trick the gentile [to avoid having to save his life] and state that 'we only violate the Sabbath for those who observe it' [although it would be forbidden to save them even if no Sabbath violation was involved] and thereby not have to multiply the seed of Amalek."[7]

Hatam Sofer addresses the issue of shittuf in his glosses to the section of the *Shulhan Arukh* where Rema cites the view that non-Jews are not proscribed from shittuf, an assertion that, as previously mentioned, was hotly contested and debated by rabbinic authorities of the seventeenth and eighteenth centuries. Sofer states, "Regarding the worshippers of the Trinity, see *Sha'ar Ephraim* and *Me'il Zedakah* and see the *Peri Megadim* in this chapter [all of whom forbid shittuf in worship], and the proper ruling [*ha-ikar*] is that non-Jews are executed for worshipping with shittuf."[8]

Furthermore, Sofer is the lone authoritative rabbinic figure in modern times to question the authenticity of the views of Meiri regarding Talmudic anti-gentile legislation. The author of *Shittah Mekubetzet* cites Meiri's assertion that "we do not show favoritism to ourselves" with respect to contemporary "nations that are restricted by the ways of religion," and that such favoritism could only be applied when dealing with ancient pagans. These comments, cited by Shittah Mekubetzet, appear on the margin of the Vilna

Talmud. Sofer was not pleased with these comments, and he writes, "It is a mitzvah to erase [those words] for they did not emanate from his [Meiri's] holy mouth, for it is the view of those who say to the wicked, 'the righteous shall live by his faith' (Habakkuk 2:4; cf. Proverbs 24:24)."[9]

Furthermore, Hatam Sofer emphasizes the metaphysical difference between Jews and non-Jews in his explication of the Talmudic dictum that "[only] you [the Jewish people] are called 'man' [*adam*] but the nations of the world are not called 'man'" (Yevamot 61a). Citing the medieval view that the nations *are* called 'the man' [*ha-adam*], Sofer explains that the difference is that with the definite article, *adam* refers to the external appearance of humanity, with respect to which there is no difference between Jews and non-Jews. However, without the definite article, *adam* refers to the inner essence of a man, namely that he is composed of the essence of God [*tokho adam penimi—helek elohai mi-ma'al*], and that is only true with respect to Jews, not non-Jews. On this basis, Sofer sees no reason to prohibit autopsies performed on gentile corpses—despite the prohibition on autopsies on Jewish corpses—since they are not true "men," although he adds that this is "in accordance with their views and faith" [*lefi da'atam ve-emunatam*], which possibly adds an element of limitation to his otherwise essentialist argument, since those non-Jews whose "views and faith" were in accord with God's demands of them *would* be considered true "men." It is not clear, though, if the halachic implications of how inclusive the term *adam* is would be impacted by the views of each individual non-Jew.[10]

It thus emerges that Hatam Sofer was not merely an advocate of separatism from non-Orthodox Jews but that he supported a harsh and exclusionary attitude toward contemporary Christians as well.[11] It is a noteworthy irony that Hirsch cites Sofer's responsum on separatism from Jewish Reformers in support of his own secessionist stance but makes no mention of Sofer's attitude toward non-Jews in any of his writings, no doubt because Hirsch's own views on this issue were diametrically opposed to those of Sofer.[12]

Hatam Sofer's father-in-law was the famous Talmudic virtuoso Rabbi Akiva Eger (1761–1837), rabbi of Posen. Rabbi Eger adopted a nuanced stance toward modernity, opposing the Reform movement but remaining open to secular disciplines.[13] His views on Christianity are not widely known since his single most important responsum treating this topic was published relatively recently and was not included in any of the earlier editions of his responsa collection.[14] The responsum was written to Eger's son, Rabbi Shlomo, and is dated July 26, 1837, only several months before his death in October of that year. Eger was informed that certain people in Warsaw, presumably including its beth din, wished to proclaim that Christians are not worshippers of AZ, for their worship is directed toward the true God, and although they also associate another entity (Jesus) with God (shittuf), this is entirely permissible for gentiles.

Eger writes that he "does not know the details of the matter nor for what purpose would they proclaim thus and what benefit would there be from doing so. The [entire] matter is strange in my eyes."[15] He then proceeds to examine the issue and comes down in favor of the restrictive interpretation of the Tosafists' comments relating to shittuf, according to which Christian Trinitarian worship is certainly forbidden for gentiles and, accordingly, the apparent leniency of the Tosafists must be confined to the narrow context of making an oath. Eger further cites the views of several earlier authorities who had also advocated a restrictive reading of the Tosafists' comments, expressing his concurrence but failing to make mention of the opposing view that interpreted the Tosafists more broadly. Eger then adds that he would really like to write his views on this matter to Rabbi Shlomo Zalman Lipschitz, head of the beth din in Warsaw, but he does not wish to impugn the honor of the learned Warsaw rabbi, who may perhaps have already ruled leniently on this matter. Eger therefore encourages his son, who was a rabbinic authority in his own right, to discreetly discuss this matter with Lipschitz perhaps persuade him not to issue a lenient ruling if he has not already done so.

The most noteworthy aspect of this responsum is the introductory remarks made by Eger before he began his examination of the issue. He appears at a loss as to why anyone would wish to make a declaration that Christians are not worshippers of AZ and instead worship the one true God. He states that he cannot see what benefit would accrue from such a declaration and adds that the entire matter is "strange" (*zar*) in his eyes. This is the worldview of a pre-emancipation rabbi. As late as 1837, a year after the publication of Hirsch's *Nineteen Letters*, Eger could not understand why Jews would wish to proclaim publicly that Christians worship the same God that Jews do. It apparently did not occur to him that by so doing, those Jews would in effect be saying, "We consider Christians to be fellow-monotheists, heirs to immortality, and they share a common heritage with Jews." Such a declaration would indicate a Jewish readiness for emancipation, a desire to integrate (but not necessarily assimilate) into European society and to view their non-Jewish neighbors as fellows in a spiritual as well as a political sense. This was a stance that certain acculturated Warsaw Jews wished to adopt but which was apparently foreign to Eger's way of thinking.[16]

An important leader of nineteenth-century East European Orthodoxy was Rabbi Naphtali Zvi Yehuda Berlin (1817–93), known as Netziv, who headed the Volozhin yeshiva for forty years.[17] He authored numerous commentaries, including a monumental work on the Pentateuch, from which the bulk of his ideology can be extracted. His view of non-Jews was nuanced. On the one hand, he stresses that the telos of the Jewish people is to serve as a "light unto the nations."[18] Netziv develops this idea in a manner that is reminiscent of the "mission theory" expressed by Hirsch and other German rabbis, albeit employing an idiom that is far less idealistic than his German contemporaries. Netziv goes so far as to suggest that the rabbinic statement that the world was created "on account of Israel [the Jewish people]" is to be understood as connoting the foundational need for a model nation that will inspire the rest of mankind to recognize God's sovereignty.[19] While most East European rabbinic authorities see this rabbinic passage as indicating that the world revolves around the Jews, Netziv is willing to undercut the exclusivist implications of the passage by inserting a universalist message.

Netziv also states that God wished for the Torah to be accessible to all nations and therefore commanded that it be translated into seventy languages. He also notes that God-fearing gentile scientists who uncover the wonders of the natural world are fulfilling a divine mandate and are to be applauded for doing so.[20] Further, Netziv writes that the Book of Genesis is sometimes described as *Sefer ha-Yashar* (book of the upright) because it depicts the life stories of the patriarchs of the Jewish people, whose lives exemplified uprightness, ethics, and compassion in their dealings with the non-Jewish nations, "even debased idol worshippers." The essential component for preservation of God's creation, writes Netziv, is to care about the welfare of others, regardless of who they are. That is why Abraham prayed for the wicked people of Sodom despite his antipathy for their lifestyle. He wants them to thrive just as a father wants even his wayward son to persevere; this why, according to Netziv, Abraham is described as the "father" (*av*) of a multitude of nations (Genesis 17:5).[21]

On the other hand, Netziv emphasizes the rarity of pious people among the non-Jewish nations, as opposed to the Jewish people, whose essence is piety.[22] Yet, Netziv does not dehumanize gentiles in his writings and is prepared to accept not only that Esau had genuine feelings of brotherly love toward Jacob in Genesis 33:4 but that this has implications for his descendants as well: "Both [Jacob and Esau] cried, which comes to teach that Jacob too was sincerely brought to affection for Esau at that moment. And so too for the generations: at a time when the descendants of Esau are aroused with a pure spirit to recognize the people of Israel and their elevated status, then so too we will be aroused to recognize Esau for he is our brother, just as Rabbi [Yehuda ha-Nasi] was a genuine friend of Antoninus, and so too many [similar cases]."[23]

This passage is remarkable for it shows that Netziv, for all his hostility to the Haskalah movement, did not doubt the sincerity of gentile advocates of Jewish emancipation. At the same time, Netziv authored a treatise on the subject of contemporary anti-Semitism, which he maintained was a divine punishment for the embrace by Jewish assimilationists of reformist programs.[24]

Noteworthy in this context is that Netziv was comfortable employing the terminology of brotherhood for the descendants of Esau, who were undoubtedly (in his view) the Christians of Europe. However, Netziv attaches an important caveat to this affirmation: non-Jews must be prepared to recognize the elevated (spiritual) status of Jews. Outside this hierarchic relationship, Netziv is not prepared to accept non-Jewish remonstrations of affection for Jews as equals. Nonetheless, Netziv's willingness to accept and reciprocate gentile affection stands in stark contrast to a contemporary who, along with him, served as Rosh Yeshiva of the Volozhin yeshiva, Rabbi Joseph Dov Soloveitchik.

Rabbi Joseph Dov Soloveitchik (1820–92), known as the Beit ha-Levi, the title of his responsa collection, was one of the most important leaders of East European Orthodoxy in the nineteenth century.[25] Rabbi Soloveitchik, together with Netziv, stood at the helm of the Volozhin yeshiva for ten years in the middle of the century; he later left and eventually became the rabbi of Brest-Litovsk, known as Brisk in Yiddish. He is regarded as the founder of the Brisk rabbinic dynasty, and he, his son Rabbi Hayyim, and grandson Rabbi Velvel were each known as "the Brisker Rav" during their lifetimes. Rabbi Soloveitchik was a fierce opponent of modernity and those whom he regarded as its agents, the maskilim. This is the standpoint from which to evaluate his attitude toward non-Jews as well. Rabbi Soloveitchik feared the negative repercussions of emancipation, which he believed would lead to large-scale Jewish assimilation.

One of his most well-known comments comes from his novellae on the Pentateuch, and it treats this theme.[26] Genesis 32:12 describes Jacob's prayer to be saved "from my brother, from Esau." Soloveitchik notes that this clause seems redundant as either of the two references to his brother would have sufficed. Therefore, Soloveitchik concludes that the message of the Torah was that Esau will sometimes play the part of Jacob's "brother" and sometimes the part of "Esau." In the latter case, Esau wishes to wage war against Jacob and kill him, whereas in the former case, Esau claims to desire to treat Jacob with respect and emphasizes their brotherhood. Jacob, however, is equally afraid of both of Esau's modes "for also Esau's goodness and love was considered to be evil by Jacob." Soloveitchik continues by noting that the events that occurred to the ancestors of the Jewish people repeated themselves in the lives of their descendants:

> So too in the Exile of Esau, he [i.e., his presumed descendants, the Christians of Europe] will conduct himself likewise with Israel in these two modes, just as he wished to do with Jacob. For in the earlier stage of the Exile, he will issue evil decrees, [including] forcible conversion and persecution and he will wage war with them and wish to eradicate them, but God in His mercy will not desert them. At the end [of the exile], he will say that he wishes to dwell in peace with Jacob, and his intention in so doing is to distance Israel from its worship of God and to make them deviate from their faith . . . For in the end, they too [Christians] will accept good principles from the faith of Israel, and they will accordingly believe in one Creator and in the Divinity of the Torah and in reward and punishment, and they wish for Jacob [i.e., the Jews] too to make some concessions from what is rightfully God's, and drop some of the aspects of their worship which pertain solely to the World to Come [i.e., distinct Jewish ritual] and instead adopt some of the ways of this world, to engage in external paths and matters, and that they should not devote themselves exclusively to the Torah.[27]

This passage is clearly a reference to the emancipation of European Jewry that was occurring in Soloveitchik's time, as well as to the two stages of Czar Nicholas I's policies (conscription and intrusion into the Jewish educational system), and his message was not to trust the gentiles as they are ill-disposed toward Jews and are not merely interested in loosening the shackles of persecution but intend to cause the Jews to defect from their faith. Even the fact that European gentiles have adopted Christianity, which includes many fundamental tenets of the Torah, such as monotheism and God's exercising the power to reward or punish humanity for its deeds, is decried by Soloveitchik as an example of how the gentiles have made a "concession" to the Jews in order to gain a reciprocal "concession" on the part of the Jews. In contradistinction to all of the leaders of German Orthodoxy, he did not necessarily regard the spread of Christianity as a positive development, although he clearly recognized that it represented a departure from the polytheism of the ancient pagans.

This one passage has been enormously influential in the yeshiva world, and Beit ha-Levi's comments are cited regularly in Haredi yeshivot.[28] The contrast between Beit ha-Levi's views and those of German Orthodoxy could not be starker. It may be suggested that Rabbi Soloveitchik expressed pessimistic views about gentile trustworthiness due to the dramatically different circumstances of nineteenth-century Russian Jewry when compared to that of contemporaneous German Jewry. The czarist policies of forced conscription with a strong subcurrent of conversionary pressure (which had no parallel in the Germanic lands during this period) certainly demonstrate that Soloveitchik's concerns were not unfounded.[29] However, it was not only the German rabbis S. R. Hirsch and his teacher, Jacob Ettlinger, who expressed optimism about the emancipation of Jewry, but even the anti-Haskalah Russian Rosh Yeshiva, Netziv, viewed the era of emancipation in quite different terms than Soloveitchik, and none of these three doubted the sincerity of gentile piety. It would seem reasonable to assert that Netziv was an exception to the previously discussed general patterns of thought among East European rabbis, in terms of universalism and attitudes toward non-Jews.

Other passages in the writings of Beit ha-Levi that relate to gentiles display a similar attitude—one of mistrust but not dehumanization. Gentiles do not perform acts of kindness for selfless reasons but rather due to ulterior motives. Furthermore, gentiles are not considered bound, body and soul, to the mitzvot that they are required to perform. Whereas with Jews, their bodies are "owned," as it were, by God, which generates their obligation to observe the Torah, gentiles are merely required to keep their mitzvot. Their observance is not generated by, nor does it engender, a close spiritual relationship with God.[30] It is for this reason that it was relatively easy for God to negate gentile property rights (in a very limited context); had God wished to do the same to Jews, it would have required a more substantive process.[31]

A survey such as the present one would be remiss if it omitted reference to Rabbi Elijah Zvi Soloveitchik (1805–81), a grandson of Rabbi Hayyim of Volozhin and an uncle of the author of *Beit ha-Levy*. Soloveitchik, about whose biography little is known, was an idiosyncratic scholar who published a Hebrew commentary on two books of the New Testament (Mathew and Mark), endeavoring to demonstrate the compatibility of Orthodox Judaism with Christianity. Soloveitchik stressed that Christians are true monotheists and are not guilty of avodah zarah. Samson Raphael Hirsch approved of Soloveitchik's work on the New Testament, as did the German Reform rabbi Nehemiah Brüll (1843–191) and the French rabbi Lazare Wogue (1817–97). However, aside from these rabbis and some limited interactions with missionaries, Elijah's work has remained almost entirely obscure and, it must be stressed, had no impact on the course of Orthodox Jewish thought of the last two centuries.[32] While this fact alone may be worthy of further study, for the purposes of the present work, Soloveitchik's views cannot be considered as in any way representative of nineteenth-century East European Orthodox thought or of modern Jewish thought more broadly conceived.

For our purposes, there is no need to go into a lengthy analysis of Hasidic attitudes toward non-Jews in the nineteenth century, because the basic outlook of this movement, which emerged in the eighteenth century, did not dramatically change in the following century, at least as far as attitudes toward gentiles are concerned.[33] Hasidic views of gentiles are decidedly more negative not only than the views of Hirsch and other Neo-Orthodox leaders but also than the outlook of non-Hasidic East European Jewry. They are predicated on an ontological distinction between the essence of a Jew, who is wholly good, and that of a gentile, who is wholly bad.[34] It seems that this essentialist distinction was not altered as a result of the Enlightenment. Hasidic views of gentiles may even have been a reaction to the Enlightenment; however, since they are based on Kabbalistic sources, which predated the Enlightenment, it is difficult to determine the degree to which views of gentiles in Hasidic thought were engendered by the historical context in which Hasidism emerged.[35] Although there were Hasidic leaders who did not accept the caricature of all non-Jews as entirely bad, and some did have a more benign image of the gentile, there were none—to my knowledge—who saw non-Jews as ontologically no different from Jews, as fellow humans of a different nationality.[36] Nevertheless, it must be stressed that Hasidic writings exhort Hasidim to treat non-Jews in an ethical fashion, purported ontological differences notwithstanding. The non-Jew is still considered human in Hasidic thought, albeit a human who possesses a different spiritual character.

Among Hirsch's contemporaries in Central Europe, several stand out with respect to their views of non-Jews. Notable among them is Rabbi Moses Schick (1807–79), known as Maharam Schick. Schick was a prominent disciple of Hatam Sofer and became one of the outstanding Hungarian halachists of the nineteenth century.[37] Like Hirsch, Schick was a staunch advocate of secession and took the lead in the fight for Orthodox independence in the Hungarian Jewish Congress of 1869. Schick opposed S. B. Bamberger's ruling permitting membership in a Reform-dominated community and sided instead with Hirsch's more hardline stance.[38] Schick seemed to distance himself from Hatam Sofer's harsh attitude toward non-Jews, instead seeing the Reformers and not the non-Jew as the main enemy of the Orthodox Jew. There are no responsa authored by Schick that systematically treat the status of Christianity or discuss the value of gentile lives.[39] However, Schick did write an undated responsum on the permissibility of making an oath to become a representative of the city in partnership with gentiles.[40] In it, Schick discusses the applicability to contemporary Christians of certain laws of idolatry.

Schick begins by examining whether the laws pertaining to making treaties with idolaters apply to any nation other than the Seven Nations explicitly included in the biblical proscriptions against such treaties.[41] Many authorities had ruled that this prohibition applies to any nation that is idolatrous, which raises the issue of how the Patriarch Abraham who, according to rabbinic tradition, fulfilled all of the mitzvot, could have entered into a treaty with Abimelech, the pagan king of Philistia described in the book of Genesis.[42] Rabbi Schick argues that an oath-treaty that is made with idolaters for nonidolatrous purposes in a time of peace is certainly permissible. Accordingly, there would be no prohibition involved in the case brought before Schick. Not content with this reasoning, Schick adds, "It seems further that even if there were a prohibition [to enter into treaties with idolaters], this would only apply to other nations, but in the state and kingdom in which we reside, in which they protect us, and we are commanded by God through the prophet Jeremiah, 'Seek out the welfare of the city to which I have exiled you' [Jeremiah 29:7], and we have been made to swear in the name of God, and we are bound by this through the force of a commandment of God, it is [incumbent] upon us not to deceive or to be traitorous with them, for they protect us . . . If so, we have already entered into a treaty with them by God, so how could there be a prohibition to make an oath to them that we will not deceive or betray them?" On this basis, Schick permits the oath to be taken by the Jewish representative of the unnamed Austro-Hungarian city.[43] Although Schick says nothing that can be seen as a substantial departure from earlier rabbinic views on similar issues, the spirit of patriotism that permeates it is noteworthy.[44] The fact that Schick appears to take for granted that the gentiles in that city, who were certainly Christians, were indeed considered to be idolaters confirms what he had written in an earlier responsum, as noted.[45] However, some of Schick's ideas were taken to a whole new level by his son.

Rabbi Joseph Schick wrote an introduction, around 1880, to the *Orah Hayyim* section of his father's responsa collection.[46] In it, he takes up the issue of why God chose the Jewish people to be "the chosen nation" and develops a position strikingly reminiscent of the "mission theory." Joseph Schick states that God gave the Torah to the Jewish people for their own benefit. Therefore, he asks, was it not unfair for God to have limited his bounty by bestowing the Torah upon the Jewish people alone and not upon the other nations? He notes that the rabbinic statement that God did offer the Torah to the other peoples who then rejected it does not suffice to explain this seeming act of discrimination.[47] Schick therefore cites a different Midrashic passage that he feels was aimed at resolving this very difficulty. According to his interpretation, the Jewish people were the recipients of the Torah solely so that the other nations might benefit from the example which they set. The Jewish people were to be a model nation, whose fear of God and ethical conduct make them stand out as a model for emulation. Schick employs the Hebrew terms *yi'ud* and *shlihut* to characterize the Jewish people's purpose; both terms signify "mission."

Joseph Schick adds that this mission of the Jewish people was not carried out properly while it had sovereignty in the Holy Land, and it was therefore necessary for God to exile them. This exile did not mean a lessening of the Jewish mission but rather a broadening of it: now the Jews were to spread faith in God and His omnipotence throughout "the four corners of the world." This entire passage bears a remarkable resemblance to Hirsch's discussion of this subject in his *Nineteen Letters*, which was published well before Schick's essay was composed. A direct influence is possible. But it is equally likely that Schick's emphasis on the universal purpose of the selection of the Jews had become commonplace among many prominent nineteenth-century Orthodox Jewish thinkers.

There is no need to look to the Reform movement or the Haskalah as a source of these views, as they were generated by the emancipation itself. Joseph Schick, who lived through the 1848 revolutions and the *Ausgleich* of 1867 and, like most Hungarian Jews, was a staunch patriot, was uncomfortable viewing Jewish chosenness in a chauvinistic fashion. Instead, he regarded it as serving the interests of mankind at large.

Interestingly, one of the architects of Ultra-Orthodoxy, and a signatory to the 1866 Michalowitz ruling, Rabbi Hayyim Sofer (1821–86), also subscribed to the mission theory.[48] In his commentary to Psalms, Sofer discusses the role of the Jewish people in the world. He states that although all nations are children of God (citing Malachi 2:10 as a source), the Jewish people were chosen to serve as guides to the world on how to properly worship God. That is the raison d'être of the Jewish people.[49] In the messianic era, rather than seeking vengeance from the nations for their persecution of Jews, the Jewish people will be happy to see that their fellow men have finally reached the stage where they worship God properly.[50] Coming from a hardliner like Hayyim Sofer, these comments indicate the degree to which all streams of nineteenth-century Judaism subscribed to the mission theory.[51] Interpreting Jewish chosenness in a more chauvinistic fashion was simply unpalatable for those thinkers who lived during this era, in which emancipation of Jews seemed like a real possibility.[52]

Another important nineteenth-century Hungarian halachist was Rabbi Yehuda Aszod (1794–1866), author of the responsa collection *Yehuda Ya'aleh*.[53] Aszod makes the remarkable assertion, in a responsum dated March 26 1866, that rabbinic proscriptions against dealing with gentile ritual objects—even according to the view of Hatam Sofer—applied only to the Hindus of India but not to contemporary Christians, whose deity is not to be classified as "foreign."[54] As already noted, Hatam Sofer clearly had Christians in mind, and not merely Hindus, in his remarks upholding the applicability of the laws of idolatry to contemporary times.

Another remarkable (undated) responsum of Aszod that displays his liberal attitude toward contemporary Christians concerned the issue of a Jew serving as a matchmaker for the marriage of two non-Jews. Aszod rules that the matter is "obviously permitted" (*milta peshita de-shari*). He takes note of a medieval authority who had written that assisting non-Jews to give birth is tantamount to "increasing the seed of Amalek," so that perhaps assisting in a marriage that will most likely result in the birth of children should also be forbidden.

Aszod states that the view of the authority cited is "perplexing" (*tamu'ah*), for why does he assume that the non-Jewish children to be born will be in the category of the wicked Amalekites—perhaps the children will be among the righteous of the nations, who will merit a portion in the World to Come? In general, Aszod avers, we must consider the possibility of worthy descendants emerging from a union, perhaps some who will convert to Judaism, as the Talmud states about the grandchildren of Haman, who were said to have converted to Judaism and studied Torah in the land of Israel.[55] But Aszod hastens to add that it is not necessary to consider the possibility of the conversion of the gentile descendants of this union, for non-Jews are not expected to convert but can be considered righteous as non-Jews, as Maimonides ruled in his code. Therefore, on these and on other grounds, Rabbi Aszod rules decisively to permit this matchmaking so long as it will not require of the Jew to eat a feast at the non-Jewish wedding, which is rabbinically prohibited due to a fear of socialization leading to intermarriage.[56]

What is especially noteworthy about this responsum is the fact that Aszod raises what may be deemed humanistic objections to the medieval authority who compared helping non-Jews give birth to increasing the seed of Amalek, although Hatam Sofer, who lived only a generation earlier in the same Austro-Hungarian environs, cited that passage *approvingly* as a basis to prohibit saving the life of a gentile. Although the difference in attitudes of these two Hungarian halachists is only speculative, it is possible that Aszod, who lived through the 1848 revolutions, saw the emancipation process differently than did Sofer and was more willing to accept at face value the good-will gestures of Hungarian fighters for civic equality.[57] To be sure, it is difficult to maintain that Aszod's halachic view of Christianity was nothing more than an outgrowth of his attitude toward emancipation; his independent investigation of the sources (among other considerations) may have simply led him to different conclusions than those arrived at by Sofer. Nevertheless, I would suggest that the more benign attitude toward gentiles that Aszod expressed in his responsum on matchmaking may have also engendered a more liberal assessment of the religion practiced by most European gentiles, namely, Christianity.

It seems appropriate to round out our discussion of the views of East and Central European rabbinic leaders of the nineteenth century by looking at the views of Rabbi Meir Leibush Malbim (1809–79), a leader of East European Orthodox Jewry, a militant opponent of the Haskalah and Reform movements, and a prolific biblical exegete.[58] Malbim's oeuvre as well as his life story make him resemble, in many respects, S. R. Hirsch, who wrote similar types of commentaries and who fought similar battles. Malbim discusses non-Jews in several places in his writings. On the one hand, Malbim notes that shittuf is permissible for non-Jews, although this was said not in the context of a discussion of Christianity but in his comments to the Books of Joshua and Kings II, with reference to the ancient pagans who worshipped God through intermediaries.[59] Nevertheless, Malbim was well aware of the implications of such a view for the halachic status of Christianity.

One ambiguous passage in the writings of Malbim is his discussion of the commandment to "Love thy neighbor as thyself" (Leviticus 19:18). Although he does not state this explicitly, it would appear that Malbim regards "neighbor" as inclusive of non-Jews.[60] If this is the case, then Malbim broke from the more widespread tendency to interpret this verse narrowly—as limiting the obligation to love the "neighbor" to fellow Jews.[61] These references indicate that Malbim, as a nineteenth-century rabbi who fought against the East European Haskalah movement, was nevertheless concerned to demonstrate that Judaism preaches significant tolerance toward those who worship the Trinity and that it carries exhortations to love non-Jews.

In a remarkable passage, Malbim formulates a striking version of the mission theory. Commenting on the narrative of the spies who scouted out the land of Israel (Numbers 13–14), Malbim notes that if not for the sin of these spies, Moses would have entered the land, constructed the Temple, and the Jewish people would have merited eternal peace without experiencing the destruction of two Temples and exile from the land. But, Malbim asserts, this "salvation" would have been limited to the Jewish people. Due, however, to the divine decree of exile that was intimately connected to the sin of the spies, the Jewish people was afforded the opportunity to be exiled across the four corners of the earth, bringing core teachings about God and religion to humanity, thereby preparing *all* of humanity for the messianic era of spiritual perfection, where all nations will serve God in unison. The destruction of the Temples and the exile of the Jews from Israel, asserts Malbim, were thus not merely expressions of divine punishment but necessary preludes that enabled the Jews to serve as a vehicle for universal salvation.[62]

On the other hand, Malbim interprets the universalistic message of the Book of Jonah in as particularistic a manner as possible, arguing that the prophecy given to Jonah to warn the non-Jewish inhabitants of Nineveh of their impending destruction was proclaimed by God not so much to secure their salvation should they repent (as they did) but rather to allow Assyria (represented by a member city, Nineveh) to purge itself of its unworthiness to serve as God's tool to punish the Jews.[63] In this respect, Malbim was following the exegesis of Abravanel. However, since Abravanel represents a minority approach to this biblical narrative, Malbim's decision to follow Abravanel—and his rejection of the ample precedent for more universalistic readings of the book—indicate his rejection of those approaches.[64]

Had Malbim fully subscribed to the views of his rabbinic contemporaries in Germany, for whom the universal purview of God's concern was a fundamental principle of Judaism—and who felt the need to consistently emphasize this point in their writings—it is likely that he would not have interpreted the Book of Jonah in a manner that ignores its straightforward message of God's concern for the well-being of all mankind. Further, Malbim interprets Amos 9:7, which compares the Jewish people to Ethiopians, "with total disregard for the plain meaning," in a manner that removes any element of universalism from the verse.[65] Despite this one example, overall Malbim demonstrated a keen awareness of some of the ethical concerns raised by nineteenth-century thinkers and did not reject the entirety of their worldview, even though he did reject the maskilic program for educational reforms.

Having discussed the predecessors and contemporaries of the German-Orthodox figures who will be examined in depth—their primary antecedents and rabbinic peers—there are several possible conclusions. Patriotism was more widespread in Central Europe, where a genuine process of emancipation for Jews was clearly taking place.[66] Hungarian rabbis who lived in the mid-nineteenth century generally rejected Hatam Sofer's negative depictions of non-Jews, although they differed with one another about the halachic status of Christianity. Rabbis in the Russian Empire were not prone to expressing patriotic sentiments, but some of them did have a moderately positive outlook on non-Jews. Beit ha-Levi, the greatest Talmudist among them, was altogether suspicious of non-Jewish overtures to Jews.

His contemporary, Netziv, who spent much of his career writing commentaries on the Bible and on the less widely studied Midrashic compilations, viewed his non-Jewish contemporaries in a more positive light. The same can be said of Malbim, who was primarily a Bible commentator and never served as a Rosh Yeshiva. Neither Malbim nor Netziv, however, expressed a truly humanistic or universalistic outlook. Thus, although some East and Central European rabbis did espouse a more liberal attitude toward gentiles, or a more tolerant view of Christianity, than many of the medieval and early modern authorities, there is still no true parallel for the views of the German Orthodox leaders that are at the heart of the present work.

4

German Attitudes toward Jews in the Eighteenth and Nineteenth Centuries

Debate Concerning Jewish Emancipation in Germany

The broader context for Neo-Orthodoxy's attitude toward non-Jews and Christianity was the desire of its leaders to prove that Jews were worthy of emancipation. Thus a discussion of the debate among German intellectuals about Jewish readiness for emancipation is central to our analysis. This debate centered on various aspects of Jewish culture and belief that were regarded as potential obstacles to emancipation. In the last decades of the eighteenth century, a debate broke out among German intellectuals over whether Jews were truly worthy of citizenship. A catalyst for this debate, though hardly the only factor, was the Edict of Toleration promulgated by Habsburg emperor Joseph II, which permitted Jews to attend non-Jewish elementary and secondary schools and expressly allowed them to attend universities, although this had not explicitly been forbidden in the past.[1] Jews were also allowed to engage in business with the same conditions that applied to Christians—thereby permitting the opening of factories by Jews—and all trades were open to them. Certain restrictions, such as their exclusion from trade guilds and acquisition of land outside established Jewish communities, remained. This was a first step toward Jewish emancipation but it did not constitute its fulfillment. What is clear is that Joseph II intended thereby, among other considerations, to encourage Jews to engage in activities that demonstrated their loyalty as citizens.[2]

This was a watershed moment in the narrative of modern Jewish history. Traditionalists among the Jews were wary of these overtures and attempted to limit their impact. Those who came to be known as maskilim, by contrast, championed the edict and attempted to bolster its authority. Most famous among them was Naphtali Herz Wessely, who was a member of Mendelssohn's circle and an accomplished Hebrew poet and author of rabbinic commentaries that were praised by the leading traditionalist rabbis in Central Europe. Wessely published a controversial pamphlet, *Divrei Shalom ve-Emet* (Words of peace and truth), which called upon Jews, on religious grounds, to send their children to general schools.

Wessely argued for the pedagogic priority of what he termed *Torat ha-Adam*, loosely translated as human knowledge, which included sciences and the humanities, over *Torat Elokim*, the religious texts of Judaism. Wessely believed that most Jewish students would never come to excel in their Judaic studies, and so life as a religious scholar was out of the question for most. On the other hand, knowledge of science and the humanities was essential for exemplary citizenship and a meaningful participation in civic life, and therefore training in these subjects must be given priority over instruction in religious subjects. This program was clearly an attack on the normative education system of the schools sponsored by the traditional Jewish communities in Europe. It was not long before leading rabbis, including Rabbi Ezekiel Landau (author of *Noda be-Yehuda*), denounced Wessely as a "wicked" and "vile" man who dared to insult the prestige of Torah scholarship and Torah scholars.[3] (As discussed in chapter 8, Wessely's reputation was, to a large degree, rehabilitated after this controversy abated.)

The controversy within the Jewish community over Wessely's ideas was eclipsed by a much broader debate among non-Jewish intellectuals, a debate that came to define the entire Jewish quest for emancipation in Western Europe. Christian Wilhelm von Dohm, a historian, authored a pamphlet in 1781 (a year before the promulgation of the Edict of Tolerance) titled *Über die bürgerliche Verbesserung der Juden*, often translated as *Concerning the Amelioration of the Civil Status of the Jews*.[4] Dohm had been approached by Mendelssohn, who was actively seeking Jewish emancipation in Alsace, to write an essay that favored emancipation and addressed the concerns of those who opposed it. Dohm engaged head on with these issues, foremost among them the alleged particularism of the Jews.

It was alleged, Dohm notes, that Jews look down upon non-Jews and that their Talmud contained a wealth of anti-gentile passages.[5] Dohm further observed that all religions contain texts that speak derisively of members of other faiths; he singled out Christianity by name. What is more important, he argued, was how much weight the Jews give to the passages that have been seized upon by critics and whether there are other passages that are more authoritative and serve to mitigate any negative repercussions that might result from the harsher passages. Dohm maintained that indeed Judaism contained such statements and that the Jewish people as a whole have never accepted as binding those statements of individual rabbis that appear to deny ethical obligations to non-Jews. Dohm goes so far as to say that Christian persecution of Jews is what engenders any misanthropic views Jews may have.[6]

Dohm's most famous critic was Johann David Michaelis (1717–91), who argued that it was the primary purpose of Jewish law to keep Jews segregated from the rest of the world. A charitable reading of Talmudic literature could not change that essential fact. Since Judaism was fundamentally a particularistic religion, the possibility of "ameliorating" (or "bettering") the Jews did not exist. Michaelis also charged that Jews do not consider themselves to be truly at home in any gentile lands because they eagerly await their messiah's arrival on a daily basis.[7] Mendelssohn felt compelled to cite a passage from the Talmud—which he did not often do in his German writings—to refute Michaelis's claims. That passage, which is based on rabbinic exegesis of several verses in the Song of Songs, states that the Jewish people are compelled by oath to take no this-worldly action that might hasten the messiah's arrival.[8] Thus, argued Mendelssohn, the Jews' belief in the coming of a personal messiah did not in any way impede their loyalty to the states in which they live in any practical sense.[9]

This entire episode, one of the seminal events in the history of the emancipation of European Jewry, demonstrated just how damaging to Jewish hopes for civic advancement was the charge that Judaism was a particularistic religion.[10] Despite being the most famous, the Dohm-Michaelis dispute was hardly the first that cited supposed Talmudic particularism as grounds for denying Jews citizenship. Indeed, Anton Büsching, one of Dohm's mentors, had written in 1779 that the majority of Jews follow "Talmudic Judaism," not "biblical Judaism," and they will therefore always maintain a sense of disdain for non-Jews. Therefore, Büsching argued, Jews should not be granted equality even if a few exceptional ones, such as Mendelssohn and the Dutch economist Isaac de Pinto, were indeed worthy of it.[11] Büsching relied heavily on Johan Eisenmenger's *Entdecktes Judentum*.

On the eve of the century in which the process of emancipation began, a German Orientalist, Johann Eisenmenger (1654–1704), authored a two-volume treatise called *Entdektes Judentum* (Judaism Unmasked). First published in 1710, this work cited, verbatim, passages from the Talmud deemed to be anti-gentile, anti-Christian, or otherwise superstitious and unreasonable, with German translations. Jacob Katz has highlighted both Eisenmenger's erudition and his ability to cite rabbinic sources in a highly tendentious fashion. His approach leads the reader to believe that Talmudic Judaism preached the most malicious misanthropy, an impression Eisenmenger created by ignoring the context and authoritativeness of the passages cited and by giving an overly literal translation.[12] Even Michaelis, the most vocal opponent of Jewish emancipation in the final third of the eighteenth century, criticized Eisenmenger's improper use of rabbinic sources.[13] Nevertheless, Eisenmenger did not advocate violent measures against the Jews. He merely wanted to retain the status quo and opposed any lessening of already extant disabilities faced by European Jews.

As Jacob Katz has noted, Eisenmenger was an adherent of classical Christian teachings regarding Jews and their antipathy to Christianity. Contrary to the arguments of certain anti-Semitic polemicists, Eisenmenger was not an adherent of Enlightenment philosophy, and his attacks on Judaism ought not to be seen as those of a rationalist philosopher critiquing an irrational religion.[14] Eisenmenger's book was quite influential in the eighteenth century and beyond. Further, the essential argument that Judaism was an unreasonably particularistic religion was echoed by many leading Enlightenment thinkers, most notably Voltaire.[15]

Thus, at the cusp of emancipation in the 1780s the entire issue of Jewish particularism resurfaced. For opponents of emancipation such as Michaelis, Jewish particularism was an incontrovertible fact that vitiated any claims that Jews could be "improved" by granting them civic rights. It was precisely this concern that reemerged when Napoleon consolidated his control over France and wished to incorporate its Jewish residents into his empire. The charge of Jewish particularism continued to be a central theme that continually resurfaced throughout the nineteenth century in the writings of German intellectuals and theologians.

German Attitudes toward Jews in the Nineteenth Century

When examining the attitude of German intellectuals and writers toward Jews in the nineteenth century, it becomes clear that Jews were preaching a far more liberal attitude toward non-Jews than non-Jews were toward Jews. Even before the emergence of racial anti-Semitism in the final quarter of the nineteenth century, German writers had a generally negative and stereotypical attitude toward Jews.[16] However, the views propagated by German intellectuals prior to the 1870s are more complex than is often assumed. In many respects, they resemble the attitude which eighteenth century Enlightenment philosophers had toward Jews. Jews were still seen as fellow human beings with a claim to fundamental human rights.

It would be a mistake to read into some of the negative passages about

Jews in nineteenth-century German literature the vituperative dehumanization of Jews that was prevalent in the Nazi period.[17] No one questioned whether Jews were human beings; they questioned whether Jews were human beings who were entitled to all of the same rights as Christians.[18] If Jews abandoned certain practices and beliefs, virtually all German intellectuals were prepared to grant them full civic equality.[19] While the demand for Jews to take such a course of action was, of course, indefensible, it was not entirely unreasonable within the context in which these writers operated.

It is precisely in this context that the views of Johann Gottlieb Fichte (1762–1814) must be understood. He famously declared, "I see no way to give the Jews civil rights except to cut off their heads in one night and replace them with heads containing not a single Jewish idea."[20] Although this hyperbolic statement was not intended to be taken literally, the visceral hatred of anything Jewish evinced by Fichte here should not be taken lightly.[21] In the same essay, Fichte insists that his comments refer only to civic rights and that the Jews "must have human rights, even if they will not grant them to us. For, they *are* human and their malevolence does not justify our becoming like them . . . If you have eaten yesterday, but are hungry and only have enough bread for today, then give it to the Jew. He hungers for it, since he did not eat yesterday. You will be doing a good deed."[22]

Fichte further expresses his indignation at the Jews' alleged double standards, one for fellow Jews and one for non-Jews. Jewish exclusivism, which insists that Jews cannot even dine together with non-Jews, is another source of Fichte's displeasure. Since Jews insist on their superiority over non-Jews, they constitute a nation that is in a perpetual war with every nation in whose midst they reside. Therefore, granting them the same rights as other citizens would be both foolish and self-destructive. Thus Fichte, like Michaelis, believed that Jewish teachings rendered Jews who adhered to them unfit for emancipation. However, like Michaelis, Fichte did not advocate imposing additional restrictions on Jews and certainly did not encourage violent measures to be taken against them. The fact that Fichte was later usurped by the Nazi regime as a kindred spirit should not obfuscate the core difference between his attitude toward Jews and that of the Nazis: Fichte encouraged his readers to perform acts of kindness for Jews.

In discussing the view of German intellectuals toward the humanity of the Jew, the words of Christian Wilhelm von Dohm, the famous advocate of Jewish Emancipation, ought to be noted here. Dohm wrote: "Der Jude ist noch mehr Mensch als Jude" (The Jew is still more a human being than a Jew).[23] Coming from the foremost advocate of Jewish emancipation, this quote indicates that those German intellectuals who were influenced by Enlightenment thinking did not accept the Jew as anything less than human. Those who opposed the emancipation of Jews, most famously Johann David Michaelis, also did not call into question the humanity of the Jew: the Jew was certainly a fellow man, just one who was not entitled to the same rights of citizenship as Christians.[24]

The bases for denying equality of rights were alleged Jewish cultural and economic patterns, supposedly engendered by the teachings of Judaism. As the case of Fichte illustrates, these conservative forces accepted the complete *humanity* of Jews and did not wish to deny them the dignity that all humans merit; however, they did wish to deny them the full rights of *citizenship*. This approach was dominant throughout most of the nineteenth century, until the emergence of racial anti-Semitism in the final quarter of that century. It would be a mistake to read Nazi ideology into anti-Jewish statements that emerged in an entirely different context.[25]

It is essential at this point to examine the views of one of the most famous late nineteenth-century German anti-Semites, Heinrich von Treitschke (1834–96). Treitschke is often categorized with Wilhelm Marr, Adolph Stoecker, Georg Ritter von Schonerer, and Karl E. Duehring, as a leader of anti-Jewish agitation in the last decades of the nineteenth century. What is striking is how starkly von Treitschke's views stand out from those of the others he is often associated with. He is at pains to emphasize that Jews can be good Germans, if only they would assimilate and link their destiny with that of the German nation. As Paul Mendes-Flohr has noted, "he did not dispute the right of truly assimilated Jews to regard themselves as Germans, culturally and politically."[26] Ironically, the same man is notorious for proclaiming that "the Jews are our misfortune," a slogan later adopted by the Nazis.[27]

What seems to emerge from von Treitschke's writings about Jews is that he rejected the nascent racial theories about Jews even while sharing the gloomy view of Jewish malevolence that was advanced by the racial theorists. He expressed genuine disdain for those Jews, like Heinrich Graetz, who dared to posit a uniquely Jewish national history. If Jews want to speak of a unique Jewish identity, then they cannot simultaneously claim to be Germans, he wrote. It is a zero-sum game, and only Jews who regard themselves as *wholly* German can legitimately make any claims to be considered authentic Germans. But, in the end, von Treitschke believed that *Jews can be Germans*. This fact alone suggests that an examination of the writings of those German intellectuals who espoused anti-Semitic ideas, especially those who wrote before the final quarter of the nineteenth century, must not start with the assumption that their attacks on Jews constitute attacks on the humanity of Jews. A glance at fictional literature of the period confirms this.

Irving Massey has demonstrated that even in works of German fiction in which the author expressed anti-Semitic views, the murder of a Jew was always treated as a high crime, one which cannot so easily be expiated.[28] Massey argues that non-Jewish feelings of guilt for persecution of Jews over the centuries were a central factor in what he characterizes as philo-Semitic tendencies among certain nineteenth-century German writers. These writers were often prone to simultaneously expressing both philo-Semitic and anti-Semitic views, as if the legacy of European anti-Semitism could not be entirely negated from their consciousness; yet they still recognized the humanity of the Jews and the great evil involved in perpetrating violent crimes against them, with the ugly record of anti-Jewish violence over the centuries etched into their minds as they wrote.[29]

Another illustration of this attitude emerges from the writings of Theodor Mommsen (1817–1903). Mommsen was a classical scholar and historian and, as a member of the Prussian and German parliaments, he was a liberal advocate of Jewish civic equality with German Christians. He was also the only German writer to publicly attack Heinrich von Treitschke over the latter's 1880 anti-Semitic treatise. Nevertheless, this attack contains an exhortation for German Jews to assimilate and to abandon any vestiges of religious independence that he considered remnants of medieval times. He was criticized by Jewish leaders for sharing too many of von Treitschke's anti-Semitic presumptions.[30] What this debate suggests is that certain ideas were common to virtually all German writers of this period, irrespective of whether they are placed in the anti-Semitic camp or any other. The humanity of the Jews was not in question. At the same time, doubts lingered about alleged Jewish exclusivism. Defenders and detractors of Jews alike regarded Judaism and contemporary Jews with some degree of wariness on account of deeply entrenched notions pertaining to Jewish particularism and clannishness.[31]

Despite the anti-Semitic feelings and anti-Jewish suspicions that were widespread during this period, verbal (and, needless to say, physical) attacks on Jews were strictly forbidden in many German states.[32] Nevertheless, anti-Jewish violence was not a rarity; there were a number of violent anti-Jewish riots over the course of the nineteenth century in these territories.[33] However, governmental authorities were in no way complicit in these violent incidents; on the contrary, they did everything in their power to quell them, and the Jewish population was generally aware of these government actions.[34] While government opposition to anti-Jewish pogroms may have factored in other premodern and contemporary incidents of anti-Jewish violence, what distinguishes the case of nineteenth-century Germany was how it was perceived.[35] The perception on the part of Jews that the German governments were not complicit in these acts distinguishes them from, say, the Jews in the Russian Empire during the same period. This important distinction generated a sense of assurance among many German Jews that, indeed, times had changed and they were now living in a more enlightened era, with only lawless rabble-rousers involved in anti-Jewish violence.

A matter that is of significant import in seeking to understand the views of Jews held by nineteenth-century German intellectuals is the then–universally held doctrine that Christianity contains a morality superior to that found in Judaism. This view was promulgated even by friends of Jews. Interestingly, even those thinkers who were more secular in orientation—and who did not wish to see the spread of Christianity—still maintained that Jewish morality was inferior to Christian morality. This critique was based on several charges. First, Judaism promoted formalistic ritualism that was devoid of genuine spiritual content. Second, Judaism advocated a tribal ethics, that is, only fellow Jews were included in its legislation concerning human rights and obligations. Third, Judaism encouraged its adherents to look to Jerusalem as their true homeland and Germany as merely a temporary domicile. Finally, Judaism encouraged unhealthy and antisocial behavior that has led to the predominance of Jews in commerce-related professions. These themes appear throughout the writings of nineteenth-century German intellectuals, just as they had appeared in similar writings from the previous century. The debate between von Dohm and Michaelis in the late eighteenth century over granting civic equality to Jews centered on these very questions.

Perhaps no German intellectual in modern times has had a greater impact on the direction of modern Jewish thought than Immanuel Kant (1724–1804). Kant occupied the unique position of being one of the foremost German Enlightenment thinkers while simultaneously serving as the most incisive critic of many of the suppositions of Enlightenment thought.[36] What concerns us here is his relationship to Jews and Judaism. Despite Kant's popularity with Jewish thinkers of all religious orientations, he expressed stinging critiques of Jews and Judaism. Kant wrote that Judaism in its original form was "really not a religion at all" but was instead a "collection of mere statutory laws upon which was established a political organization."[37] Kant, following certain contemporary trends in biblical criticism, further alleged that Judaism "in its purity" (by which Kant meant its biblical form) never accepted a belief in an afterlife and this is another reason why Judaism "is not a religious faith at all."[38]

Kant's most trenchant criticism of Judaism and the one most relevant to our discussion was his view about Judaism's alleged particularism. Kant states that Judaism "actually exclude[d] from its communion the entire human race, on the ground that it was a special people chosen by God for Himself—[an exclusiveness] which showed enmity toward all other peoples and which, therefore, evoked the enmity of all."[39] This line of attack in particular proved to be quite decisive in the formulation of Reform Jewish ideology. Samuel Holdheim, as discussed in the next chapter, insisted that the father of all humanity be substituted for the father of one nation; other Reform thinkers shared Holdheim's sentiment. Since Kant was revered by German Jews, it was inconceivable for them to allow his criticism of Jewish particularism to go unanswered.

Kant also wrote that "the pure moral religion is the euthanasia of Judaism" (*Euthanasie des Judenthums*).[40] His views of contemporary Jews were no brighter. The Jews are "a nation of swindlers," he wrote, who benefit from "deceiving the people who grant them protection." Further, their immoral behavior demonstrates that they "do not aspire to civic virtue." On the contrary, there is a "spirit of usury which holds sway amongst most of them." Jews are "sharpers," said Kant, and they are "bound together by ancient superstitions." Since their nation is "composed merely of merchants, that is to say, of unproductive members of society," non-Jews cannot expect better from them.[41]

It is astonishing that Kant's Jewish admirers in Germany felt compelled to respond to his critique of Judaism but failed—to the best of my knowledge—to forcefully challenge his pejorative statements about Jews.[42] Isaac Breuer, a grandson of S. R. Hirsch, had a reverential attitude toward Kant, declaring that Jews should make a special blessing thanking God for having created the philospher.[43] Breuer's religious philosophy is couched in Kantian terminology, indicating both his indebtedness to the philosopher as well as his sensing the need to seriously grapple with Kant's ideas if one wishes to have an impact on skeptical young German-Jewish intellectuals. Breuer here followed the widespread veneration of Kant among German Jews of all stripes.[44] Yet there does not seem to have been any righteous indignation on the part of Breuer over Kant's anti-Semitism.

At this point, mention must be made of Georg Wilhelm Friedrich Hegel (1770–1831), one of the most influential of nineteenth-century German philosophers and a writer whose style (at least) had an influence on Samson Raphael Hirsch. As demonstrated by Yirmiyahu Yovel, Hegel was a consistent supporter of Jewish emancipation, but his views regarding Judaism vacillated significantly over the course of his life. In general, Hegel, like other Christian philosophers, ancient and modern, was a harsh critic of Judaism. Even more pertinent in this regard is the charge made by Hegel that Jews hate other nations, a hatred which stems from their conception of themselves as God's chosen people. Unlike Spinoza, who notes both Jewish hatred of other nations and the said nations' hatred of the Jews, Hegel mentions only the former, even using the Hebrew-Yiddish word "goyim" in this context.[45]

Yet despite these criticisms, Hegel does not qualify as an anti-Semite, according to Yovel, since he did not utilize his theological-philosophical criticisms of Judaism as a weapon against contemporary Jews. On the contrary, in the two places in his *Philosophy of Right* where he mentions Jews, he unequivocally supports Jewish political equality. "To exclude the Jews from civil rights . . . would be blamable and reproachable . . . Experience has shown that so to exclude them [Jews] is the silliest folly, and the way in which governments now treat them has proved itself to be both prudent and dignified."[46] Thus, like Schleiermacher, Hegel supported Jewish emancipation and opposed practical manifestations of anti-Semitism even as he criticized Judaism for its alleged particularism.[47] This should be kept in mind when examining the universalistic sentiments expressed by German Orthodox rabbis such as Hirsch.

As will be demonstrated more fully, the views of Friedrich Schleiermacher (1768–1834), the most prominent German Protestant theologian in the first third of the nineteenth century, are essential to a proper understanding of Jewish reactions to charges of Judaism's alleged tribalism. What makes Schleiermacher particularly noteworthy in this regard is his stance on anti-Semitism. He had well-known friendships with several assimilated German Jews, defended the potential for Jewish virtue, and proffered an unqualified denunciation of anti-Semitism. He characterized anti-Semitism as "an old bias" and "one of the miserable prejudices." Further, "Schleiermacher attended the Jewish salons and felt at home there."[48] When some of his contemporaries were lambasting Jewish exclusivism, Schleiermacher pointed to the existence of "educated and informed Jews," whose acquaintance he recommended Christians should make. Schleiermacher was wont to attend the synagogue and make comments to the preachers about their style.[49] This would have been unimaginable for a modern anti-Semite, and therefore his criticisms of Judaism ought to be seen as emerging from the tradition of European Christian critiques of Judaism and not as a manifestation of modern anti-Semitism.

Schleiermacher, like Kant before him, regarded Christianity as superior to Judaism on rational, and not just dogmatic, grounds, declaring that Judaism "is a dead religion and those who at present still bear its colors are actually sitting and mourning beside the undecaying mummy and weeping over its demise and its sad legacy."[50] Furthermore, when apprised of David Friedlander's plan to convert masses of Jews to Christianity on the condition that they would not have to accept Christian dogma, Schleiermacher responded—admittedly, not unreasonably—by calling this an attempt to "Judaize" Christianity.[51] Thus, despite his moderate approach to Jewish participation in European society and his qualified support for emancipation, Schleiermacher remained a triumphalist Christian and a proud German nationalist.[52]

In examining critical remarks about Judaism (and even about contemporary Jews) made by nineteenth-century German thinkers, it becomes clear that the humanity of Jews was not called into question by German writers of this period, even those with anti-Semitic leanings. The primary charge made against Jews prior to the final quarter of the century was that their religion was overly particularistic and that it promoted unproductive occupational patterns and negative moral traits. The universalist ethos of the Enlightenment, which had been dominant during the eighteenth century, was replaced by a more triumphalist German nationalism during the course of the nineteenth. Jews remained the targets of scorn but were welcome to join the German nation if they "corrected" the flaws they were charged with. Even von Treitschke, a leading anti-Semitic agitator, did not deny that Jews were capable of becoming "true" Germans. The notable exceptions to this summary are the late nineteenth-century racialist thinkers, whose views emerged long after the Neo-Orthodox rabbis had already formulated their basic conception of a thoroughly traditional, and simultaneously humanistic, Judaism.

Despite the lack of dehumanization of Jews by nineteenth-century German thinkers, there can be little doubt that anti-Semitic stereotypes of Jews were very much the norm throughout the century. Pre–World War II Germany simply did not produce that many non-Jewish thinkers who were genuinely liberal, especially when compared to contemporaneous English or American culture.[53] But for the Jews living in Germany, this did not seem to matter.

5

Jewish Intellectual Currents in the Eighteenth and Nineteenth Centuries

German Jews and Bildung

This book's examination of German Orthodoxy's view of non-Jews would be deficient if it did not consider the enormous role played by the conscious desire on the part of German Jews of all denominations to acquire broad culture and education. The term *Bildung* refers to this concept in its broadest sense and cannot be translated narrowly as "education."[1] David Sorkin states that "self-formation" is a better definition of Bildung as it suggests "a notion of the integral development of personality through a concept of form."[2] Bildung encompassed a sense of internal self-development, a process whereby one develops one's character holistically—wherein "the whole man would fully develop his inherent form by transforming all his faculties, mind and body, into a harmonious unity."[3] The pursuit of Bildung necessarily impacted attitudes of German Jews, including Orthodox ones, toward general culture as well as their unwillingness to tolerate forms of discrimination and prejudice toward non-Jews.

By the advent of the nineteenth century, German Jews were engaged in the process of acculturation, which they viewed as integral to their quest for emancipation. German Christian intellectuals repeatedly wielded the argument that Jews were not ready for emancipation since they confined themselves to economically deleterious occupations and were, more generally, uncivilized and untrustworthy. The desire to prove them wrong was instrumental in generating the enthusiasm that German Jews displayed for virtually all aspects of German culture.

Jacob Katz argued that German Jews pursued the cultivation of Bildung even more avidly than their Christian neighbors: "They were more avid readers of literature; they frequented theaters and concert halls in numbers far greater than their proportion of the population; and they were statistically overrepresented in all cultural activities."[4] Yet despite the preponderance of Jewish involvement in German cultural pursuits, Jews remained a group apart, noticeable to onlookers, both sympathetic and hostile, as Jews.[5] Katz expresses uncertainty as to the primary explanation for this disproportionate Jewish involvement in German culture, particularly the arts.[6] It seems, however, that the reason lay in the desire on the part of German Jews to prove their worthiness for emancipation, even if not all individual Jews who engaged in artistic pursuits consciously regarded themselves this way.[7]

Furthermore, the fact that German advocates of emancipation for Jews were also leading German enlightenment figures—luminaries such as Lessing and Schiller—created a linkage in the minds of German Jews between their own achievement of civic equality and participation in general cultural endeavors.[8] Among the endeavors that German Jews were especially fond of were German literature and music. Steven Lowenstein notes that even rural Jews from small towns were more educated and cultured than their non-Jewish peers; by the mid-nineteenth century this was reflected in the higher representation of Jews in institutions of secondary and higher education. By the late nineteenth century, Lowenstein notes, "rural Jews were more likely than their non-Jewish counterparts to read the German classics, know French, play the piano, or otherwise participate in urban German culture."[9] Thus, for these Jews, Bildung did not merely signify the acquisition of a rudimentary secular education but encompassed the broad sphere of German cultural activity. This pursuit ought to be seen within the framework of German Jews' quest for emancipation.

Most pertinent to our question is the fact that German Orthodox Jews valued Bildung no less than did their more liberal coreligionists.[10] Thus, prominent rabbis of the Neo-Orthodox mold such as S. R. Hirsch, Esriel Hildesheimer, and Marcus Lehmann all engaged in the sort of cultural activities that would have been foreign to their East European counterparts. For example, Hirsch attended classical music concerts, Hildesheimer was fond of German Lieder, including Heine's poetry, and visited Berlin's museums with his children, and Lehmann enjoyed swimming and horseback riding.[11] This is not intended to suggest by any means that Orthodox Jews attempted full cultural *integration* as much as their non-Orthodox peers. As already noted by Mordechai Breuer, Orthodox Jews not only had fewer opportunities for social intercourse with non-Jews than did non-Orthodox Jews but also "neither needed nor desired such living together . . . From the very beginning Orthodox Jewry renounced the social dimension of emancipation."[12] A distinction in this regard must be made between acculturation and integration (and, all the more so, assimilation). Orthodox Jews valued the former only, but they did so with no less fervor than non-Orthodox Jews.[13]

Taking this estimation as the starting point, it is clear that the premodern prejudices toward non-Jews were regarded as outdated and inapplicable to the nineteenth century. A prominent Orthodox teacher and Wissenschaft scholar, Abraham Berliner (1833–1915), even advocated the removal of the morning blessing thanking God for "not making me a gentile" and its substitution of a blessing in the affirmative, thanking God for "making me an Israelite."[14] Berliner also insisted that Judaism does not distinguish between Jew and non-Jew in the realm of love of fellow and interpersonal ethics.[15] Berliner's formulation almost appears to be a direct reply to the charge discussed by Von Dohm in his essay in favor of Jewish emancipation.[16] Other rabbis made concessions to Christianity that would have been unimaginable in an earlier century.[17] Thus, despite German Orthodox Jews' disinterest in integrating with their Christian environment, they certainly adjusted their cultural orientation in their quest for acceptance, here narrowly defined as being granted emancipation.

The very fact that German Orthodox leaders consciously strove to achieve full emancipation indicated a break with the past. Previously, many traditionalist rabbis expressed fear about the prospects of gaining full civic equality, as this might weaken adherence to religious observances and cleaving to the Jewish collective. (Hatam Sofer in particular voiced these doubts.) By contrast, nineteenth-century German Orthodox rabbis, led by S. R. Hirsch, actively worked toward emancipation in the hope that it would grant Jews the ability to carry out their religious duties unhampered by persecution and allow them to serve as a "light unto the nations."[18] This concept, which originates in the Book of Isaiah (e.g., 42:6) and came to the fore in the thought of some pre-nineteenth-century rabbinic authorities, achieved an emphasis and centrality that it had rarely attained before and was construed somewhat differently from how earlier rabbinic figures had construed it.[19] The proactive quest to be seen as cultured German citizens left an indelible mark on the ethos of German Neo-Orthodoxy.

In fact, prior to the emergence of Neo-Orthodoxy as a distinct response to the Reform movement, earlier traditionalist rabbis who had occupied some of the same rabbinic posts later occupied by Hirsch evinced similar attitudes toward modernity. Michael Miller's study of the rabbinate of Rabbi Mordechai Benet (1753–1829), Hirsch's predecessor in Moravia, sheds light on this question.[20] Benet, whom Noah Rosenbloom characterizes as "saintly" in contrast to Hirsch, who he (without evidentiary basis) says appeared to many elderly Moravian Jews as "not much different from a Reform rabbi," displayed a more progressive approach than is generally thought.[21] Benet approved of Herz Homberg's *Bnei Zion*, a German-language catechism of the Jewish religion. Although his endorsement of the book has been characterized as "lukewarm," he did clearly state (in German) that the book is in accord with the Bible, Talmud, and "all of the great teachers of our nation from ancient and modern times."[22] Further, Benet favored the pursuit of secular knowledge in a limited form and was known to have studied Mendelssohn's *Biur*. He actually authored an approbation to a Viennese edition of the *Biur* and referred to Mendelssohn as the "wise German translator."[23]

Therefore, heretofore accepted views as to the dichotomy between the traditionalist rabbis of the first generation of Orthodoxy and the leaders of "Neo-Orthodoxy" must be revised.[24] The same social forces that drove the Neo-Orthodox group to adapt to the cultural trappings of nineteenth-century German society also engendered a similar, though more conservative, reaction on the part of those Orthodox rabbis who possessed no formal secular education, did not pursue Bildung, and did not espouse an ideology of *Torah im Derekh Eretz*. Thus, despite the differences between the Neo-Orthodox and their predecessors, they shared a common outlook with respect to accepting at least some aspects of modernity; neither group considered modernity to be something that must be opposed in its totality.[25]

David Sorkin, in his seminal study of German Jewry, discusses the emergence of a "subculture" within German society comprised of Haskalah-oriented Jews, who stood out from traditionalist Jews but also from their Christian contemporaries.[26] While this group retained its outsider status during the eighteenth century and the first decades of the nineteenth, by the middle of the century, the pursuit of Bildung had become the common denominator of all German Jews, Orthodox and Reform alike.[27] The focus on Bildung ensured that German Jews of all denominations would not espouse views that were seen as incompatible with their self-perception of being cultured and morally educated people. Thus, from the point of view of nineteenth-century German Jews—even Orthodox ones—the anti-gentile hostility found in some medieval Jewish writings was, largely, without any contemporary relevance or application.

The pursuit of Bildung undoubtedly played a significant role in shaping the philosophy of the leaders of German Orthodoxy.[28] However, by itself, it accounts only for the absence of overtly anti-gentile prejudice among these rabbis. However, the consistently liberal universalism with respect to Judaism's view of non-Jews that is found in the writings of these men was generated by more powerful social forces. While some of the factors that can account for these rabbis' positions have already been outlined, additional factors to be discussed played an even greater role.

The Napoleonic Sanhedrin

The most highly publicized events that affected how traditionalist Jews in Central and Western Europe viewed their non-Jewish contemporaries were undoubtedly the 1806 Assembly of Notables and the 1807 Napoleonic Sanhedrin convened in its aftermath in Paris. These events were later used by partisans of the Reform movement to justify the proposed changes to Jewish law that it advocated. By contrast, Orthodoxy never expressly cited the Napoleonic Sanhedrin as the basis for its own position on Jewish law. Nonetheless, it seems likely that this event made a significant impact on the thinking of Orthodox leaders in the modern era. The impetus for the Sanhedrin was Napoleon's desire to verify the worthiness of French Jews for civic equality, with his most serious reservations concerning the attitude of Jews toward Christians with respect to such issues as loyalty to the state, intermarriage, and usurious practices. He believed that a convention of the most outstanding rabbis and lay leaders of the time could address these issues in a satisfactory manner.

There is ample literature on the background of how the Sanhedrin came to be convened.[29] One point that should be stressed from the outset is the anti-Jewish propaganda that emerged in the period preceding the calling of the Assembly of Notables. Accusations that Jews were disproportionately involved in usurious practices were rampant. Napoleon, who had earlier courted an amicable relationship with Jews who had come under his control, was now faced with the dilemma of how to ensure that the Jews of France would prove themselves loyal and patriotic citizens. His advisors suggested that a series of questions pertaining to some of the most controversial aspects of Judaism—or, at least, the manner in which Judaism was perceived—be posed to the leaders of French Jewry, both lay and rabbinic.[30] Here, it is helpful to focus on how one of the key questions was addressed by the rabbis who presided over the Sanhedrin to see to what extent their views served as a precedent for the later views of the German Neo-Orthodox leadership.

The question and answer pertaining to intermarriage between Jews and Christians were enormously influential on how later generations of Jews related to this issue. Rabbi David Joseph Sinzheim (1745–1812), supreme halachic authority and president of the Sanhedrin, carefully formulated his response so as to preserve the image of Jewish fellowship with Christians even while holding fast to the clear prohibition against such marriages that is found in the halachic literature. The translated text reads:

> The law does not say that a Jewess cannot marry a Christian, nor a Jew a Christian woman; nor does it state that the Jews can only marry among themselves.
>
> The only marriages expressly forbidden by the law are those with the seven Canaanite nations, with Amon and Moab, and with the Egyptians . . . The prohibition in general applies only to nations in idolatry. *The Talmud declares formally* that modern nations are not to be considered as such, since they worship, like us, the God of heaven and earth. And, accordingly, there have been, at several periods, intermarriages between Jews and Christians . . . but we cannot deny that *the opinion of the Rabbis* is against these marriages. According to their doctrine, although the religion of Moses has not forbidden the Jews from intermarrying with nations not of their religion, yet, as marriage, according to the Talmud, requires religious ceremonies called Kiddushin, with the benediction used in such cases, no marriage can be *religiously valid* unless these ceremonies have been performed. This could not be done towards persons who would not both of them consider these ceremonies as sacred; and in that case the married couple could separate *without the religious divorce*; they would then be considered as *married civilly but not religiously.*
>
> Such is the opinion of the Rabbis, members of this assembly. In general, they would be no more inclined to bless the union of Jewess with a Christian . . . than Catholic priests themselves would be disposed to sanction unions of this kind. The Rabbis acknowledge, however, that a Jew who marries a Christian woman, does not cease on that account to be considered as a Jew by his brethren, any more than if he had married a Jewess *civilly and not religiously.*[31]

Later partisans of Reform utilized this as a basis to deny that Jewish law forbids marriage between Jews and monotheistic gentiles (i.e., Christians).[32] Hatam Sofer, in his eulogy for Sinzheim, praised the latter for "not allowing others to rule over him" and not being "seduced into following them, God forbid. After he revealed one handbreadth, he concealed two handbreadths."[33] The latter clause refers to a Talmudic passage that admonishes the religious teacher to be careful in his application of Jewish law in difficult circumstances.[34] Sofer was saying that Sinzheim never compromised his halachic integrity and that even where he phrased something in a manner that was pleasing to his listeners, he simultaneously withheld from them more information they would not appreciate.

In the case of intermarriage, although Sinzheim emphasized that Judaism recognized civil marriages, he was careful not to state that such marriages were permissible, only that they are forbidden with pagans but that they are known to occur between Jews and Christians and that the Jewish partner would continue to be recognized as a Jew in such a case.[35] Sinzheim thereby concealed the fact that the entire corpus of halachic literature up until his time recognized that there was at least a rabbinic prohibition on Jews marrying non-Jews, pagan or monotheistic, and the fact that the Jewish partner would still be regarded as a Jew was of almost no relevance to the question presented to the assembly.

More noteworthy was the speech given by Sinzheim after ratifying the proceedings of the Sanhedrin. In this speech, Sinzheim declared that Jews were under obligation to adhere to all the laws of their country of residence, applauded the Sanhedrin's declaration about the brotherhood of mankind, and stated that the decisions of the Sanhedrin constituted a social pact between God's people and contemporary nations who regard Jews as equals. He then called upon mankind to recognize that the halacha was perfect and not in need of any reforms. He thanked the commissioners for their help and Napoleon for convening the Sanhedrin in the first place.[36]

Throughout the discussions leading to the decisions of the Assembly of Notables, the idea that contemporary Christians ought to be removed from the category of pagans, both in theory and in practice, was brought up repeatedly. Sinzheim may have been in favor of adopting this view so long as laws relating to intermarriage with gentiles were not abolished. The French commissioners who oversaw the assembly expressed dissatisfaction with what they regarded as the disingenuousness of the wording of the replies. With respect to the question of whether Jews considered Frenchmen to be their brothers, the answer given included copious citations from rabbinic literature promoting hospitality and love toward all men in addition to an expression of deep loyalty to France as the homeland of French Jews. The commissioners felt that this response was simply too vague: the real issue was whether biblical and rabbinic *law* authorized Jews to regard as brothers people who could not claim any Jewish ancestry or association with Judaism, with all the legal ramifications that this title carries. Thus, the question of whether there was a form of Jewish tribalism that justified discrimination against non-Jews was simply unanswered.[37]

Although the answers provided by the assembly were eventually ratified and the minister of the interior rebuffed the commissioners for their doubts, the substantive issues raised were never really resolved. Sinzheim, who presided over the proceedings, was careful to ensure that none of the answers of the assembly betrayed Jewish law. While there should be little doubt of his sincerity with respect to French patriotism and his positive regard for the morals of his Christian contemporaries, he did not explicitly adopt the view of Meiri, for example, which excluded in principle all Christians and Muslims from the disabilities that the Talmud places upon the gentile.[38] For Sinzheim, as a matter of practicality, Christians were to be accorded the highest level of respect, but no systematic reevaluation of the relationship between Jews and the gentile nations was to be undertaken. This next, more revolutionary, step was first undertaken by the early ideologues of Reform Judaism, whose views will be examined next.

Particularism and Universalism in German Reform Judaism

Perhaps the single most important factor in evaluating the views of German-Orthodox rabbis regarding non-Jews and Christianity is the stance adopted by the leading ideologues of German Reform Judaism to whom the German Orthodox rabbis were responding.[39] It was the leaders of Reform who made the "mission theory" of the Jewish people into a central creed of Judaism. Hirsch's classmate and later ideological antagonist Abraham Geiger (1810–74) developed the idea of the universal mission of Israel more thoroughly than anyone else.[40]

The roots of this ideology can be traced back to Mendelssohn's circle in mid-eighteenth-century Berlin. Mendelssohn himself argued that Judaism was fully compatible with Enlightenment rationalism as well as natural religion, and that it had no dogmas—in the Christian sense of the term—that were essential to salvation and known only via revelation.[41] Mendelssohn's ahistorical mode of thinking caused him to reject his friend Lessing's view of history as the divine "education of the human race."[42] Nevertheless, Mendelssohn did stress the centrality of the Jewish people to the moral betterment of mankind. In his view, the Jewish people were chosen by divine providence "to be a *priestly* nation, that is, a nation which, through its establishment and constitution, through its laws, actions, vicissitudes, and changes was continually to call attention to sound and unadulterated ideas of God and his attributes. It was incessantly to teach, to proclaim, and to endeavor to preserve these ideas among the nations, by means of its mere existence, as it were."[43]

Mendelssohn thereby laid the groundwork for the ideology that would later become central to all streams of German Judaism.[44] As important as this idea was to his Weltanschauung, it was greatly expanded by many of his followers in the Berlin Haskalah. Some began to further develop the mission theory in response to the raised historical consciousness of the Jewish intelligentsia in the early nineteenth century. The philosophy of Johann Gottfried Herder (1744–1803), in particular, paved the way for a stronger sense of the historical purpose of the Jewish people among German Jews. Herder's views regarding the peculiar role that each national group plays in history were influential in shaping the philosophy of nineteenth-century Jewish intellectuals across the religious spectrum. The emergence of the Wissenschaft des Judentums movement in the second decade of the nineteenth century brought about a tendency toward contextualization of Jewish texts, but it may also have served as an impetus for the popularization of the mission theory.[45] The first explicit expression of this theory after Mendelssohn is difficult to trace. The maskilic journal *Sulamith*, which paved the way for the Reform movement through some of the views expressed in its columns from the end of the first decade of the nineteenth century, discussed an "essence" of Judaism that must be separated from excess accretions to it.[46] But there appear to be no overt references to the mission theory in *Sulamith*.[47]

The position of Reform Judaism was formally expressed at the 1844 Brunswick Reform rabbinical conference. At the tenth session, on June 18, 1844, the committee of Reform rabbis agreed to adopt the following text, modeled on the answers given by the Napoleonic Sanhedrin: "The Jew considers members of the people with whom he lives his brethren." Abraham Jacob Adler (1813–56) then stated that it should be made known that "the Jews consider not only the people with whom they live as brethren, but all mankind. Do not all men, according to the prophets, have but one Father?" A discussion followed about the prudence of emphasizing the ties to the Jew's countrymen over mankind as a whole. All members of the committee, however, agreed that love of mankind and especially members of the "fatherland" of the Jew ought to be a central principle of Judaism.[48] Thus, Reform Judaism, centered in Germany, officially endorsed both patriotism and love of all non-Jews as core Jewish beliefs.[49]

What proved to be even more pertinent to the formation of Neo-Orthodox views was the acceptance by Reform ideologues of critiques of Judaism rendered by leading non-Jewish thinkers.[50] Several leading Reform thinkers strove to demonstrate that although these criticisms were valid, they were inapplicable to the Judaism of the nineteenth century because Judaism was a constantly evolving religion.[51] Thus, Kant's view of Judaism as isolationist and even misanthropic was accepted by certain Reform thinkers as true of *temporary* features of Judaism in certain periods of its evolution which no longer apply to present-day Judaism. Michael Meyer has observed that while German rabbis of all denominations tried to reinterpret passages in Jewish texts that were seen as morally problematic, "only the Reformers were willing to suggest that their reinterpretations were grounded in a morality that had transcended that of the Bible itself."[52]

Salomon Ludwig Steinheim (1789–1866), "the most original and least influential" of the systematic Jewish thinkers who emerged in the first half of the nineteenth century, was "a universalist who stressed that the Jewish religion, including its messianic teaching, was free of particularism."[53] Clearly, then, the intellectual climate of nineteenth-century German Jewry was inhospitable to any forms of Jewish particularism. It is thus unsurprising that the Neo-Orthodox camp strove to demonstrate by means different from those of Reform ideologues that Judaism was indeed a universalistic religion.[54]

One of the most radical of Reform ideologues, Samuel Holdheim (1806–60), fully accepted the critique of the concept of the Jews as "the chosen people" and therefore argued that it was time for Judaism to substitute "the holy God and Father of humanity for the holy God of Israel, the holy human race for the holy people, the covenant between God and humankind for the covenant between God and Israel."[55] Holdheim was clearly familiar with the critiques leveled by German intellectuals charging that Judaism preached a tribal morality. Instead of challenging them, he accepted the criticism entirely. This was in keeping with Holdheim's approach to Judaism in general. For example, when Samuel Adler, a leading speaker at the third Reform synod in Breslau in 1846, argued for the emancipation of the Jewish woman based on Talmudic sources, Holdheim rejected that approach entirely. He authored a volume arguing that women were not given a very exalted position in Talmudic Judaism.[56] Holdheim posited that "the elements and conditions of our age are so utterly different from those of rabbinic Judaism that the Jew has only the alternative either to be a rabbinic Jew and live outside of time or to live in time and cease to be a rabbinic Jew."[57]

Having taken this standpoint on Judaism, Holdheim had no compunctions about conceding to the critics of Judaism that the classical rabbinic, and even biblical, sources paint a chauvinistic view of God's ties to one particular nation.[58] It was the views of people like Holdheim that engendered Hirsch's unique approach to preserving (what became known as) Orthodoxy: Hirsch argued that Judaism must be understood based on what its texts say about its ideals and not judged by criteria that are external to Judaism.[59] Yet he took issue with the rabbinic leadership prior to the emergence of Neo-Orthodoxy for failing to properly understand the spirit of Judaism even as they observed its laws.[60]

It was in this context that Hirsch developed his unique version of the "mission theory." Hirsch is well-known as an advocate of this idea, and it has been suggested that he borrowed the idea from Reform thinkers or, at the very least, that his views regarding the Jewish mission were identical to those of Reform Judaism.[61] The importance of this ideology for German Jews has been well expressed by Michael Meyer:

> All streams of German Judaism also shared a fundamental doctrine: the "mission of Israel" . . . As early as the eighteenth century Moses Mendelssohn argued that the Jews were chosen by Providence to be a priestly people, whose task among the nations was to call attention to its unadulterated idea of God and high morality. Following Mendelssohn, Hirsch's writings from the very first repeatedly expressed this idea . . .
>
> The mission of Israel was the most extreme response to the alleged depravity of the Jewish religion argued by the enemies of emancipation; it was, in effect, the chosenness of Israel turned outward. No matter that in practical fact few Christians believed they still had anything to learn from the Jews; for the Jews themselves the mission of Israel was the most powerful doctrine of self-justification. Thus Jewish particularism ceased to be an end in itself, becoming instead the means toward a greater goal: the universal acknowledgement of the God of Israel and God's moral precepts for humanity. And thus the survival of the Jews became more, not less, significant in an age of emancipation.[62]

In fact, the "mission theory" hardly remained the property of German Judaism.

As noted, Central European Orthodox leaders of the nineteenth century who experienced the emancipation process and remained optimistic about its chances for success embraced this idea as fervently as their German coreligionists. Thus, Rabbi Zvi Hirsch Chajes (1805–55), writing in the first half of the nineteenth century, was at pains to emphasize that the Jewish people were selected by God to be the bearers of Godly ideals amid mankind. God intended no favoritism to the Jews in choosing them; He intended to make them responsible for a greater task than He asked of the rest of mankind.[63] Rabbi Joseph Schick, in his 1880 introduction to his father's responsa collection *Maharam Schick* makes the same point, as did Malbim.[64]

Thus, the mission theory is not a peculiar innovation of the Neo-Orthodoxy of S. R. Hirsch or of the Reform Judaism that he opposed; it was instead the product of the social process that all Western and Central European rabbis—of all denominations—experienced. However, among the Orthodox, it was formulated most forcefully and consistently by the segment that engaged in anti-Reform polemics, namely, the German Neo-Orthodox.

Another prominent feature of nineteenth century Reform Judaism was its denationalization of Judaism. No longer were the Jews a nation; they ceased to be one when the Second Temple was destroyed and they were scattered across the earth. Judaism was entirely a matter of faith, and the Jews were a faith community only. This meant that German Jews were "Germans of the Mosaic persuasion" rather than members of the Jewish nation. The same could be said of the Jewish communities of other West European countries such as Holland, France, and England. Abraham Geiger famously wrote that he was concerned for the Jews of Damascus, after the 1840 blood libel there, as a human being, but it was not their Jewish identity that engendered his concern; only the spiritual progress of other Jews was of concern to Geiger as a Jew. Although he later modified his views somewhat, the basic concept of Judaism as a faith and not a nationality was central to Reform ideology up until the 1937 Columbus Platform.[65]

Although the Neo-Orthodox were unable to accept that Jews were not a nation but a faith-community only—this is examined in chapter 8—they identified with Germany as the "Fatherland" as enthusiastically as their Reform counterparts did. The Jews were a unique nation, they believed, whose nationality was based on shared religious goals rather than on common territory. Thus, a sense of kinship with German Christians as fellow citizens of the "Fatherland" was central to the self-identity of German Orthodox Jews. It necessarily followed that rabbinic texts that appear to allow for discrimination between Jews and non-Jews could not possibly have any application in modern times.

The framework for the Neo-Orthodox paradigm shift with respect to views of non-Jews and Christianity is thus: Jewish chosenness could no longer signify a Jewish monopoly on divine favor; nor could it allow for invidious discrimination between human beings. Thus, though it was inevitable that citizens of Germany who adhered to different faiths would disagree about theology, there could be no question about their common humanity. Mystical conceptions of Jews as a distinct species that are found in certain medieval and early modern Jewish texts were therefore regarded by the Neo-Orthodox as simply irrelevant (and, possibly, even as a distortion of Judaism).

Nineteenth-Century German Christian Theology

The German-Orthodox rabbis who formulated their views on Christians and Christianity did so with a sound—even if only rudimentary—knowledge of Christian doctrine and practice. All of the rabbis examined here attended German universities, and Hildesheimer, Lehmann, and Horovitz attained doctorates. They were all exposed, in differing degrees, to Christian theology as it was developed by their contemporaries. Hirsch in particular is known for his knowledge of the ideology of the Protestant theologian Friedrich Schleiermacher. It would be impossible to evaluate the assessment that these rabbis made of Christianity without giving a general overview of the currents of nineteenth-century German Christian theology, particularly as it relates to conceptions of the Trinity and the incarnation.[66]

Among the most prominent German Christian theologians of the mid-nineteenth century were Gottfried Thomasius (1802–75), Isaak August Dorner (1809–84), and Alois Emanuel Biedermann (1819–85); their theologies have been anthologized by Claude Welch.[67] What makes these individuals important is the fact that they were reacting to what they regarded as the excesses of rationalism, which denied a place to the miraculous in human history. They wanted to restore belief in the classical doctrine of the incarnation to the liberal-minded Protestants among whom they lived. To the extent that the views of these three men were known by the rabbis under survey here, it would have been clear that all three accepted the classical doctrine of the incarnation of God in human form in the person of Jesus. What these thinkers grappled with was how precisely to interpret the meaning of this incarnation for those who are rationally inclined and thereby to explicate how it relates to the individual (Christian) believer's daily life.

The issue, then, for the German Orthodox rabbis was how to relate to their Christian colleagues' belief in the doctrine of the incarnation. Whether this doctrine is compatible with Enlightenment rationalism or not—the issue to which Thomasius, Dorner, and Biedermann devoted themselves—it would seem to run afoul of the prohibition of AZ for gentiles. Perhaps the Orthodox rabbis believed, as Michael Wyschogrod has argued, that the concept of incarnation, though not in its Christian form, was not incompatible with Jewish teachings.[68] The extent to which nineteenth-century Christian theologians were willing to reinterpret the concept of incarnation would surely have played a role in the rabbis' view of it. For, if by incarnation, Christians did *not* conceive of Jesus as a man-God in a literal sense, then no issue of AZ would have come into play merely because the Godhead was referred to as a Trinity. The mere affirmation of a tripartite relationship within the Godhead would not necessarily entail the violation of the proscription against AZ, at least as far as gentiles are concerned.[69]

Friedrich Schleiermacher discussed the doctrine of the Trinity in his writings and developed a nonliteral conception of the incarnation. Karl Barth, the author of a monumental work discussing the main themes of nineteenth-century Protestant theology, criticized Schleiermacher's conception of the Trinity as being too unitarian (i.e., placing too much weight on the unity of God to the detriment of God's triune nature).[70] Schleiermacher had argued that the person of the Father constitutes the essence of the Godhead and that the other two persons of the Trinity were created by the Father.[71]

This transforms the concept of Jesus as "the son of God" into a more literalist idea of God having fathered a son with a human mother. It follows that the son was not primordial (and was not present at the world's creation). He was created. This corresponds to the manner in which the seventeenth-century author of *Olat Tamid* presented the doctrine of the Trinity.[72] Notwithstanding Barth's criticisms, Schleiermacher remained a venerated figure for theologians such as Barth due to the former's significance in reviving and modernizing Protestant theology in the nineteenth century.

Despite the important role played by Schleiermacher in general German intellectual and religious history, it is not at all certain that this influence extended to German Jews. It seems that even S. R. Hirsch, the most philosophically sophisticated of the German Orthodox rabbis examined here, was not intimately familiar with the nuances of contemporary Christian theology. He was quite familiar with Schleiermacher's romanticist approach to religion, which Hirsch believed posed a danger for traditional Judaism. He was therefore interested in countering this view as forcefully as possible in his writings.[73] However, he gives no indication in those passages that he exerted any effort to understand Schleiermacher's conception of the Trinity. Whatever view Hirsch held of his Christian fellow citizens, it was not based on a careful analysis of all aspects of their Trinitarian theology.

There is, however, one passage in which Hirsch expresses concern about Trinitarianism and shittuf and which may indicate awareness of Schleiermacher's conception of the Trinity. This passage was written in Hirsch's youth and in Hebrew, which he rarely used, and was left unpublished at the time of Hirsch's death.[74] This is the only passage in his writings where he directly addresses the issue of shittuf for non-Jews.[75]

The medieval halachic codifier Rabbi Moses of Coucy had written that the second of the Ten Commandments prohibits Jews from accepting other entities as divine beings even if one does not substitute such entities for God.[76] Hirsch specifically cites this passage in his Pentateuch commentary (which was composed in German and thus available to the non-Jewish public), which is clearly treating the parameters of acceptable notions of God *for Jews*.[77] But in this Hebrew manuscript, Hirsch directly addresses the view of halachists that non-Jews are not proscribed from shittuf. Hirsch argues, on the basis of BT Sanhedrin 63a, that shittuf is a *more grievous sin* than pure idolatry.[78] If so, he asks, how can shittuf be permissible for non-Jews?

To resolve this difficulty, Hirsch proposes that there are actually two types of shittuf: the first is where one merely cites God in conjunction with another being, although that being is not accepted as "an outright deity" (*ke-eloah gamur*). This is the form of shittuf permissible for non-Jews. The second type of shittuf, forbidden even to non-Jews, is where an entity is accepted as a deity, even though the worshipper also worships God. That form of belief is "certainly in the category of avodah zarah," writes Hirsch. Hirsch ends this passage with the abbreviation for "and the matter needs further elucidation," indicating his own ambivalence about interpreting the Talmudic source relating to shittuf in this manner.

The most relevant aspect of this passage, however, is Hirsch's citation of and acceptance of the view of the author of *Olat Tamid*, who had permitted a form of Trinitarian worship for non-Jews—just the sort of Trinitarian worship espoused by Friedrich Schleiermacher, the leading Protestant theologian of nineteenth-century Germany. Apparently, this passage, written early in Hirsch's life and not intended for publication, represents Hirsch's first grappling with the issues involved in Christian worship but it was hardly his last word on the subject.

Hirsch authored a responsum later in life—it is undated—in which he implicitly states that a Christian woman who is loyal to her faith would be regarded as an observer of the Seven Noahide Laws. The issue brought before him was whether to permit the circumcision of a boy born to a Jewish father and a gentile mother. Since such a child would be considered halachically non-Jewish, performing a circumcision for the sake of conversion would ruin the child's chances of salvation, for as a Jew he would be bound by many more commandments and restrictions than as a non-Jew and, in the post-emancipation era, the likelihood that this child would faithfully carry out all of the mitzvot was very slim. By contrast, if he adhered to "his mother's faith, he would then be given the possibility of conducting his life in a manner that is pleasing to God through his observance" of the Noahide Laws.[79] Obviously, if Christianity runs afoul of the AZ prohibition, Hirsch could not have stated this. Hirsch was essentially reiterating the position he had already emphasized in his other writings, namely, that Judaism does not demand adherence to its doctrines to ensure salvation. Instead, leading a moral life, defined as observing the universal Noahide Laws, guarantees salvation.

It therefore seems justified to assert that despite the severe limitations in German Orthodox rabbis' understanding of Christian theology, they nevertheless developed a theory of religious tolerance that included pious Christians. They simply did not concern themselves with the precise contours of their Christian contemporaries' religious beliefs. Given that the rabbis under examination here, especially Hirsch, were not followers of Maimonides's philosophical system, according to which one's intellectual grasp of the essence of God is the highest level of religious worship that can be achieved, it is unsurprising that they did not submit their Christian contemporaries' theological beliefs to any rigid litmus tests.[80] They essentially accepted the view of earlier halachists who had classified Christian Trinitarian worship as shittuf and adopted the lenient stance according to which such worship is permissible for non-Jews. This seems to be the only plausible explanation for why no attempt was made by the leading German Orthodox rabbis of the nineteenth century to delve into the precise nature of their Christian neighbors' theological beliefs.

6

Rabbi Jacob Ettlinger

Rabbi Jacob Ettlinger as a Pioneer of Neo-Orthodoxy

Rabbi Jacob Ettlinger (1798–1871) is rightly regarded as a pioneer of German Neo-Orthodoxy along with his friend and colleague Rabbi Isaac Bernays (1792–1849). Both rabbis were among the first in Europe to give sermons in the vernacular and to don the canonical robes worn by Christian clergy. Both attended university and, though neither received a degree, both recognized the value of secular knowledge from a religious point of view. More than Ettlinger, Bernays has remained something of an enigma for scholars. Although it is known that he combined the most rigid traditionalism with a very broad humanitarian and cultured outlook, he left behind no significant writings that can be attributed to him with certainty.[1]

Heinrich Graetz said of Bernays that he was "the first to recognize in a much profounder manner than Mendelssohn the importance of Judaism in the history of the world, and at a glance to take an accurate survey of the range of its literature."[2] Hirsch, who was one of Bernays's most famous students (along with Hildesheimer), said of his teacher, "He was the greatest shining light of Jewish thought of his time, and were he alive today, the same would still be true."[3] Despite his vehement opposition to the emerging Reform movement, Bernays was deeply immersed in the intellectual currents of his day and exerted a powerful influence on some Christian contemporaries.[4]

Rabbi Bernays was perhaps the first leader of Orthodoxy, understood as an early nineteenth-century movement, to regard the broader non-Jewish world as a matter of great import for Judaism. The view, prevalent in Eastern Europe, that Judaism was concerned primarily with Jews was regarded by Bernays as a distortion of authentic Jewish teachings. Although Bernays's authorship of *Der Biblische Orient* has been contested, there is no doubt that Bernays authored, in German, a critical review of a scholarly work by a Protestant Bible scholar that was published in a Protestant journal of theology.[5] Furthermore, Bernays befriended the liberal Christian theologian J. A. von Kalb and the two studied texts from each other's religion together, a most uncommon pastime for traditionalist rabbis of any century.[6]

Kalb actually wrote a letter of recommendation on behalf of Bernays, in which he stated that Bernays was unique among Jews in his deep knowledge of the world, human history, and politics.[7] Thus, Bernays represented a break with the premodern rabbi whose dealings with the non-Jewish intellectual world, if there were any, were of a more pragmatic nature (such as rabbis who were hired to teach Hebrew to Christians) or, in some cases, polemical. Bernays regarded the broad world of European culture as within the purview of a rabbi and in fact central to the Weltanschauung of Orthodox Judaism.[8]

Bernays had an enormous impact on Hirsch's intellectual development, as Hirsch himself testifies.[9] However, contrary to Rosenbloom, Bernays was a thoroughly rabbinic Jew, not a maskil.[10] The German maskilim of the eighteenth century and the Russian maskilim of the nineteenth century had anticlerical views; they wished to reform Jewish society on the basis of non-Jewish critiques of that society; they wished to bring European culture to their more traditionalist brethren; and they generally (with Wessely as a notable exception) did not treat *all* Talmudic and halachic texts with reverence. Bernays was undoubtedly more open to modern culture than his traditionalist predecessors, but that does not make him a de facto maskil: he did not share any of the four aforementioned points with the maskilim. His primary goal was to defend what then became known as Orthodox Judaism from its modernist critics.[11] As there was no Haskalah in Germany in the nineteenth century, it would also be anachronistic to label Bernays as a maskil.

One of Bernays's closest friends and colleagues was Rabbi Jacob Ettlinger, a Talmudist of the highest rank and the last German Rosh Yeshiva. The two studied religious texts together while they were taking classes at the University of Wurzburg. Ettlinger eulogized Bernays upon the latter's passing.[12] To be sure, Ettlinger had some misgivings about Bernays's philosophical lectures and generally discouraged students from attending them. However, this is not because Ettlinger harbored doubts about the Orthodoxy of Bernays's beliefs but rather because he believed single-minded devotion to Talmudic studies was the only way genuine success could be achieved in that field. He made exceptions for students like Esriel Hildesheimer, who he was convinced would not neglect his Talmudic studies as a result of attending these lectures.[13] When Bernays was attacked for his opposition to the renewal of the Hamburg Reform prayerbook in 1841, Ettlinger immediately came to his defense. There can thus be no doubt that Bernays, despite his broad culture, was fundamentally a rabbinic Jew, that is, someone whose worldview was formed primarily by a reading of authoritative rabbinic texts, such as the Talmud and codes of halacha, and not by critiques of traditional Jewish society made by those outside it.

Whatever doubts have been raised regarding a relationship to Haskalah in the case of Bernays certainly do not apply to Ettlinger, who was thoroughly immersed in traditional Talmudic studies for his entire life. He was also introduced to the Kabbalah by his father and retained a lifelong veneration for Jewish mysticism.[14] His magnum opus was his multivolume work of Talmudic novellae, *Arukh la-Ner*, which is considered a classic in the genre to this day. His second most important work is his collection of responsa, *Binyan Zion*, and it was as a rabbinic judge in the beth din of Altona (which retained its civil status until 1863) that Ettlinger found his greatest fulfillment. Ettlinger was indeed a rare combination of old and new, combining the mysticism and Talmudic studies of old-school Orthodoxy with a university education and a broad outlook on the problems facing nineteenth-century Jewry. Although he did not receive a formal degree, certificates and affidavits from professors testify to his diligence in his study of philosophy at the University of Würzburg.[15]

Kaufmann Kohler has stated with respect to Ettlinger, "Ettlinger was a remarkable personality . . . Having been one of the earliest German rabbis of academic training and having become one of the most prominent and strictest upholders of Orthodoxy in all its practices and beliefs, the saying was that Satan made him go through the university and come forth immune and loyal so as to lure the rest of modern rabbis to pursue those studies which caused their disloyalty to traditional Judaism. He was a pronounced mystic and spent hours in prayer . . . He dwelt chiefly on the Halakhic discussions [of the Talmud], pointing out difficulties in the most naïve fashion."[16] What Kohler seemed unable to grasp was how Ettlinger managed to combine his university training with his more "old-fashioned" traits such as mysticism, intense prayer, and traditional Talmudic studies. In reality, the tension Kohler perceived was due to Ettlinger being sui generis, the first of his type. In the following generations, figures such as Esriel Hildesheimer, Marcus Horovitz, and David Zvi Hoffmann would combine some of the same qualities Ettlinger was known for and would no longer be considered as figures characterized by irreconcilable contradictions.

Rabbi Ettlinger's comments on the value of secular studies are ambivalent. On the one hand, he criticized those who would give undue weight to these studies based on spurious arguments from isolated rabbinic passages. He emphasized the superiority of Torah study above all other knowledge. However, he conceded that value may be derived from limited pursuit of these studies, which could even serve to bolster Torah knowledge.[17] The fact that he himself attended the university of Würzburg for nearly three years, devoting himself particularly to the study of philosophy, combined with his support for rabbinical seminaries that incorporated a secular curriculum, serves to mitigate the criticisms he issued in his homiletic sermons.[18] The schools that he founded in Altona taught secular subjects to both girls and boys.[19] It is apparent that when secular studies were pursued under rabbinical supervision and within clearly defined limits, they met with his full approval, his written reservations applying only to those who might diminish their desire for the acquisition of Torah knowledge as a result of secular pursuits.

Ettlinger's approach of preaching in pure German and donning modern clerical gowns was imparted to his students, Hirsch and Hildesheimer foremost among them. As a young rabbi, Ettlinger expressed the sort of patriotic sentiment that Hirsch would later espouse. In an 1824 sermon, he stated, "Therefore always faithfully follow and punctiliously obey the laws and duties of the states that, with paternal mildness, allotted you their gifts. Regard them as your fatherland, just as you formerly regarded the Promised Land of your patriarchs (*Betrachte sie als dein Vaterland, wie es dir früher das gesegnete Land deiner Erzväter war*)."[20] Just how much of this was a genuine religious exhortation and how much was a reflection of Ettlinger's youthful German patriotism cannot be determined with certainty. Ettlinger certainly did not mean that Germany ought to be regarded as the replacement for Palestine as the Jews' homeland. This was the view of partisans of Reform, against which Ettlinger devoted significant effort. In fact, in his last will, he expressed veneration for the land of Israel and insisted that although it would not be feasible to be buried there, he at least wished to be buried with soil that he had purchased (and stored in his attic) from that land.[21] Clearly, Ettlinger's promised land remained the land of Israel, not Germany.

Ettlinger probably intended to arouse his audience to a strong sense of identification with the land of their birth. Indeed, Ettlinger was consistently patriotic throughout his life and, further, expressed optimism that he was living at the dawn of a new era. He applauded the "sun of Enlightenment which has banished the dark clouds of religious prejudice" as evidenced by the civic emancipation of Jews.[22] This optimism would be passed on to his student, S. R. Hirsch, who expressed similar patriotic sentiments in his *Horeb* (published in 1837), written both after Hirsch's studies with Ettlinger and the publication of the latter's youthful sermons.[23]

Ettlinger's Views of Non-Jews and Christianity

Rabbi Ettlinger expresses his view of the era in which he lived in several places in his posthumously published sermon collection, *Minhat Ani*.[24] In one passage, he describes the two stages of the Jewish exile (*Galut*): the first is the stage of persecutions and humiliations, in which the trial is to remain faithful Jews despite the difficulties. The second stage is the era in which he lived, when persecutions have come to an end and Jews "dwell in tranquility under the protection of benevolent states."[25] The test here is whether Jews will sacrifice their tradition for the sake of material advances or whether they will remain faithful to the Torah despite the allure of European civilization. Samson Raphael Hirsch, Ettlinger's student, expressed precisely the same view in his journal, *Jeschurun*.[26] Ettlinger also expressed optimism that the benevolence of his times would make it easier for Jews to observe the Torah.

Ettlinger emphasized that the relationship of the nations of the world to the Jewish people ought to be considered as parallel to that of a priest to the laymen. The selection of the Jewish people by God did ***not*** imply a rejection of the rest of humanity but a choice of one group to serve to advance the interests of all of mankind. Just as a *kohen* (the Jewish priest) is not exempt from the obligation to love his fellow Jews, so too the Jews are not exempt from their duties of love towards all of mankind. Both the priest and the Jewish people are expected to act in the interests of the larger "community" and neither can claim special favoritism toward them on the part of God. "And only in this matter and with this condition is the separation of Israel from the nations [to be understood]."[27] This theme is a central motif in all of the writings of Ettlinger's student, S. R. Hirsch, whereas in Ettlinger's writings it is merely one idea among many that makes an occasional appearance. Although it is not a centerpiece of his worldview, Ettlinger's particular formulation of the distinction between the Jewish people and the non-Jewish nations is noteworthy. Most of his colleagues in Central and Eastern Europe—the case of Netziv stands out as a notable exception—conceived of the chosenness of Israel in a far more exclusivist fashion.

Ettlinger does indirectly refer to the monotheistic status of Christianity in several places in his writings when discussing the issue of shittuf. In a responsum dated June 3, 1858,[28] he was asked about the permissibility of transforming a building originally built for nonreligious purposes and then used for a number of years as a church into a synagogue or study hall. Ettlinger begins this responsum with the assumption that the church indeed constitutes "accessories to avodah zarah" but then proceeds to argue against a prohibition on different grounds. Still, he suggests that it may be preferable to avoid using the building in question. At this point, Ettlinger states that the church is not truly a place used for AZ because non-Jews are not proscribed from shittuf and, further, no actual idolatrous objects were brought into the building. Ettlinger then questions the relevance of the fact that non-Jews violate no prohibition when they worship in a church by noting that Jews certainly do violate the AZ proscription by worshipping there; accordingly, *for Jews* the building is a "house of AZ." He therefore cautions against using the building as a synagogue, while still maintaining that there are sufficient grounds for leniency because the building was not originally built for religious purposes.

What is noteworthy about this responsum is that Ettlinger takes for granted that non-Jews violate no prohibition by engaging in shittuf worship. He was certainly aware of the controversy over this point and had read the views of those authorities who contested this assertion and who maintained that only when taking an oath was no prohibition infringed but worshipping the Trinity was certainly prohibited even for non-Jews. Ettlinger may have had other grounds to base a prohibition to use the building in question but it was not because he had any doubts in his mind as to whether Christianity was sufficiently monotheistic for non-Jews. This interpretation is corroborated by comments from Ettlinger's Talmudic novellae, *Arukh la-Ner*.

The Talmud states that one of the demands that was made by Naomi of Ruth when she expressed a desire to join the Jewish people was the prohibition of AZ.[29] The commentators wonder why this demand would have been placed on a convert if non-Jews are already prohibited from AZ on the basis of universal Noahide law. Rabbi Ettlinger responds that there is one form of worship that is considered AZ for Jews but not for non-Jews and that is shittuf. It was this form of worship that Ruth was being told to abjure. As a proof text, he refers to the oft-cited *Tosafot* to Sanhedrin 63b, which as noted was the source of much controversy. Ettlinger simply takes for granted that the *Tosafot* unambiguously ruled that worshipping God along with partners—which is the halachic view of Christian Trinitarian worship—is permissible for non-Jews.[30]

In other places in his novellae, Ettlinger repeats his contention that *shittuf* is permissible for non-Jews. Commenting on the *Tosafot* to Sanhedrin 63b itself, Ettlinger states that the commentators have stated that the subject of *Tosafot*'s declaration that non-Jews are not prohibited "on this [*al kach*]" refers to shittuf. He then notes that it is unnecessary to emphasize that shittuf is what *Tosafot* is permitting because gentiles are not forbidden from swearing in the name of actual AZ, so certainly swearing in an "association" would be allowed.[31] Clearly, Ettlinger accepted the view that Christian Trinitarian worship was permissible. In another passage from his *Arukh la-Ner* Ettlinger notes that non-Jews are permitted to engage in shittuf worship, stating that this is the normative halacha.[32] Once again, in a case where Ettlinger had the chance to *challenge* the contention that non-Jews are not proscribed from shittuf, he instead made a point of *affirming* that this is indeed normative Jewish law.

Aside from these passages in his halachic and Talmudic writings, Ettlinger did not directly address the standing of Christians or of Christianity. The period in which he lived would have made such discussions sensitive at best and potentially ruinous for any prospects of emancipation at worst. Ettlinger was content to emphasize the duty of brotherly love that the Jew owes towards all his fellow men and to note that the selection of the Jewish people by God was intended to further universalistic aims. By taking for granted the nonidolatrous status of Christians in his halachic writings, despite the controversy that surrounded this question among latter-day authorities (*aharonim*), Ettlinger made it clear to his readers that he regarded Christians as fellow men who were capable of achieving immortality.

Still, he stopped short of directly confronting centuries of Jewish-Christian polemic; nor did he grant Christians a specific role in his philosophic scheme. Since Ettlinger was primarily a Talmudist, this is unsurprising. His more philosophically inclined student, S. R. Hirsch, did address the role of Christianity in the divine scheme in a manner consistent with his style of idealistic prose that was employed only rarely by Ettlinger (in his German language sermons). However, another of Ettlinger's students, Esriel Hildesheimer, who was primarily a Talmudist, developed some of Ettlinger's ideas a bit further and it is to him, and to some of his contemporaries, that we now turn our attention.

7

Rabbi Esriel Hildesheimer and Other Nineteenth-Century German Orthodox Leaders on Non-Jews and Christianity

Rabbi Esriel Hildesheimer (1820–99) was the most prominent leader of Neo-Orthodoxy in the second half of the nineteenth century, aside from Hirsch. Hildesheimer was Rabbi Jacob Ettlinger's close student, having forged a closer and deeper relationship with him than did Hirsch. The age gap between Hildesheimer and Ettlinger (twenty-two years) far exceeded that between Hirsch and Ettlinger (ten years). Further, Hildesheimer began his studies with Ettlinger in 1837 when Ettlinger was older and a more renowned scholar than he was when Hirsch studied with Ettlinger in 1828.[1]

Consequently, Hildesheimer's relationship to Ettlinger was almost like that of a son and indeed in one of Ettlinger's responsa he refers to Hildesheimer as "my son."[2] Further, Hildesheimer studied with Ettlinger for more years than did Hirsch and, by temperament, he was more closely aligned to Ettlinger's Talmudic disposition than was Hirsch, whose scholarly activity concentrated more on Jewish thought and ethics than on advanced Talmudic studies.[3] Thus, Hildesheimer's approach to the problems facing Orthodox Judaism in the modern era more closely resembles that of Ettlinger than does Hirsch's.

On the issue of patriotism, however, all three rabbis appear to have held virtually identical positions. Ettlinger's patriotic statements have already been discussed, and Hirsch's will be examined in chapter 8. Hildesheimer, who was born in Germany but spent a number of his younger years in Hungary, seemingly felt an attachment to his birthplace that was comparable to Hirsch's, although the latter lived there for all but four years of his life.[4] Although

Hildesheimer's correspondence does not appear to contain characterizations of Germany as *der Vaterland* (an expression that appears in Hirsch's writings), Hildesheimer nevertheless did not regard Germany as a land of "bitter exile" (as a correspondent of his claimed) and instead maintained positive "personal feelings for his homeland."[5] Further, his daughter, Esther Cavalry, described her younger years when Hildesheimer used to sing German Lieder to her while she sat on his lap, having a special fondness for those of Heine.[6] Nevertheless, in response to Abraham Geiger's claim that "Europe is our Jerusalem," Hildesheimer responded that "Europe is not our Jerusalem"; rather, "Israel is our homeland [*Heimatland*]."[7] But this concept was understood by Hildesheimer, like Hirsch, in a spiritual sense; in the here and now, Jews ought to be devoted to their lands of residence and must not try to hasten the Final Redemption.[8]

Rabbi Hildesheimer authored only one responsum that directly relates to Christianity, dated November 29, 1885.[9] He was informed by the rabbi of the Bavarian city of Burgpreppach, Shimon Zvi Deutsch, that a new teacher had been hired to teach history at the local Jewish school. That teacher was said to have repeatedly uttered the name of Jesus in his classes. When asked why he did not avoid making explicit reference to Jesus, he stated that Jesus's name was cited in a textbook on reading and he did not wish to deliberately avoid saying his name so as not to offend the two Christian students in the class. Rabbi Deutsch told this teacher that he did the right thing and that it would have been a profanation of the divine name (*hillul Hashem*) had the teacher been "strict" on a matter that only involves an act of piety (*midat hasidut*). Still, he cautioned the teacher to examine the reading materials in advance of his classes to avoid having to mention Jesus's name with too much frequency. Deutsch was then notified that "another rabbi" had taken issue with his ruling that mentioning Jesus's name is only an infringement of an act of piety and is not an outright halachic violation. Therefore, Deutsch decided to write to Hildesheimer to obtain his ruling on this matter.

Deutsch spelled out his reasoning for being permissive in the text of his query. He noted that an earlier authority had written that only names that directly refer to the divinity of a deity are forbidden to be mentioned, but general names that happen to be deities are not forbidden.[10] This earlier authority had further noted that the Talmud itself makes reference to Jesus and his disciples on numerous occasions "and there is no greater [false] deity than him." Deutsch adds that these Talmudic references, as well as citations of Jesus's name in many other rabbinic works, are limited to the name "Jesus" alone (with a few exceptions). It would thus seem that the use of Jesus's name in the Jewish school should be permissible without reservation.

Hildesheimer responded with an affirmation of Deutsch's position. He notes that the Talmudic references to Jesus say only "Yeshu" but never "Christ," or the equivalent, since that refers to his messiahship. Hildesheimer expresses his bewilderment at the fact that many of his contemporaries were strict about employing the word Jesus while they were lenient when it came to the name Christ, which presents a far greater halachic impediment. He commends Deutsch for clearly presenting a preference for the use of only the name Jesus. Hildesheimer then states that the fact that the term "messiah" (in reference to Jesus) and "messianists" (in reference to his followers) is used in a handful of rabbinic works does not indicate any permissiveness to refer to Jesus as the messiah in speech.

Hildesheimer continues his response by noting that the vast majority of early modern and modern rabbinic works were printed in Christian countries. Jews in Muslim countries, however, may well avoid referring to Muhammad by name. In any case, Hildesheimer avers, there is simply no comparison between the two since Muslims have never regarded Muhammad as anything other than a prophet, unlike the Christian belief in the divinity of Jesus. He further notes that Rabbenu Nissim (Ran) is of the view that gentiles are not proscribed from shittuf (i.e., Trinitarian worship), a view that is also codified by Rema in his glosses to the *Shulhan Arukh*. Despite the weight of this view, Hildesheimer makes a point of noting that there are divergent opinions on this matter. Although he does not spell out what those views are, he does cite several authorities who argued that shittuf is not a permissible form of worship for gentiles. This is perhaps the most noteworthy part of the responsum: Hildesheimer's willingness to entertain the view that Trinitarian worship may actually be forbidden for non-Jews.[11] Nevertheless, that is not the view that he personally endorses, just as his teacher Ettlinger, who was aware of the controversy surrounding shittuf, ultimately sided with the liberal view.[12]

Another responsum by Hildesheimer deals with the issue of non-Jews innovating religions. Maimonides had written in his code that just as the Talmud declared Sabbath observance and Torah study off-limits for gentiles, so too any innovative religious practice—beyond observance of the Seven Noahide Laws—is forbidden for them.[13] Yet Maimonides also ruled that non-Jews may perform Jewish ritual acts (mitzvot) for the sake of receiving reward although they are clearly not commanded to perform such acts.[14] Various commentators have grappled with Maimonides's source for extending the Talmudic proscriptions to any new religious practice. (Some medieval authorities, such as Meiri, rejected the assertion that gentiles are forbidden to innovate religions.[15])

Hildesheimer offers a novel interpretation of Maimonides's view, predicated on his approach to reconciling Maimonides's aforementioned two rulings. He suggests that the prohibitive stance of Maimonides was referring to a case of a non-Jew who persists in worshipping avodah zarah and wishes to associate ritual commandments of the Torah with his pagan religion; that is prohibited. But a monotheistic gentile who has totally abandoned avodah zarah and wishes to perform Torah commandments in order to receive reward is certainly allowed to do so. Hildesheimer bases this interpretation on Maimonides's use of the term *akum* (an abbreviation for *Ovdei Kokhavim u-mazalot*, i.e., idolators)—which is the censored version of the term found in uncensored texts, namely, *goy*—in the proscriptive ruling and Maimonides's change to the term *ben Noah* (a Noahide law-observing gentile) in his permissive ruling.[16] Maimonides intended to suggest that only pagans were not allowed to observe Jewish rituals; morally upright non-Jews may certainly do so. Hildesheimer then adds these key sentences:

> And in this [way] Maimonides has satisfactorily resolved that which [has caused] many of the sages of the nations of the world [to] have cried out against the Talmud, which states that a gentile who observes Sabbath is liable to death. To this, Maimonides places sound reasoning, [that the case refers to a gentile] who has fabricated a religion from his heart and does not observe the Sabbath for the sake of the Torah but instead invents a religion based on human intellect alone and not the religion of our God, may He be blessed, and he remains simultaneously an idolator, as Maimonides begins his words 'an *akum* who studies Torah . . .' This [clearly] indicates that he remains an idolator and [yet] studies the Torah in order to invent a new religion. And this is destructive to anyone with connection to religion [*ba'al dat*], and he is like one with no faith at all. That is why he is liable to death, and is worse than other *akum*. For one [the observant Noahide] has, at least, the religion of his fathers, whereas the other [the pagan] has no religion at all. And understand this, for this is good as a response to a heretic.[17]

The expression "response to a heretic" is often used in rabbinic literature in cases where the assertion associated with it is not an authentic presentation of rabbinic law or ideology but is merely presented to satisfy critics of Judaism. However, it would be a mistake to understand Hildesheimer's use of this expression here as indicative of a lack of sincerity to the interpretation that he offered. It is quite clear from the tenor of Hildesheimer's remarks, and from the fact that nowhere else does he proffer insincere readings of rabbinic texts to placate hostile critics, that he considered the interpretation that he advances to be a compelling one. What he means by "this is a good response to a heretic" is that he is aware that Maimonides's ruling here has been criticized by those hostile to Judaism—Jews and non-Jews—and is satisfied that he has presented a satisfactory reading of Maimonides that simultaneously undercuts the basis for those who regarded Maimonides's statements as an expression of religious intolerance.[18]

In a different responsum written to Hildesheimer pertaining to the conversion of a child born to a Jewish father and Christian mother, Rabbi Zvi Hirsch Kalischer (1795–1874) expressed a version of the mission theory when he writes that God loves all of humanity and certainly wishes to benefit all of it; that is why the Torah was first offered to other nations. But despite their refusal—according to rabbinic homily—to accept the Torah, the Jewish people remains "like the priests of all of humanity, so that when you [the Jews] come close to Me [God] they too [the rest of humanity] will see the light, as indeed actually occurred, for all believers among the nations [i.e., non-Jewish faiths] are rooted in the holy Torah . . . and since the Blessed One wishes to benefit his creations and they have not thus merited [by accepting the whole Torah]," it is beneficial to allow them to convert to Judaism with as few obstacles as possible.[19] This desire to more fully carry out the priestly mission of the Jews to humanity by spreading the light of Torah as widely as possible by converting gentiles was not shared by Hildesheimer, who rejected Kalischer's halachic view that this child ought to be circumcised and thus converted to Judaism.[20] This, however, was not because Hildesheimer did not endorse the mission theory but rather because he did not believe that it entailed a mandate to convert non-Jews to Judaism whenever feasible; on the contrary, Hildesheimer preferred those born as non-Jews to lead exemplary lives in keeping with the Noahide Code.

Although Hildesheimer did not often express idealistic assessments about the Jewish mission to the world, he could be quite pragmatic when it came to Jewish-Christian relations. He (along with S. R. Hirsch) was sent a query as to whether it might be permissible for a rabbi to attend the cornerstone-laying of a church. He (along with Hirsch) answered in the affirmative.[21] At the same time, Hildesheimer cautioned against the wearing of a decoration in the form of a cross.[22] It would seem that the latter scenario would not have involved a breach of proper etiquette if the decoration was not worn whereas there would have been such a breach if Orthodox rabbis refused to attend ceremonies associated with the dedication of churches since it was not uncommon for priests to attend similar ceremonies at the founding of synagogues.[23] Furthermore, the potential halachic violations involved in the latter case were more significant than those of the former case.

Hildesheimer also took a firm stance with respect to the issue of *hukkot ha-goyim*, the prohibition against imitating certain gentile practices. When a group of Hungarian rabbis met in the town of Michalowitz in November of 1865 to issue a series of prohibitions against what they deemed to be unjustified accommodations to modernity that had been made by the Neo-Orthodox, Hildesheimer did not remain silent. He wrote a rejoinder to the Michalowitz ruling arguing that the aesthetic adjustments made in Neo-Orthodox synagogues, though designed to modernize these synagogues, were not an attempt to mimic Christian services and therefore no prohibition applied to these actions.[24] The fact that Orthodox synagogues would have certain features of their prayer services in common with Christian churches was of no concern to Hildesheimer.

It is noteworthy that in his private letters Hildesheimer did sometimes refer to non-Jews in a manner that does not distinguish him from earlier rabbinic authorities.[25] In a letter to Moshe Mendelsohn-Frankfurter of Hamburg (1782–1861), a Hebrew poet who had a sympathetic view of the earlier Haskalah, and who was an uncle of S. R. Hirsch, Hildesheimer decries the religious laxity of his era and wishes for the day when, "with God's help, the wicked will return to the grave, all nations that are forgetful of God."[26] The latter clause comes from the Book of Psalms (9:18) and it was the focus of the Talmudic passage discussing the righteous of the nations.[27] Although Hildesheimer clearly accepted Maimonides's ruling endorsing the view of Rabbi Joshua, namely, that righteous gentiles are heirs to paradise, he did not make a point of noting in this letter that he lived in a new era where morality was common among gentiles or where most non-Jews venerated the Bible and adhered to its moral code, something Hirsch would likely have done.[28]

This does not indicate a departure from Hirsch, who made a point of emphasizing those ideas in his published writings. Since Hildesheimer's letter was a private correspondence, which he did not intend to publish, it does not weaken our central argument about German Orthodox rabbis of the nineteenth century. What Hildesheimer expressed in private when corresponding with a broadminded Hebrew poet is quite different from what he wrote in responsa or novellae intended for publication. He felt no need to demonstrate Judaism's universalism or its recognition of Christianity's contribution to civilization when writing in confidence to a man who was already convinced of these points. In this case in particular, Hildesheimer may have felt that Mendelsohn-Frankfurter was a bit too enamored of German culture and therefore deliberately expressed his longing for a messianic era where wickedness—which necessarily exists within a secular culture not predicated on the fear of God—no longer existed. Unlike the ideologues of Reform Judaism, Hildesheimer regarded the messianic era as yet to come.

Even more striking in this regard is Hildesheimer's 1884 protest against a declaration made by sixty-eight leading non-Orthodox rabbis.[29] The declaration contained three statements. The first was that Judaism affirmed ethical obligations toward all non-Jews, who are duty-bound to follow the prophet Micah's admonition, "It has been told of you, man, what is good, and what the Lord requires of you: to do justice, to love mercy, and to walk humbly with your God" (Micah 5:8). Two key verses from Leviticus (19:18 and 24:22) were also cited as a basis for Judaism's universalistic ethics. The declaration further alleged that any particularistic statement found in rabbinic literature that would seem to contradict the principle of universal love must be understood as an individual opinion only, one which was engendered by an atmosphere of anti-Jewish persecution. The rise in German anti-Semitism in the 1880s gave renewed vitality to the charge that Judaism prescribes dual ethics: one for how Jews treat fellow Jews and one for how they treat non-Jews. Thus, these non-Orthodox rabbis wished to publicly refute that charge.

The non-Orthodox declaration, in its second statement, noted the need for raising religious awareness and education among Jews so that Jews may better understand what Judaism demands of them, and also so that they may better respond to the disparagers of Judaism. Finally, the declaration expressed hope for a meeting of rabbis from all denominations with the hopes of creating an interdenominational alliance of all German rabbis that could work together on common causes.[30]

Interestingly, Hildesheimer led a group of fifty-nine Orthodox rabbis who protested against this statement. They argued that the declaration by the liberal rabbis was simply incorrect. Non-Jews are bound by the Noahide Laws, not by the verse in Micah that was cited. In order to be considered a righteous individual, a gentile would need to do more than follow the vague directive of Micah; he/she would have to be committed to a specific lifestyle, one that is permeated by the observance of those universal laws to which all descendants of Noah are perpetually bound. In particular, Hildesheimer was incensed by the omission from the non-Orthodox declaration of any obligations expected of non-Jews in the realm of sexual morality.[31] Thus, these Orthodox rabbis, led by Hildesheimer, felt that the liberal declaration misrepresented a key teaching of Judaism, namely, the moral obligations to which non-Jews are bound. Naturally, Hildesheimer considered it obligatory for Jews to treat *all* non-Jews with the highest standards of ethics and consideration. But the obligation of brotherly love (mandating actively sustaining one's fellow) was predicated upon observance of the Noahide Laws, which

Hildesheimer suggested was something that observant Christians, as monotheists, adhered to.[32]

Hildesheimer's counterstatement also declared that the second plank of the non-Orthodox declaration was misguided because in order to raise Jewish religious awareness, the normative texts of rabbinic Judaism, such as the Talmud, would have to be studied as authoritative texts, and the liberal rabbis regard the Talmud as nonbinding. Finally, stated Hildesheimer, non-Orthodox rabbis do not have the capacity to speak on behalf of Judaism, and there can therefore be no interdenominational agreement between Orthodox and non-Orthodox rabbis. The latter's nonbelief in the divinity of the Torah rendered them unqualified to issue religious declarations. Hildesheimer and the other Orthodox rabbis who signed this alternative statement thus affirmed their acceptance of S. R. Hirsch's principles concerning the relations between Orthodox and non-Orthodox clergy.[33]

In his analysis of this statement, David Ellenson has concluded that the decisive factor that generated Hildesheimer's counterstatement was liberal Judaism's lack of qualification to issue statements pertaining to Jewish law and practice, and this appears to be correct.[34] It seems highly unlikely that Hildesheimer would have publicly refused to sign the aforementioned sort of declaration of universalism had the declaration originated with fellow Orthodox rabbis. Even though Hildesheimer still would not have agreed with the assertion about non-Jewish obligations being limited to the verse in Micah, the pressing need to respond to anti-Semitism would most likely have engendered a more sympathetic reaction on his part. In particular, there would have been no pressing need to take a public stand that could have been seen as limiting Jewish universalism.[35]

What is particularly interesting about this episode is that S. R. Hirsch did not sign Hildesheimer's counterstatement, a matter upon which they corresponded. Hirsch stated that Hildesheimer's protest letter conceded "too much recognition of the men who personify the total opposites of the inalienable Jewish truth." Furthermore, Hirsch felt that the proposed meeting of German rabbis mentioned in the non-Orthodox declaration was likely not to occur, and by making a public statement about it, the Orthodox are unwittingly giving credence to the whole idea. The best approach, Hirsch averred, was silence, which would ultimately lead to the demise of the entire project.[36] Hirsch was particularly upset with Hildesheimer's agreement to further discuss the possibility of an arrangement between the Orthodox and non-Orthodox even after issuing the counterstatement; Hirsch blamed this on the Reform rabbi Rudolph Ungerleider, who pressed Hildesheimer about the matter. Negotiating with Reform rabbis about a potential rapprochement constituted "a crime against the holiness and truth of our cause."[37]

Clearly, Hirsch shared Hildesheimer's view about the incapacity of non-Orthodox rabbis to issue declarations pertaining to Judaism's teachings; to Hirsch, the very fact of Hildesheimer's engagement with the liberal rabbis regarding this matter was, at best, a tactical error and, at worse, a tacit recognition of the legitimacy of non-Orthodox Judaism. However, when it comes to the specific issue of Judaism's expectations regarding the conduct of non-Jews, it is questionable whether he agreed with Hildesheimer's counterstatement. Although he clearly considered the Noahide Laws to be the basis for non-Jewish society, he may have felt that the verse in Micah cited by the non-Orthodox does, in its unique way, encapsulate these laws, and that it may therefore have been a fitting manner to convey the Jewish view of non-Jewish obligations to a general public, particularly in a time of heightened anti-Semitism. Hirsch does not appear to address this issue in his correspondence with Hildesheimer.[38]

It is clear that Hildesheimer was the Orthodox rabbi who took it upon himself to gather the signatures for the Orthodox counterstatement, the effect of which was—even if only unintentionally—to mitigate somewhat Judaism's universalism. This indicates, I believe, that Hildesheimer did not place as great a priority on expressions of universalism as did Hirsch, although it may not necessarily point to a diminution of Hildesheimer's conception of Jewish universalism. Some suggestions that may account for this difference between these men are discussed later.

Another letter written by Hildesheimer demonstrates a keen awareness of German anti-Semitism. This letter, written to members of the Jewish community of Kishinev, Russia, in the aftermath of the devastating pogroms there, discusses the feasibility of emigrating to various countries to escape the threat of anti-Semitic violence. Hildesheimer notes that Chancellor "Bismarck himself is undoubtedly inclined toward antisemitism."[39] This assessment of Bismarck is noteworthy because Bismarck is sometimes regarded as having been favorably disposed toward Jews.[40] Hildesheimer clearly did not share this assessment. Further, Hildesheimer does not recommend that the Kishinev Jews enlist the aid of a German organization that was created to help emigration and relocation for persecuted individuals.[41] Hildesheimer felt that if this organization was aware that the petitioners were Jewish, it would have no interest in helping them due to anti-Semitic sentiments held by its leaders.[42] Thus, despite Hildesheimer's tolerant disposition when it came to non-Jews and Christianity, he was not naive regarding the prevalence of German anti-Semitism in the late nineteenth century.[43]

Hildesheimer's limited remarks pertaining to non-Jews or Christianity are insufficient for us to render any sweeping judgments concerning the importance of universalism to his religious ideology. Nevertheless, a few preliminary observations may be made. Hildesheimer was not a revolutionary in terms of Jewish views of non-Jews. He followed those whom Jacob Katz has characterized as "the enlightened halakhists" of the early modern period in considering Christians to be monotheists. It is implicit in his writings that Hildesheimer did not consider Talmudic anti-gentile discrimination to be applicable to his Christian contemporaries. Further, Hildesheimer was sensitive to Christian sensibilities, allowing the mention of Jesus's name and attendance at the dedication of a church.

These latter two examples verify the observations of David Sorkin and David Ellenson about the role of Bildung among German Jews of all denominations during this period.[44] Yet despite Hildesheimer's affinity for German culture and (somewhat guarded) recognition of Christian monotheism, he still harbored suspicions about the goodwill of German Christians. Anti-Semitism was not, in the mind of Hildesheimer, a thing of the past. The messianic era was still an unrealized goal, and Jewish life in nineteenth-century Germany was just a temporary stop on the way toward that prophetic utopia. Further, he believed the non-Jewish public ought not to be misled by liberal rabbis into believing that gentile religious obligations are exhausted by simply being just, merciful, and humble: the Noahide Laws are the basis for assessing gentile conduct. Still, the exact role he assigned to non-Jews in the schema of Judaism remains unclear because Hildesheimer was reluctant to express programatic ideological statements regarding this matter. Some of his contemporaries did not share that reluctance.

Rabbi Marcus Lehmann (1831–90) was a younger contemporary of Hirsch and a student and colleague of Hildesheimer who became the rabbi of the Separatist Orthodox community of Mainz in 1854.[45] Lehmann possessed a doctorate in philosophy from the university of Halle and was a leading advocate of the Neo-Orthodox ideology. He is famous for his historical novels aimed at young adults, and he also published a medieval commentary on the Jerusalem Talmud with his own notes. Additionally, he edited the important Orthodox journal *Der Israelit*. However, his commentaries to the Passover Haggadah and Tractate *Avot* are his two most noteworthy works as an exegete. In them, Lehmann presents a lucid commentary and analysis of the texts, often touching upon contemporary events. His attitude toward non-Jews is also evident in these works.

Commenting on the Mishnaic passage often printed at the beginning of *Avot*, "All Israel(ites) have a portion in the World to Come," Lehmann writes that one might think that the words *kol Yisrael* exclude everyone except Jews from immortality and the World to Come, but he insists that such exclusion is not compatible with Jewish belief (*Eine solche Ausschliesslichkeit liege den Glauben Israels durchaus fern*).[46] Lehmann then goes on to cite the Talmudic passage in which the potential for non-Jews to receive immortality is debated (though citing only the view affirming this potential) and notes that the view that gentiles will receive immortality if they are upright is the normative halacha, as indeed it is.[47] After citing Maimonides, who also notes that righteous non-Jews will receive immortality, Lehmann concludes his comments by noting that although the words *kol Yisrael* do not exclude non-Jews from eternal happiness, they do suggest that everyone fortunate enough to be born a Jew has a clear path and life mission that will enable him to achieve closeness to God.[48]

Lehmann's certainty that exclusion of non-Jews from immortality is incompatible with Jewish belief is hardly revolutionary given Maimonides's codification of the view that upright non-Jews do receive immortality. It is more in the tone of Lehmann's remarks that one detects special pleading: a need to assert, for the record, that Judaism is not exclusionary, nor could it be. This is quite characteristic of nineteenth-century German Orthodoxy. Other remarks in Lehmann's *Avot* commentary further attest to this tendency.

Commenting on *Avot* 1:12 ("*Ohev et ha-beriyot*"), Lehmann assumes that *beriyot* encompasses all of humanity and adds that the most noble principle of Judaism is love of one's fellow man.[49] His commentary to *Avot* 3:18 indicates that Lehmann interpreted Leviticus 19:18 ("Love your neighbor") as inclusive of non-Jews, in contrast to Hirsch. Both, however, considered love of all mankind to be a prime imperative of Judaism. Hirsch's position may be similar to that of a twentieth-century rabbinic authority who explicitly distinguished between the imperative of Leviticus 19:18 and Avot 1:12, where the latter is inclusive of non-Jews while the former is not.[50]

In his commentary to *Avot* 2:16 (*ve-sin'at ha-beriyot*), Lehmann notes that the term *beriyot* means God's creatures and that the lesson of this Mishnah is that we should love all human beings because they were created by God (*und es wird daraus erwiesen, dass man alle Menschen ale die Geschöpfe unsres Gottes betrachten und deshalb lieben soll*). He later notes that "in modern times, class suppression and race hatred" (*der Klassenhass und Rassenhass in unsren Tagen*) corroborate the Sages' claim that *sin'at hinam* (baseless hatred) was the cause of the destruction of the Second Temple.[51]

Lehmann develops his most forceful exposition of the value of humanity in his commentary to Avot 3:18 (*Haviv adam she'nivra be-tzelem*). There he states that this Mishnah was revolutionary for its time in declaring that all human beings, without distinction of race, nationality, or creed, are created in the image of God. The divinity contained within every human became a fundamental tenet of Judaism. Judaism insists that even a criminal condemned to capital punishment does not lose his divine image. The idea of a divine soul contained within every human being, asserts Lehmann, is the basis for human rights according to traditional Jewish teaching.[52]

Lehmann continues his explication of this Mishnah by citing from the commentary of Naphtali Herz Wessely, which discusses the Tannaitic debate between Rabbi Akiva and Ben Azzai as to whether "love thy neighbor" (Leviticus 19:18) or "this is the book of the generations of man" (Genesis 5:1) is a greater principle of the Torah. In this discussion, Lehmann endorses the view of Wessely that "love thy neighbor" is inclusive of non-Jews and that the Tannaim mentioned were not debating whether Jews are expected to love non-Jews; both agreed that they are so required on the basis of this verse in Leviticus. Their debate concerned which text is more suitable to generate a command to love one's fellow. Ben Azzai considered the verse from Genesis to be preferable in this regard because it characterizes man as made in the "likeness of God" (*be-demut elohim*) and the term "likeness" demands a higher degree of love than do other terms.[53]

While the lofty status of human beings is immutable, Lehmann argues that, on some level, the special status of the Jewish people is conditional: "If they deviate from God's ways, [and] are no longer a holy nation or a kingdom of priests, they have no advantage over the other nations."[54] His comments are cited here at length to emphasize that Neo-Orthodox rabbis such as Marcus Lehmann attached much importance to the divine dignity of all human beings and were at pains to emphasize that this dignity is not restricted to Jews. They further conceived of the chosenness of the Jewish people as being conditional on their conduct, as demonstrated by Lehmann's already cited comments, and not as a metaphysical advantage that Jews are born with. While obvious to rabbis such as Lehmann, these principles were not consistently upheld by many contemporaneous East and Central European rabbis.

In Lehmann's Haggadah commentary, he treats the most problematic passage—from the point of view of Jewish attitudes toward non-Jews—in that book, namely, the verses beginning with *shefokh hamatkha el ha-goyim* (pour out thy wrath upon the nations), which is taken from the Book of Lamentations and Psalms. Commentators had dealt with these verses in a variety of ways, but the most noteworthy, as far as Jewish views of non-Jews are concerned, is the approach of Rabbi Eliezer Ashkenazi (1512–85). Jacob Katz has noted that it was Ashkenazi's attitude toward Christians (and Muslims) that made a dramatic impact on the way European rabbinic authorities began to reassess Christianity in the sixteenth and seventeenth centuries. The principled distinction that Ashkenazi drew between ancient pagans, on the one hand, and contemporary monotheistic gentiles, on the other, was later used in halachic contexts by European halachists.[55]

Lehmann provides a full and literal translation of Ashkenazi's remarks, which had been written in Hebrew. Lehmann is at pains to emphasize that fact, among others, as proof that Ashkenazi had never intended it for non-Jewish readers.[56] The first point made by Ashkenazi is that the verses cited make it clear that only those nations that refused to recognize God even after all the miracles that God performed for the Jewish people at the time of the Exodus are the subject of this passage. After all, the passage reads "pour out thy wrath upon *the nations that do not recognize Thee*." Thus, prima facie, monotheists such as Christians and Muslims cannot be the intended reference of that passage.

Lehmann further cites Ashkenazi's assertion that Jews cannot possibly have Christians in mind when they recite this passage in the Haggadah because Jews regularly pray for the well-being of Christian government officials and it would be inconceivable for Jews to simultaneously ask God to pour His wrath upon Christians while also protecting them! Ashkenazi notes that the simple meaning of the text recited makes it clear that "we are saying specifically that God should *not* exercise His wrath upon those who *do* know His name . . . Our Christians, and equally the adherents of Islam, do know God and recognize the fact of the exodus from Egypt. It would therefore be quite wrong to imagine that our laws require us to seek to revile them." Furthermore, he notes that it may sometimes occur that a Jew will curse those that persecute him, which is unlawful from a Torah point of view, despite being understandable. However, cursing an entire people on account of the wrongs that some have done is entirely opposed by the laws of Judaism. Ashkenazi cites several biblical verses as prooftexts for this claim. Ashkenazi ends by repeating that the prayer "Pour out thy wrath" is directed solely against pagans who do not recognize God but is inapplicable to Christians.

Lehmann's citation of this passage in its entirety (in translation) is followed by his own comment that he is stressing this distinction between pagans and Christians because "to this day" (*auch in unserer Zeit*) the accusation that Judaism reviles Christianity is still made.[57] Lehmann then notes that S. R. Hirsch, in his commentary to Psalms, noted that the text reads "el [aleph-lamed] ha-goyim" (*toward* the nations), rather than "al [ayin-lamed] ha-goyim" (*upon* the nations). Therefore, the meaning should be understood as: may God let His displeasure reach up toward these heathens, but *not*: may His wrath be poured upon them. This again demonstrates Lehmann's acute sensitivity to the issue of how Orthodox Jews view non-Jews. He was not content to note that Christians were excluded from the passage recited in the

Haggadah. He felt the need to further mitigate the impact of the "wrath" of God upon those nations who *are* included in this prescription. Even those pagan nations, he says (citing Hirsch), will only experience God's displeasure *reaching* them, but they will not experience God pouring out His wrath *upon* them. In other words, Jews do not pray for God to do something as brutal as obliterating even pagan nations.

Perhaps the most interesting passage in Lehmann's Haggadah commentary was not penned by him but was included by his family, who published his commentary after his death. Rabbi Tevele Bondi (d. 1882) was related to the Mainz family of Frankfurt-am-Main.[58] (Lehmann was married to the daughter of Rabbi Samuel Bondi, who was apparently Tevele's brother.[59]) Bondi wrote a commentary to the concluding sections of the Haggadah; at one point, he writes:

> Our enemies are not usually satisfied with theoretical impatience. They turn it into deeds, deeds that must evoke the disgust and indignation of all right-minded people, if there are still any such when Jews are to be the victims. If only those of other faiths were once faced with the roll of the murdered and the beaten who fell victim to their intolerance, they would sink into the ground in shame, and curse the memory of those who turned the world into a great cemetery. The weapons of human slaughterers are obviously not always the same. In civilized circles today it would no longer be suggested that Jews should be simply murdered (*Man würde heute in zivilisierten Kreisen wenigstens nicht mehr die Losung ausgeben, Juden einfach zu ermorden*), but no one is concerned even today about blocking their means to sustenance. Laws were not invented without purpose; they are on occasion quite a good substitute for the slaughterer's knife![60]

This passage is striking for what it reveals about the attitude of strictly Orthodox German Jews regarding the degree to which German Christians, as civilized people, would not contemplate murdering Jews. The author, an elderly Orthodox rabbi, charged Germans with a lack of concern about Jewish sustenance, going so far as to suggest that laws constricting Jewish occupations were a more acceptable substitute for "the slaughterer's knife." Yet at the same time, Bondi is convinced that civilized Germans would not think of resorting to violence against Jews. It would be incorrect to suggest that Bondi is writing sarcastically, really intending to imply that murder of Jews was on the minds of Germans, but that they could only express those intentions through more moderate measures. Rather, Bondi accepts that German (and, more broadly, non-Jewish) civilization has moved past the point where it is acceptable to kill Jews. This view was not upheld by many of Bondi's East European colleagues, who remained suspicious about non-Jews and their lack of empathy even for Jewish lives.[61] The fact that Lehmann's family included this passage in his Haggadah commentary may be taken to mean that they concurred with Bondi's comments.

As far as Christianity is concerned, Lehmann is quite blunt in asserting that early Christianity, following the teaching of the Essenes, encouraged seclusion and continuous prayer. While "such a view may seem enticing and captivating to the pious mind, it is [however] in contradiction to the fundamental beliefs of Judaism."[62] Lehmann's forthrightness in characterizing Christian doctrine in this manner is in keeping with Hirsch's blunt criticism of Christian doctrines. Both rabbis were more concerned with explaining to their Jewish readers why Judaism rejects certain key Christian teachings than with avoiding any pointed criticism of Christian belief. While Mendelssohn felt the need to write respectfully even in his criticism of Christianity, when written for a public audience, the legacy of not insignificant Jewish conversion to Christianity in the generation following Mendelssohn's death compelled the Orthodox rabbis of the nineteenth century to adopt an unrestrained approach in their critiques of Christian doctrines (though their Reform contemporaries were even more scathing in their denunciation of Christianity).[63] Nevertheless—and this is key to our argument here—the Orthodox rabbis accepted the sincerity of Christian piety and emphasized Judaism's humanistic concern for the welfare of all of humanity.

One of the most important halachists in nineteenth century Germany was Rabbi Seligman Baer (Yitzhak Dov) Bamberger (1807–78), who later became embroiled in a dispute with Hirsch regarding the *Austritt* law. Bamberger represented South German "old Orthodoxy"—those Orthodox rabbis who had not participated to a significant degree in German culture and who did not place any particular value on Bildung.[64] He did not write philosophical essays treating the status of non-Jews in Judaism. However, in his halachic works he does treat this issue, even if only tangentially. In the first responsum printed in his *Yad HaLevy*, Bamberger writes that the prohibition of delaying the burial of the dead certainly applies in full force to the bodies of non-Jews. As proof, he cites several verses in the book of Joshua.[65] This is a rather unconventional approach for a halachist, since the Bible, unmediated by rabbinic texts, was rarely used as a direct source for halachic rulings.[66]

Bamberger does not treat the halachic status of Christianity in his responsa. Indeed, he rarely touches upon any halachic issues relating to avodah zarah. However, his son Rabbi Simha (1832–97), an important halachist in his own right, did treat this issue in his responsa *Zekher Simha*.[67] Rabbi Simha was asked by his brother Zekl whether it is permitted to rent one's home to Protestants who wish to hold religious services there. In his question, Zekl mentions a passage found in several medieval rabbinic sources (based on a Talmudic passage) that states that contemporary gentiles (i.e., Christians) are not to be considered worshippers of avodah zarah since they are merely following ancestral custom.[68] He states that this fact could not serve as a factor that might permit the renting of the Jewish house for Christian religious services (citing an earlier source as his basis for this position). Implicit in this discussion is the assumption that Christianity is considered avodah zarah and that Christians violate the proscription against such activity. Thus the question of whether the Jewish home owner violates the proscription against *lifnei i'ver* (lit. not placing a stumbling block before the blind) came into play when discussing contemporary Christians (even Protestants, who do not use icons in the manner in which Catholics do).[69]

In Rabbi Simha's reply to his brother Zekl, reference is made to a commentary to the *Shulhan Arukh* that questions whether Christians are indeed considered worshippers of AZ, or if they may actually be considered genuine monotheists.[70] Later in the responsum, Simha Bamberger cites a responsum written by his father, Yitzhak Dov, who wrote that it is certainly forbidden for Jews to produce crosses to sell to Christians who will use them in their worship. The prohibition involved is that of *lifnei iver*. (He then grants limited permission to do so under specific circumstances.) Thus, it is clear that both Rabbis Bamberger considered Christianity to constitute avodah zarah even for non-Jews (although they did not draw any inferences from this to questions pertaining to ethical conduct between Jews and non-Jews).

The Bambergers were not alone in this assessment. Rabbi Benjamin Zvi Auerbach (1808–72) published a controversial edition of the *Sefer ha-Eshkol* with his own commentary.[71] The charge was later made that this work was forged.[72] Be that as it may, in his commentary, Auerbach explicitly rejects the view that shittuf is permissible for non-Jews. He writes that there are ironclad proofs that even non-Jews are forbidden from worshipping in a shittuf manner, namely, worshipping the Trinitarian God of Christianity. He makes a point of rejecting those proofs that had been brought for the more liberal view regarding shittuf.[73] Auerbach does not otherwise address the potential for salvation that Christians possess, and his view on this question is a subject for speculation.

What emerges from the cited examples is that, in general, those German Orthodox rabbis who did not subscribe to the Neo-Orthodox ideology were more likely to classify Christians as idolators. They were less concerned with the implications that such a classification may have for the salvific potential of

Christians. Rabbi Auerbach seems to occupy an intermediate position on the spectrum of approaches to modernity. On the one hand, he was university-trained and possessed of a doctorate and preached in High German.[74] On the other hand, he opposed the notion that pursuit of secular studies is an ideal, he mistrusted Jewish scholars whose educational background gave undue weight to the study of secular disciplines (which he characterized as being quite distant from Torah studies), and he rejected Hildesheimer's overtures to him to participate in the Berlin Rabbinical Seminary. He seems to have considered certain elements of the Neo-Orthodox program to be exigencies demanded by the times.[75] Auerbach's guarded embrace of modernity did not engender a view of Christianity that differed decidedly from that of many of his premodern predecessors.

Now that we have delineated the different approaches to modernity among the German Orthodox rabbis, what can be inferred from their writings? It would seem that while the quest for emancipation and the value accorded to the cultivation of Bildung among the Neo-Orthodox influenced their perception of Christians, some halachists valued these concerns more than others. For many, the entire emancipation project—premised as it was on the idea of equal citizenship for equals, Jews and Christians alike—led to the internalization of the idea that Christians were fellow monotheists, with all the halachic and philosophic implications that demarcation carried. In contrast, some rabbis, such as B. Z. Auerbach, for example, were not particularly sensitive to the social implications of their halachic rulings pertaining to non-Jews.

It may be suggested that the value that many of the Neo-Orthodox rabbis placed on Bildung also made it unattractive to classify their fellow citizens of a different persuasion as worshippers of avodah zarah simply based on the latter's erroneous theology. By contrast, those rabbis who were less concerned about both emancipation and Bildung were also less conscious of the social implications of their classification of Christians as worshippers of avodah zarah. This interpretation resembles David Ellenson's explanation for why Hirsch and Hildesheimer championed secession while Bamberger downplayed its significance. Ellenson suggests that the more acculturated German Orthodox rabbis were more likely to recognize the danger posed to Orthodoxy by communal association with Reform Judaism in cities (like Frankfurt and Berlin), whose cultural milieu was more modernized than was the more rural area which was the environs of Bamberger's rabbinate.[76] Picking up where Ellenson left off, the more acculturated rabbis in the larger cities may well have been more self-conscious about matters that could impact the perception of Jews in the German state, such as their view of non-Jews and their religions.

However, no sweeping conclusions can be drawn from this survey. Rabbi Auerbach apparently placed his own reading of the halachic sources pertaining to avodah zarah above any other considerations, and it is possible that those rabbis who arrived at a more liberal assessment of Christianity than his did so based on their reading of the halachic sources and not due to any social or cultural considerations.

Returning to Hildesheimer, it is noteworthy that he was not consistently universalistic in his writings. As someone who was primarily a Talmudic scholar and institution-builder, and who wrote primarily in Hebrew, Hildesheimer did not regard himself as the leading spokesperson for Orthodox Judaism in Western Europe in the nineteenth century. By contrast, the more philosophically inclined and idealistic S. R. Hirsch, a prolific author who wrote thousands of pages in High German pertaining to—what he regarded as—the authentic Jewish view of virtually every issue relevant to nineteenth-century Jews, was more conscious of the perception of Judaism by those on the outside. Hirsch was more committed to demonstrating Judaism's humanism and universalism than any of his Orthodox contemporaries. It is to him that we now turn our attention.

8

Rabbi Samson Raphael Hirsch

The Framework

Hirsch and the Haskalah

More has been written about Hirsch's religious philosophy than about that of any other Orthodox rabbi of the last two centuries.[1] There is, unfortunately, a substantial amount of misunderstanding regarding several central aspects of his ideology, notably the *Torah im Derekh Eretz* (henceforth: TIDE) and *Austritt* principles. In some cases, ideological biases on the part of writers have led to this problem. In others, an overemphasis on contextualization has, ironically, led to anachronistic interpretations of Hirsch's views.[2] Other studies simply suffer from tendentiousness. This study does not need to reexamine the two central tenets of Hirsch's philosophy in depth.

It will suffice to note that TIDE, for Hirsch, entailed the religious Jew's involvement in the culture of the civilization in which she finds herself. The Torah is the supreme guide for all confrontations that may arise from such cultural engagement, but Hirsch regarded cultural isolation as a departure from the true ideal of the Jew's vocation to serve as a "light unto the nations."[3] Hirsch's views on separatism, while only fully expressed in the final two decades of his life, are so central to his Weltanschauung that it would be erroneous to assert, as some have, that they are not essential to his ideology or that they represent a break with his open-mindedness in the cultural sphere.[4] In short, Hirsch called upon the religious Jew to disassociate herself from, and to shun all manifestations of, institutionalized heresy. Thus, a Jew cannot be a member of a community that is legally controlled by Reform clergy; nor should a Jew join any Jewish organization that does not accept the divinity of the Torah.

Before proceeding with a delineation of the dilemma posed by Hirsch's thought with respect to non-Jews, a broader issue, namely, Hirsch's relationship to the Haskalah, must be addressed. Was Hirsch a latter-day maskil, that is, was he motivated by the same ideals that motivated observant maskilim of the previous century, such as Mendelssohn and Naphtali Herz Wessely? (Though Wessely had a mindset that was not consonant with that of less religious maskilim, there is no doubt that he wanted to incorporate the full spectrum of the humanities into the Jewish educational curriculum, and he tended to downplay the centrality of Talmudic studies.[5])

Noah H. Rosenbloom answers this question in the affirmative: Hirsch was a religiously observant maskil who tried to implement some of Wessely's educational reforms. The primary evidentiary basis that Rosenbloom adduces for his thesis is the fact that Hirsch ("euphemistically," in Rosenbloom's words) characterized his parents as *erleuchtet religiös* ("enlightened religious") in his *Nineteen Letters*.[6] Additionally, in his teenage years, Hirsch was sent to a German grammar school and later a Gymnasium, hardly typical of traditionalist Ashkenazi education. Furthermore, members of Hirsch's family, such as his grandfather, great-uncle, and uncle, as well as his teacher, Isaac Bernays, all admired Wessely's works.[7] His grandfather personally knew Moses Mendelssohn and respected him. Further, Hirsch was in possession of all of Wessely's manuscripts and books.[8] It therefore seems reasonable to assume that when Hirsch called for an educational program of *Torah im Derekh Eretz*, he was following the model first established by Wessely.[9] In fact, according to Rosenbloom, Hirsch went even further than Wessely had in his *Divrei Shalom ve-Emet* in advocating a humanistic curriculum, since Wessely had allegedly only advocated the study of practical subjects.[10]

There are serious grounds on which to contest Rosenbloom's thesis. First of all, it is erroneous to write about a nineteenth-century Orthodox rabbi in a manner suggesting that the challenges he faced were identical to the eighteenth century's "conservative maskilim." The latter were not active in the rabbinate, and their primary goal was not to galvanize a defense of tradition against those who had encroached upon it. Quite the contrary. By contrast, nineteenth-century Orthodox rabbis like Hirsch were at the forefront of formulating the response of Orthodoxy to deviations from tradition. The intellectual milieu of the maskilim and that of Hirsch was similar in that both took cognizance of contemporary non-Jewish intellectual currents, but their respective attitudes toward the rabbinic tradition and their senses of mission and purpose were so different from one another as to eclipse the significance of any possible similarity of ideas. The difference in time, context, and motivation is key.[11] The Berlin maskilim of the eighteenth century wished to reform

Judaism, even if they accepted the authority of the Bible and Talmud. Mordechai Breuer's analysis is worth citing here: "Mendelssohn turned to a Jewry that was still almost completely rooted in the living tradition, and he wanted to draw them close to culture. Hirsch saw himself in the midst of a Jewry that had already taken great strides on the road to culture and whose loyalty to tradition and Torah he wanted to renew and preserve. Mendelssohn led the old Jewry toward culture; Hirsch led the new Jewry to the Torah . . . Every page of his [Hirsch's] writings testifies to that."[12]

When comparing Hirsch's view to Wessely's, it should be noted that Wessely advocated the incorporation of the gamut of the sciences and humanities into the Jewish curriculum, as is evidenced by his definition of *Torat ha-Adam*: "ve-hen ha-devarim she-ba'avuran ba'aleihen re'uyin le-hikare' be-shem 'adam" (and these are those matters on whose account those who master them are worthy of being called by the title "man"). Wessely includes etiquette, the ways of morality and good character, civility, and clear graceful expression, history, geography, political science, arithmetic, geometry, zoology, botany, anatomy, medicine, and chemistry as essential components of *Torat ha-Adam*.[13] On the face of it, Wessely's program exceeded Hirsch's in scope and in content. It seems fair to suggest that Wessely hoped to better educate the culturally insular, traditional Jews of eighteenth-century Central Europe.[14] For his part, Hirsch mentions world history, physics, geography, psychology, anthropology, and arithmetic as subjects to be studied in order for the Jew to better understand the Torah's conception of the Jew's task in this world.[15] Hirsch hoped to inspire the cultured Jews of nineteenth-century Oldenburg to apply their knowledge of these subjects to their study of the Torah, in order to see the hand of God in the development of history and in the natural world. While both men were influenced by the Bildung concept, Hirsch emphasized that general knowledge must always remain "subsidiary" to Torah study.[16] In contrast, Wessely appears to have attributed inherent value to the acquisition of worldly knowledge which, *in his own formulation*, makes a Jew worthy of the title "man."[17]

This general assessment of Rosenbloom's interpretation of Hirsch fundamentally impacts the broader questions this book seeks to answer, namely, the degree of Hirsch's attachment to the Haskalah and whether it can account for his liberal attitude toward non-Jews. Noah Rosenbloom has portrayed S. R. Hirsch as a man deeply indebted to the Haskalah for his religious ideology. But, as noted, the differing contexts and motivations for the respective careers and writings of Mendelssohn and Hirsch render the attempt to portray Hirsch as having been more of a maskil than a rabbinic Jew untenable. It is because Hirsch *was* fundamentally a rabbinic Jew that his attitude toward non-Jews merits further scrutiny.

Rosenbloom actually goes further and asserts that there has been a concerted effort by Hirsch's admirers to cover up his ties to the Haskalah, including the allegedly close ties of his father to the Haskalah.[18] As for Hirsch's nineteenth-century contemporaries, Rosenbloom contends that Hirsch had more in common with leaders of Reform Judaism than with those of other forms of Orthodox Judaism. In making this argument, Rosenbloom relies heavily on Hirsch's relationship to the writings of Moses Mendelssohn and Naphtali Herz Wessely. Hirsch, Rosenbloom claims, was brought up by conservative maskilim who admired Mendelssohn and Wessely. According to Rosenbloom, neither Hirsch nor his parents can be considered mainstream rabbinic Jews, that is, they were adherents of a modernizing movement and their loyalties to European values eclipsed, or at least equaled, their attachment to the venerated texts—such as the Talmud and Shulchan Arukh—upon which present-day Orthodox Judaism is based. If this interpretation of Hirsch's family is correct, then there is no need to account for Hirsch's view of non-Jews: they were obviously generated by his internalization of European sensibilities and not by his genuine understanding of what classical Judaism teaches. Since Rosenbloom develops this thesis in a highly tendentious fashion through a selective citation of those sources that buttress his view, those sources will be examined presently.[19]

The first issue is Hirsch's relationship to Wessely. Rosenbloom notes that Wessely was decried by the foremost rabbinic authorities of his time for the educational program he called for in his *Divrei Shalom ve-Emet* of 1782, and yet Hirsch still saw fit to cite Wessely's works in his own writings. "Although Hirsch seldom credited his sources, in this case he had no misgivings in citing the leading Maskil in Germany," writes Rosenbloom.[20] What Rosenbloom does not tell his readers is that Wessely was held in high regard, and was cited by name, by numerous leading Torah scholars in Western, Central, and even Eastern Europe.[21]

Hirsch's teacher, Jacob Ettlinger, the greatest living Talmudist in Germany during Hirsch's lifetime, referred to Wessely in laudatory language reserved for esteemed rabbinic scholars. Ettlinger wrote of Wessely, "Come and see the wonders of the world which were achieved by the poet, scholar, and linguist whose name is known for praise in all the camps of the Hebrews until the corners of the world, his honor, our master, Rabbi Naphtali Herz Weisel, may the memory of the righteous be for a blessing [*zekher zaddik le-brakhah*], in his beautiful works which are founded upon the pillars of our tradition, and express the beauties of the figures of speech [in Scripture]. There is nothing problematic in them [his writings]."[22] Since there can be no question that Ettlinger was a mainstream rabbinic Jew, his praise for Wessely, which far exceeds anything that Hirsch ever wrote about him, renders it highly problematic to prove Hirsch's maskilic leanings from his citation of Wessely.

Further, a number of other prominent rabbinic predecessors and contemporaries of Hirsch held Wessely in similarly high regard. Rabbi Israel Lipschutz (1782–1860), rabbi of Danzig and author of a monumental commentary on the Mishnah (*Tiferet Yisrael*), cites Wessely a number of times and in one place in his commentary to Tractate Avot states, "I have based my interpretation of this Mishna, as I did with many others, on the *Yeyn Levanon* [Wessely's commentary on Avot], whose words are sweet and true."[23] Rabbi Zvi Hirsch Kalischer, whom Jacob Katz has characterized as more of a traditionalist than Hirsch, cited Wessely's work and referred to Wessely as "the wondrous sage" and "the rabbi, the celebrated sage."[24] Rabbi Jacob Zvi Mecklenburg also frequently cited Wessely's works and authored an approbation to a reprinting of Wessely's commentary to Leviticus, which was his contribution to Mendelssohn's *Biur* project.[25]

Rabbi Hirsch's antagonist in the *Austritt* debate, Rabbi Isaac Dov Bamberger, "the Würzburger Rav," who was perhaps the last champion of old-school Orthodoxy in nineteenth-century Germany, also cited Wessely's works. Bamberger refers to Wessely as "the sage, Rabbi Naphtali Herz Weisel."[26] Even Rabbi Moses Schick, the most outstanding pupil of Hatam Sofer (who was the source of the adage *hadash assur min ha-Torah*—anything innovative is biblically prohibited), cited one of Wessely's works by name in at least one public speech.[27] Other disciples of Hatam Sofer also cited Wessely's works, in some cases using rather laudatory terms to describe him.[28] Apparently, Hirsch was not so daring after all.

It should further be noted that Hirsch corresponded with his uncle, Moshe Mendelsohn-Frankfurter of Hamburg, who was an avid admirer of Moses Mendelssohn (after whom he modified his surname), and it is likely that his uncle shared with Hirsch the following anecdote (which Wessely had told to Hirsch's uncle). Wessely had studied in the yeshiva of Rabbi Jonathan Eyebeschutz. At that time, Wessely authored a commentary on the rabbinic Midrash to Leviticus, *Torat Kohanim*.[29] Eyebeschutz became aware of this work and beseeched Wessely to share it with him. Despite his reluctance, Wessely acceded to reading portions of it to Eyebeschutz. After reading several sections, Eyebeschutz "stood up from his chair, raised his hands, and said 'Your words are as if given from [God to Moses on Mt.] Sinai.'"[30] The fact that Hirsch's grandfather had studied in Eyebeschutz's yeshiva increases the likelihood of such an intrafamily discussion about one of Eyebeschutz's most famous students, Wessely.[31]

Rosenbloom makes much of the fact that Hirsch's grandfather, Rabbi

Mendel Frankfurter (1742–1823), gave a seal of approval to Wessely's works, which indicates, in Rosenbloom's view, that Hirsch's entire family had maskilic leanings, in opposition to the majority of traditionalist German Jewry.[32] It would seem that such a conclusion is unwarranted. Hirsch's grandfather served as the chief *dayan* (rabbinic judge) in the community of Altona in the latter part of his life. His approval of Wessely was hardly revolutionary. Virtually all rabbis living in Germany and Western Europe during the nineteenth century held Wessely in similarly high regard.[33]

As far as Hirsch's relationship to Mendelssohn is concerned, Rosenbloom says the following: "In his first published work, Hirsch referred to Mendelssohn, already anathema in Orthodox circles, as a 'brilliant, respect-inspiring personality.'"[34] It is altogether strange to cite Hirsch's introductory remarks concerning Mendelssohn from his *Nineteen Letters* and entirely omit the withering criticism to which Hirsch subjected Mendelssohn immediately thereafter![35] There was nothing controversial about acknowledging Mendelssohn's brilliance or the fact that he inspired respect among Jews and non-Jews of all circles. Hirsch's following attack on Mendelssohn is what was more surprising, given the reverence in which Mendelssohn was held by the masses of German Jews, to whom Hirsch's book was addressed.

Further, it is not at all clear that Mendelssohn was "anathema in Orthodox circles" in the 1830s. Quite the contrary: reprintings of Mendelssohn's *Biur* were given approbations by the leading rabbinic authorities of the time, such as Rabbi Mordechai Benet, Rabbi Akiva Eger, and Rabbi Jacob Zvi Mecklenburg in the period immediately preceding the publication of Hirsch's *Nineteen Letters*.[36] Mordechai Breuer noted, "Many Orthodox circles went far beyond Hirsch's reserved appreciation of Mendelssohn in their admiration for the philosopher . . . Leading rabbis of the old school, among them Seckel Wormser, the Baal Shem of Michelstadt, [Zvi] Hirsch Kalischer in Thorn, and Abraham Sutro (1784–1869) in Münster, had accepted Mendelssohn as a Jewish thinker and diligently studied his *Biur*."[37] Thus, a significant element in Rosenbloom's portrayal of Hirsch as a maskil, one who evinced an attitude to controversial Haskalah figures that was at odds with the attitude of his Orthodox contemporaries, is simply without merit.

A recent study of Hirsch by Michah Gottlieb advances an approach that, in some respects, resembles Rosenbloom's but vastly improves upon it, as it is far more multifarious and nuanced than Rosenbloom's and is decidedly not tendentious. Gottlieb's painstakingly researched study is an invaluable resource for understanding the role of Hirsch's Bible commentary in the context of other German-Jewish Bible projects.[38] However, there are a few assertions that seem unpersuasive. Gottlieb argues that Hirsch was deeply impacted by the Haskalah, as his entire family were devotees of the movement and imbued him with its values. Gottlieb further argues that when Hirsch made his entry on the scene of German Judaism in the 1830s, he was not yet committed to Orthodoxy but was instead a man of "no party" (a term Hirsch himself uses in *The Nineteen Letters*), who surveyed the "partial truths" presented by four approaches to Judaism then available, selecting the parts of each that he accepted as correct. These four approaches were: the Wissenschaft movement, the Haskalah, Reform Judaism, and "Jewish traditionalism."

Gottlieb notes that Hirsch's very decision to study in a yeshiva was surprising ("countercultural") since maskilim didn't value Talmud study that much, and that is what is studied in a yeshiva.[39] On his way to Ettlinger's yeshiva in Mannheim, Hirsch spent time in and around Frankfurt, meeting with both traditionalists and Reformers. "The radically different people Hirsch visited suggests that he was seeking to clarify his own religious position and was open to a wide range of viewpoints." Judging Hirsch only by *The Nineteen Letters*, written in 1836, he could "never have been considered an implacable foe of Reform," since his criticism of it is tempered by "a remarkable sympathy for it, even adopting the label [Reform] for himself."[40] Only later, in the 1850s, does Hirsch "become Orthodox," and later yet, he becomes a militant and sectarian Orthodox leader.

This thesis is problematic. There was simply no Haskalah in nineteenth-century Germany, and so whatever Hirsch's father, uncle, or grandfather may have thought about the eighteenth-century German Haskalah, Hirsch cannot be considered even a partial devotee of Haskalah when he began his career in the 1830s. There is no doubt whatsoever that Hirsch read the writings of Mendelssohn and Wessely and that he agreed with some of their views. There is nothing particularly striking about this fact; very few rabbis in Western Europe who lived during the nineteenth century would have summarily rejected anything that had to do with these figures. On the contrary: Orthodox writers tended to claim Mendelssohn as one of their own, arguing that he has been wrongly misappropriated by Reformers. Hirsch himself said as much.[41] There is thus no basis for the contention that Hirsch was, somehow, a nineteenth-century maskil or, as Gottlieb describes him, someone with "maskilic sensibilities."[42]

While Hirsch was unquestionably an openminded rabbi, willing to learn from a variety of sources, he was very much a partisan of Orthodoxy from the beginning of his rabbinical career. There is a virtual consensus among historians that Orthodoxy in Germany began no later than 1819.[43] When Hirsch applied for a rabbinical post in Oldenburg in 1830, he was seeking to be the Orthodox rabbi of this principality. His predecessor was Rabbi Nathan

Adler (1803–90), who—unlike Hirsch—had received a doctorate, and was committed to upholding strict Orthodoxy.[44] Hirsch's candidacy was backed by the wealthy Baron Amschel Rothschild, who was known as a defender of Orthodoxy and who wanted to stem the tide of the growth of the Reform movement.[45] This is why Leo Trepp notes that Hirsch was known to Oldenburg government officials as a staunch defender of Orthodoxy when he first filled the rabbinic position there, and this perception of Hirsch exacerbated his tense relations with these officials. Hirsch was interviewed for the position by Adler, who queried Hirsch concerning his theological views, his views concerning reward and punishment, the prophecy of biblical prophets, and the divine revelation of Jewish doctrines, among other issues. Only after Hirsch satisfactorily answered these questions was his candidacy accepted.[46]

It is true that Hirsch uses more conciliatory language with respect to Reformers in *The Nineteen Letters* than in his later writings. Rather than being the result of a transformational shift in Hirsch's ideology, this shift in Hirsch's idiom is easily accounted for by the more assertive posture of the Reform movement in subsequent decades. In the 1830s, Hirsch still held out hope that Reform might recognize the error of its ways. After the Reform synods of the mid-1840s, it seemed clear that Reform was here to stay and that its leaders not only had no intention of backing down but arrogated to themselves (from the perspective of the Orthodox) the authority to initiate formal change to key aspects of Jewish law. Hirsch was asked by the militantly Orthodox editors of the polemical pamphlet *Torat ha-Kena'ot* to contribute a Hebrew essay denouncing the first Reform synod in Brunswick in 1844. If Hirsch was regarded as open to different types of Judaism available to German Jews, as Gottlieb asserts with respect to Hirsch's time in Oldenburg (which ended in 1841), it is indeed strange that Hirsch's aid would have been sought in this matter only three years later. When, exactly, was Hirsch recognized as a champion of Orthodoxy? Further, Hirsch obliged and composed a sharply worded Hebrew essay denouncing the Reformers in vituperative language—and this was the second essay published in the book![47] Hirsch, in this essay, comes across as a militant champion of Orthodox Judaism, or what Gottlieb characterizes as "Jewish traditionalism." Gottlieb suggests that Hirsch was not yet Orthodox at this time (though in the process of a gradual shift toward Orthodoxy); if this were true, then this episode would be somewhat bewildering.

The reference to being a man of "no party" made by the fictional character Naphtali—the stand-in for Hirsch—in *The Nineteen Letters* was part of Naphtali's effort to demonstrate to the perplexed young man to whom he was writing (Benjamin) that he arrived at the convictions about the divine character and eternality of the Torah as a result of much investigation and consideration, not due to following the "party line" or the calling of his profession.[48] As Naphtali encouraged Benjamin to think for himself and examine Judaism from its own sources, it is but natural that Naphtali would characterize himself as a man with "no party." But, by any definition of Orthodoxy, Naphtali (i.e., Hirsch) was clearly an Orthodox rabbi, albeit one unafraid to critique shortcomings he found in the entrenched Orthodoxy that he encountered in his adolescent years.

For these reasons, the present study is founded on a different premise than Gottlieb's. Hirsch, like his teachers Bernays and Ettlinger, was a "rabbinic Jew"—that is, someone whose worldview was shaped primarily by rabbinic texts, who saw it as a sacred task to uphold the binding authority of the rabbinic tradition among his contemporaries, and who denied the possibility of making adjustments to observances that have been codified in the medieval codes of Jewish law. This sets Hirsch apart from both maskilim and also moderate Reformers like Zechariah Frankel.[49]

Further, as demonstrated previously, the charge that Hirsch and his family (unlike ostensibly more traditional Orthodox Jews) had a controversially favorable view of Haskalah figures like Wessely and Mendelssohn, is untenable. Wessely was not regarded as antitraditional by many more "right-wing" Orthodox rabbis than Hirsch, while Hirsch criticized Mendelssohn more forcefully than many of his rabbinic contemporaries did. Thus, we are back where we started this chapter: Hirsch was raised by pious and traditional parents; Hirsch himself did not evince more of an affinity for the Haskalah movement than other European rabbis of the time; Hirsch's education was unconventional but it was not "maskilic." There are thus no facile explanations of Hirsch's universalism (e.g., that he was a maskil, and so, like all maskilim, had universalistic sentiments). The explanation must lie elsewhere. However, accounting for Hirsch's universalism is a task that is not easily undertaken.

The Dilemma Posed by Hirsch's Thought

Now to delineate the primary dilemma that Hirsch's thought poses with respect to the subject of this book. Hirsch consistently reiterated the centrality of "Sich selbst begreifendes Judentum," that is, that Judaism must be viewed organically, from its own literary sources.[50] A Jew must not attempt to analyze Judaism based on preconceived notions regarding the nature of Judaism that have been imbibed from foreign sources. Hence, Hirsch criticized Maimonides for accepting Aristotelian philosophy in his *Guide of the Perplexed* and interpreting the Torah in a manner that does not conflict with those views.[51] Aware of this basic tenet of Hirschian philosophy, here is a question that has perplexed scholars for generations: did not Hirsch himself accept many tenets of eighteenth- and nineteenth-century German philosophy and, as a result, construct his conception of Judaism in such a manner that it did not conflict with those views? In the context of this study, this question becomes all the more urgent.

In his first published work, Hirsch argued that Judaism, if properly understood, presents a world in which "one glorious chain of love . . . unites all creatures . . . Love is the message which all things proclaim" to the Jew.[52] Hirsch explicitly includes the Jewish obligation of love and concern for all of mankind in this "chain of love."[53] He states further in that work that "Judaism, correctly conceived and conveyed, constitutes a bond of love and justice encompassing all creatures."[54] How was he so sure that this is what Judaism demanded? Did he arrive at this conclusion *solely* on the basis of the Bible, Talmud, and Midrash—the three sources he said Jews must examine without preconceptions in order to properly understand Judaism? Numerous rabbinic sages and savants have arrived at very different conclusions regarding the Jewish view of non-Jews.

Rabbi Abraham of Posquieres (Ra'avad; 1125–98) stated that "the Gentiles are like animals; they do not become impure and cannot defile, 'a people who are like donkeys,' 'behold, the nations are as a drop of a bucket,' and the wind will blow them all away, and one who thinks of them as something [worthwhile] will gather the wind in his fist."[55] Hirsch actually refers to Ra'avad as "one of the most Jewish of our thinkers" (*einer unserer jüdischsten Denker*).[56] What did Hirsch think of these comments—were they rooted in "Judaism organically understood" or were they based on preconceived notions? The fact that Ra'avad's remarks are based on passages in the Jerusalem Talmud and the Midrash makes this question even more pressing (even though those passages do not say exactly what Ra'avad says).[57]

Rabbi Aharon Lichtenstein (1933–2015) saw a disconnect between Hirsch's humanism and his Judaism, and he went so far as to assert that the former is "an element that has been engrafted" onto the latter, although he maintained that Hirsch himself saw his universalism as "of the woof and warp of *Yahadut* [Judaism]."[58] This latter point is of central importance. Hirsch saw "love and justice for all creatures" as lying at the heart of Judaism. What compelled him to adopt this view, given his own opposition to arriving at conclusions about Judaism based on notions derived from sources that are external to it? Perforce, in Hirsch's own estimation, a universalist outlook must be mandated by the authentic sources of rabbinic Judaism.

Several of Hirsch's contemporaries, convinced as was he that Judaism preaches love for all of mankind, resolved the difficulties posed by certain exclusivist rabbinic texts by stating that those texts are not authoritative and do not represent genuine Jewish teachings regarding the Jewish people's relationship to mankind. Samuel David Luzzatto (1800–65), sometimes referred to as a leader of Italian Neo-Orthodoxy, argued that the fundamental purpose of Judaism is to "generate a love of the entire human family."[59] In Luzzatto's own words, "The compassion that Judaism commends is universal. It is extended, like God's, to all of His creatures. No race is excluded from the Law, because all human beings, according to Judaism's teaching, are brothers, are children of the same Father, and are created in the image of God."[60] As for the Talmudic passages that do not seem to reflect this sentiment, Luzzatto states, "Whatever proposition or story that could be found in the Talmud . . . which would be in opposition to the sentiments of universal humanity and justice—which are suggested equally by nature and by Sacred Scripture—must be regarded as neither of the dictates of Religion or of Tradition, but as regrettable insinuations of the calamitous circumstances, and of the public and private vexations and cruelties to which the Jews were subjected in the barbaric centuries."[61] Luzzatto's formulation clearly extends to Talmudic passages that are halachic (pertaining to Jewish law) and not merely aggadic (homiletical), which raises the question of his views on the origins and authority of the Oral Law. If the Oral Law was divinely revealed just as the Written Law was, as Hirsch believed, then there is no room for Luzzatto's view about the historical context of the Talmudic anti-gentile laws.[62]

Michael Friedlander (1833–1910), a British Orthodox scholar and the principal of Jews' College, the Orthodox theological seminary founded by Hirsch's friend and colleague, Nathan Marcus Adler, expressed views similar to those of Luzzatto. In his monumental work *The History and Philosophy of the Jewish Religion*, Friedlander writes,

> We meet in the Talmud and works based on the Talmud with dicta which seem at first sight to exclude Gentiles (*Akum, Nakhri*, or *Goy*) from our duty of love towards our fellow-men. This, however, was never intended. Sayings of this kind originated in days of warfare between the oppressor and the oppressed, and were outbursts of feelings of pain and anger, caused by an enemy who was not restrained from tyranny and cruelty by any sense of justice and humanity. But this state of affairs has ceased, and such sayings have since entirely lost their force and meaning, and are practically forgotten . . . But having led, and being still likely to lead, to errors and misunderstanding . . . they ought to be eliminated in future editions of any of these works by Jewish censors.[63]

Friedlander thus advocated the extirpation of all anti-gentile texts from current editions of the Talmud and Talmudic works. Even if Friedlander's comments were confined to nonlegal statements concerning gentiles—which is clearly not the case—it would be unimaginable to envision Hirsch advocating the same course of action. Given that Friedlander clearly had in mind halachic passages such as "'thy brother'—this comes to exclude the gentile," which are found scattered throughout Talmudic literature, there is no doubt that Hirsch would have vigorously opposed this suggestion as another attack on the divinity of the Oral Law.[64] But Hirsch fully shared the humanistic sentiments expressed by Friedlander and Luzzatto, so how would he relate to those Talmudic passages? This seems to be the most pressing problem in analyzing Hirsch's worldview.

Katell Berthelot has argued that biblical or rabbinic texts that seem to exclude non-Jews from ethical obligations or from the privileged status of Israelites present no problem for exegetes, who are free to interpret those texts in a more inclusive manner.[65] The most obvious example, discussed by Berthelot, is the injunction in Leviticus 19:18 to "love thy neighbor as thyself." Maimonides excludes non-Jews from the category of "neighbor," while many modern Jewish thinkers have deliberately included non-Jews in this biblical command.[66] In this case, Hirsch sides with Maimonides in interpreting the verse in Leviticus restrictively.[67] However, Hirsch—unlike some of his East European contemporaries—does not consistently interpret seemingly universalistic biblical passages in a restrictive manner.

As noted by Shlomo Chertok, Hirsch departs from rabbinic exegesis in his elucidation of two of the biblical passages relating to the *ger*, notwithstanding the fact that throughout the rest of his biblical commentary Hirsch is at pains to stress that the *only* legitimate interpretation of scripture is that which is found in the Oral Law, not the rationalist readings of moderns.[68] As further noted by Chertok, Hirsch vehemently opposed the historicist readings of the Bible that were advanced by Luzzatto, since Hirsch maintained that the Oral Law was revealed in its entirety to the Jewish people *before* they received the text of the Pentateuch.[69] Therefore, it would be out of the question for Hirsch to have believed that the *original* intent of the Bible, when referring to the *ger*, was to any non-Jewish stranger that dwelled among the Jews, and that only later did the rabbis engage in exegesis that narrowed the meaning of *ger* to a convert to Judaism. Indeed, in several places Hirsch clearly understands the meaning of *ger* as a convert to Judaism, which he bases on the rabbinic passages that make this assertion.[70] Therefore, a different explanation must be sought for Hirsch's deviation from the rabbinic reading in these specific cases, since it would have been untenable for Hirsch to deviate from the Talmud on the basis of humanistic considerations.

In another section of his biblical commentary, commenting on the verses that express the prohibition of oppressing the *ger* and refer to the Jewish experience as *gerim* in Egypt, Hirsch clearly regards the *ger* as being any non-Jew who accepts the Noahide Laws.[71] His entire argument rests on the understanding that what the Jews experienced in Egypt serves as a reminder to behave differently to those in a parallel position in a Jewish state. He states that "a heathen born and bred, as soon as he attaches himself to Judaism by simply acknowledging the Jewish principle of the conception of God, can demand the fullest equality and the full equal rights in Law with any Jew." This fact, avers Hirsch, emphasizes the Jewish teaching that "it is not race, not descent, not birth or country or property, altogether nothing external or due to chance, but simply and purely the inner spiritual and moral worth of a human being, which gives him all the rights of a man and of a citizen."

Hirsch highlighted the Torah's humanistic approach to the "stranger" in an essay penned in 1841.[72] In that year, there was a large fire in Hamburg (less than a year before the Great Hamburg Fire of 1842). F. Mallet, a leading cleric in Bremen, published a pamphlet arguing that the fire was the work of God, to punish Hamburgers for their sins. Adolph Stahr responded by charging that Mallet had no right to judge in this manner. A controversy broke out, and Stahr ultimately laid out two fundamental questions underlying this discussion: Is the Jewish God also the God of Christians? And is the Old Testament valid for Christians?

In response, twenty-two Protestant pastors, including Mallet, issued a statement that recognized Christianity's debt to Judaism and the Old Testament. They stated that God's word is indivisible and includes both the Old and New Testaments. If man leads a life enlightened by God's word, then the scriptures can be properly understood. The Bible has clearly spelled out the basis for blessing and curse in human life, and the Christian apostles merely carried on that teaching. Although this essentially justified Mallet's position, a conservative Protestant responded to these twenty-two pastors with an attack on Judaism charging that its values pale in comparison with Christianity's moral sensibilities.[73] The charge that Judaism is tribalistic in its morality in this case was coupled with claims that Judaism does not recognize moral autonomy, in the Kantian sense, among other claims against Judaism.

Hirsch refuted each charge but devoted the greatest portion of his response to the charge of tribalism. He utilized the various exhortations of the Torah regarding proper treatment of the "stranger" as his primary evidence against the claims of the anonymous Protestant author. "You, dear Mr. Protestant," Hirsch exclaimed, "ought to read this [regulations concerning the "stranger"] and be ashamed!"[74] Hirsch then contrasted the Jewish compassion for the stranger with the long history of Christian brutality toward Jews, despite Christianity's claim to be the religion of love. There can be no doubt that Hirsch, at least for the purposes of this essay, did not regard the biblical "stranger" as a convert to Judaism but rather as a non-Jew living as a minority among Jews, much like the status of Jews in Christian Europe.

Hirsch's insistence that Judaism must be organically understood, *aus sich selbst*, coupled with his insistence that the Oral Law is no less divine than the Written Law, makes this problem even more acute. Hirsch could not have believed that the Pentateuch should sometimes be understood in a manner that conflicts with the halachic interpretation of the text based on "external" considerations, such as a desire to prove the humanism of the Torah.[75] Therefore, his interpretation of the passages relating to the *ger* is all the more perplexing. If Rosenbloom's thesis that Hirsch was, largely, unlearned in rabbinic literature (having mastered only the Bible) were correct, then it could be assumed that the rabbinic interpretation of *ger* was not at the forefront of Hirsch's thoughts. But this is extremely unlikely: Hirsch was an expert in the Talmud and displayed remarkable familiarity with the various branches of Talmudic literature.[76] Did he deliberately ignore the rabbinic interpretation of *ger* in certain instances because he believed there to be room for an alternative view? That alternative would have to have some basis in the Talmudic or Rabbinic literature, and I have not seen such a view in the cases under study.

Since Hirsch never systematically treated the issue of the relationship between *peshat* (the simple meaning of a biblical verse) and *derash* (homiletic exegesis of a verse), what can instead be suggested is that Hirsch believed that there was room for the simple meaning of the verse (*peshuto shel mikra*) in cases where the rabbinic interpretation was not intended by the Talmudic rabbis to be the *only* legitimate reading but was instead viewed by them as the nonliteral (*derash*), additional, meaning of the verse. Thus, in the two passages cited by Chertok, Hirsch believed that the literal meaning of the verses, based on the context, was intended as a lesson in how to treat *any* stranger, whether or not they had converted to Judaism. The rabbinic interpretation, though imbued with halachic weight, was never intended by the rabbis to negate the simple meaning of the verses.

Reading the verses this way did not raise the specter of interpreting Judaism based on external criteria—which Hirsch so opposed—because unlike some of the biblical exegetes of the rationalist Andalusian tradition, who reinterpreted biblical verses based on scientific or philosophical ideas that seemed to clash with the text, here the motivation for reading these verses in this manner was the desire to understand the simple meaning of the text in its original context. Since the Bible associates the command to treat the *ger* equitably with the Jewish experience in Egypt, the primary intent must have been to any foreigner or minority residing among the Israelites, regardless of their religious affiliation.[77]

The comments of Nahmanides on one of these verses, which seem to suggest that Nahmanides understood the meaning of *ger* as any stranger living among Jews, may have served as precedent for Hirsch's approach to (at least) that verse, particularly given Hirsch's veneration of Nahmanides, though Ibn Ezra's understanding of the term, not just in this verse but in others as well, is an even clearer precedent for Hirsch.[78]

Further, Hirsch's citation of several other biblical references to the "stranger" in his 1841 polemical essay were not intended to be the correct halachic interpretation of those passages.[79] Hirsch was surely balancing a fine line here.[80] However, he presumably felt that even those verses could be understood as general admonitions to be kind toward all strangers.[81] In addition to this plain meaning, there was also the rabbinic interpretation according to which the halacha forbids mistreatment of converts to Judaism.

Understanding Hirsch's approach in this manner resolves the potential conflict between Hirsch's views on the authority of the Oral Law and his understanding of these two verses relating to the *ger*.[82] What is left to determine is what factors were decisive in shaping Hirsch's attitude toward the gentile Other, although the context of the 1841 essay provides us with some clear indications.

Hirsch's Relationship to Humanism, German Nationalism, and Jewish Nationalism

Much has been written about Hirsch's affection for German culture and the degree to which his thought is imbued with the humanism that permeated the writings of the German idealists. There has been a common, if not quite regnant, view in academic circles that Hirsch was first and foremost a German patriot and was only secondarily a rabbinic Jew. Noah Rosenbloom expressed the most extreme version of this viewpoint in his 1976 study of Hirsch.[83] As already indicated, according to Rosenbloom, Hirsch was not very learned in the field of rabbinic literature, having mastered only the Bible. Hirsch's attendance at the yeshiva of Jacob Ettlinger, the foremost Talmudist in Germany at that time, and the rabbinic ordination Ettlinger conveyed upon him, is interpreted by Rosenbloom as indicative of the low stature of rabbinic learning in early nineteenth-century Germany.[84]

Further, the well-known comments of Rabbi Abraham Samuel Benjamin Sofer (known as Ketav Sofer), son of Hatam Sofer and dean of the illustrious Pressburg yeshiva, in which Sofer commended Hirsch on his mastery of the Talmud and codes and deemed Hirsch a *lamdan* (Talmudic virtuoso) of significant stature, are dismissed by Rosenbloom as having been said in jest, although he adduces no support for that conjecture.[85] Rosenbloom's view had been suggested by some earlier writers and it was repeated by some later scholars.[86]

However, the publication of Hirsch's responsa and Talmudic novellae in 1992 has seriously called into question the tenability of Rosenbloom's thesis.[87] Since Rosenbloom's portrayal of Hirsch as first and foremost a German nationalist and only secondarily a rabbinic Jew rests largely—in Rosenbloom's estimation—on the view that Hirsch was not very well-versed in rabbinic literature, instead founding his intellectual conception of Judaism on his reading of the Bible, which Jews share with Christians, the untenability of that view seriously undermines the related assertion that Hirsch was primarily a German nationalist. Related to the latter claim is the view, so often asserted, that Hirsch denied the nationality of the Jewish people, deeming them a religious community only, a view it is said he had in common with Reformers. That view too can no longer be sustained, as Mordechai Breuer and Matthias Morgenstern have demonstrated.

Hirsch emphasizes in his writings that the teachings of the Torah are *not* merely religious in nature; rather, they constitute national training for the national vocation of the Jewish nation. In this context, it is worth citing a passage that Hirsch wrote that stands in tension with the views of those scholars who have portrayed Hirsch as one who denied the national component of Judaism. The Bible (Exodus 6:1–7) has God telling Moses to tell the Children of Israel that He will free them from Egyptian bondage and will take them to be a nation for Him (*li le-am*). Hirsch comments:

> *Li le-Am*, in these two short words, by which here, for the first time, the whole future destiny of Israel is expressed, lies the specific difference, the speciality of Judaism, in which it is so absolutely unique. People thoughtlessly choose to include what they so unfittingly call 'the Jewish religion' in the category of religions generally, as being also a kind of religion . . . *Li le-Am*, to God—to be a People! This itself already tells us that Judaism, Judaism founded by God, is, in no wise, a religion (*Darin ists schon gesagt, dass das Judentum, das von Gott gestiftete Judentum, mit nichten eine "Religion" sei)*. . . . Here God founds not a Church, but a Nation, a whole national life is to form itself on him. As a nation, **not merely as a religion**, is Israel His (*Hier aber stiftet Gott keine Kirche, sondern ein Volk, ein ganzes Volksleben soll sich von ihm aus gestalten. Als Volk, **nicht als blosse Konfession**, ist Israel sein*) [. . .] While other nations have their national bond in their country, the Jewish nation have theirs in their common God.[88]

It seems that some earlier scholars may have conflated Hirsch's staunch patriotism and his opposition to an activist approach to messianism and the building of the land of Israel with the denationalization of the Jewish people. While partisans of Reform adopted just such a position, Hirsch and the rest of the Neo-Orthodox rabbinic leadership opposed it. Hirsch went further than most Neo-Orthodox leaders in his adoration of the Hebrew language and his view that a thorough grounding in Hebrew etymology should be a fundamental requirement in the most elementary Jewish education.

Hirsch's view of Hebrew as a "living language" in the nineteenth century certainly calls into question the theory that he favored the denationalization of Judaism.[89] His opposition to the activist approach to messianism (as exemplified by his opposition to Zvi Hirsch Kalischer's proto-Zionist initiative) ought to be understood as a reflection of Hirsch's self-perception as a guardian of tradition and is in keeping with the hardline stances he took regarding the issues of Orthodox Wissenschaft (as represented by the Hildesheimer Rabbinical Seminary) and secession.[90] Hirsch did believe that despite the national character of Judaism, during the period of the exile, when the Jewish people were dispersed across the world, they ought to devote themselves wholeheartedly to furthering the well-being of the nations in whose midst they resided.[91] But Hirsch opposed the view, advanced by Reform thinkers, that Jews living in Germany were "Germans of the Mosaic persuasion."

Hirsch viewed loyalty to the country of one's residence, including all actions undertaken to further the welfare of that country, as a religious obligation, "a duty imposed by God and no less holy than all the others (*nicht minder als alle übrigen heilige, von Gott geordnete Pflicht*)."[92] Hirsch further asserted that "this outward obedience to the laws must be joined by the inner obedience: i.e., to be loyal to the State with heart and mind, loyal to the kings, to guard the honor of the State with love and pride, to strive with enthusiasm wherever and whenever you can so that the nation's institutions shall prosper, so that every aim which your country has set as its national goal shall be achieved and furthered."[93] Hirsch added that "this duty is an unconditional duty and not dependent upon whether the State is kindly intentioned toward you or is harsh . . . [in either case] you shall not neglect your duty."[94]

Howard Levine has taken Hirsch to task for these words, claiming that he went too far in his adoration of the German state and his demand for unconditional patriotism, even to a regime that treats its citizens harshly.[95] Judith Bleich has speculated that perhaps Hirsch got carried away in the patriotic rhetoric of the times.[96] However, Leo Trepp has examined Hirsch's career as rabbi of Oldenburg, during which time he wrote the *Horeb*, and has drawn some conclusions that directly pertain to this issue.[97] His analysis leads to an inversion of the widely held conceptions with respect to Hirsch's impetus for the composition of his first two works.

Trepp shows that Hirsch's position as Landesrabbiner of Oldenburg was fraught with difficulties from the start. The Grand Duchy of Oldenburg established this position in 1827 and the first occupant was Nathan Adler, who held that title for only one year.[98] The official function of this position was to "acculturate the Jews of the Grand Duchy to the ways of the western world and society."[99] Adler was successful in initiating this task and, upon leaving, was asked for a suitable replacement to finish what he started. He chose Hirsch. As noted, Hirsch (unlike Adler) did not possess a doctorate and, further, was known as a militant defender of Orthodoxy.[100] Only the fact that Hirsch did attend university classes (but only for a short time and without obtaining any degree) allowed for his consideration by the Oldenburg government.[101] By state law, Hirsch had to undergo an examination before a state board, which was presided over by the Protestant Superintendent of Churches. Adler, who was chief examiner, aided Hirsch in supplying answers that were satisfactory.

The first collision came when Hirsch's salary did not arrive regularly, as it had for Adler. The Oldenburg congregation was apparently unhappy with Hirsch's rigid Orthodoxy. The government saw this as its opportunity to derail Hirsch's position entirely, using the issue of salary as a pretext. Although the duke of Oldenburg did not accept the government's recommendation to fire Hirsch, he did enact strict supervision over Hirsch to monitor all his movements and activities. Thus, Hirsch's impetus for writing *The Nineteen Letters* and *Horeb* a few years after his installation as Landesrabbiner may have been more than, as is generally assumed, a desire to enlighten German youth about the relevance of halachic Judaism for the modern age. Hirsch was simultaneously proving to his employers that he intended to do nothing in his capacity that would be deleterious to the government's stated goal of acculturating the Jews—even as he remained a champion of strict Orthodoxy.

This would explain the presence of two elements in those early writings that, though not entirely absent from his later writings, are far more prominent and pronounced in the former: his staunch German patriotism and his choice of terminology in referring to non-Jews. Nowhere in his later writings does Hirsch speak of the duty to not only be loyal to "the Fatherland" in deeds but to internalize a sense of loyalty to everything associated with it. Faithful adherence to the laws of the host country is an obligation that is found in the Talmud and has been codified as normative Jewish law.[102] The internalization of loyalty to one's host country is not explicitly found in earlier sources. But given Hirsch's tenuous position, it is unsurprising that he would have made that statement in the very first work he composed (in 1835, but published only after *The Nineteen Letters*).[103]

Another noticeable peculiarity of Hirsch's two earliest works is the terminology he employs for non-Jews: "your non-Jewish brethren" (*deinen nicht-jüdischen Bruder*). Although Hirsch always wrote respectfully of non-Jews and the obligations of Jews toward them, he did not employ this particular terminology in any of his later writings.[104] Yet they appear throughout *The Nineteen Letters* and *Horeb*. Hirsch was obviously aware of the ever-watchful eye of Oldenburg's governmental authorities.[105] However, it must be stressed that the argument here is about style, not substance. Hirsch remained a German patriot throughout his life (even when his optimism about the position of Jews somewhat subsided in his later years), and he also sincerely regarded all of humanity as brethren. He consistently stressed that God's love extends to all mankind and that the Jews are merely the trailblazers, forging a path for all humans to claim their place as God's beloved children. The tenor and idiom, though, do change somewhat in his later writings.

This understanding of the context for Hirsch's position in Oldenburg sheds light on some of his unpublished letters.[106] They reveal that in his correspondence with governmental officials he displayed a reverential and deferential attitude toward the authorities. In one letter, Hirsch requests that his two oldest sons be allowed to attend the gymnasium in Nikolsburg. He adopts a humble and deferential posture (e.g., by writing: *mit der inständigen und ehrerbietigen Bitte* [with fervent and reverent plea]). Hirsch employs hortatory language in his letter, entreating the Moravian government to accept his request, which Hirsch suggests is a matter of basic rights.[107]

Hirsch's tone suggests that he believed that Jews and Christians in Moravia ought to be regarded as equal citizens in all respects. It is difficult to imagine Hirsch's East European colleagues writing in this manner. They took it for granted that gentiles hated Jews and would never be willing to accept Jews as equals. An examination of Netziv's essay on anti-Semitism confirms this supposition. Netziv argues that God ensures that hatred for Jews develops in non-Jewish nations so as to prevent Jewish assimilation. The granting of complete equality would have upset this divine scheme.[108] But for Hirsch, it was a matter of basic human dignity, which recognizes no distinction between Jews and non-Jews.

Another letter displays Hirsch's reverence for the government authorities in delicate situations, and it is difficult to determine if this is primarily a result of his concern for the situation or if they are authentic representations of Hirsch's patriotism. In this letter, Hirsch asks the Frankfurt government to ease restrictions on Jewish soldiers.[109] Hirsch writes that these soldiers are dedicated to serving their homeland, but sometimes a collision of two duties (*Collision der Pflicht*) arises: between their obligation to the state and their obligation to follow God's laws, such as keeping the Sabbath and the dietary restrictions. If the food provided by the military to the soldiers is not kosher, this puts the soldier in a very delicate situation, seeing that he is grateful for the food graciously provided. A struggle within the conscience of the soldier ensues, writes Hirsch. Therefore, he implores the proper authorities to do their best to prevent such struggles of the conscience (*dieser Gewissensangelegenheit*) from arising.

The style of these letters is in keeping with Hirsch's idealistic prose. They do not appear to reveal anything new about Hirsch's relations with the German or Moravian governments that was not previously known.[110] In short, Hirsch adopts a deferential attitude toward whatever government official he is corresponding with, and he frames the Jewish point of view that he is championing, whether it is of a personal nature, or if it impacts the masses of Jews, as a matter of rights and conscience. It would seem that Hirsch believed that the Moravian and Frankfurt governments were fair players when it came to the interests of their Jewish subjects, and if Hirsch could present his case in the most persuasive and respectful manner possible, his remonstrations would not go unheeded.

It should be noted here that despite Hirsch's deferential posture when dealing with the local government, he was hardly an enthusiast of the autocratic nation-state. He emphasizes, in his commentary to Exodus, that it was the Egyptian government, and not its people, that stirred up hatred against the Hebrew people in order to deflect attention from the oppressive system of government that all Egyptians suffered under. Hirsch notes that this pattern has repeated itself throughout history, especially during the Jewish Middle Ages, when "Jew-Laws" were promulgated that served to indemnify the various medieval tyrants against the oppression they perpetrated against the Christian populations.[111] It must be noted, however, that this commentary was composed when Hirsch was no longer the Landesrabbiner of Oldenburg but was instead the rabbi of an independent congregation in Frankfurt. To Hirsch, the less interventionist local government there was apparently not a cause for concern, and he felt free to write his trenchant critique of the corruption of centralized autocratic regimes, a characterization that Hirsch may have felt was applicable to ascendant Bismarckian policy.

In his *Horeb*, composed while in Oldenburg, Hirsch, employing passionate language, urged his coreligionists to welcome all steps toward reconciliation on the part of non-Jews and to forget past persecution. The passage is worth citing in its entirety. In commenting on the biblical verse that exhorts Jews not to "abhor an Egyptian because thou wast a stranger in his land" (Deuteronomy 23:8), Hirsch comments that the persecution inflicted by Egypt upon the Jews ought to be forgotten:

> The good shall you remember, the evil forget (*des Guten sollst du gedenken, vergessen das Böse*). There is a lesson in this for the Jewish people who are once more scattered over the face of the world. Learn to forget the centuries of oppression and misery, of the inhuman scorn and the inhuman degradation *which folly and lack of understanding brought upon you* in your wandering in the *Galuth* [exile], and remember gratefully the good that you found everywhere—and still find. And when you, yourself, find merely an abode, are allowed only a pitiful existence, even for that be thankful, show gentleness and love to every citizen of those States that have welcomed you and given you their protection; *let him learn from you the love that he has denied you* (*er lerne von dir die Liebe, die er dir versagt*). And now, Jew of today, now, when God has put into the hearts of the princes and the people a spirit of kindness, justice and humanity, and the yoke is lifted, and the chains are unbound and the scorn and the degradation disappear and, through tender justice, *the sons try to atone for the harsh unkindness with which their forefathers treated your people*: with what heartfelt love and gratitude would you advance to meet your non-Jewish brother (*mit welch herzlicher Liebe und Dankbarkeit müsztest du entgegen kommen deinem nichtjüdischen Bruder*), if you only pondered carefully the full implication of this Divine commandment.[112]

The passages in italics indicate a sincere belief on Hirsch's part that the centuries of anti-Jewish Christian persecution were coming to an end and that the perpetrators of those acts were misguided individuals whose descendants yearn to atone for their ancestors' inhumanity. By showing kindness to his non-Jewish fellow citizens, the Jew will be teaching Christians the love that their ancestors had denied him. Although this text appears to be influenced by Enlightenment ideals espoused by non-Jews who favored helping Jews to achieve emancipation, Hirsch was neither the first nor the last to express this view.[113]

In 1819 dozens of Orthodox rabbis contributed to the volume titled *Eleh Divre ha-Berit*, in which they denounced the nascent Reform movement and its halachic innovations. Rabbi Eliezer of Triesch composed several letters for that collection, and in one he refers to the biblical prohibition against hating an Egyptian. He emphasizes that although the Egyptians had done much evil to the Jewish people, it was only the good that they had earlier done that Jews were to remember.[114] Although the rabbi of Triesch does not explicitly refer to the efforts of his Christian contemporaries to lift anti-Jewish measures (as Hirsch later did), he does note that "the nations amongst whom we dwell do only good [things] for us" and that we should therefore repeatedly refer to those good deeds carried out by these nations.[115] Clearly, he intended for his audience to understand that while Reform innovations were proscribed, the principle of love of mankind that was advocated by Reform leaders was in fact demanded by authentic rabbinic Judaism. Thus, there was nothing radical about Hirsch's stance on this issue. He merely reformulated ideas that had been found in earlier rabbinic writings (that is, texts written by rabbis who regarded the Talmud as the authoritative source for Jewish belief and observance) using the idiom of German idealism; his style is particularly indebted to the Romanticism of the early nineteenth century, but the ideas are firmly rooted in classical Jewish texts.

The text of *Horeb* was composed in 1835, a full thirteen years before disillusionment would set in among European liberals in the wake of the failed 1848 revolutions and the reactionary policies that followed. Nevertheless, Hirsch continued to remain hopeful even during that stormy period, which coincided with his tenure as the Chief Rabbi of Moravia. It was only with the rise of German anti-Semitism in the final third of the nineteenth century that Hirsch's faith in progress collapsed.[116]

In keeping with his approach, Hirsch, in his petitions on behalf of the emancipation of Moravian Jewry (which occurred some two decades prior to the surge in German anti-Semitism), urged "our Christian brethren" to fulfill their divine task in removing burdensome restrictions on Jewish life.[117] Although Hirsch was no doubt sincere in his expressions of optimism that Christians, motivated by their "sense of justice," would grant civic equality to Jews, his choice of terminology was obviously influenced by the circumstances.[118] He was well aware of the handicaps faced by his coreligionists in many German states—which his "Christian brethren" chose not to lift.[119] His approach to emancipation in Moravia reflected both a tactical decision as well as a heart-felt conviction regarding the beneficence of his Christian contemporaries.

Mention must be made at this point of Hirsch's well-known "Mensch-Yisroel" concept. This idea first appears in Hirsch's first-published book.[120] Some have suggested that this was Hirsch's version of Mendelssohn's demarcation of human and Jewish identities.[121] Mordechai Breuer, however, argues that this is a serious misunderstanding of Hirsch's views. On the contrary, Hirsch recognized no such bifurcation. "Hirsch's concept did not signify a combination of the external universal aspect with the internal Jewish aspect of the Jew, but the Jewishness of human values and the universal validity of Jewish values . . . 'Israel' is 'Man' on a higher plane."[122]

Matthias Morgenstern has argued that Hirsch regarded nineteenth-century Prussia as the ideal vehicle for the realization of the aspirations of independent Orthodoxy. Having waged a struggle for legal independence from the Reform-dominated Gemeinde in Frankfurt, Hirsch believed that the Prussian state would guarantee freedom of religion for the Orthodox better than his Liberal co-religionists would. Morgenstern suggests that there is a connection between Hirsch's championing of engagement with German culture and his idealized views about the Prussian state, whose dominance Frankfurt fell into while he served as rabbi of the IRG. Whether or not such a linkage can be definitively corroborated, there can be little doubt that—despite his favorable opinion of the Prussian state—Hirsch did not deny the national element of Judaism.[123] On the contrary, he emphasized that Judaism is *not* merely a religion but a nationality and that the training of the Israelites by God in the Bible was meant to create a nation that would last for all eternity.[124]

Even when Hirsch was purportedly still in his "liberal" phase, he emphasized the centrality of the Hebrew language in educating a child to be a faithful member of the Jewish people.[125] In a later essay, published in 1866, Hirsch made the following emphatic declaration:

> While Christianity, for instance, sees in itself a religious doctrine that finds its concrete representation in the Church, the goal of Judaism is to build a nation (*ist das Judentum ein volkbildendes Element*). The Jewish nation, in every aspect of its historical reality, is the product of Judaism, and the national endeavors that have engaged an entire people through the ages are set forth in the literature of Judaism. Judaism does not view Hebrew literature as part of theology. This sacred Hebrew literature is the literature of the Jewish nation (*Sie ist die jüdische Nationalliteratur*), just as Greek literature is the literature of the Hellenic people and German literature is that of the German nation (*wie die deutsche die der deutschen Nation*).[126]

Several years earlier, Hirsch had penned a series of essays titled "Jewish Weltanschauung: An Attempt to Develop the Jewish Outlook on the World and Life from the Hebrew Language and Literature of the Jewish People."[127] In it, he repeatedly refers to Hebrew as the national language of the Jewish nation, demonstrating that he saw Judaism as more than merely a religious denomination. Furthermore, while Hirsch and likeminded German-Orthodox leaders did share with their Reform counterparts an enthusiasm for Bildung, the Orthodox did not internalize a European set of values that they could then use as a basis for determining which aspects of rabbinic Judaism were still binding in modern times, as their Reform colleagues had done. Hirsch's writings, in contrast to those of his Reform coreligionists, evidence a sense of Jewish national consciousness; assertions that Hirsch denationalized Judaism are thus untenable.

This analysis leads us to a question of significant import to the interpretation of Hirsch's ideology: what was his relationship to nascent Zionism?[128] He was opposed to the proto-Zionist Hibbat Zion movement, but his very conception of Jewish nationhood needs clarification. As noted, some authors have argued that Hirsch's conception of the Jewish people as only a spiritual nation places him in a category almost identical with the Reformers.[129] Since in the worldly realm the Jews were members of the German nation, there is in that case no fundamental disagreement with Reform thinkers on the question of nationality. Further, they argue, Hirsch strove to demonstrate that there is no organic link between the Jewish people and the land of Israel.

It is true that, unlike Mendelssohn, who described the centrality of the land of Israel to Judaism during the period when Jews exercised national sovereignty, Hirsch minimizes the significance of the land from the very inception of Jewish peoplehood. They were given the Torah in the desert and were given a land only for a temporary period. In fact, according to Hirsch, they were expelled from the land, in order to demonstrate that there is only one factor that binds the people together—its loyalty to God. Even Abraham was forced to leave his homeland to seek God. The temporary reunion between the Jews and the land of Israel was purely spiritual and was never intended to last. Hirsch is said to have alluded to Heinrich Heine's conception of Judaism as a religion with a "portable homeland." Thus, it is argued, Hirsch's conception of Jewish nationalism was no less radical than that of his Reform nemesis, Abraham Geiger.[130] Accordingly, Hirsch did not accept traditional notions of Jewish national identity or, as Michael Meyer has stated, "Hirsch was not a traditionalist by principle."[131]

However, only by examining Hirsch's positions alongside those of his non-Orthodox German-Jewish contemporaries can Hirsch's views be appreciated in their proper context. Abraham Geiger, the most influential German Reform thinker, argued that the essential characteristic of Judaism was its spirit. When the Jews exercised political sovereignty, this was in order for their spirit to be dispersed among the surrounding nations. Once Jews lost their sovereignty, there was no longer any relevance to Jerusalem or the land of Israel. The Jews practice their mission of diffusing pure humanity wherever they live. Therefore, wherever a Jew lives *is* his homeland. There will be no future ingathering of Jews to the land of Israel and Jerusalem no longer holds any significance for contemporary Jews.[132] Further, Geiger believed that there was no essential connection between Judaism and the Hebrew language.[133]

By contrast, Hirsch emphasized that the physical return to Zion was a fundamental tenet of Judaism.[134] He wrote that the Torah is the national training book of the Jewish nation. Given the proscription on messianic activism, which Hirsch regarded as normative halacha, it would not have been possible to maintain that Palestine was the homeland of contemporary Jews, since mass settlement of Palestine would have violated Hirsch's understanding of this law.[135] Furthermore, Hirsch believed that Jews must be patriotic and engaged citizens of the lands of their residence, in order to preach "pure humanity" (*reines Menschtum*), though not Judaism, to their non-Jewish fellow-citizens.[136] Thus, even if Hirsch had supported an activist approach to messianism, there would have been an additional impediment to regarding Palestine as the homeland of the Jewish people and Germany as merely a temporary abode: Hirsch's philosophy of the Jewish people as *Jeschurun*, the most upright sector of humanity, militated against the possibility that Jews can simultaneously regard two lands as their homelands since this would have precipitated the dual loyalty charge. Hirsch's entire conception of Judaism did not allow for such a possibility.

Several scholars have argued that Hirsch opposed any form of Jewish nationalism on the basis of a comment made by Saemy Japhet in 1948. This is what Japhet wrote: "He [Hirsch] was opposed to any form of Jewish nationalism as well as to Zionism and one of his versions of the translation of '*ki mi-Zion*' was 'from where the Tauroh emanates, there is my Zion.' He sternly rejected the order B'nai B'rith."[137] As a result of Japhet's assertion, Hirsch has been described as sharing the views of the Reform movement regarding Jewish nationalism.[138] In this interpretation, just as many Reform ideologues argued that Berlin was the new Jerusalem, so too Hirsch considered any place from which the Torah emanates to be the new Zion. The problem with this characterization is that the translation Japhet refers to cannot be found in any of Hirsch's writings. Apparently, Japhet was repeating what he may have heard his father (who was a member of Hirsch's Frankfurt congregation) cite in Hirsch's name, but there is no way to verify this. Since statements that Hirsch makes in his published writings contradict this idea, we cannot accept the accuracy of Japhet's citation (which, in any case, is quite vaguely described as "one of his [i.e., Hirsch's] versions," with no reference to when Hirsch may have proffered this idea).[139]

A well-known passage from *The Nineteen Letters* sheds light on Hirsch's view of Jewish national identity:

> Land and soil were never Israel's bond of union, but only the common task of the Torah; therefore, it still forms a united body, though separated from a national soil (*darum ja auch eine Einheit noch, wenn auch fern vom Lande.*) Nor does this unity lose its reality, though Israel accepts everywhere the citizenship of the nations amongst which it is dispersed. (You may call this unity by the Hebrew terms *am* and *goy* but not by the German word "Volk," unless we are able to separate from this German term the concept of common territory and political power.) [This is the case] until one day when God will again reunite the Jews outwardly too as a people gathered on its soil (*bis sie einmal Gott auch äusserlich als Volk auf einem Boden vereinigen*), and the Torah will again form the constitution of a state, serving as a model and a manifestation of God and the human mission.[140]

This idea is repeated by Hirsch in several other places, and he seems to have placed much significance on the inapplicability of the German term *Volk* to contemporary Jews.[141] Yet he maintains, by implication, that the Jews once were, and will once again be, a *Volk*. It is the absence of common territory and political power that make this term inapplicable to nineteenth-century Jews. What is striking is that Hirsch insists that all present-day Jews constitute an *Einheit*, a unit. He does not distinguish here between Orthodox and Reform Jews: all are part of the same national unit. There can thus be little doubt that Hirsch did espouse a unique form of Jewish nationalism, and he by no means advocated the denationalization of the Jewish people. Even later Zionist Jewish thinkers would most likely accept Hirsch's definition of the Jewish nation, with the important caveat that they would insist that Jews *ought* to do everything in their power to once again constitute a *Volk*.

But if Hirsch considered all Jews as members of the same *Einheit*, why did he champion secession of the Orthodox from the Reform-controlled community? Does this not prove that the sole criterion of Jewish national identity in Hirsch's view is religious affiliation? A careful examination of the controversy regarding secession renders such a reading untenable.[142] The fact that Hirsch repeatedly stated that the religious differences dividing Orthodoxy from Reform are far greater than those which divide different Christian denominations ought not to be understood as indicating that Hirsch considered Orthodoxy a religious confession like one of the churches.[143] Hirsch's emphatic declaration that God founded *not a Church but a Jewish nation* has already been discussed. The key issue in the secession controversy was the structure and purpose of a Jewish *kehillah*: it is to be the representative of Jewish truth, which is the divine Torah.[144] Since what Orthodoxy regards as truth, Reform regards as false (the divine origin and eternality of the Torah), the two camps cannot be united in a communal structure.[145] But they are certainly members of one nation—the important caveat being that one camp (the Orthodox) was faithful to its national calling, while the other (Reform) was not. Hirsch's emphasis on this point during his debate with Rabbi S. B. Bamberger regarding secession in Frankfurt in 1877 lends weight to this interpretation of Hirsch's view of Jewish nationhood.[146]

9

Hirsch's Views on Non-Jews and Christianity

Non-Jews

Many of Hirsch's ideas regarding non-Jews have already been discussed. In particular, his embrace of the mission theory has been examined. It is worth noting here that the fact that this view is rooted in rabbinic sources from an earlier period, as noted, has sometimes been considered as immaterial, given the similarity of Hirsch's views—particularly their formulation—to those of Mendelssohn and the later Reformers. A further examination of Hirsch's writings on this subject should shed light on this question.

In his first published work, *Die Neunzehn Briefe über Judentum* (1836), Hirsch develops the framework for subsequent writings on this topic. Mankind had lost its sense of purpose, which had been to build national lives in accordance with divine dictates of holiness and morality. It thus became necessary to create a model nation that would build its national life in this manner and would serve as a beacon of light to other nations. God saw that the descendants of Abraham, Isaac, and Jacob were most suited to this task and He therefore sent them into Egypt as a training ground for their physical perseverance and spiritual fortitude. When God saw that they were up to the task, they were liberated from their oppression in a miraculous manner and were made to wander in the desert for forty years, during which time they received the Torah.

God did this to demonstrate that Jewish nationality is dependent not on a common land but on a common spiritual possession. The land of Israel was given to the Jews on the condition that they implemented the Torah on a national scale on that territory. After the Jewish people demonstrated they were unfaithful to their calling during the period of political sovereignty in their land, they were exiled. The dispersion of Jews around the world was indeed a punishment for Jewish sinning but it was more than that: it was an opportunity to demonstrate the faithfulness of the Jews to the Torah even when they lacked that which made other nations great. By coming into contact with diverse streams of mankind, the Jews ultimately spread to mankind at large essential Jewish teachings about God and man's responsibilities to Him. The emergence of Christianity and Islam demonstrated that the Jewish mission had begun to achieve success since those religions propogated many of the key teachings of Judaism, albeit in a flawed manner.[1]

The concept of the Jewish people as "priests" of humanity, teaching the latter fundamental truths about divine providence is, of course, first found in the book of Exodus, where God tells Moses that Israel was to be "a kingdom of priests and a holy nation" (Exodus 19:6). The precise meaning of the term "priests" (*kohanim*) in this verse is not made clear by its context. Thus, it could be construed to mean that the Jewish people were to become exceedingly pious, like priests. However, Maimonides, according to the recollection of his son, Rabbi Abraham Maimuni, maintains that the meaning here is that just as the priests among the Jews serve to teach and guide the rest of the people about what is pure and impure, right and wrong, so too Israel was to be the priest among the nations, guiding them in the direction of all that is holy.[2] That was the purpose of Israel's selection as God's "treasured people" (Exodus 19:5), according to Maimonides. Rabbi Ovadia Seforno, living in Renaissance Italy, also maintained that this verse connotes the priestly mission of Israel with respect to the other nations.[3]

As far as Hirsch's views on this matter and those of Reform ideologues is concerned, Jacob Haberman has stated, "Concerning the 'mission of Israel' there is little to choose between Hirsch and the Reformers. One could transpose sentences, even paragraphs, from Hirsch's Reform opponents and interchange them with Hirsch's words and not notice any *hiatus* or break in the continuity of thought."[4] Hirsch's teacher, Jacob Ettlinger, had also written of the mission of the Jewish people to the nations but, according to Judith Bleich, "in expounding the mission theory Hirsch goes far beyond Ettlinger." Bleich adds that Ettlinger's treatment of this issue is "more restrained and more firmly rooted in traditional sources."[5] There seems to be a consensus that Hirsch's views on the mission theory exceed what could demonstrably be extracted from traditional rabbinic sources, and move into the (at least) rhetorical territory of nineteenth-century German Reform Judaism.

It appears that Hirsch's views are a direct expression of what he was taught by his other teacher, Isaac Bernays. Bernays, as discussed, had a broad historical picture of Judaism's importance for advancing the welfare of mankind. Since the concept of the Jewish people serving as a "light unto the nations" had ample biblical and rabbinic precedent, Hirsch, inspired by Bernays, further developed this idea as far as its application to post-emancipation circumstances is concerned. He argued that during the period of the ghettos it was impossible for Jews to fulfill the "mission" aspect of their vocation; in contrast, in the period of emancipation, Jews were especially called upon to serve as beacons of morality to the world at large.[6]

The precise nature of what the Jews ought to be teaching the nations is at the heart of the confusion surrounding the origin and use of the mission theory by the Neo-Orthodox. For Geiger and Holdheim, the essence of Judaism is "ethical monotheism." The entire purpose of post-exilic Judaism was to spread this concept among non-Jewish nations. This is why Reform ideologues believed that they were living in an era that constituted a fulfillment of messianic prophecies: the lifting of the ghetto restrictions, which enabled Jews to participate in European cultural life and to serve as role models, was deemed to be the advent of the final period of Jewish history, wherein Jews and non-Jews lived as equals. Accordingly, prayers for a restoration of the Jewish people to Palestine were nothing short of treasonous because the concept of a *national* homeland of the Jews was entirely a matter of the past. The task for the present was the dissemination of Judaism's essence—ethical monotheism—amid the nations among whom Jews lived.[7] This is a fundamentally different perspective from that of the Neo-Orthodox leaders.

While the Neo-Orthodox shared the Reform enthusiasm for the granting of civic equality, they believed that the basic tasks of the Jew remained fundamentally unaltered: the preservation and observance of the Torah commandments, whether they were ethical or ritual in nature. The mission to the nations was one of the most significant reasons for why God ordained the particular commandments that He did, but the immediate goal was the upkeep of those commandments, not the spread of Judaism to the nations. Jewish ideals would inevitably be spread among the nations only if the Jews loyally observed all the minutiae of the legal portions of the Torah. The existence of a nation that submits its entire national life to the dictates of God's will—and of individuals who dedicate every facet of their daily lives to divine authority—would serve as a source of inspiration to the other nations to seek to carry out God's will for them in their own national lives.[8]

This brings us to an issue that has perplexed scholars for generations: Hirsch's abolition of the *Kol Nidre* prayer while he was rabbi of Oldenburg. On the one hand, a number of scholars have cited this as proof of Hirsch's moderate reformist tendencies.[9] Others, however, have apologetically defended his actions.[10] Roland Tasch has examined the views of those who advocate the former approach and considers them either inadequate or unacceptable. Can Hirsch's bold action with respect to *Kol Nidre* really be understood as a result of his "enlightened background and aesthetic sensibilities," as Rosenbloom suggested? Can it be understood any better as acquiescence to the overtures of a twenty-two-year-old Heinrich Graetz, whose tumultuous personality was then in a narcissistic stage, as Heinemann suggested?

Instead, Tasch advances an approach that focuses on Hirsch's concern about charges of Jewish duplicity and its impact on the ability of Jews to take oaths in German courts. Hirsch was acutely aware of the attacks on the *Kol Nidre* prayer in Germany since Eisenmenger had, in his 1700 *Entdecktes Judenthum* popularized the allegation that Jews ritually nullify their vows to non-Jews yearly.[11] These attacks caused the trustworthiness of Jewish oaths to be called into question. As the rabbi of a province whose government wished to acculturate its Jews, Hirsch could not allow this situation to deteriorate further. By abolishing the *Kol Nidre* prayer, he made it clear that Jews had no intention of negating promises made to their fellow citizens of a different faith, and that therefore oaths that Jews took in German courts could be trusted absolutely.[12] This act was an exception to Hirsch's general aversion to liturgical reforms, as he did not engage in any other significant liturgical reforms after this episode.[13] Indeed, Hirsch contemplated even this one act carefully, and Tasch suggests a possible reading of the rabbinic sources that Hirsch, based on his own treatment of vows in his *Horeb*, may have developed, according to which the *Kol Nidre* prayer could be abolished in pressing circumstances such as the one he faced.[14]

Tasch argues that it was only in retrospect that Hirsch's abolishment of *Kol Nidre* came to be viewed as a venture into religious reforms. Viewing German-Jewish history through the prism of the Holocaust, scholars scoured Hirsch's record for signs of accommodation to German cultural values. The only negative reaction engendered at the time, notes Tasch, was that of Hirsch's family in Hamburg.[15] Indeed, Tasch's analysis is rendered even more compelling in light of the fact that Hirsch, early in his rabbinic career, had already acquired a reputation for religious militancy and was by no means seen as a moderate reformer.[16] That being the case, the *Kol Nidre* episode must be seen in light of the delicate political circumstances of Jews in 1830s Oldenburg, a time and place where emancipation had not yet been fully achieved. Jewish oaths were still suspect. Hirsch therefore tried to demonstrate that Orthodox Jews, no less than Reform Jews, were sensitive to the charge of untrustworthiness and had no special annulment ceremony for their vows.

This liturgical modification was reported, first by the Reform leader Samuel Holdheim and, later, in the German-Jewish press. Hirsch himself, in his one letter addressing this issue, is vague about the reasons for his abolishment, saying only that it was justifiable *al pi ha-din* (acceptable according to Jewish law) and that he regretted making this decision without first consulting other rabbinic authorities. He therefore reinstituted the prayer for subsequent years.[17] As seen, Hirsch was acutely sensitive to charges made against Judaism, and this concern applied as much to claims regarding Judaism's alleged tribalism as to Jews' alleged disregard for promises they made to non-Jews. His action concerning the *Kol Nidre* prayer ought to be understood within this context.[18]

Before proceeding to examine aspects of Hirsch's universalism, it is worth noting an apparent exception to the patterns thus far delineated. In his commentary to Numbers, Hirsch emphasizes that the Torah elaborated upon the story of Balaam in order to vindicate the assertion of the Sages that God ceased "to shower His Holy Spirit (*ruah ha-kodesh*) on men of other nations" after Moses implored Him to do so, according to a Midrash.[19] "Balaam was one of those who received it and see how he misused his spiritual gift."[20] Hirsch points out that while the Jewish prophets were interested in the welfare of all mankind and never utilized their proximity to God to further their own egoistic and base desires, that was precisely what Balaam did.

Thus, Hirsch regarded the biblical Jewish prophets as morally superior to their non-Jewish counterparts specifically *on account of their universalism.* Hirsch paraphrases a Midrash when he writes, "The prophetic spirit of Israel's prophets was filled with pity and commiseration with both Israel and the nations; Isaiah's inside vibrated like the strings of a harp over Moab's woes, Ezekiel wailed lamentations over the fall of Tyrus, while Balaam—wanted to ruin a whole innocent nation with his curse."[21] Hirsch asserts that the most famous non-Jewish prophet described in the Pentateuch was egomaniacal and misanthropic, whereas Jewish prophets were imbued with a love of mankind that caused them to experience distress upon learning of the suffering of nations regarded as enemies of the Jewish people. Thus, Hirsch's seemingly exclusivist assertion about the limits of non-Jewish prophecy was effectively a formulation of his deeply ingrained religious humanism.

In assessing Hirsch's views of non-Jews more broadly, it must be stressed that he consistently emphasized that there is no essentialist distinction between Jews and non-Jews. In his view, Jews were given a special mission by God, but they are regular human beings like everyone else. Menachem Kellner has argued that Maimonides—in contradistinction to the Zohar and medieval authorities such as Rabbi Judah Halevi—denied there was any essentialist, ontological distinction between Jews and non-Jews.[22] There can be no doubt that, despite Hirsch's acerbic criticism of Maimonides in the eighteenth letter of his *Nineteen Letters*, he completely shared Maimonides's perspective on this particular issue. While this is evident in virtually every reference to non-Jews in Hirsch's writings, two passages in his Pentateuch commentary make this view abundantly clear.

Commenting on the violent conduct of Simeon and Levi toward the inhabitants of Shechem (Genesis 34), Hirsch writes that the close juxtaposition in the Bible of the temporary humaneness displayed by Esau (in the preceding chapter of Genesis) and the cruelty manifested by Simeon and Levi teaches the Torah's readership "the fact that brightens Jewish history, namely, that though we have ultimately become the nation to whose hands the least spilled blood sticks, if we have become the mildest, most soft-hearted of nations, this is not due to any inherent weakness on our part . . . We *can* wield the sword of Esau, we can also become bloodthirsty. Our humaneness and mildness are the fruits of the education which God has given us through our history and through His Torah."[23]

For Hirsch, not only are Jews not inherently predisposed toward compassionate behavior—the fact that the Torah here stresses that Jews have only become this way as the result of an educative process serves to brighten Jewish history. If Jews were inherently possessed of a predisposition for gentle behavior, then they do not deserve to be laureled on account of their having shed relatively little blood. The rabbinic statement that the Jewish people are distinguished by three traits—they are compassionate, bashful, and known for performing deeds of kindness—was presumably understood by Hirsch, as well as Maimonides, as descriptions of how present-day Jews conduct themselves, *based on Torah teachings*, not as a metaphysical depiction of some essentialist Jewish quality.[24]

In the biblical narrative of Korah's rebellion against Moses, the Torah places into the mouth of Korah the assertion that "the entire community [of Israel], every one of them, is holy and God is among them" (Numbers 16:3). The majority of classical Jewish Bible commentators, from the medieval and modern periods, seem to accept the premise of Korah's claim. Indeed, all Jews *are* inherently holy and God dwells among all Jews. Nevertheless, some other aspect of Korah's conduct in this episode is deemed to be sinful. However, Hirsch completely undercuts this approach by insisting that the entire premise of Korah's claim is false:

> For the premises on which Korah based his revolt were false and the deductions in their application to the circumstances to which he referred, no less false. "The entire community, every one of them" were by no means "holy" already. They were "men of a holy calling" [Exodus 22:30], "holy shall ye be"

> [Levit. 19:2], they have the calling to become holy, and just by this calling are "holy unto your God" [Numbers 15:40], are a "holy people unto God" [Deut. 7:6], are men hallowed to God, belong with every fiber of their individual and national life exclusively to God. But *kedoshim*/holy, that they are not yet. And just so that they always work themselves indefatigably up to their holy calling, *so that they do not mix up what they are with what they should be, do not imagine themselves already holy because they are hallowed to a holy calling*, but that they should rather keep this holy calling of theirs always before them as the goal set by God for all their endeavors, just for that, their holy calling was given a symbolic representation of its ideal realization in the Sanctuary . . . The whole ranking of the nation into Kohanim, Levites, and Israelites, and the Sanctuary fenced off in the center, *preaches to all, "thou shalt be holy!" but not yet, "thou art holy!"*[25]

Here, Hirsch makes it abundantly clear that Jews are *not* inherently holy, but that they are called upon by God to *become* holy by their way of life.[26] This is precisely the Maimonidean view as well.[27] There are no passages in Hirsch's writings that suggest he accepted any conception of inherent Jewish holiness or innate spiritual superiority over non-Jews (not to mention any kind of racial superiority).

This is in sharp contradistinction to the views prevalent in Eastern Europe during Hirsch's time, which were rooted in the teachings of the sixteenth-century Jewish thinker Maharal. Maharal consistently reiterated that "the [non-Jewish] nations" and "the Jewish people" constitute two metaphysically different entities that only appear similar externally. Internally, however, they are like two different species.[28] Maharal writes that the famous rabbinic passage concerning God offering the Torah to all the nations, wherein all nations except for the Jews reject the Torah, is not to be understood literally.[29] In his interpretation, what the Talmud actually means is that *God examined the essence of the nations and determined that they were unsuitable to receive the Torah.* Given their inherent proclivity to physicality and sensuality, the non-Jewish nations could not have upheld the Torah even if they had chosen to accept it. Thus, observes Maharal, we find no prophets communicating with the nations offering them the Torah. Instead, God determined that only the Jews, who are inherently predisposed to virtuous conduct, would be worthy recipients of His Torah.[30]

Hirsch, by contrast, stresses that the Jewish people are just as capable of barbaric behavior as any other nation. *Only the education afforded the Jews by the Torah has trained* them to become the most humane of peoples. Hirsch does not merely affirm this point but characterizes it as a fact that "brightens

Jewish history." As noted, this passage demonstrates Hirsch's rejection of any metaphysical differences between Jews and non-Jews and is in line with the Maimonidean outlook.

Furthermore, the teachings of Rabbi Moses Hayyim Luzzatto (1707–46), which were popularized by the Mussar movement of the mid-nineteenth century, emphasized that the selection of the Jewish people constituted a rejection of the rest of mankind. Even in the World to Come, Rabbi Luzzatto averred, the minority of righteous gentiles can only hope to cleave to the Jewish people as clothing cleaves to the body. They will not attain independent salvation.[31] Hirsch's teachings on these matters were diametrically opposed to those of both Maharal and Luzzatto. To Hirsch, the selection of Israel was solely for the benefit of mankind, and "the achievement of nearness to God is equally within the reach of the Lapp in Lapland as to that of the Greek in Greece."[32]

Thus, it is clear that Hirsch's consistent emphasis on the universal purview of the Torah stands in stark contrast to the views that were popular during his lifetime among East European Jewry (as discussed).[33] His emphasis on the universal salvific character of the Torah is perhaps the most striking element in his writings relating to non-Jews. A characteristic example of Hirsch's views on this matter is the following declaration:

> The truth is that the attitude of Judaism toward all other religious faiths and all human intellectual pursuits differs basically from the attitude of other religions. Judaism is probably the only religion that does not declare *extra me nulla salus*, that happily welcomes any intellectual or moral advance, no matter what its origin. Indeed, the timeless words of the Jewish prophets look with firm assurance to the ever-growing, ever-spreading spiritual and moral ennoblement not only of the Jews, but of all mankind. Judaism is probably the only religion that teaches its followers to view . . . the sight of any human being great in wisdom or knowledge, no matter what his nationality or religion, as a revelation of the Divine . . .
>
> Now what about the attitude of Judaism toward other religious faiths? Again, Judaism is probably the only religion that does not presume to reign supreme over all other religions. Judaism perceives itself as an instrument working for all mankind, but not as a dictate to be obeyed by all men on earth. It welcomes any human, spiritual, or ethical advance brought about by other religious faiths; indeed, it hails every such triumph of truth and goodness as a triumph of its own mission on earth. The attitude of Judaism toward other religions may be compared to that of a true mother toward her daughters . . . Similarly, Judaism rejoices, and has a right to rejoice, in

> the harvest of light and goodness produced by its daughter religions in the civilized world for the benefit of universal human happiness and culture, just as if the accomplishment had come directly from Judaism. Judaism regards these advances as triumphs of the concepts that are to be brought to the rest of mankind by the Divinely-selected Jewish people.[34]

A related, and equally instructive, point is that according to Hirsch nothing was fundamentally altered with the revelation of the Torah at Mount Sinai.[35] While many traditional Jewish thinkers regard that monumental event as marking—forever—a profound distinction between Jew and non-Jew, for Hirsch it merely marked the most decisive step in God's plan to achieve salvation for all of mankind. While prior to Sinai there may have been the possibility that humanity as a whole could achieve its goal of sanctifying the world as the habitation of God, the advent of Sinai meant that this task was placed on the shoulders of one people, who had been crafted from its origins—the time of the biblical patriarchs—to serve as a model for the rest of mankind to emulate. The ultimate goal, however, remained exactly the same: the submission of all mankind to God's will.

Hirsch emphasizes that in messianic times the distinction between Israel and the nations will diminish but adds the following qualification: "Yet, in keeping with their separate historical development and the differing nature of their qualifications for the fulfillment of the destiny of mankind, Yisrael and the nations will still remain two separate entities. *Both are equally near to God in dignity and worth*, and both stride forward in equal measure toward the attainment of the goals of all mankind; nevertheless, they will remain two separate entities."[36]

Hirsch's image of the Jewish people uniting with the nations in messianic times is a central theme of his *Nineteen Letters*. In fact, the most recent English translation of this work incorporates footnotes by Rabbi Joseph Elias (1919–2014), including one that seeks to mitigate the implication of Hirsch's references to the nations "joining with Yisrael" in messianic times. Elias rightly cites the previously quoted passage from Hirsch's Siddur commentary, which makes it clear that a difference will still exist between the two groups—and then erroneously cites Rabbi Moses Hayyim Luzzatto's assertion that the revelation at Mount Sinai created "a permanent difference in roles and destinies between Yisrael and the other nations."[37] The passage that Elias cites makes it clear that Hirsch and Luzzatto were not by any means expressing the same idea but were rather expressing completely opposite ideas.[38] For Luzzatto, Sinai signaled the *end* of the nations' ability to achieve nearness to God.[39] For Hirsch, Sinai marked the *beginning* of a phase whose goal it was to restore the original purpose of creation—the unity of mankind in the service of God.

It is precisely this fundamental difference between Hirsch and many earlier and contemporaneous thinkers that has proven so confusing for commentators. For some, like Elias, Hirsch was merely formulating in different terminology what earlier rabbinic authorities had already written. For others, Hirsch was espousing the Reform mission theory, according to which at the end of days no difference at all will exist between Israel and the nations, a view contravened by Hirsch's comments in his previously quoted Siddur commentary.

Despite the assertion of some difference between the Jewish people and other nations remaining even in messianic times, it must be stressed that a recurring theme in Hirsch's writings is the centrality to Judaism of the brotherhood of mankind and the universal purpose of the people of Israel. This basic idea runs like a thread from *The Nineteen Letters* to his posthumously published commentary to the Siddur. What does change is the idiom. In his earliest two works, *Horeb* and *Nineteen Letters*, Hirsch's idiom sounds more reminiscent of the Reform mission theory than does the language he employs in his Pentateuch, Psalms, and Siddur commentaries, which were composed thirty to fifty years later.

What might account for that change? As noted, when serving as rabbi of the province of Oldenburg, Hirsch was ever mindful of the watchful eye of the Oldenburg government, which actively sought to promote culture and enlightenment among its Jewish citizens. Thus, Hirsch liberally employs the term "your non-Jewish brethren," which is conspicuously absent from his later writings. However, there was another, perhaps far more crucial, change. The later commentaries were all composed when Hirsch was rabbi of the Frankfurt Israelitische Religionsgesellschaft (IRG). At that time, Hirsch was an embattled leader, either working with Prussian governmental officials to allow for secession from the Gemeinde or serving as the rabbi of a secessionist congregation in the unified German Reich. In either case, although the universal mission of the Jewish people remained unchanged, the flowery and idealistic prose inevitably gave way to a more sober manner of expression.

Despite the change in idiom, Hirsch's universalist conception of Judaism remained as essential to his worldview in his later writings as it was in his earliest writings. An examination of his posthumously published Siddur commentary demonstrates this point. One of the most controversial sections of the Orthodox prayerbook, and one which to the present day troubles many egalitarian-minded Orthodox Jews, is the section containing the morning blessings where men thank God for not having made them gentiles, slaves, or women. As noted earlier, a prominent Orthodox scholar in early twentieth-century Berlin had advocated the recitation of an alternate text that expresses a more positive affirmation. In fact, the classic medieval commentators on the Siddur have expressed puzzlement as to why Jews do not recite the text thanking God for "having made me a Jew" rather than the negative "for having not made me a gentile." They were not guided by a concern for egalitarianism but rather by a desire to understand why a blessing would be formulated in the negative rather than in the positive, a formulation that renders this blessing distinct from other blessings. Hirsch implicitly responds to the criticisms of these blessings with the following remarks: "This is not a prayer of thanks that God did not make us heathens [i.e., non-Jews], slaves or women. Rather, it calls upon us to contemplate the task which God has imposed upon us by making us free Jewish men, and to pledge ourselves to do justice to this mission. These three aspects of our own status impose upon us duties much more comprehensive than those required of the rest of mankind."[40]

The *Aleinu* prayer at the end of the three services was one of the first texts to be modified by the early Reform movement.[41] Its first paragraph is a proud affirmation of Jewish distinctiveness. It emphasizes that God has not made the Jews "like the peoples of the lands" and has given them a position unlike "the families of the earth," for God "did not let our portion be like theirs nor our lot like that of all their multitudes." There is an additional text, removed by external and internal censors but still recited by some, which declares that the other nations "bow to vanity and nothingness and pray to a god that cannot save."[42] While Hirsch's prayer book omits that text, it retains the preceding statements.[43] Knowing full well the reaction they generated among his Reform contemporaries, Hirsch provided a sensitive and nuanced interpretation of these statements: "'*Shelo asanu*': It was in a very unusual manner that God made us into a nation, '*velo samanu*': and He gave us a unique position among the families of mankind. '*helkenu*': Our unique portion on earth is rooted in our unique relationship to God and to His Law, and it is for this reason that '*goralenu*,' our fate, too, is unique."[44] With these comments, Hirsch emphasizes that the difference between the Jewish people and the other nations is not metaphysical. Rather, the historical development of Israel differs from that of the rest of humanity. Hirsch is thus careful to clarify that this oft-recited passage from the Jewish liturgy carries no chauvinistic connotations.

Hirsch also made a point of denying that there is any implication in the second paragraph of the *Aleinu* prayer that Jews expect non-Jews to convert to Judaism in messianic times. This whole question was the subject of controversy among medieval Jewish thinkers and there is no consensus to be found in their writings.[45] Hirsch was not interested in providing his readers with an analysis of what medieval authorities had written; instead, he presents a view that is consistent with the universalism that permeates his writings and also echoes the Mendelssohnian approach. After noting that the prayer calls for all men to return to the service of God, Hirsch states, "According to the teachings of Judaism, however, such a hoped-for 'return' is not meant to be identical with a mass conversion of all men to Judaism; it will be no more than the conversion of all mankind to true humanity. It merely means that all men will then recognize God . . . and do Him homage forever by living a life of loyal obedience in accordance with the universal moral law which has been handed down in the Torah of Judaism for all the rest of mankind as well to follow."[46]

Hirsch's commentary to Tractate *Avot* is included in his Siddur commentary. Notable is his citation of Wessely in his comments to the very first Mishnah. Hirsch's commentary follows Wessely's *Yeyn Levanon* in certain key respects. Both authors stress the continuity of the Mishnayoth; both stress the broad themes treated in the tractate. Most noteworthy, however, is that both emphasize the ethical teachings of the rabbis to a degree greater than was commonplace in medieval and early modern commentaries to *Avot*.

In particular, Hirsch is at pains to stress the humanistic outlook of the Mishnaic sages, and stresses each comment found in *Avot* that could be interpreted in a universalistic fashion. Thus, commenting on *ohev et ha-beriyot* (meaning "loves the *beriyot*") (1:12), Hirsch writes that *beriyot*, "lit. creatures, is a term embracing all of mankind without distinction."[47] As noted, Hirsch limited the commandment "Love thy neighbor as thyself" to fellow Jews; thus, here was an opportunity to highlight a rabbinic passage that makes the love of all mankind a rabbinical mandate. When the term *beriyot* makes its second appearance in 2:16 (*sinat ha-beriyot*—hatred of *beriyot*—is condemned), Hirsch emphasizes that the Sages were concerned with the misanthropist who sees only evil in other people and overlooks "the good which is never entirely absent in any human being." Hirsch then adds a soliloquy about the term *beriyot*: "The Sages use a beautiful expression to describe men in their admonitions to us to love mankind and to shun malice. They call our fellowmen *beriyot*, 'creatures' of God, and they employ this term to include all men, without exception, thus stressing the motive which is at the basis of the behest to love all men. We are to respect in a human being, whoever and whatever he may be, the 'creature of God' and we must not deny this love to any fellowman, seeing that we were all made by the same Creator."[48]

Similar comments can be found in Hirsch's commentary to the Pentateuch. Chapter 5 of Genesis begins with a genealogy of mankind, stating, "This book is of the developments of Adam. On the day on which God created Adam, He formed him in the likeness of God." The Tanna Ben Azzai regarded this verse as encompassing a fundamental principle of Judaism, even more fundamental than the command to "Love thy neighbor as thyself."[49] Hirsch explains what Ben Azzai meant by classifying this verse as a fundamental principle of the Torah:

> Here a much greater, much higher union of all men is given. This verse looks on the greatest criminal, the greatest degeneration, the greatest bestiality, all as *toldot ha-adam*, all as developing out of the one Adam, the one creation in the likeness of God, all together entered in God's great Book of the World in which he enters mankind. *Toldot*, written *haser* [missing the second *vav*], even the deficient, imperfect products of humanity are still *toldot ha-adam*!
>
> So ALL men are human beings, the image of God is never completely lost, that is the first Truth which stands at the head of the history of Man.[50]

While these sentiments are not radical from the perspective of Jewish thought, their unmistakably humanist undertones bear the marked imprint of the nineteenth century.[51] More precisely, Hirsch was here responding to the charges that Judaism is a parochial religion. If one of the fundamental principles of the Torah is the inalienable humanity of every single human being, all of whom are created in God's image, then the Jews could not have been a people who regarded themselves as the sole beneficiaries of God's grace.

Hirsch didn't merely stress universalism in the abstract; he developed humanitarian approaches to biblical passages that sounded harsh to nineteenth-century ears. His treatment of the biblical episode of Dinah and Shekhem (Genesis: 34)—noted previously—is an illuminating example of this type of exegesis. The actions of Simeon and Levi, who slaughtered the entire city of Shekhem in retaliation for the kidnapping and rape of their sister Dinah by Hamor, son of the lord of the city (named Shekhem), have long perplexed commentators. Most medieval and early modern commentators justified the conduct of Simeon and Levi by explaining how all inhabitants of Shekhem were actually guilty of capital crimes. The most famous example of this approach is that of Maimonides, who writes that non-Jews are obligated to establish courts that enforce the other six Noahide commandments. Failure on the part of any non-Jewish resident of any locale to establish such courts renders that individual liable to death. Since the inhabitants of Shekhem did not try Hamor or his father Shekhem for their involvement in the abduction of Dinah, they were all subject to capital punishment.[52]

Nahmanides takes issue with Maimonides's assertion that failure to establish courts renders non-Jews liable to death, maintaining that only violation of negative commandments can cause non-Jews to be liable. However, he hastens to add that there is no need to search for a basis for the inhabitants of Shekhem having been liable to death since they were known as idolators and adulterers, both capital crimes for non-Jews. Nahmanides notes that it was not the responsibility of Jacob's sons to impose upon Shekhem's inhabitants the penalties to which they were technically liable.[53] However, Nahmanides does not characterize the behavior of Simeon and Levi as morally reprehensible.

Hirsch's approach is strikingly different from that of his predecessors. Commenting on the killing of the city's inhabitants he states, simply, "Now the blameworthy part begins, which we need in no wise excuse. Had they killed Shechem and Chamor [the individuals guilty of Dinah's abduction] there would be scarcely anything to say against it. But they did not spare the unarmed men who were at their mercy, yea, and went further and looted, altogether made the inhabitants pay for the crime of the landowner. For that there was no justification. For that Jacob too reproached them: You have 'clouded' me, our reputation, our name, our honor, which was clear as crystal you have besmirched . . . And just as you have dealt unjustly so have you dealt unwisely, we are so few in number, etc."[54] These comments demonstrate Hirsch's sensitivity to charges that the founders of the Jewish nation were immoral and barbaric. In his view, the Torah does not hide the flaws of even its greatest protagonists.[55] Therefore, he read the passage dealing with Simeon and Levy's slaughter of the town of Shekhem as an example of the Torah revealing the flaws of these children of the Patriarch Jacob.[56]

Another case of a biblical imperative to practice what would have been seen by modern Jews as barbarism is the injunction in Deuteronomy 7:16–24, where the Israelites are commanded to destroy the nations inhabiting the land of Israel when they conquer it. Hirsch writes that the correct understanding of the war enjoined by the Torah "would be not so much a war of objective destruction [but instead] the destruction of the [pagan] nation for the purpose of self-preservation." Hirsch continues, "The repeated admonitions not to have any mercy on the Canaanite population shows how much such a merciless procedure goes against the grain to the Jewish people and is against what they are meant to be, which is, and is to remain, the predilection to protect all living creatures. They are to regard this merciless procedure against the Canaanite population as an exception, expressly commanded by God, to be done at His bidding because of the special circumstances."[57] For Hirsch, then, there could be no possibility of the Torah countenancing barbaric behavior as a norm, even in ancient times. The Jewish people's raison d'être, he says, is to serve as protectors for all of humanity and, indeed, all of creation. Thus, the command mentioned here must be understood as an "exception" that was "expressly commanded by God," generated by "special circumstances."[58]

Convinced that he had demonstrated that rabbinic Judaism contained no provisions in opposition to the spirit of humanism, Hirsch proceeded to develop his conception of the universal mission of the Torah. A particularly illuminating example of his universalism is the introduction that he wrote to his Psalms commentary, published in the last decade of his life, the 1880s. In the introduction, Hirsch emphasizes that "[the Torah] also demonstrates to us that the founding and the destiny of our people is most intimately linked with the course of the history of mankind as a whole, which is no less guided by God than is our own. It teaches us to recognize that the purpose of our founding and our introduction into the midst of the nations was that we might teach mankind, and reclaim mankind for the knowledge and recognition of God, and of its own destiny and task as assigned it by Him. At the very beginning, Abraham was appointed to be 'the spiritual father of the multitude of the nations.' It was through him, and through the generations that would follow him, that blessings were to come 'to all the families of the earth.'"[59]

Hirsch continues by noting that David's purpose in authoring the Psalms was not merely to effect the spiritual edification of his own people. Rather, David felt that his purpose was to advance ideas of divine kingship and universal justice among all the nations. Hirsch continues, with words that could not have been written by his East or Central European contemporaries or by those in the Middle East: "One aspect of the efficacy of his psalms . . . has been gloriously vindicated even now, after so many centuries, in that the Psalms have been disseminated with telling effect [not only among Jews] . . . but also among all the other peoples known to us (*sondern unter sast alle uns bekannten Völker ihre glänzende Bestätigung gefunden*). For, far beyond the confines of the Jewish people, even today, the psalms still serve to lift up to God the emotions of all those who seek Him, to bring them enlightenment, consolation and strength, and to inspire them to show self-sacrificing devotion in their conduct on earth."[60]

For Hirsch, then, the idea that God selected a people as well as unique individuals in order to secure salvation just for themselves was unacceptable. The ultimate purpose of the creation of the Jewish people was to bring about the salvation of all of mankind. The other nations are to ultimately accept the universal teachings of Judaism, that is, those teachings that are essential for all human beings. The unique Jewish ritual law was intended to fashion a people that could better serve this purpose. Thus, the emergence of Christianity on the world scene was a triumph for the Jewish people's mission, as Hirsch states in *The Nineteen Letters*. The fact that by the late nineteenth century, the

Book of Psalms was read by people around the world in order to lift up their spirits to God was proof of the efficacy of David's Psalms.[61]

Hirsch's claim that the history of mankind as a whole is no less guided by God than the history of the Jewish people is another bold—though not radical—idea. The traditional view, based on Midrashic sources, is that the non-Jewish nations are guided by various angels and heavenly hosts, whereas the Jewish people are guided by direct divine providence.[62] Hirsch does not directly contradict this idea since he is careful to formulate his view in teleological terms, looking at how God guides history to serve His purposes and, in that respect, the history of the nations is no less a part of God's plan than that of the Jewish people. Hirsch does not state that God is directly involved in the day-to-day affairs of all nations—Jewish and non-Jewish—to the same degree. This is probably because Hirsch was careful not to contradict ideas that are found in rabbinic sources. Yet, one cannot escape the impression that Hirsch's words are intended to stress the equal love and care of God toward *all* human beings.

Effectively, Hirsch's position was that the Jewish people were a first among equals, that is, they were the first among the nations to dedicate themselves to God, but they are not regarded as innately superior to the other nations.[63] At the end of days, all nations will pay homage to God in absolute unity. Although Hirsch envisions a separate, unique role for the Jewish people at that time due to the distinct path they charted throughout history, they will remain the equals of the other nations. This basic view of Hirsch is a bold contrast to the view of his East European contemporaries. It also stands out from the view of most of his predecessors, although Rabbi Obadiah Seforno (Italy; 1470–1550), whom Hirsch has characterized as "one of our most thoughtful commentators" (*eines unserer denkendsten commentatoren*), expressed a similar viewpoint.[64] Unlike Seforno, however, Hirsch makes this idea a central doctrine of his Weltanschauung, recurring repeatedly throughout his writings.

The key biblical prooftext used by Hirsch to support his view regarding the relationship of the Jewish people to mankind is Exodus 4:22. There, God tells Moses to tell Pharaoh that the Israel is "my son, my firstborn" (*beni bekhori*). Several medieval commentators had noted that this phrase implies that indeed all of the nations are considered God's children, but the Israelites are considered to be His firstborn son.[65] Hirsch goes a step beyond this and elaborates on the reason for the metaphor of a firstborn son being applied to the Jewish people:

> *Bekhor* is not the one who has become free, but the one who makes free . . . The forces of the mother's womb which up till now have been bound, closed, are freed, opened by him . . . He is not *bekhor* for himself, but for

> what follows him. With him, the mother enters her calling as "mother," for the future. He breaks the ice. His holiness lies therein, that through him, the home first gets children, through him the womb becomes holy and everything that passes through this portal afterwards is "holy to God"... So that when God speaks of Israel as *beni bekhori* it expresses the idea that with Israel, the mother womb of humanity is opened, with Israel is commenced the list in which the names of all the nations should appear as my sons. So that in your name and in the name of the whole of humanity I come to you. Israel is My first but not My only child, *it is only the first nation that I have won as Mine* . . . Not as *beni bekhori* but as *beni* (verse 23), do I demand freedom for Israel, as I would for any nation that gave itself to Me as My son. *Israel is not the first in rank, but the first in time.*[66]

Hirsch alludes to another biblical verse in that passage, which he feels corroborates his interpretation. That verse (Leviticus 20:26) has God stating to the Jewish people, "And I have separated you from the nations to be mine" (*va-avdil etkhem min ha-amim li'heyot li*). Hirsch's commentary to this verse states:

> Further on our verse we find in the *Yalkut* [a Midrashic collection], at the end of *Kedoshim*, the great saying of R. Berakhiya in the name of R. Abahu: "were it to say 'I have separated out the nations from you,' there would be no hope of a future for the nations, but it says 'I have separated you out of the nations:' it is as one who first picks out the best from the lesser good, and then goes on and on picking out the good ones; but one who picks the bad out of the good, throws the bad away, and has nothing more to do with them." So that in no wise does Jewish thought look on the choice of Israel as a rejection of the rest of humanity. It regards the choice of Israel [as] only a beginning, only the restarting of the spiritual and moral rebuilding of Mankind, only the first step to that future where [Hirsch cites, in Hebrew, Zechariah 2:15] many nations will attach themselves to God, and become His People, and Israel's Sanctuary will not only be the central heart of Israel but the center of Mankind who will have found their way to God.[67]

Clearly, for Hirsch, the idea that God selected the Jewish people to foster a privileged tribal relationship with them to the exclusion of the other nations, was anathema. This universalism is central to Hirsch's ideology, and he describes the opposing view as one which has been made by critics of Judaism but which is demonstrably false. The primary example he cites to refute that view is the conduct of Abraham after his circumcision (Genesis 18:1–8). At that time, despite his debilitating weakness, Abraham insisted upon seeking out pagan wayfarers to shower with his generosity. The connection between Abraham's circumcision and his acts of benevolence is explained by Hirsch:

> How this inheritance of Judaism and its bearers, the Jews, have been falsely and maliciously charged with its [Judaism's] very opposite! How these "circumcised ones" are supposed to imagine themselves the favored "only ones" of their God. How just this segregating sign is supposed to strip them of all cosmopolitan feelings and thoughts for mankind in general, and to constrict the God of all human souls to the exclusive God of their corner of the world, and to the national God of their race!
>
> And now there sits the first circumcised Jew! . . . and although circumcised he remained in his behavior to the non-Abrahamitic world entirely unaltered. Abraham's one worry was—so those old rabbis, those true sons of Abraham, teach—and this drove him out into the burning sun, that now, after his circumcision, people might draw away from him. They teach this, to impress on his sons by Abraham's example, the dictum "to receive wanderers hospitably is greater than to stand before the Presence of God." And what kind of wanderers! Uncircumcised idolators—for no others could Abraham expect—Abraham hurries away from before God to practice on them the duty of brotherly love! . . .
>
> This picture comes immediately following the circumcision. *The Abrahamites flourishing in the circumcision-isolation are to be the most humane mortals.* They form the most definite contrast to the world in general but nevertheless they are always to be found ready for all general humane purposes. For fostering such humaneness they are set apart . . .
>
> And not for nothing did Abraham hasten into the glowing sunshine in front of his tent. If his sons, the defamed Jews, have inherited anything from him, this spirit of general benevolence and universal charity they certainly have had as their heritage from him. That, at least, has never been denied them. Where open hearts, open houses, open hands are sought for, where readiness for sacrifice of time, energy and money for general humane purposes is required . . . even today, even the disparagers of Judaism turn in the first place to Jews.[68]

This passage is cited at length to demonstrate how conscious Hirsch was of non-Jewish critics of Judaism when he wrote his Pentateuch commentary. Unlike *The Nineteen Letters*, *Horeb*, and the essays from his *Jeschurun* journal, the Pentateuch commentary contains Hebrew-language excursions on Talmudic topics and is replete with citations, in Hebrew and Aramaic, from various texts of Talmudic and post-Talmudic rabbinic literature. It was clearly intended *primarily* for a Jewish audience. Nevertheless, when it came to topics as sensitive as the chosenness of the Jewish people, Hirsch wrote in a more popular and polemical style, echoing his earliest works.[69] He noted that "even the disparagers of Judaism" turn first to Jews when seeking support for humanistic endeavors.

Hirsch's universalistic conception of Jewish peoplehood must therefore be placed within the context in which he wrote: as a reaction to the criticism of Judaism as a tribalistic religion, a charge leveled at it by critics of all stripes during the nineteenth century. Schleiermacher, for example, argued that Judaism limited "the love of Jehovah to the race of Abraham," thereby betraying an "affinity" with pagan doctrine, according to which the tribal god loves only its tribe.[70] Bruno Bauer (1809–82), a radical nineteenth-century German philosopher and a disciple of Hegel, argued vigorously that Judaism, even in its biblical form, promoted the love of fellow Jews only. Hatred of mankind, even war against mankind, was part of the warp and woof of Judaism, he argued.[71] Interestingly, Bauer conceded that Christianity too was highly exclusivist, no less so than Judaism. But Christianity's exclusivism was a peculiar kind of exclusivism, in Bauer's view, because it distrusts all of humanity. By contrast, Judaism posits the more pernicious notion that its own people may be trusted while all other people are excluded from its bond of trust. This makes Judaism more "immature" than Christianity.[72] Bauer's views were met with responses by both supporters and opponents of Jewish emancipation.

On the Jewish side, Reform Jewish thinkers responded to Bauer by employing the same Hegelian methods Bauer had used and by internalizing his critiques—accepting that classical Jewish texts were indeed overly exclusivist and hostile toward non-Jews.[73] Since the controversy engendered by Bauer had significant repercussions for nineteenth-century German Jewry's self-perception, the comments of Orthodox rabbis like Hirsch must be seen as an implicit response to his views.[74]

Another German writer who, unlike Bauer, was a Protestant theologian and who leveled the same charge against Judaism, was Friedrich Wilhelm Ghillany (1807–76). In his 1843 book *Die Judenfrage*, Ghillany argued that Judaism, in its traditional rabbinic form, evinced the vilest hatred of humanity, limiting God's love to the Jewish people alone. It is thus the task of the humanist to oppose emancipation of the Jews, as they constituted the segment of mankind most hostile to humanism. Ghillany makes no apology for his reliance on Eisenmenger's reading of Judaism here. For Ghillany (unlike Schleiermacher), this was sufficient ground to deny the Jews emancipation.[75]

There can be little doubt that Hirsch was aware of these critiques and that he felt compelled to respond to them. Hirsch's teacher, Isaac Bernays, had engaged in critical discussion of the relevance of Judaism to the modern world in light of contemporary Christian critiques. Hirsch too believed that authentic Torah Judaism must not sit on the sidelines while the leading Protestant theologian of the nineteenth century (among others), who was an opponent of anti-Semitism, mistakenly charged Judaism with errors of which it was innocent. Seen this way, it is unsurprising that Hirsch reiterated the themes of the universality of Judaism and God's concern with the well-being of all of mankind throughout his writings.

This lays the groundwork for better understanding Hirsch's East and Central European rabbinic contemporaries. For them, such critiques of Judaism were of little concern for two fundamental reasons. First, many of those rabbis did indeed affirm that Judaism was concerned primarily with Jews; thus, there was nothing malicious about this critique. More importantly, even for those East European rabbis such as Netziv, who maintained that the telos of the Jewish people was to serve as a light unto the nations, the framework for this was conceived in a more rigidly hierarchical fashion, in which Jews are the superiors in their relations with the other nations.[76] This was so because the Jews of Eastern Europe generally had a more assertive posture in their relations to non-Jews; they were not actively seeking emancipation as distinct religious minorities, as was the case for West European Jews—nor was emancipation available to them. The latter circumstance generated a more deferential and defensive posture on the part of German Jews.[77] Therefore, from the East European rabbinic perspective, if a non-Jewish theologian such as Schleiermacher issued critiques of Judaism as a religion inferior to Christianity, the very legitimacy of the critiques is undercut, for he fails to recognize the superiority of Judaism. For Hirsch, who saw the brotherhood of mankind as a Jewish ideal and championed emancipation for Jewish minorities in non-Jewish states (Moravia and Prussia), there could be no question of such a relationship between the Jewish people and other nations. Therefore, the challenges issued by non-Jewish intellectuals had to be taken seriously and a theological response had to be formulated.

Having established the context for Hirsch's writings, let us turn our attention to Hirsch's championing of the brotherhood of mankind as a Jewish ideal. The Talmud and Midrashic literature contain few statements that could be construed as indicative of such a view.[78] Hirsch explicitly lauded this principle in his 1859 speech in honor of Friedrich Schiller.[79] Schiller had also criticized Judaism, and Hirsch notes this fact when he says that had Schiller understood the true ideals taught at Jewish schools, he "would have corrected his misconception of the mission of Moses" and would have been able to find in Judaism the lofty ideals that he couldn't find in Greek culture. Further, according to Hirsch, "if Schiller had been a Jew," he would have found in Judaism the ideals that he valued and "would have walked the earth a much happier and contented man."[80] In other words, according to Hirsch, Schiller truly appreciated authentic Jewish ideals; he just didn't understand Judaism well enough to recognize its greatness.

Particularly striking, given what has been outlined thus far, is a shortcoming that Hirsch found in Schiller: he accused Moses of turning a universal God—the one Sovereign of the universe—into a national Jewish God. This view, advanced by Schiller in his 1789 lecture *Die Sendung Moses*, was part of Schiller's argument for the superiority of a universal religion of reason over more primitive forms of religion, such as Judaism and Christianity. It should be stressed that Schiller's perspective is distinct from that of later German writers who denounced alleged Jewish particularism, as Schiller's focus here was not on Jewish particularism. In Schiller's view, Moses himself contributed to the development of a more rational form of thought than the superstitions he encountered among his own people. However, Schiller denies that Moses received an actual revelation from God. Rather, Moses transformed the highly philosophical and abstract mysticism of the elite Egyptian priests into a national religion. But Moses was only able to unite the uneducated and pagan Hebrews around the idea of monotheism due to his Egyptian education.[81]

Schiller's views concerning Moses are in such dissonance with the strict Orthodoxy that Hirsch championed that it seems incongruent that Hirsch could still applaud Schiller. Despite Hirsch's militant posture toward what he perceived as heresy within the Jewish community (as evidenced by his literary battles with Heinrich Graetz and Zechariah Frankel), he was apparently far more tolerant of expression of ideas that could be considered heretical (from an Orthodox Jewish perspective) if they emanated from non-Jewish sources. He felt that distortions of Judaism by Jews were far more spiritually toxic for Jewish readers than were misrepresentations of Judaism by non-Jews.[82]

Thus, Hirsch not only read the transcription of the aforementioned speech by Schiller, he was prepared to embrace Schiller as a righteous gentile—and a true Sage over whom the Talmudic rabbis would have recited a blessing—despite Schiller's mistaken views about Moses and his indebtedness to Egyptian religion.[83] Furthermore, the fact that even so liberal a thinker as Schiller also expressed the view—however tangentially—that Judaism transformed a universal God into a national one further buttresses the argument that Hirsch and his rabbinic colleagues were conscious of this charge when they formulated their own philosophy of Judaism. The ubiquity of the accusation demanded a response, and Hirsch provided it.

In the 1859 speech Hirsch praised Schiller for propagating "Jewish truths" in his writings. One of these was the ideal of the brotherhood of mankind. This idea is already found in *Die Neunzehn Briefe*. There, he states: "Findet Jissroel nicht sein Ziel in Allverbruderung der Menschheit?" (Does not Israel consider the universal brotherhood of mankind to be its goal?)[84] Unlike Bernard Drachman's translation of *Die Neunzehn Briefe* (later followed by Jacob Breuer), Hirsch does not state that the "most cherished ideal" of Judaism is the brotherhood of mankind but rather that this is its ultimate *goal* (*Ziel*).[85] In other words, Hirsch was reiterating what the prophets had stated on numerous occasions, namely, that the ultimate goal of history is for all of mankind to unite in the worship of God.[86] This is not the universal humanism of secularist thinkers of the eighteenth and nineteenth centuries, who saw the unity of the human race as an end unto itself; it was a reiteration of prophetic ideals, couched in humanistic terminology. In Hirsch's view, Schiller had expounded upon this prophetic ideal and disseminated it among European peoples.

To be sure, Hirsch's exaltation of Schiller must be attributed to more than a feeling of affinity for a kindred spirit who happened to be Christian. At the time of Hirsch's speech in honor of Schiller, Hirsch had served as rabbi of the IRG for eight years and the entire German nation was celebrating the centenary of the birth of one its national heroes. As a leading spokesperson for Orthodox Judaism, Hirsch would have been remiss in ignoring this monumental event.[87] Once Hirsch decided to participate in the Schiller festivities, he devoted his intellectual and oratorical abilities to extolling the values that Schiller had stood for and which, in Hirsch's view, were simply expressions of Jewish ideals. Nonetheless, Hirsch's enthusiasm for Schiller, the sincerity of which cannot be called into question, sets him apart from his rabbinic contemporaries elsewhere in Europe, who could not have expressed such effusive praise for a Christian writer who had issued criticisms of Judaism.[88]

Another central feature of Hirsch's attitude toward non-Jews was his consistent rejection of any form of parochialism in relationship to the world beyond the Jewish people. Hirsch emphasizes that "it is just the most isolated Jew who bears in his breast the most universal thoughts and sentiments."[89] Furthermore, the Jew knows that "the upright and pure in all societies of men are working with him for the kingdom of God on earth." His Judaism teaches the Jew "to find in every new truth which is propounded a welcome contribution to the clearer revelation of God in nature and in history and to see in every new art and in every new science a welcome addition to the means for rendering perfect service to God." Hirsch goes on to note that the Jew will welcome any art, science, or culture which is genuinely edifying and serves to "promote the welfare of mankind." The authentic Jew will follow the advice of "the Sages" to receive the truth from whatever source it comes.[90] Hirsch's conception of the universality of truth and his opposition to Jewish parochialism foreshadows what Rabbi Kook expressed nearly a century later, but it was a rather unconventional view for Orthodox rabbis in Hirsch's time.[91]

Hirsch incorporates his ethical universalism into his treatment of the non-Jewish slave (*eved kena'ani*) in Jewish law. His Pentateuch commentary is the only one written prior to the twentieth century that discusses the ethical dilemma posed by the concept of Jews owning non-Jews as slaves. This passage appears immediately upon the first biblical reference to this type of slavery, namely, in Exodus 12:44. There Hirsch writes:

> The consideration of certain circumstances is necessary, correctly to understand the fact that the Torah presupposes and allows the possession and purchase of slaves from abroad to a nation itself just released from slavery. No Jew could make any other human being into a slave. He could only acquire by purchase, people who, by the then universally accepted international law, were already slaves. But this transference into the property of a Jew was the one and only salvation for anybody who, according to the prevailing laws of the nations, was stamped as a slave . . . The home of a Jew was to them a home of freedom. There, he was protected by law against mishandling, the law courts were accessible to him, and—this cannot be sufficiently valued—had the option if he wished (Yebamoth 48b) of joining, by circumcision and immersion, the Jewish bond with God in conjunction with the rest of the household. He would then become like the children, a member of the home.[92]

These comments are unique.[93] Other biblical commentators, including Hirsch's nineteenth-century contemporaries, did not express discomfort with the idea that a nation just freed from slavery would acquire non-Jews as slaves.[94] Hirsch was not only concerned with the ethical issues involved but demonstrates an acute awareness of contemporary writings on the status of slavery in the Hebrew Bible. Hirsch's contemporary, Moses Mielziner (1828–1903), authored a treatise demonstrating that the biblical and Talmudic view of slavery was guided by an overriding humanitarian goal, aimed at humanizing and eventually abolishing slavery. Mielziner specifically mentions the fact that the Israelites had experienced slavery firsthand in Egypt and thus were acutely sensitive to the dehumanizing tendencies of this institution—precisely the point alluded to by Hirsch.[95] Hirsch's commentary to the Pentateuch was published between 1867 and 1878, shortly after the appearance of Mielziner's study, and Hirsch was likely familiar with it.

This is made clear by Hirsch's comments to Exodus 21:21, which states that a master who fatally strikes his slave is liable for capital punishment only if the slave did not survive a day or two; if he did, the master is exempt, "for he is his property" (*ki khaspo hu*). Hirsch comments that "this reason given cannot be taken to mean that he is in some way of a lower degree of humanity than an ordinary free man."[96] According to late medieval Jewish thinkers such as Maharal, this may be precisely what the biblical text means. But for Hirsch, this was inconceivable.

Hirsch was further troubled by the statement in Leviticus 25:46: "You shall leave them [non-Jewish slaves] as inheritance to your children after you as inherited property, you shall keep them permanently as bondmen; but over your brethren, the children of Israel, one over the other, you shall not rule with vigor." The Talmud interprets the statement about keeping the slaves "permanently" as a positive injunction—to retain the slaves and not free them. Hirsch notes that the status of non-Jewish slaves has already been treated elsewhere in his commentary, and then adds:

> The same motive—as worked out there—which underlay the continuance of slavery in the Jewish State, would also be the motive of "you shall keep them permanently as bondmen," which is taken as a positive command (Gittin 38b). Nevertheless, for the purposes of mitzvot and for the reasons of general morality (*und aus Sittlichkeitsgründen*),[97] giving them freedom was allowed. And the Halacha learns from this "you shall keep them permanently as bondmen' that 'you only have a claim of servitude from them" (*Torat Kohanim*), that your right over them extends purely and solely to work, but you have no right to mishandle them, to hurt their feelings, or put them to shame (Nidda 47a), and Jewish writings are full of features showing characteristic kindness, mildness and humaneness which marked the treatment of slaves. See Maimonides at the end of the Laws of Slaves.[98]

Catherine Hezser has argued that the writings of people like Mielziner reflect the fact that their authors were grappling with the charge made by Christian thinkers that Judaism was lacking in morality when compared with Christianity.[99] She cites Michael Meyer's essay (discussed earlier) on the subject of Reform Jewish thinkers responding to charges of Judaism's immorality.[100] What needs to be added to this assessment is the fact that Neo-Orthodox thinkers like Hirsch were no less interested in refuting those charges. Hirsch's approach is more subtle since he does not mention the views of non-Jewish thinkers; nor does he develop a systematic approach demonstrating Judaism's progressive approach to slavery. But it is clear from reading several crucial passages in his works that this was his goal.

As with many aspects of his Weltanschauung, when discussing this issue, Hirsch writes as though what he is saying is elementary and there is no disagreement on the matter, except on the part of critics of Judaism. In this one-sided presentation he was not alone; Jacob Katz has written that by the period between the 1860s and 1870s "even learned Jews sincerely maintained that Judaism had always taught universalistic ethics only."[101] However, Hirsch was surely aware of the sources that paint a different picture, as his rabbinic knowledge was quite significant. Further, it is quite likely that he read the first edition of David Zvi Hoffmann's *Der Schulchan Aruch und die Rabbinen über das Verhaltnis der Juden zu Andersgläubigen*, published in Berlin in 1885, a work that contained a lengthy discussion of the rabbinic sources that seem to express a less-than-tolerant attitude toward non-Jews. Even if Hirsch regarded the anti-gentile comments from rabbinic literature cited by German anti-Semites to have been taken out of context or mistranslated, he was surely aware of their meaning in their original context, and this meaning did not always square with Hirsch's universalism.

This brings us to the most sensitive aspect of evaluating Hirsch's views on non-Jews, mentioned previously: how did he view the anti-gentile statements found in rabbinic literature? It would seem that Hirsch, like Hoffmann after him, endorsed the views of Meiri (1249–1316), according to which the statements in question are not, in fact, anti-gentile but anti-pagan. Since there were no longer any pagans in Hirsch's time, the problematic statements were simply irrelevant. However, since Hirsch did not have access to the entirety of the Talmud commentary authored by Meiri, he would have had to rely on two citations of Meiri by Rabbi Bezalel Ashkenazi (1520–91), in his *Shittah Mekubetset*.[102]

The volume of *Shittah Mekubetset* that contained statements of Meiri distinguishing between ancient pagans and Christians is the commentary to Tractate *Bava Kamma* of the Babylonian Talmud. This volume was published several times in the nineteenth century, including an 1810 publication in Zhovkva and an 1876 publication in Lemberg. Hirsch would have had to have access to the 1810 publication for he formulated his "enlightened" view of gentiles in his earliest works from the 1830s. Excerpts from Rabbi Ashkenazi's citations of Meiri are also printed in the Vilna edition of the Talmud, first printed in the 1870s. Further, Zvi Hirsch Chajes cites the passage of Meiri excluding Christians from anti-pagan legislation in his 1840 pamphlet denouncing the blood libel.[103] Hirsch would likely have read this, although it must be emphasized that he seems to have formulated his views prior to the publication of this pamphlet.

Another source for Hirsch's views could be Moses Rivkes's widely known comments, discussed previously. Rivkes's comments would have been found in any edition of the *Shulhan Arukh* that Hirsch would have used. The sources that Azriel Shohat has collected indicate that this distinction between the ancient pagans and contemporary Christians with respect to discriminatory legislation was made by virtually all German halachists in the first half of the eighteenth century, a full century before Hirsch's earliest writings.[104] One authority in particular stands out: Rabbi Shlomo ben Moshe of Khelm's (1715–78) *Merkevet ha-Mishneh*, a commentary on Maimonides's *Mishneh Torah*. In one key passage, Rabbi Shlomo explicitly exempts Christians and Muslims from Talmudic anti-gentile discrimination.[105] As Rabbi Shlomo was a teacher of Solomon Dubno (1738–1813), who was almost certainly admired by Hirsch's parents, it is likely that his books were studied by the young Hirsch, who would thus have been exposed to this view from childhood.[106] His parents and teachers would then most likely have taught, presumably consistently, that the non-Jews among whom they lived were not to be viewed or treated as the pagans referred to in the Talmud.[107] Once this was taken for granted by Hirsch, he was free to elaborate on his view of the importance of the non-Jewish nations in the schema of Judaism; his other "liberal" views of gentiles would also have been regarded as not being in opposition to any halachic principles.

Perhaps more important than any earlier precedents are the views of Hirsch's teacher, Rabbi Jacob Ettlinger, discussed earlier. Since Ettlinger ruled that Christian Trinitarian worship does not render Christians "idolators," Hirsch understood that anti-gentile passages in the Talmud and other rabbinic writings do not refer to them. Recall that this was stated explicitly by the seventeenth-century halachist Rabbi Yair Hayyim Bacharach in his *Havot Yair*: "The gentiles of our time are not considered to be worshippers of Avodah Zarah for all matters [*le-kol mili*] since they believe in the creator of heaven and earth, may His name be blessed, and any negative [statements] about non-Jews that are found in the Talmud and Codes do not apply to them."[108] Hirsch cites this book (though not this passage) in his *Humash* commentary, so it is likely that he was familiar with the passage.[109]

Furthermore, Hirsch's other primary teacher, Rabbi Isaac Bernays, who did not author any halachic works, clearly regarded his Christian contemporaries as moral beings worthy of salvation. There can be no doubt that he did not consider them to be akin to the pagans of the Talmud. For Hirsch, then, there was little doubt that there was no halachic impediment to incorporating Christians into a conception of Judaism that offers them salvation. He was free to take the next step of highlighting the centrality of non-Jewish service to God, which specifically included the rise of Christianity, in his interpretation of history.

Christianity

As noted by Moshe Schwarz over fifty years ago, the more liberal and assimilationist a German-Jewish thinker was, the more severely he criticized Christianity.[110] Thus, Abraham Geiger and Ludwig Steinheim had more vituperative words for Christianity than did Hirsch. Unlike Geiger, for example, Hirsch was not interested in establishing an alternative narrative of the role of Christianity in Western civilization. Susannah Heschel has argued that Geiger specifically focused on the figure of Jesus, a figure so central to Western, and not just Christian, thought and attitudes for nearly two millennia. Geiger argued that Jesus had been wrongly usurped by Christianity and fashioned after its own image. That is, Christianity according to Geiger, was the religion *about* Jesus, whereas Judaism, as Geiger conceived it, was the religion *of* Jesus, a thesis intended to buttress his own liberal interpretation of Judaism.[111]

Hirsch, by contrast, was an Orthodox rabbi who often took hardline positions on matters pertaining to proper belief. Therefore, it is Hirsch's genuine appreciation for Christianity's contribution to civilization that is striking. In Hirsch's first-written (but second-published) work, *Horeb*, the view that Judaism recognizes the moral worth of righteous Christians is implicit when he states that "Israel can rejoice today in the midst of the peoples among whom it mostly lives. Behold, Israel, how the holy light which God placed among you at Sinai has spread far and wide and has already scared away from a great part of humanity the delusion and abomination of idol worship. Rejoice that in Europe, in America, and in part of Asia and Africa non-Jewish peoples also have become illumined by the Revelation of the One God given to you and have adopted a doctrine which teaches them to perform the seven duties which according to your doctrine are binding on all men—to worship no idols . . . [and the other six Noahide laws]."[112] There can be no doubt that Hirsch was referring to Christianity and its adherents. (As will be shown, it is characteristic of Hirsch's writings to refer to Christianity without explicitly referring to the name of the religion.) Since he states that Christianity teaches its adherents to renounce idolatry, it is certain that Hirsch did not consider Trinitarian worship to be idolatrous as far as non-Jews are concerned, his misgivings about the precise nature of shittuf notwithstanding.

There are numerous references to Christianity scattered throughout Hirsch's writings although in most cases he does not explicitly state the subject of his reference. Most of these references are polemical in nature: Hirsch alludes to various flaws in Christian doctrine and indicates the superiority of Judaism with respect to those beliefs. In contrast to the tone of medieval Jewish anti-Christian polemic, Hirsch writes in a respectful tone and does not denigrate Christian believers but merely indicates why a particular Christian belief is mistaken and falls short of the heights that Judaism has attained.[113] In this respect, Hirsch's remarks on Christianity bear a resemblance to the comments about Judaism found in the writings of Hirsch's Christian contemporaries; they too, for the most part, did not denigrate Jews for accepting the teachings of Judaism but stressed the superiority of Christian teachings.

A notable exception is a comment that Hirsch made in his journal *Jeschurun* in 1858. A teacher in Hirsch's school had tried to suppress references to Christianity in a textbook the school used. Hirsch censured this teacher and stated that it is perfectly harmless for Jewish children to be exposed to Christian concepts since they will anyway encounter them later in life. Furthermore, added Hirsch, there is a positive value in exposing Jewish children to Christian ideas, for this will enable the Jewish youth to examine these ideas from a Jewish standpoint and come to recognize that the truth to be found in Christian teachings emerges from the fact that Christianity is a "messenger of Judaism." He even deemed descriptions of Christmas Eve to be innocuous, since the family celebration of Christmas Eve should be recognized by Jews as, effectively, an echo of Jewish bliss (i.e., Jewish holiday observances). (Hirsch limited this approval of exposure to Christian ideas to those Jewish children who had received an authentic Jewish education at home or in their schooling.)[114] One contemporary observer has noted how distant Hirsch's comments about Christmas Eve was from prevailing views in Eastern Europe about the same evening, which was termed *nitel nacht* and during which Torah study was prohibited by some authorities due, among other reasons, to the perceived contamination (*tumah*) that rises to the celestial spheres during this night.[115]

While Hirsch rejected a number of Christian doctrines—especially original sin —one of his strongest critiques of Christianity was that it abandoned the Law. Given the nineteenth-century context, it is not surprising that Hirsch did not get into discussions about the identity of the messiah; instead, he responded to the critique of Judaism that had become de rigueur by his time, namely, that slavish adherence to the Law stifles spirituality. Since this was an implicit argument of the Jewish Reform movement as well, it is unsurprising that Hirsch devoted much effort to attacking this line of thought. In Hirsch's view, it was precisely *because* Christianity had abandoned the Law that it has not succeeded in removing the shackles from mankind's misery.[116]

Hirsch's other primary critique of Christianity was of its "otherworldliness." Its emphasis on the imperfection of this world and longing for the next world has succeeded in shackling mankind in perpetuity to a hopeless world-view. If man is born into sin and can only achieve salvation by the acceptance of a particular dogma, how can mankind at large achieve happiness?[117] Like his critique of the abandonment of the Law, the critique of otherworldliness was also directed against the Reform movement, which had asserted that rabbinic Judaism denigrated this world and advocated asceticism.[118] According to Hirsch, Judaism stands in stark contrast to Christianity on the issue of the value of this world. Whereas Christianity denigrates the physical and sensual aspects of human existence, Judaism embraces them—within defined boundaries. The Torah wishes human beings to enjoy sensual pleasures if such enjoyment is regulated by the Law. Were it not for the Law, such indulgence would rightly be characterized as animalistic, but within the parameters of the Law, such enjoyment is to be celebrated. Hirsch has harsh words for those who maintain that Judaism looks upon innocent laughter as sinful.[119]

Thus, Hirsch boldly confronted the challenge Christian thinkers posed to Judaism by turning the tables and placing the onus of misdirecting the spiritual potential of the Hebrew Bible on Christianity rather than on rabbinic Judaism, as other nineteenth-century European thinkers had argued. This was not a case of religious polemics (which Hirsch reserved for the Reform movement) but rather of defending the legacy of historic Judaism against its detractors. Hirsch had the greatest respect for sincere Christian piety, as evidenced by his insistence that descriptions of Christmas Eve ought to be respected by Jews.

Another example of this respect emerges from Hirsch's response to the complaints of a baker during his tenure as chief rabbi of Moravia. The baker had been censured by Hirsch for keeping his business open on the Sabbath. He tried to justify his conduct on the grounds that his Christian customers would not patronize his shop all week if they could not also depend on his shop for their Saturday shopping. Further, they would not understand his motivation for closing on Saturday and instead of regarding the Jewish people, as did Moses, as a "wise and understanding nation" (Deuteronomy 4:6), they would instead scorn the Jewish religion. Hirsch replied that the Sabbath is worth a great deal more than one's monetary compensation and that the latter is surely worthy of being sacrificed for the sake of the former. Hirsch added, at the very end of his letter, "Be aware that you are mistaken about the Christian, the true Christian, just as you are mistaken about the truly loyal Jew, and may the good Lord open your eyes."[120] Such a statement, reflecting Hirsch's view that a "true Christian" has respect for Judaism, would have been virtually unimaginable from a rabbi of the old school (although Jacob Emden did express a similar sentiment in the eighteenth century).[121]

At this point, note should be made of perhaps the most foundational component of Hirsch's ideology: that Judaism served a world-historic purpose and thus *could not possibly be* tribalistic in its ethos or its purview. The spread of authentic Jewish teachings to mankind at large—though not actual missionizing—would advance God's plan for the world. Thus, for Hirsch, the emergence of Christianity (and, later, Islam) "represented a major step in bringing closer the goal of all history" *(grosser Schritt zur Förderung des Ziels aller Geschichte)*, as he put it in his first published book.[122] This idea is based on a statement of Maimonides but it represents an enlargement of Maimonides's thought beyond its original meaning. Maimonides had noted that God works in mysterious ways and that even Christianity, which had (in Maimonides's view) wrought so much damage, was ultimately destined to play a positive role in bringing the knowledge of the Torah to mankind.[123] Like other nineteenth-century writers, Hirsch focused exclusively on the positive aspect of Maimonides's assessment and made it into a central element of his Weltanschauung. In this respect, Hirsch's view represents something unique to modern rabbinic personalities, with the notable exception of Jacob Emden.[124]

Though unique to Orthodox leaders, this view of Hirsch regarding the positive role played by other religions was shared by prominent Reform thinkers. Salomon Formstecher (1808–89), whose lifespan is virtually identical to Hirsch's, expressed the same view when he declared that Christianity and Islam "are the northern and southern missions of Judaism to the pagan world, they are the means used by Providence to overthrow the deification of nature and to aid the generations of man to the apex of perfection."[125] Although Abraham Geiger had a different perspective on Jesus and the religion established in his name, and despite his sometimes vituperative attacks on Christianity, he largely agreed with the view that Judaism was able to spread its message of ethical monotheism through Christianity and Islam. This, then, was the view of these religions that was widely held among non-Orthodox nineteenth-century German Jews, and it was shared by Hirsch. The question of who influenced whom may remain unanswered. However, developments in eighteenth-century Jewish intellectual history, especially the views of Jacob Emden, exercised considerable influence on the thinkers of the following century, and this makes it likely that those Orthodox thinkers who upheld this view arrived at it independently of the Reform thinkers who also expressed it.

Matthias Morgenstern has drawn attention to the fact that Hirsch was faced with the same dilemma that confronted Moses Mendelssohn in his correspondence with Jacob Emden: how can the Noahide laws be regarded as a universal covenant with mankind if a prerequisite to make their observance salvific was acceptance by non-Jews of the authenticity (and, implicitly, the superiority) of the revelation of the Torah to Israel, as formulated by Maimonides?[126] Emden had insisted that Maimonides was correct and that only non-Jews who accepted that the Noahide laws were revealed by God to Moses could be considered faithful Noahides. Significantly, for Emden acceptance of Christianity (and, apparently, also Islam) was an automatic qualifier for this status since Christianity (and Islam) accepted the historicity of the biblical account of the Sinaitic revelation. Mendelssohn was troubled by the implications of Maimonides's view for the majority of mankind, which had no knowledge of the Hebrew Scriptures at all. How can they be denied salvation if they led upright lives, Mendelssohn asked. At first, it may appear as if Hirsch's views are identical to those of Emden in this matter (though Emden still outdid Hirsch in his enthusiasm for Jesus and Paul). Morgenstern argues that, in fact, Hirsch found a creative way to universalize the Noahide laws in such a manner that Mendelssohn's dilemma would likely be resolved.

This is how Hirsch achieved this: he expended much effort in drawing attention to the relationship between Edom, regarded in post-Talmudic literature as the representative of Christianity, and Israel. Hirsch turned the standard dichotomy between Edom and Israel, often found in Jewish polemical works, on its head. Through the use of his speculative philology, Hirsch connected the Hebrew word for "man" (*adam*) with "Edom."[127] Hirsch opposed the idea that the word *adam* was derived from the word for "earth" (*adamah*), which would mean that man's primary characteristic is that he is earthborn. Quite the contrary, asserted Hirsch, man is the one creature that did not entirely originate from the earth, but the breath of God made him into a human being. Instead, *adamah* is derived from *adam* since the earth is the platform on which man can accomplish his task for creation. *Adam* itself is derived from *adom*, which is the word for red, signifying the "least broken ray of the spectrum of the pure ray of light, i.e., the nearest revelation of the divine on Earth."[128] The connection, then, between *man* and *Edom* (Christianity) is readily apparent: Christianity is Man after he has reached his historical goals through God's "education of humanity," Lessing's terminology that Hirsch alluded to in his writings. Thus, Christians participate in the divine covenant with mankind in a unique manner befitting their close relationship to the Jewish people.[129]

As noted, Hirsch's attitude toward Christianity sets him apart from his ideological nemesis in the Reform movement (and erstwhile friend), Abraham Geiger.[130] Geiger, the foremost Jewish polemicist against Christianity of the nineteenth century, launched a full-scale attack on the Christianized Jesus, arguing instead that Jesus was a rabbinic Jew with reformist tendencies. In doing so, Geiger hoped to wrest control of the symbolic power of Jesus for European civilization and "return" it to its rightful source: Judaism and the Jewish people. This was a bold strategy of seizing upon a potent symbol of Western civilization and (re)claiming it for the Jews. Geiger ultimately failed in this endeavor. German Christian scholars rejected his interpretation of Jesus, and when modern anti-Semitism emerged in the final third of the century, Geiger's ideas about Jesus's Jewishness played no role whatsoever in mitigating the anti-Jewish assault. Even opponents of anti-Semitism, such as the Hebraist and missionary Franz Delitzsch, could not accept a portrayal of Jesus that saw him as a Jewish reformer guided by the principles of Judaism and thus *almost* on a par with the Mishnaic sage Hillel. Delitzsch insisted that Jesus was the primary critic *of Judaism*, whose Weltanschauung paved the way for Christianity, unlike Hillel, who represented ancient Judaism.[131] Some anti-Semites such as von Treitschke even took umbrage at the presumptuousness of Jewish writers who (in his view) dared to claim symbols of Christian/Western civilization for themselves.[132]

Delitzsch, in his defense of Jews from August Rohling's anti-Semitic attacks, expressed his frustration with contemporary Jews, who deny "Christianity even the recognition as the religion of fulfilled wisdom and essential salvation—we deplore that."[133] In his critique of Rohling, Delitzsch refers to nineteenth-century Jewish Wissenschaft scholars such as Zunz, Rappaport, S. D. Luzzatto, and Steinschneider, but no mention is made of Hirsch.[134] Indeed, unlike Geiger and other Wissenschaft scholars, Hirsch's approach was far more modest. He was not interested in demonstrating that the most potent symbol of Western civilization for thousands of years was actually Jewish. For Hirsch, one of the essential purposes of Judaism was to spread truths about God among the nations. The spread of Christianity partially fulfilled this goal. Yet Hirsch did insist that Christians recognize the rightful place and role of Jews and Judaism, just as Delitzsch had asked for the same recognition of Christianity on the part of Jews.

In one essay, Hirsch notes that Christians are still taught of the rejection of the Jews by God due to their sins. Simultaneously, however,

> to the Christian, the Jews are still the first and only Nation to which God revealed Himself, the one which God chose for the sake of the redemption of mankind. To the Christian, every one who yearns for truth, consolation and peace must try to meditate upon the ideas that come from this Nation and attain its levels of inspiration!
>
> The Jews are said to be a sinful nation, and yet it is the Jewish World of Right and Truth on which nations and sovereigns build their sovereignty and national life![135]

As far Jesus is concerned, Rabbi Hirsch did not go as far as Rabbi Jacob Emden, who had embraced Jesus as a Pharisaic rabbinic scholar almost on a par with the Tanna'im.[136] Nor did he accept Geiger's vision of Jesus as a reformist rabbinic Jew whose contribution to civilization is almost without peer. Rather, Hirsch describes Jesus in respectful terms that one could hardly expect to be found in the writings of most of his East European rabbinic contemporaries. In his comments to the Pentateuch, Hirsch notes that one particular passage was written in the Torah specifically to counter Christian contentions regarding Jesus's divinity. In making this point, Hirsch has the following to say about Jesus: "We know well enough how, in later times, a Jew whose genealogical table was not available, and because it was not available, and because he brought the world a few sparks of light borrowed from the man Moses, became to be considered by nations as begotten of God, and to doubt his divinity became a capital crime."[137]

Despite Hirsch's concession that Jesus "brought the world a few sparks of light," the fact that those sparks were borrowed from Moses was what was key in Hirsch's thinking. That is, Christianity has no claim to any original spiritual teachings that have aided mankind. Whatever teachings it did bring to the world that ultimately advanced civilization were simply borrowed from Judaism. In this respect, Hirsch, despite his greater respect Christianity, was following the approaches of his ideological nemeses Graetz and Geiger, and his views were in opposition to those of even the most benign to Jews of nineteenth-century German Christian writers.

Hirsch also insults Christian sensibilities by asserting that Jesus's genealogical table "was not available" and claiming further that it was this supposed unavailability that engendered Christian claims about his divinity. Although far from the mocking tone of the medieval *Toledot Yeshu*, which developed a detailed narrative about Jesus's origins from illicit sexual liaisons, Hirsch is suggesting that it was the lack of clear knowledge about the identity of Jesus's father that led early Christians to make fantastical claims about his origins, which would not have been accepted had more about his background been known.[138]

References to Jesus elsewhere in Hirsch's writings are few and far between.[139] Hirsch was not interested in developing a Jewish alternative to the Christian narrative of Jesus and therefore did not expend much energy in discussing him. For Hirsch, Jesus's importance lay in the fact that he was the first Jew to carry out the sacred Jewish mission of spreading Jewish ideas about God and man to the world. Though Jesus and his followers did this in a flawed and, in Hirsch's view, sometimes garbled, manner, their achievement in advancing the course of history must not be overlooked. Hirsch was, generally, a follower of Lessing's teleology—albeit in its Jewish version—and thus for him it was highly significant that biblical and rabbinic ideas had become the property of large segments of mankind who would, in Hirsch's optimistic view, further spread these ideas as a panacea to a suffering mankind.[140] This is what enabled Hirsch to admire Christianity's contributions to the development of humanity.

Nevertheless, Hirsch was not without misgivings about Christian monotheism. In an essay from his journal *Jeschurun*, written with a non-Jewish audience in mind, Hirsch wrote the following: "Nations of the world: let the concept of the One and Only God in its pure form, with which you are familiar for thousands of years by observing the Jewish example, overwhelm you and guide you. *He needs no intermediary*. Let our Guardian finally become your Guardian in truth and in fact. Let His words of sanctification, righteousness and love become your Guide, so that *the false belief of salvation through faith may fade* and the Redemption through Law begin—the Law that governs every facet of daily life."[141]

When Hirsch speaks of "the Law that governs every facet of daily life," he refers to the halacha, which was intended for the Jews. However, the central idea behind the halacha is that human beings ought to submit themselves, in all manifestations of their existence, to their Creator. Therefore, even non-Jews are missing something very essential when they are taught that faith is the most important dimension of their spiritual lives. In fact, even for them, strict obedience to the laws that God has designated for them is key to their spiritual bliss, not mere faith alone.

He also wrote in another essay that "pure Mosaic monotheism was itself diluted and endangered by the Christian doctrine of the Trinity (*Der reine mosaische Monotheismus der Juden fand sich vielmehr durch die Trinität der christlichen Lehre getrübt und gefärdet*) and, therefore, from the very outset, had to abandon all hopes of making any great headway among the Jews."[142] Thus, despite his acceptance of the monotheistic status of Christianity from a halachic point of view, Hirsch was quite critical of the fact that Christianity diluted pure monotheism by developing the doctrine of the Trinity. In this respect, there is nothing unusual about Hirsch; no other rabbinic authority or scholar would have denied that the doctrine of the Trinity represented a departure from the strict monotheism of Judaism.

In summation, Hirsch's attitude toward Christianity contained nothing revolutionary. Jacob Emden, writing in the previous century, far exceeded Hirsch in his enthusiasm for Christianity and for Jesus. What makes Hirsch's views noteworthy is his consistent acceptance of the moral virtue of pious Christians. He accepted that they too are heirs to immortality, notwithstanding any misgivings he may have had about their theology. The fact that he did not shy away from polemicizing against certain Christian ideas—in the context of nineteenth-century German Jewry's struggle for recognition and validation—is an indication of his boldness, although it still pales in comparison to that of Abraham Geiger and German Reform thinkers. Hirsch's view of the role that Christianity plays in the divine scheme for the education of mankind is the most important contribution of his thought to modern Orthodox approaches to Christianity. It was the context in which he lived that allowed for such an assessment to be made and consistently adhered to.

Some Conclusions

Marjorie Lamberti has argued that "Orthodox Jews made little contribution to the Jewish struggle for civil equality."[143] While that claim may be true insofar as active involvement in politics is concerned, the Orthodox leaders made their own significant contribution to the quest for emancipation, albeit passively, by affirming the universalism of Judaism and its respect for Christianity. Thus, Lamberti's assertion must be somewhat tempered, as the embrace of non-Jews and the avowed respect for their religion on the part of the German-Orthodox must be seen as inextricably linked to the quest for emancipation and the effort to demonstrate the superiority of Orthodox Judaism over Reform Judaism.

In a somewhat different context, Mordechai Breuer wrote, "German Jews wanted to prove that they were able and worthy of emancipation. Among the Orthodox, this apologetic self-perception was much more complicated because they had to do more than defend one front only, that is, vis-à-vis the Germans. Orthodox Jews had to reassure themselves, over and over, of Jewish values in German culture, but, above all, they had to establish their legitimacy as thoroughly cultured people in the eyes of liberal Jews."[144]

This need to be seen as "thoroughly cultured people" left an indelible impact on the attitudes toward non-Jews that the Orthodox adopted. The inapplicability of many of the rabbinic statements regarding gentiles to their Christian contemporaries was taken for granted even when not openly stated. Orthodox Jews would have been accepted neither by German Christians nor by Reform Jews had they espoused a tribalistic conception of Jewish chosenness or advocated the practical applicability of many of the disabilities faced by non-Jews in Talmudic literature.

The battle between partisans of Orthodoxy and those of Reform for the allegiances of nineteenth-century German Jews served as a catalyst for the leading spokesmen of Orthodoxy, who desperately wanted to retain as many Jews within the fold of (what they termed) "Torah-true" Judaism as possible, to present the most palatable vision of Judaism to the general public. Essential to the palatability of Judaism was the oft-repeated assertion, whether in the form of the mission theory or otherwise, that Orthodox Judaism was no less universalist than Reform Judaism.

Thus, the writings of Hirsch, who was, far and away, the leading spokesman for Orthodox Judaism in Germany from the 1830s until his death in the late 1880s, are devoid of any expressions of Jewish chauvinism and are instead replete with exhortations about the broad humanitarianism and universalism of traditional rabbinic Judaism. This remained the same whether he was writing primarily for Jewish or non-Jewish audiences. Notwithstanding the previously outlined pressures that bore down upon him, Hirsch was genuinely convinced that Judaism constitutes a system of universalistic ethics, and this is the view that he championed. The covenantal relationship between God and the Jewish people does not signify any vitiation of the universality of human rights. Jews were chosen by God to carry an extra burden and, ultimately, to bring about the moral regeneration of all mankind.

Hirsch's views regarding the equality of all men and the universality of human rights have resonance in contemporary social and political thought. For example, the debates in the United States concerning immigration reform can be better informed by recourse to Hirsch's views. In Hirsch's Bible commentary, the following passage can be found: "The absolute equality in the eyes of the Law between the native and the foreigner forms the very basic foundation of Jewish jurisdiction . . . This principle, this respect for human beings as such, apart from all chance of birth and fate, is proclaimed everywhere in the Torah by remembrance of what was experienced in Egypt."[145] Likewise, debates in Israel regarding its Arab minority as well as its conflict with the Palestinians would be illuminated by utilization of Hirsch's ideas.[146]

While Hirsch made a point of stressing universalistic sentiments, those rabbis who composed primarily Talmudic and halachic essays—and did not achieve renown in German literary circles as did Hirsch—did not feel the previously noted pressures nearly as acutely; they did not feel compelled to issue programmatic statements about Judaism.[147] Thus, Rabbis Ettlinger and Hildesheimer, while affirming a tolerant assessment of the prospects for salvation of observant Christians (implicit in their endorsement of the view that shittuf is permissible in non-Jewish worship), felt no need to repeatedly emphasize a universalistic ethos. They accepted the mission theory but only rarely promulgated it.

This, then, is the crux of nineteenth-century German Orthodoxy's encounter with modernity as it pertains to religious tolerance and Orthodoxy's willingness to embrace non-Jews. Somewhat surprisingly, the negative shift in

German attitudes toward Jews that occurred in the final third of the nineteenth century engendered a similarly robust affirmation of the universalism of Judaism by the next generation of leaders of German Orthodoxy, as a form of response to the charges that Jews preach and live by a tribalistic ethos. In the preceding period, the stress placed on universalism was an affirmation of the worthiness of Jews for the emancipation that they were in the process of receiving. In the latter period, with the rise of anti-Semitism, the stress on universalism was effectively a plea to not revoke the emancipation that had already been granted.[148] In both cases, it was representatives of the most traditionalist sector of the Jewish community that endeavored to demonstrate that love of humanity transcends the constraints that would seem to emerge from still-venerated ancient texts—not by rejection of their authority but rather by their inapplicability in the modern context.

10

The Impact of Hirsch's Universalism on the Next Generation of German Orthodoxy and Beyond

The pressures of demonstrating worthiness for emancipation, which contributed to the formulation of Hirsch's universalism, were not present after the unification of Germany and the granting of complete civic equality for Jews in 1871.[1] However, a byproduct of the granting of emancipation was the emergence of modern anti-Semitism, both political and racial. Many Jewish leaders, both Orthodox and non-Orthodox, exerted much effort to combatting the new forms of anti-Semitism.[2] One particularly persistent charge, which emerged during several trials of anti-Semitic agitators in the 1880s, was the claim that the Talmud and subsequent rabbinic literature was anti-Christian, considering Christians to be idolators who were not entitled to full human rights in Jewish law.

The most scholarly response to this charge among the Orthodox was David Zvi Hoffmann's (1843–1921) *Der Schulchan Aruch und die Rabbinen über das Verhältnis der Juden zu Andersgläubigen*.[3] Hirsch, who died in 1888, likely read the first edition of this book that appeared in 1885, though not the more influential second edition of 1894. The work employs the methodology of the Wissenschaft des Judentums movement, which Hirsch opposed, and his reaction to this book is unknown. However, it seems reasonable to assert tentatively that Hoffmann's reading of the rabbinic sources in this volume was influenced by Hirsch's universalism.[4] Mention should also be made of three other important Jewish leaders, one a German Neo-Orthodox rabbi whose ideology was diametrically opposed to Hirsch's with respect to the issue of secession, one a Polish Hasidic woman active in the first third of the twentieth century, and one an East European rabbi who had been trained at the elite yeshivas there before moving to Germany just before the First World War. All of these individuals were deeply influenced by the universalistic ethos of Hirsch's brand of Orthodoxy, and this chapter will examine their views concerning non-Jews.

Marcus Horovitz

In the last two decades of the nineteenth century and the early years of the twentieth, two disciples of Rabbi Esriel Hildesheimer, Rabbi David Zvi Hoffmann (1843–1921) and Rabbi Marcus Horovitz (1844–1910), distinguished themselves as preeminent halachists whose counsel was sought throughout Germany. Both of these men were, like their teacher, primarily Talmudists, and neither developed a systematic Jewish philosophy, as did Hirsch. Nevertheless, in different contexts both were confronted with the issue of Judaism's attitude toward Christianity—as noted regarding Hoffmann—and both responded in a manner that was consistent with the approach developed by the leaders of Neo-Orthodoxy in Germany in the previous generation.[5] This section will examine Horovitz's views.

Marcus Horovitz was a close disciple of Hildesheimer, and Hildesheimer referred to him as "an outstanding student and *zaddik*, whose like can hardly be found among all the youth of this generation."[6] Horovitz reciprocated that esteem by dedicating the first volume of his responsa collection, *Matteh Levi*, to his teacher Hildesheimer, whom he called a "prince of Torah and pillar of piety." The closeness of their relationship can be gauged by the fact that despite Hildesheimer's advice to Horovitz not to accept the position of rabbi of the Gemeindeorthodox synagogue in Frankfurt, when Horovitz nevertheless took that position, Hildesheimer (upon Horovitz's request) personally dispatched a ritual slaughterer to Frankfurt and delivered a sermon in Horovitz's synagogue.[7] Together with Hoffmann, Horovitz was one of the major halachic authorities in late nineteenth-century Germany. Of note is the fact that the Hungarian-born Horovitz was also a student of Rabbi Hayyim Zvi Mannheimer (1814–86), who was a close disciple of Hatam Sofer; the two remained in contact throughout Mannheimer's life.[8]

Rabbi Horovitz's responsum on Christianity is the most thorough presentation of the "liberal" halachic position on this issue ever written.[9] Dated February 12, 1891, when Horovitz served as the rabbi of the Communal Orthodox synagogue in Frankfurt, the responsum treats the question of the permissibility of donating money to be used for the building of a Catholic church. A member of Horovitz's congregation was approached by a group of

Catholics who, at the time, were a religious minority in Frankfurt and who wished to build a church in the city. The Catholic priest had praised the generosity of Jews when it came to helping their coreligionists in sacred matters and hoped that this too would qualify as such a cause. The priest was attempting to solicit donations from the Jewish population that could be used to pay for the expense of building the church. The congregant was inclined to respond affirmatively but sought Horovitz's counsel first.

Horovitz began his response by making a programmatic statement about how halachists generally treat these types of issues. He notes that many have been permissive in these matters due to concerns of avoiding animosity (*eivah*) or to further peaceful relations (*darkhei shalom*), which has resulted in two basic approaches to issuing rulings regarding Jewish-Christian relations. Those who are stringent express such views only in theory but are inclined for practical reasons to be permissive. Many who issue permissive rulings do so solely out of pragmatic concerns and thereby contradict their own views regarding what the correct theoretical halacha ought to be. These remain two separate spheres: the theoretical truth of halacha, on the one hand, and the way it ought to actually be implemented in the real world, on the other. Horovitz states, "As for me, my whole life I have seen that there is only one truth, and that which cannot be practically implemented is also not the correct [theoretical] halakhah. Therefore, I state that I will not budge from the truth due to concerns of either [preserving] peaceful relations or due to animosity. However, after careful consideration it appears that the law is the law of truth and all the ways of the Torah are genuinely the 'ways of pleasantness' and all the pathways of the Law are 'peace'" (Proverbs 3:17).

Horovitz then proceeds to examine the sources that treat the status of Christianity in halacha. He starts with the passage from the Talmud in *Sanhedrin* 63b, which gave rise to the comments of the Tosafists regarding shittuf. Horovitz states that the Tosafists repeat these comments in other places and notes that Rema based his permissive ruling regarding shittuf on the statement of the Tosafists.[10] To preempt a narrow interpretation of Rema, he proceeds to cite the ruling given by Rema in his *Darkei Moshe* that permits the sale of incense to Christians for use in their religious worship.[11]After citing this ruling, Horovitz states that "no one opened their mouth or argued [with this view] until two great Jewish luminaries arose to contend this point." He then cites two of the early modern authorities who disagreed with the "liberal" interpretation of the Tosafists' statement, as already outlined.[12] His main issue is with the claim made by the author of *Me'il Tzedakah* that there is no basis to distinguish between the laws of AZ that apply to Jews and those that apply to non-Jews. On the contrary, asserts Horovitz, the primary Talmudic discussion of the issue suggests the very opposite point of view, namely, that there is only a source that forbids shittuf for Jews, but there is no source that prohibits non-Jews from this type of worship.[13] Further, the Talmud clearly indicates that those who engage in shittuf are not outright idolators.

The trouble for Horovitz at this point is the fact that Maimonides appears to take a different approach in one passage which seems to state that the "root" of idolatry is, in fact, associating other beings with God—shittuf.[14] Horovitz exerts much effort in demonstrating that Maimonides did not intend to assert that the primary form of idolatry is shittuf worship. In fact, Maimonides was not issuing a halachic pronouncement at all in that passage but was rather expressing "words of wisdom," outlining the historical background to the development of polytheism: first, people who recognized the supremacy of the one God erred in thinking that it was an honor to Him to worship other celestial beings that serve a purpose in the universe.[15] Once that error was made, it was only a matter of time before people began to forget God and place all of their emphasis on the other beings that they worshipped. But, insists Horovitz, Maimonides never intended to suggest that the *primary* form of polytheism was shittuf.

According to Horovitz, Maimonides's analysis of idolatry in his *Guide of the Perplexed* sheds much light on his approach to the issue. In one passage in that work, Maimonides emphatically states that no idolators ever believed that their man-made fetishes had created the world. Instead, they saw in them some representation of the deity, which could serve as an intermediary between humans and God. In fact, Horovitz claims that it was Maimonides's piety that persuaded him of this view: "Maimonides in his exalted intellect, and his great wisdom, and in his pure heart did not recognize nor realize how ignorant the outlook of idolators was, and [therefore] did not believe that there [could] be a man walking on this earth, under the heavens, who did not recognize his Creator. To his exalted soul, he regarded this as an impossibility. However, in truth, not one [halachic] decisor in Israel has [ever] said that outright idol worship is not the main form of AZ, and there has been no sage aside from Maimonides who would accept his view that no person has ever engaged in truly polytheistic worship."[16]

Horovitz then examines another passage from Maimonides's work, which seems to suggest that Maimonides did regard shittuf as AZ, but he suggests that an alternative interpretation is a more compelling reading of that passage. According to Horovitz, then, there is nothing in Maimonides's writings to suggest that he regarded shittuf as AZ for non-Jews (though for Jews it is certainly forbidden). He then cites the statement of Rabbi Samuel Landau who claims that the masses have misunderstood the comments of the Tosafists and

Rema regarding shittuf for, he asserted, in truth only if a non-Jew makes an oath in the shittuf manner is the act acceptable, but they are not permitted to worship in that manner. Landau added one substantial challenge to the ones that his predecessors had already raised regarding the liberal reading of the comments of the Tosafists. Landau noted that the Talmud in *Sanhedrin* 56b states, as a matter of course, that any idolatrous act for which a Jew would be liable to the death penalty, is forbidden for non-Jews. Since a Jew who worships God in partnership with another entity (shittuf) would be so liable, this act must therefore be forbidden for non-Jews.

Horovitz responds to this charge by delimiting the contours of the Talmudic passage discussed by Landau. Accordingly, only those acts associated with idolatrous worship that are performed in veneration of an entity that has been established to be a foreign deity (avodah zarah) are the subject of the passage from *Sanhedrin* 56b that Landau had cited. On the other hand, worshipping God in partnership (shittuf) is clearly, according to Horovitz's reading of *Sanhedrin* 63a, something that is entirely permissible for non-Jews and, therefore, there is no basis on which to declare such worship forbidden for non-Jews based on the passage that Landau cited from *Sanhedrin* 56b.[17]

Having defended the view that Trinitarian worship is absolutely permitted for non-Jews, Horovitz ends the responsum by stating that it has hereby been established that no sin whatsoever would be transgressed by aiding the Catholics in worshipping, such as by contributing to the building of their church. On the contrary, adds Horovitz, there is actually a mitzvah to do so:

> The law follows my friend [the questioner] that there is also a mitzvah here, namely, that of sanctifying His great Name [Horovitz notes the example of Moses Montefiore, who aided in the building of a church in Ramsgate] through His people Israel, so that all the nations of the world may see that we Jews are always prepared to sacrifice ourselves with love . . . on behalf of our holy faith, for we all agree that this mitzvah [accepting absolute monotheism] is specifically for us and no other nation. *And we all agree that someone who is not Jewish can become one of the pious and great ones of the world and heirs to paradise* [emphasis added], if they observe the Seven Noahide Laws which were given to the entire world.

Horovitz qualifies his permissive ruling by stating that if there are Jewish converts to Christianity to be found "among our non-Jewish brethren who are building a house of worship," then it would be forbidden to aid in the building of the church, for the prohibition of not placing a stumbling block before the blind (i.e., facilitating the commission of a sin) would be transgressed—that is, if no other church can be found in "that place." He adds that such "apostates" have always been "reckless destroyers of all peace amongst us regarding all aspects of life." Further, they only convert due to ulterior motives *(ahavah ha-teluyah ba-davar)* and "if not for them, who are persistently our enemies, all the nations would see and recognize that we are trustworthy friends."

This responsum, written less than two decades after the unification of Germany, is the most remarkable halachic analysis of Christianity ever penned by a major halachic authority.[18] Unlike so many others, including Hoffmann, Horovitz takes the liberal view of Christianity to its logical conclusion: if Christianity is not AZ for gentiles, then helping Christians (even Catholics who use icons in their worship) build a church is absolutely permissible and can even be regarded as a kiddush Hashem. He does not engage in what Jacob Katz has characterized as the "halakhic casuistry" so common among the medieval and early modern halachists who had distinguished between Christians and pagans in limited circumstances only but failed to allow this position to impact cases where (what Jacob Katz calls) the "emotionally conditioned repugnance to the visible symbols of the alien religion" comes into play.[19] Horovitz was not concerned about the possibility of even greater social intermingling, and possible intermarriage, between Jews and Christians once Jews are encouraged to aid in the building of churches. His only concern was with Jewish apostates.[20]

The only thorough analysis of this responsum thus far is that of David Ellenson.[21] Ellenson argues that Horovitz "departed dramatically" from the approach of his colleague, David Zvi Hoffmann, who had ruled that it is forbidden for a Jew to donate money for the building of a church.[22] While Hoffmann was concerned about "the dangers of syncretism" if Jews adopted a liberal approach toward Christianity, Horovitz eschewed such considerations. Horovitz was more concerned with turning potential anti-Semites into friends of Jews, which he hoped might be achieved by the gesture of aiding in the building of a church. Furthermore, Horovitz had a genuine appreciation for Christianity and considered Christians to be people who, "like Jews, were engaged in the task of doing God's work in the world." For Ellenson, this responsum by Horovitz and the restrictive one by Hoffmann demonstrate the "pluralistic" nature of the halachic system since two halachists who came from similar backgrounds, and lived in the same cultural milieu, reached diametrically opposed conclusions on the same question.

Marc Shapiro takes issue with Ellenson's interpretation. Shapiro argues that Hoffmann's view was not a departure from earlier, tolerant assessments of Christianity since earlier authorities had never directly addressed the issue of donating money to be used for the building of a church, and they certainly did not issue a permissive ruling regarding this question.[23] Whether one follows Ellenson's or Shapiro's positions on this matter, there is no doubt that Horovitz's responsum is remarkable for its display of religious tolerance.[24]

Although non-Jews make an appearance in several other of Horovitz's responsa, in none of those cases are there statements that could not have been found in the writings of other halachists who were not known for espousing a liberal view of Christianity. It is in Horovitz's other writings that his tolerant approach to non-Jews stands out. In his monumental study of the rabbis of Frankfurt, his most famous contribution to Wissenschaft literature, Horovitz examines the life and oeuvre of Rabbi Jacob Joshua Falk (1680–1756), author of the celebrated Talmudic commentary *P'nei Yehoshua*.[25] In one passage, Horovitz notes that Falk placed a note in his work that distinguished between pagans and Christians, saying that all references to *akum* and the like in the Talmud and Codes refer only to ancient pagan nations but not to contemporary non-Jews. Horovitz notes that this type of disclaimer was found in many other Jewish books published during that period. Yet the fact that Horovitz saw fit to highlight this point suggests that his own view was in agreement with the views of Rabbi Falk as expressed in the disclaimer.[26]

Further, in his sermons, Horovitz emphasized the universalism of Judaism. In one sermon from 1891, he states that Judaism is the priestly religion of mankind.[27] The entire purpose of the selection of Israel was for the ultimate redemption of all mankind for God's service. Horovitz makes a point of citing the rabbinic statement that "the righteous among the nations have a share in the world to come" and sourcing it as being from Tractate *Sanhedrin* 105a.[28] Unmentioned is the fact that the Talmud there actually records a dispute about whether righteous non-Jews will be granted bliss in the afterlife. Further, Horovitz's broad German translation of the rabbinic statement that he cited in Hebrew (*Die Frommen aller Völker der Erde haben Anteil an der zukünftigen Welt, an der Ewigkeit und Seligkeit*; the pious of all nations have a share in the future world, one of eternity and bliss) indicates an effort to formulate rabbinic ethics as being in line with contemporary humanism. Horovitz continues by noting that the great Jewish martyrs who died on German soil held to these universalistic teachings, according to which every human being who adheres to the Noahide laws will be amply rewarded. This is true of all sections of humanity, be they the descendants of Shem, Japeth, or Ham. These martyrs understood that the main purpose of the Jewish people was to spread universal brotherhood and peace to the world and to invite *all* people to enter into the Holy of Holies with Israel for the purpose of accepting God's dominion.

This sermon is certainly reminiscent of those of S. R. Hirsch, Horovitz's nemesis on the issue of *Austritt*. Horovitz had been one of the only Orthodox rabbis who refused to express his support for a law of secession for Jews that would be modeled on the one that was passed for Christians in 1873.[29] As noted, Horovitz accepted the rabbinical post in the Communal Orthodox synagogue in Frankfurt against the objections of his teacher, Esriel Hildesheimer. When Horovitz came to Frankfurt, he wished to meet with Hirsch, but Hirsch did not receive him.[30] It is further said that Hirsch's son-in-law, Rabbi Salomon Breuer, refused to stand in the same room as Horowitz.[31] Yet, despite the fundamentally different outlooks of Hirsch and Horovitz when it comes to Jewish unity and community structure, the two men were likeminded when it came to Judaism's universalism and its tolerance of non-Jewish religions. Horovitz appreciated Hirsch's efforts on behalf of winning back the youth to traditional Judaism, and he no doubt read many of Hirsch's books and essays.[32]

Thus, Hirsch's humanistic view of non-Jews made an indelible impact even on his ideological opponents. This fact should come as no surprise. Hirsch's views were not developed in a vacuum. The social and cultural contexts—the quest for emancipation and the pursuit of Bildung—impacted both men equally. Although Horovitz wrote at a time when emancipation had already been granted to the Jews of the Second German Reich, the cultivation of Bildung still lived on, as did a desire to prove that the anti-Semites were wrong when they charged Judaism with preaching tribalistic ethics. By Horovitz's time, it had become the hallmark of German Neo-Orthodoxy to express religious tolerance. As we will soon see, there were other Jewish leaders who were not interested in either emancipation or Bildung but who nevertheless were so influenced by Hirsch's writings that they expressed the same universalism that he so consistently upheld.

Sarah Schenirer

At this point, it would be illuminating to examine a case of the influence of Hirsch's universalism that lies outside the sphere of German Neo-Orthodoxy. Although the ideology discussed in this book was developed in the German states over a period of roughly a century, and the conditions that engendered the development of this outlook were different in other locations and during other time periods, the legacy of German Orthodoxy was not confined to these parameters. This movement has had a dramatic impact on the Modern Orthodoxy of mid-twentieth-century America as well as on different permutations of Haredi Orthodoxy.

One movement whose connections to German Orthodoxy are well-documented but insufficiently known among its followers is the Bais Yaakov school movement. Its founder, Sarah Schenirer (1883–1935), was a Polish woman from a Belzer Hasidic family that had relocated to Vienna during the First World War. There she was exposed to the sermons of Rabbi Dr. Moshe David Flesch (1879–1944), a student of Salomon Breuer, Hirsch's son-in-law and rabbi of the Frankfurt congregation after Hirsch's passing. Flesch, who was the rabbi of the Tempel-und-Schulverein Stumpergasse in Vienna, introduced Schenirer to the Hirschian teachings, and she told Isaac Breuer, one of Salomon's sons, that Hirsch's early writings (*The Nineteen Letters* and *Horeb*), which discuss the education of women, inspired her to create a movement of schools for Jewish girls and young women.[33] Schenirer's attachment to Hirsch and his ideas was so strong that, on one occasion, when she was sitting alone in the salon of Hirsch's grandchildren and skimming through a family album, she boldly wrote on the last—blank—page that though she was not a biological descendent of Hirsch, she was his spiritual descendant, and considered herself as "someone who carried on the work of a brilliant person [Hirsch]."[34]

Less known than this background to Schenirer's sense of mission are her views regarding non-Jews. One of her essays treats this issue extensively and it is worth translating here:

> My precious daughters! Now we will discuss our obligations towards the humans who inhabit this world of God with us. It is incumbent on every girl to know these matters well.
>
> When we say that it is a mitzvah to love human beings, there is no distinction at all as to who the person is, whether Jew or non-Jew, for anyone called a human is indeed one.
>
> The Torah teaches us, "God is good to all and His compassion extends to all His works" (Psalms 145:9) . . . We also learn in the Torah that man is created in the image of God. When we disparage any human being, we thereby, God forbid, disparage the Creator in whose image man was created.
>
> This alone forbids us from distinguishing between different human beings. All of mankind originates from Adam and Eve, and therefore all humans are brothers, children of one father and one mother. What suffering is endured by parents when peace does not reside between [their children] brothers and sisters! Even greater, then, is the suffering of the Creator when His children, mankind [*b'nei ha-adam*], do not dwell with one another in peace.
>
> Our holy Torah commands us: "And you shall love your fellow as yourself" (Leviticus 19:18) and it ends this command with the words "I am God!"—[meaning] I have created you all as equals, and for my own sake alone you must have warm feelings for and love your fellow human being.

> It is incumbent upon you to love every single human being, both those that are near and those that are far, and [must] express extra tenderness for the stranger, for you were strangers in Egypt. It is forbidden for you [Jews] to hate members of other religions.
>
> Only through love and friendship will it be possible to draw the hearts of the other nations to Judaism.[35] And indeed in many places in the Bible we learn of how the Jewish people and its leaders related to other nations, by expressing to them love and tenderness.
>
> [Schenirer proceeds to cite examples from the Bible where Jewish leaders treated non-Jews with respect and love.] And we can find many more such examples from various different epochs, all of which teach us that it is a mitzvah to truly love every single human being and to rejoice in the joy of others and to experience their suffering with them—as though it were our own joy and suffering.
>
> And since man was created in the image of God, there is no distinction between those of beautiful appearance and those of unpleasant appearance, whether they are of sound mind or insane. It is in all cases a very grave sin to scorn or embarrass any human being, such being considered as outright murder.[36]

Schenirer appears to regard her ideas about the brotherhood of mankind and the humanism that Judaism mandates to be noncontroversial. Her remarks about love of all mankind are headed by the title "You shall love your fellow as yourself," and she clearly endorses the view that the love ordained by this command of the Torah is inclusive of non-Jews. Furthermore, she maintains that God's compassion extends equally to all of humanity. All human beings are equally created in God's image. These humanistic remarks are worthy of analysis.

Sarah Schenirer's religious education did not include the study of Talmud.[37] The educational revolution for Jewish girls that she initiated did not include Talmudic studies in its curriculum.[38] Schenirer attended a Polish public school as a child. Her upbringing in a Hasidic home did not appear to have inculcated her with the negative view of gentiles that is commonly found in many Hasidic writings. Her limited exposure to the Talmud and the rabbinic literature it spawned meant that she was largely unaware of negative remarks about "goyim" found in those writings.[39] The rabbis discussed in this book grappled with those texts and interpreted them as referring solely to ancient pagans, but not to their Christian contemporaries.[40] Schenirer, unaware that there was any tension between her humanism and the strict Orthodoxy that she propagated throughout her life, expressed these views matter-of-factly and unselfconsciously.[41]

By contrast, the rabbis encountered in this study were well-versed in the Talmud. One of them, David Zvi Hoffmann, was acutely sensitive to the tension between the universalism that he championed and some of the classic texts of rabbinic Judaism. He authored a volume dedicated to demonstrating that a proper reading of those texts leaves no room for anti-gentile animus. The other examined rabbis did not deal with this issue in the same manner that Hoffmann did, but they did consistently preach a universalistic ethos that implicitly rejected the applicability of seemingly anti-gentile passages in rabbinic literature to their Christian contemporaries.

Rabbi Samson Raphael Hirsch, in his writings and speeches, was more committed to demonstrating the humanism and universalism of Judaism than any traditionalist rabbi prior to him. Unlike Hoffmann, he did not author a treatise examining the applicability of seemingly exclusivist rabbinic texts to contemporary non-Jews. But, as demonstrated, he was undoubtedly conscious of the tension that existed between the humanism that he insisted was integral to Judaism and some of the classic texts of rabbinic Judaism. In his own way, he resolved that tension. This was not achieved through systematic exegesis or historical contextualization. Instead, Hirsch highlighted those passages found in Talmudic literature that expressed genuinely universalistic sentiments, and he downplayed the significance of passages that seemed to paint a different picture. He insisted that love of all humanity, indeed of all creation, lay at the heart of Judaism. As shown, he implicitly accepted the halachic distinction between the ancient pagans, on the one hand, and Christians and Muslims, on the other. This was almost certainly the view of his parents and teachers as well.

Thus, when a young idealistic Polish-Jewish woman came across the writings of the idealistic German-Jewish fighter for Orthodoxy, she found in him a kindred spirit. Since Hirsch was preaching primarily for a lay audience and not for the rabbinic elite, his writings were perfectly suitable for Schenirer's target population of religiously uneducated Jewish girls. Thus, these two great Jewish leaders, despite the differences in their gender, education, region, and the times in which they lived, among other significant distinctions, were both preaching Jewish universalism to the same receptive audience.

Yehiel Yaakov Weinberg

Rabbi Yehiel Yaakov Weinberg (1884–1966) was a unique figure in Orthodox Judaism of the twentieth century. He was the product of the East European yeshivot, with a particular attachment to the Mussar (Ethical) teachings of the Slabodka academy, who made his way to Germany where he encountered—initially, with great suspicion—the Torah im Derekh Eretz approach ubiquitous in German-Orthodoxy. He ultimately emerged as the leading rabbinic authority in Nazi-era Germany and one of the few internationally renowned rabbinic authorities to survive the Holocaust, whose counsel was sought across the globe in the last two decades of his life. Uniquely, though, he continued to champion the Hirschian Torah im Derekh Eretz approach even when its detractors far outnumbered its supporters in the postwar Orthodox Jewish world. He maintained close ties to both leading Haredi luminaries and to figures more entrenched in the world of Modern Orthodoxy. Weinberg remains a rare figure, venerated in both segments of the Orthodox Jewish community.[42]

Weinberg's comments about non-Jews in both his published writings and unpublished letters bear the unmistakable imprint of Hirsch's humanistic approach. Though undoubtedly Weinberg's sensitive and ethical personality played a decisive role in the development of his views regarding this issue, it would be hard to imagine that such views could have been expressed had Weinberg not first experienced contact with Hirschian Neo-Orthodoxy.

Early in his rabbinic career, when his exposure to Hirschian teachings was still limited, Weinberg authored an essay in response to a German critic of Judaism who published a critique of Judaism's alleged tribalistic ethos. Weinberg wrote that it is not worthwhile to respond to anti-Semites themselves as they will not change their views due to Jewish defenses of Judaism. However, an unnamed German-Jewish man had written to Weinberg asking for an explanation of Judaism's ethic and whether it was truly guilty, as charged, of preaching dual standards of ethics for Jews and non-Jews. Weinberg stated that it is essential for Jews to properly understand Judaism, and that is why he wrote back to this man with an explication of Jewish ethics. Weinberg noted that Professor David Zvi Hoffmann's work treating halacha's view of non-Jews is absolutely correct; that work's primary thesis that Judaism distinguishes between pagan and nonpagan gentiles is accurate.

Weinberg then stressed that the anti-gentile discrimination found in the Talmud has no application in the present day. Referring to the position of Meiri as though it were representative of all medieval rabbinic writings on the subject, Weinberg insisted that there is no practical application of gentile disabilities when it comes to contemporary Christians.[43] At the same time, Weinberg was adamant that Meiri's view is representative of Jewish law, more generally. Halacha does not countenance discrimination against people on the basis of their nationality or religion; it does, however, treat primitive pagans with a dual ethic: theft and bodily harm are absolutely prohibited to pagans as much as anyone else but retaining extra change they mistakenly give or keeping their lost items that are found is acceptable, but only due to their deplorable lifestyle, not the accident of their birth.[44]

Thus, in terms of the legal standing of non-Jews in halacha, Weinberg unreservedly endorsed the position of Meiri, according to which there is no discrimination against non-Jews qua non-Jews in any area of ethics; only pagans, who no longer exist, are subject to such discrimination. (In the purely ritual sphere, there of course remain legal distinctions between Jews and non-Jews.) In a private letter, Weinberg expressed frustration that this position of Meiri was not taught properly in certain yeshivot where, he says, Meiri's view is presented as having been written to please the censors, when in actuality it was Meiri's sincere position, and one which should be adopted as normative Jewish law.[45]

This enthusiastic embrace of Meiri's position should be contrasted with Hatam Sofer's rejection of this view, which he found so objectionable that he doubted Meiri actually expressed it, suggesting that the words be erased from the later texts that cite this view in Meiri's name. The reader may recall the earlier discussion of Hatam Sofer, who did not subscribe to the "enlightened" view of non-Jews that was fairly prevalent among his rabbinic contemporaries.

Likewise, in the case of Weinberg, the tolerant view of non-Jews was by no means ubiquitous among mid-twentieth century rabbinic authorities. While some certainly did champion this approach, others, such as the venerated Rabbi Isaac Zev Soloveitchik (aka Rabbi Velvel), known as "the Brisker Rav" (1886–1959), did not.[46] As Marc Shapiro notes, Weinberg's tolerance toward non-Jews was not merely theoretical; his personal friendship with his university mentor, Dr. Paul Kahle (1875–1964), surely played a role. After the death of Kahle's wife, Weinberg wrote to his teacher to pay tribute to her memory. In that letter, Weinberg's respect for her Christian piety is evident.[47] Weinberg could not assess the legal standing of non-Jews from an ivory tower, as many of his rabbinic contemporaries did. They knew only of anti-Semitic Lithuanians or Poles, who were perhaps complicit in the Holocaust or prewar anti-Semitic pogroms. Weinberg had firsthand knowledge of gentile piety, and he could not accept the caricature of the "wicked goyim."

What role did Hirsch's writings play in the formulation of Weinberg's views? While this question cannot be definitively answered, it is quite evident that Weinberg's writings bear the unmistakable imprint of Hirsch's ideas.[48] Further, Weinberg's caustic formulation, with respect to a view of halacha that does not endorse Meiri's position, is illuminating: "Can the nations resign themselves to such a deprivation of rights?"[49] Classical Jewish civil law does not utilize the term "rights." Instead, there are responsibilities and obligations. Whether or not he was the first, Samson Raphael Hirsch was the most influential Jewish thinker to introduce the term "rights" into discourse about Jewish civil law in his Pentateuch commentary. Hirsch insists that the Torah *does* recognize rights and that it asserts individual rights in the most extreme cases to allow us to extrapolate the application of these rights to more mundane scenarios.[50]

An East European halachist or yeshiva dean analyzing the application of Jewish law to contemporary non-Jews would have been very unlikely to agonize about the "deprivation of [gentile] rights." Aside from Weinberg's humanistic concern with the standing of non-Jews, in itself unique for rabbis with his background, his *formulation* of that agonizing demonstrates an internalization of Western sensibilities he likely imbibed from reading Hirsch's writings. However, it must be stressed that neither Hirsch nor Weinberg regarded their views as reflecting *any* external set of values—this book has endeavored to demonstrate that classical Jewish sources were understood by Hirsch and his colleagues as mandating a universal love of mankind.

It has been argued that a halachist's view of the legal status of Christians is very likely impacted by his view of non-Jews and the relationship of the Jewish people to the other nations. In this regard, it is clear that Weinberg accepted Hirsch's view that the election of Israel was intended to enable it to carry out a spiritual mission to the nations and that "the Jewish people possess no inherent superiority over other nations."[51] Weinberg did praise many qualities he found evident in the Jewish people and he did consider Judaism the only *fully* true religion. But he did not consider non-Jews to be inferior to Jews in any way and considered Christianity a perfectly appropriate conduit for non-Jewish spirituality.[52]

Unlike Sarah Schenirer, whose exposure to the Talmud was limited, Weinberg was fully aware of the limitations to gentile rights that the Talmud *seemingly* endorsed. That is why he insisted on fully embracing Meiri's halachic position that there exists no discrimination whatsoever in the sphere of ethics between Jews and non-pagan non-Jews. Though, as David Berger has shown, there were a significant number of prominent rabbinic authorities of the nineteenth and twentieth centuries who endorsed Meiri's position, this view has nevertheless not become a consensus position among contemporary halachists, certainly not in the Haredi world.[53] Pragmatic arguments about the need to maintain amicable relations with contemporary non-Jews are still widely disseminated. The principled and idealistic stance of Weinberg—encapsulated by his enthusiastic embrace of Meiri's position and his denigration of the contrary position—is remarkably similar to the stance that Hirsch championed throughout his career.

If Sarah Schenirer championed a humanistic stance toward non-Jews due to having had limited exposure to Talmudic literature, Yehiel Yaakov Weinberg championed it because he was convinced that the Talmud and rabbinic literature—of which he was one of the twentieth century's greatest masters—never intended to discriminate between Jews and non-Jews in the realm of rights and ethics. Though Weinberg was not a fighter for emancipation, as Hirsch had been, he was just as convinced that all human beings are equally created in the image of God and are thus all equally entitled to the same human rights.[54] These rabbis thus both teach the vital lesson that Orthodox Judaism, though regarding itself as uniquely privy to divine truth, is as universalistic in its outlook as is the religion's Creator.

Conclusion

The struggle for emancipation of Jews in nineteenth-century Germany was waged rather uniquely by the Orthodox minority when compared with the greater political activism of the non-Orthodox majority. While the latter was prepared to assimilate in terms of abandoning its commitment to halachic observance, the Orthodox retained its commitment to the binding character of Jewish law. Nevertheless, the Orthodox were no less "German" than their more liberal coreligionists. They too valued culture and education (Bildung). They too internalized the ethical sensibilities of nineteenth-century Europeans, and they did this even in one area where those sensibilities *appeared* to clash with Jewish tradition: the classical view of the Jewish people as the Chosen People, with its potential implications of non-Jews possessing only limited capacity for spirituality as well as the various forms of legal discrimination in the realm of ethics that the Talmud and later rabbinic works *appeared* to subject non-Jews to.

The course of this analysis has demonstrated that the Jewish tradition was never as monolithic with respect to these issues as it seemed to its internal and external critics. Whereas non-Jewish critics of Judaism as well as non-Orthodox thinkers generally maintained that classical Judaism was overly particularistic—even tribalistic—in its ethos and its laws, the leaders of nineteenth-century German Neo-Orthodoxy argued against this interpretation. Their arguments were not, for the most part, carried out in a systematic or scientific way.[1] Instead, the leading spokespeople for Orthodoxy, Marcus Lehmann and, especially, Samson Raphael Hirsch presented traditional Jewish teachings in a highly universalistic manner, and they consistently reiterated that Judaism countenances no discrimination in the realm of ethics between people of different faiths. Other rabbinic leaders who were less prone to write in German or to issue ideological proclamations, such as Esriel Hildesheimer and his teachers and his students, subtly presented rabbinic material relating to non-Jews in a sensitive way, thereby undercutting the charges of Jewish chauvinism.

The Jews in Germany were thus not, as Gershom Scholem would have us believe, "shouting to themselves."[2] There were quite a few German Christian scholars in the late nineteenth and early twentieth centuries who devoted themselves to an objective study (by the standards of their time) of the Jewish religion and the Talmud and later rabbinic texts; many of these defended the Talmud from anti-Semitic critics. The endeavor, started by Hirsch, and further developed by scholars such as Hoffmann, to present Jewish law as universalistic and humane toward non-Jews, almost certainly influenced these Christian scholars to develop a more charitable reading of Jewish texts than that championed by detractors of Judaism.

Christian scholars such as Franz Delitzsch (1813–90) and Hermann Strack (1848–1922), as well as some of their successors such as August Wünsche (1838–1912), Hugo Gressmann (1877–1927), and Johannes Müller (1864–1949), were clearly influenced by the manner in which rabbinic texts were understood by German-Jewish scholars. Strack was on friendly terms with the leading scholars of fin de siècle German Orthodoxy, and he was familiar with their writings. Rabbi Dr. Joseph Wohlgemuth, a leading rabbinic figure in early twentieth-century German Orthodoxy, wrote an obituary for Strack, where he expressed his gratitude for the latter's defense of Jews and Judaism.[3]

These Christian scholars opposed the anti-Talmudic agitation of people like August Rohling and defended Jews from anti-Semitic attacks—though a number of them harbored Christian supersessionist outlooks, which were integral to their missionary efforts. Yehiel Yaakov Weinberg's teacher, Paul Kahle, was a celebrated Orientalist who, together with his wife, fled Nazi Germany due to their anti-Nazi activities.[4] There is no question, then, that the dialogue was *not* one-sided.

But perhaps even more importantly than the "dialogue" that opened between traditional Jewish scholars and Christian Hebraists is the impact made by Hirsch's universalism on how Orthodox Judaism understands itself. The most traditionalist sector of the German-Jewish community reevaluated its own understanding of venerated religious texts in the context of the emancipation struggle. Aside from emancipation itself, which was successfully achieved and remained largely stable for more than sixty years, Neo-Orthodoxy's legacy with respect to how Judaism views non-Jews was later embraced by two important Orthodox leaders (Sarah Schenirer and Yehiel Yaakov Weinberg) whose influence was (and is) felt far beyond the confines of the remnants of the prewar German Orthodox communities.

If German Christians during the nineteenth century, for the most part, did not reciprocate the humanistic sentiments that were being promulgated by Germany's Orthodox leaders, the efforts of the Neo-Orthodox were not in vain. Orthodox Judaism of the twenty-first century now has a rich storehouse from which to draw in its task of defending traditional religious values while affirming the inalienable dignity and value of the billions of human beings who do not accept those values. Should these people ultimately choose to embrace these values—which are embedded in the Seven Noahide laws—the "mission" of Judaism, as understood by Samson Raphael Hirsch, will have been accomplished.

Notes

Introduction

1. Jacob Katz has characterized "the transformation of [European] Jewish society from its prerevolutionary state" as "perhaps the greatest upheaval of any sector of European society at that time." *Out of the Ghetto: The Social Background of Jewish Emancipation, 1770–1870* (Cambridge, MA: Harvard University Press, 1973), 4.

2. See, for example, Michael A. Meyer, *Response to Modernity: A History of the Reform Movement in Judaism* (New York: Oxford University Press, 1988); Andreas Brämer, *Rabbiner Zacharias Frankel: Wissenschaft des Judentums und konservative Reform im 19. Jahrhundert* (Hildesheim: G. Olms, 2000); David Ellenson, *Rabbi Esriel Hildesheimer and the Creation of a Modern Jewish Orthodoxy* (Tuscaloosa: University of Alabama Press, 1990); Michael K. Silber, "The Emergence of Ultra-Orthodoxy: The Invention of a Tradition," in *The Uses of Tradition*, ed. Jack Wertheimer (New York: Jewish Theological Seminary, 1992), 23–84.

3. An excellent study that encompasses both the German and Hungarian Jewish communities is Jacob Katz, *A House Divided: Orthodoxy and Schism in Nineteenth-Century Central European Jewry*, trans. Ziporah Brody (Hanover, NH: University Press of New England, 1998). An important and more in-depth study of the role of German Neo-Orthodoxy in this schism is Adam Ferziger, *Exclusion and Hierarchy: Orthodoxy, Nonobservance, and the Emergence of Modern Jewish Identity* (Philadelphia: University of Pennsylvania Press, 2005). Other valuable studies that address this issue include Matthias Morgenstern, *From Frankfurt to Jerusalem: Isaac Breuer and the History of the Secession Dispute in Modern Jewish Orthodoxy* (Leiden: Brill, 2002) and Roland Tasch, *Samson Raphael Hirsch: Jüdische Erfahrungswelten im Historischen Kontext* (Berlin: De Gruyter, 2011).

4. In classical Jewish texts, there is the notion of a Written Torah (or Law), which refers to the Hebrew Scriptures, and an Oral Torah (or Law), which refers to the rules of Jewish law, originally unwritten, which were later presented in the Talmud. At least the Pentateuch and the core interpretation of it that is found in the Talmud are regarded by Orthodox Judaism as having been revealed by God to Moses during the Revelation at Mount Sinai described in the Book of Exodus.

5. The most comprehensive account of this episode from Hirsch's point of view is that of Eliyahu Meir Klugman, *Rabbi Samson Raphael Hirsch* (New York: Mesorah, 1996),

240, 254–62. For Frankel's point of view, see Brämer, *Rabbiner Zacharias Frankel*, 364–81. See also David Ellenson, *After Emancipation: Jewish Religious Responses to Modernity* (Cincinnati: Hebrew Union College Press, 2004), 172–76, 249–51. For an incisive exposition of the intellectual context of Frankel's thought, see Uriel Tal, "German-Jewish Social Thought in the Mid-Nineteenth Century," in *Revolution and Evolution: 1848 in German-Jewish History*, ed. Werner E. Mosse, Arnold Paucker, and Reinhard Rürup (Tübingen: Mohr Siebeck, 1981), 312–20.

6. The *Wissenschaft des Judentums* movement began in Germany in the second decade of the nineteenth century with a declared goal of reading classical Jewish texts in their historical contexts as opposed to the ahistorical approach of traditional Talmudists. Orthodox reception of this movement was mixed. See Asaf Yedidya, "Orthodox Reactions to '*Wissenschaft des Judentums*'," *Modern Judaism* 30, no. 1 (February 2010): 69–94. My assertion here is not that Hirsch opposed a scientific study of Judaism but that he opposed the approach of the nineteenth-century Wissenschaft movement. See further Mordechai Breuer, *Modernity within Tradition*, trans. E. Petuchowski (New York: Columbia University Press, 1992), 185–86; Klugman, *Rabbi Samson Raphael Hirsch*, 262–64.

7. Ferziger, *Exclusion and Hierarchy*, esp. 90–185.

8. On the role of the Mishnaic rabbis in developing a notion of an Other defined simply by not being Jewish, see Adi Ophir and Ishay Rosen-Zvi, *Goy: Israel's Multiple Others and the Birth of the Gentile* (New York: Oxford University Press, 2018). It is precisely the argument of the present book that nineteenth-century German Orthodox rabbis—and their intellectual heirs—rejected the binary dualism of Otherness that Ophir and Rosen-Zvi impute to the Mishnaic rabbis. Though that dualism still remains for the purpose of certain religious rituals (e.g., observance of Shabbat), in the realm of ethics and, more broadly, a sense of spiritual companionship, these rabbis followed the lead of Meiri (examined in chapter 2 and chapter 9) in assessing non-Jews by their outlook on the world and their conduct rather than on the fact that they are not Jewish.

9. For example, the Talmudic debate, Bava Kamma 113a–b, over *gezel akum* (lit. "theft from an idolator") is conspicuously absent from the responsa of the German-Orthodox rabbis.

10. The exception is Rabbi David Zvi Hoffmann. See chapter 10. Hoffmann, the most illustrious Orthodox proponent of Wissenschaft, was open to a certain degree of historical contextualization of Jewish law, even though he upheld the absolute authority of the medieval Codes of halacha.

11. I am using these terms as Alan Brill applies them to Judaism in his *Judaism and Other Religions: Models of Understanding* (New York: Palgrave Macmillan, 2010). They were originally employed by Alan Race and popularized by John Hick in the context of general theology. Brill, together with Rori Picker Neiss in "Jewish Views of World Religions: Four Models" (in *Jewish Theology and World Religions*, ed. Alon Goshen-Gottstein and Eugene Korn [Oxford: Littman Library, 2012], 41–42), notes that Jewish thinkers rarely fit neatly into one of the schools of thought, which are merely theoretical constructs. Indeed, the rabbis under study here borrowed elements from all the schools discussed by Brill, with the possible exception of the "pluralist" school, since they did not affirm that all religious truths are equally valid. See also Avi Sagi, *Jewish Religion after Theology*, trans. Batya Stein (Boston: Academic Studies Press, 2009), 3–42; Suzanne Last

Stone, "Tolerance versus Pluralism in Judaism," *Journal of Human Rights* 2, no. 1 (March 2003): 105–17.

12. Eugene Korn, *To Be a Holy People: Jewish Tradition and Ethical Values* (Jerusalem: Urim Publications, 2021), 219–47.

13. See David Sorkin, *The Religious Enlightenment: Protestants, Jews and Catholics from London to Vienna* (Princeton, NJ: Princeton University Press, 2008), 14–15, 167–213; cf. Sorkin, "Jews, the Enlightenment and Religious Toleration—Some Reflections," *Leo Baeck Institute Yearbook* 37 (1992): 3–16.

14. Ellenson, *After Emancipation*, 57–59.

15. Ruth Langer, *Cursing the Christians? A History of the Birkat HaMinim* (New York: Oxford University Press, 2012), 12, draws attention to the need for Jewish scholars to examine the effect that these problematic texts, many of which have been restored in the early twenty-first century (after having been omitted due to censorship), have had on the Jewish community. The present book aims to examine how a particular Jewish community grappled with these texts in light of the social and political pressures exerted upon it in a very tumultuous time.

16. William Kolbrener, *The Last Rabbi: Joseph Soloveitchik and Talmudic Tradition* (Bloomington: Indiana University Press, 2016), xi.

Chapter 1

1. Cited in Enzo Traverso, *The Jews and Germany: From the "Judeo-German Symbiosis" to the Memory of Auschwitz* (Lincoln: University of Nebraska Press, 1995), 6. (Traveso endorses Scholem's pessimistic assessment.)

2. Gershom Scholem, "Jews and Germans," *Commentary Magazine*, November 1966, available at *Commentary*'s website.

3. Meir Simha of Dvinsk, *Meshekh Hokhmah* [to Leviticus 26:44] (Riga: Even Yisrael, 1927, 244–45). On page 245, Rabbi Meir Simha specifically refers to those who consider Berlin as the replacement for Jerusalem. Interestingly, Rabbi Hyle Wechsler (1843–94), a German Orthodox rabbi with whom Hirsch corresponded, likewise had a pessimistic prognosis concerning the future of Jews in Germany. However, unlike the views of Rabbi Meir Simcha, Wechsler's views remained largely obscure. See M. P. E. Wechsler, *Ein Wort der Mahnung an Israel*, ed. Rivka Horwitz (Jerusalem: Dinur Center, 1991).

4. See David Biale's biography of Scholem, *Gershom Scholem: Master of the Kabbalah* (New Haven: Yale University Press, 2018), esp. 156–79.

5. The *Sonderweg* thesis posits that Germany, unique among European states, developed an advanced economy without concomitant advances in its system of government. Retaining authoritarian rule even as it advanced in the technological and economic spheres retarded Germany's maturation into a society in which democracy could flourish. This argument is used to explain the ease with which Germany morphed into a brutal fascist state under the Nazis that utilized its technological and military prowess to carry out the largest-scale genocide in human history. This thesis has been hotly debated since it was first advanced after World War II. See, for example, Jürgen Kocka, "German History before Hitler: The Debate about the German *Sonderweg*," *Journal of Contemporary History* 23, no. 1 (January 1988): 3–16, and the literature cited there.

6. George Y. Kohler, "Manuel Joel in Defense of the Talmud: Liberal Responses to Religious Antisemitism in Nineteenth-Century Germany," *Hebrew Union College Annual* 79 (2008): 141–63. As evidence of the charge being as old as the Talmud itself, Kohler cites the narrative in the Jerusalem Talmud (*Baba Kamma* 19b), in which Roman officials were unhappy with a case of anti-gentile discrimination found in early rabbinic law. One may add the parallel narrative in the Babylonian Talmud (*Baba Kamma* 38a).

7. Samson Raphael Hirsch, *The Collected Writings*, vol. 9, *Timeless Hashkafah* (New York: Feldheim, 2012), 137–52.

8. Mordechai Breuer, *Modernity within Tradition*, trans. E. Petuchowski (New York: Columbia University Press, 1992), 47–48, 290–91.

9. Marion Kaplan, ed., *Jewish Daily Life in Germany, 1618–1945* (New York: Oxford University Press, 2005); Kaplan, *The Making of the Jewish Middle Class: Women, Family, and Identity in Imperial Germany* (New York: Oxford University Press, 1991). Kaplan does not make the assertion presented here. However, these classic studies prioritize that which can be gleaned from everyday routines over ideological pronouncements from the elite religious leadership.

10. For a thorough treatment of Hirsch's activities during this period, see Michael L. Miller, *Rabbis and Revolution: The Jews of Moravia in the Age of Emancipation* (Stanford: Stanford University Press, 2011), 138–320.

11. A possible rival would be Hirsch's Italian contemporary Rabbi Elijah Benamozegh (1823–1900). Benamozegh's writings were, however, not nearly as influential as Hirsch's, and his most universalistic text, *Israël et l'humanité*, was published posthumously, by a non-Jewish disciple, Aimé Pallière, in Paris in 1914. For a more recent study of Benamozegh's religious universalism, see Clemence Boulouque, *Another Modernity: Elia Benamozegh's Jewish Universalism* (Stanford, CA: Stanford University Press, 2020). A more recent rival is Rabbi Jonathan Sacks (1948–2020). Neither Benamozegh nor Sacks wielded much influence in Haredi Orthodox circles, while Hirsch, in a variety of ways, still does.

Chapter 2

1. Halacha is used here to refer to the corpus of Jewish law, presented in a theoretical framework in the Talmud, and codified as binding norms for observant Jews in the classic medieval Codes of Jewish law, particularly Maimonides's *Mishneh Torah* and Rabbi Joseph Karo's and Rabbi Moses Isserelis's *Shulhan Arukh*.

2. David Berger, *Persecution, Polemic, and Dialogue: Essays in Jewish-Christian Relations* (Boston: Academic Studies Press, 2010), 381–82. For an insightful discussion of this issue in the context of Maimonides's views, see Dror Fixler and Gil Nadel, "Are Contemporary Christians Worshippers of Avodah Zarah?" *Tehumin* 22 (2002): 68–78 (in Hebrew). Another discussion that reorients the focus of Maimonides's position regarding the status of Christianity is David Novak, "Maimonides' Treatment of Christianity and Its Normative Implications," in *Jewish Theology and World Religions*, ed. Alon Goshen-Gottstein and Eugene Korn (Oxford: Littman Library, 2012), 217–33. For further perspectives on the philosophical and theological issues with AZ, see Moshe Halbertal and Avishai Margalit, *Idolatry*, trans. Naomi Goldblum (Cambridge, MA: Harvard University Press, 1992).

3. Maimonides, *Mishneh Torah*, Laws of Idolatry 9:4 and Laws of Forbidden Foods 11:5; Maimonides, *Perush ha-Mishnayot*, Tractate Avodah Zarah 1:1. All these references can only be found in uncensored editions of Maimonides's works, such as the Shabbetai Frankel edition of *Mishneh Torah* (New York: n. p., 1975) and the Yosef Qafih translation of the *Perush ha-Mishnayot* (Jerusalem: Mossad haRav Kook, 1968). For background on the views of medieval halachists concerning Christianity, see Jacob Katz, *Exclusiveness and Tolerance* (New York: Behrman House, 1961), 24–36. For a recent collection by a halachist of medieval authorities who considered Christianity to be AZ, see Yehuda Herzl Henkin, *Shu"t Bnei Banim*, vol. 3 (Jerusalem: n. p., 1997), 116–23. Many of the sources have been collected in the notes to *Hiddushe ha-Ritva al Massekhet Avodah Zarah*, ed. Moshe Goldstein (Jerusalem: Mossah HaRav Kook, 1978), 15–16n147.

4. See Israel Jacob Yuval, *Two Nations in Your Womb: Perceptions of Jews and Christians in Late Antiquity and the Middle Ages*, trans. Barbara Harshav and Jonathan Chipman (Berkeley: University of California Press, 2008), 92–134.

5. On Meiri, see Katz, *Exclusiveness and Tolerance*, 114–28; Gerald Blidstein, "Menahem Meiri's Attitude toward Gentiles—Apologetics or Worldview?" in *Binah 3: Jewish Intellectual History in the Middle Ages*, ed. Joseph Dan (Westport, CT: Praeger, 1994), 119–33; Gary Remer, "Ha-Me'iri's Theory of Religious Toleration," in *Beyond the Persecuting Society: Religious Toleration Before the Enlightenment*, ed. John Christian Laursen and Cary J. Nederman (Philadelphia: University of Pennsylvania Press, 1998), 71–91; Moshe Halbertal, *Between Torah and Wisdom: Rabbi Menahem ha-Meiri and the Maimonidean Halakhists in Provence* (Jerusalem: Magnes Press, 2000), 80–108 (in Hebrew). For an excellent analysis of Meiri that convincingly integrates his philosophical views and their historical context with his views of non-Jews, see Gregg Stern, *Philosophy and Rabbinic Culture: Jewish Interpretation and Controversy in Medieval Languedoc* (Abingdon, UK: Routledge, 2009), particularly 85–93. Another examination of Meiri's views that takes personal considerations into account is Yaakov Elman, "Meiri and the Non-Jew: A Comparative Investigation," in *New Perspectives on Jewish-Christian Relations in Honor of David Berger*, ed. Elisheva Carlebach and Jacob J. Schacter (Leiden: Brill, 2012), 265–96.

6. Katz, *Exclusiveness and Tolerance*, 35–36. Cf., however, J. David Bleich, *The Philosophical Quest: Of Philosophy, Ethics, Law and Halakhah* (Jerusalem: Koren, 2013), 36–40.

7. Tosafot to Sanhedrin 63b s.v. *Asur*; Tosafot to *Bekhorot* 2b s.v. *Shema*. It is not certain which Tosafist was the original author of this statement. See Katz, *Exclusiveness and Tolerance*, 35. The view of Shalom Albeck, as cited in Katz, *Exclusiveness and Tolerance*, 35n2, is that the author of this Tosafist passage is Rabbenu Yitzhak, the nephew of Rabbenu Tam. "Later repeated by Rabbenu Asher": Rabbenu Asher to Tractate Sanhedrin, chapter 7, note 3; "and Rabbenu Yeruham": Rabbenu Yeruham ben Meshulam, *Sefer Toldot Adam ve-Havvah* (Venice, 1553), 17:5.

8. The term used is *aherim*, which is often used in rabbinic literature to refer to non-Jews, such as in Mishnah *Bekhorot* 1:1 and Babylonian Talmud *Pesahim* 5b. However, it is not necessary to read the text of the Tosafists in that manner; it may simply mean others, whoever they may be. "Not placing a stumbling block before the blind": Leviticus 19:14, interpreted by the Babylonian Talmud, *Pesahim* 22b, to refer to causing others to sin.

9. Hereon, *shittuf* will be used to refer to the association of God with an entity not regarded by Jews as God. Specifically, shittuf will refer to the Christian worship of Jesus as the Son of God, which is precisely how this term has been—and still is—used by halachists.

10. Babylonian Talmud, *Sanhedrin* 56a–b. See David Novak, *The Image of the Non-Jew in Judaism*, 2nd ed. (Oxford: Littman Library, 2011), 11–35, for a discussion of the period during which these laws emerged as a rabbinic norm. It should be noted that Novak's historical investigation, modeled as it is on Wissenschaft methodology, would have been meaningless to the medieval and early modern rabbis under discussion, who were traditionalists and considered the Noahide Laws to be part of the divinely revealed Oral Law. The Noahide Laws were considered to have preceded the Sinaitic revelation by many centuries, as it was regarded as the norm for mankind *prior* to the giving of the Torah. On this point, see Suzanne Last Stone, "Sinaitic and Noahide Law: Legal Pluralism in Jewish Law," *Cardozo Law Review* 12 (1990–91), 1166–71.

11. Responsa *Noda bi-Yehudah, Tinyana, Yorah Deah* (Vilna, n.d.), no. 148, p. 93. (*Beraita* refers to a rabbinic text from the Mishnaic period that was not included in the Mishnah. Such texts are often cited in the Talmud, and they are generally regarded as authoritative.) Alan Brill (*Judaism and Other Religions: Models of Understanding* [New York: Palgrave Macmillan, 2010], 189–91), cites this passage as evidence that Rabbi Samuel Landau abandoned the tolerant view of Christianity that his father, Rabbi Yehezkel, championed (a point to be discussed later in this chapter). However, this claim does not seem warranted since nowhere does Rabbi Yehezkel state that Christianity is not considered to be, in a halachic sense, AZ, and nowhere does Rabbi Samuel deny his father's assertion that Christians share with Jews many fundamentals of religion, such as creation of the world, prophecy, etc. Rather, Rabbi Samuel simply does not agree with the view that Trinitarian worship is forbidden for Jews and yet permissible for non-Jews. Thus, father and son may have been in complete agreement. There seems to be no basis for Yosef Salmon's assertion that Rabbi Yehezkel's comments about Christianity's acceptance of many fundamentals of religion "is undoubtedly an extension of an accepted halakhic principle," namely, that shittuf is permissible for gentiles and that Christianity is not to be considered a form of AZ. See Yosef Salmon, "Christians and Christianity in Halachic Literature from the End of the Eighteenth Century to the Middle of the Nineteenth Century," *Modern Judaism* 33, no. 2 (May 2013): 129.

12. The question of the degree to which halachists are guided more by the social implications of their rulings than by the texts they are analyzing is an old one. David Ellenson has consistently advocated the former view and his approach is formulated most recently in David Ellenson and Daniel Gordis, *Pledges of Jewish Allegiance: Conversion, Law, and Policymaking in Nineteenth- and Twentieth-Century Orthodox Responsa* (Stanford, CA: University of Stanford Press, 2012), 102: "Halakhic decision-making, as observed elsewhere, is as much a matter of social policymaking as it is jurisprudential analysis." Marc B. Shapiro, "Review Essay: Sociology and Halakhah," *Tradition* 27, no. 1 (Fall 1992): 77–79, has questioned Ellenson's position (expressed earlier), though he too believes that there are "meta-halakhic considerations" at the heart of a *posek*'s analysis. See Shapiro, *Between the Yeshiva World and Modern Orthodoxy* (Oxford: Littman Library, 1999), 205–21. It is not my intention here to take the side of either view, though

it should be noted that Orthodoxy regards the second position as more reflective of its own methodology.

13. Katz, *Exclusiveness and Tolerance*, 166, suggests that the climate of "non-Jewish religious tolerance" (i.e., the emergence of theories of religious tolerance between Christian denominations in the aftermath of the Protestant Reformation and the ensuing religious wars) impacted these halachists no less than it influenced the maskilim. Although this may be an exaggeration, the essential point seems to be correct. Katz discusses the economic considerations in *Exclusiveness and Tolerance*, 24–36. For a more recent overview of the changing positions of halachists regarding Christianity, see Eugene Korn, "Rethinking Christianity: Rabbinic Positions and Possibilities," in Goshen-Gottstein and Korn, *Jewish Theology and World Religions*, 189–216.

14. Although Isserles was the first—and most authoritative—halachist to rule that worship of shittuf in the manner of Christians was permissible, he does not state this explicitly, as will be discussed later in this chapter. "Samuel comments:" Samuel ben Joseph, *Olat Tamid* to *Shulhan Arukh Orah Hayyim* 156 (Jerusalem: n. p., 2003), note 3. It is interesting to note that despite the tremendous controversy engendered by Samuel's interpretation of Isserles's ruling, his book received numerous approbations from the leading rabbis of both Cracow and Amsterdam prior to its publication. See the same work, introduction by the editors, 27–29. It is noteworthy that one of the rabbis who wrote an approbation was Jacob Sasportas, the famed anti-Sabbatian fighter, who writes in his *Kitzur Tzitzat Novel Tzvi* (Altona, 1757), 25b, that "even non-Jews are forbidden in shittuf." Despite his disagreement with Samuel ben Joseph on this matter (assuming that he had read the latter's comments relating to shittuf in his book, which is indeterminable), he emphasized in his approbation that "the rabbis, geonim, and sages who have signed their names in this place [the approbation to *Olat Tamid*] have not done so in a hyperbolic manner as is the case in other places" but instead genuinely recognize the greatness of Samuel's book. Cited in *Olat Tamid*, introduction by the editors, 29.

15. "Ignorance of classical Christian doctrine:" Cf. Elijah J. Schochet, *Rabbi Joel Sirkes: His Life, Works and Times* (New York: Feldheim, 1971), 124. "Heirs to paradise": As Eugene Korn, "Gentiles, the World to Come, and Judaism: The Odyssey of a Rabbinic Text," *Modern Judaism* 14 (1994): 265–87, has argued, many of the rabbinic discussions regarding which gentiles would merit a portion in paradise were forums for value judgments regarding the value of gentiles' moral lives and culture in *this* world. If their religions were deemed to be in consonance with the Noahide Laws, this meant not only that the religion's adherents were worthy of an afterlife but that their lives in this world were meaningful and salvific.

16. Yair Hayyim Bacharach, *Havot Yair* (Frankfurt am Main, 1699), no. 185; see also *Havot Yair*, no. 1 *hasagot* 11–12.

17. This clause is taken from Psalms 79:6.

18. Eliezer Ashkenazi, *Ma'asei Hashem* (Warsaw, 1871), part 2, 36b–37a.

19. David Zvi Hoffmann, *Der Schulchan Aruch und die Rabbinen über das Verhältnis der Juden zu Andersgläubigen*, 2nd ed. (Berlin, 1894), 135–37n3.

20. *Shulhan Arukh*, *Orah Hayyim* 156, glosses of Rema (end). The mere fact that Rema chose the text of Rabbi Yeruham does not prove what his position on Trinitarian worship would be since Rema, lacking the antecedent found in the text of the Tosafists,

had no choice but to end his statement with an explicit reference to shittuf. It is Rema's position on the selling of incense that is revealing.

21. Rabbi Moses Isserles, *Darkhei Moshe* to *Tur*, *Yoreh Deah* 151.

22. Shakh to *Shulhan Arukh*, *Yoreh Deah* 151n7. Ironically, this note has been truncated in some editions by censors, who were apparently unaware that Shakh was expressing a tolerant view of Christianity with this statement. (Shakh's full comment can be found in the Jerusalem: Vagshal, 2007, edition of the *Shulhan Arukh*.)

23. *Pithei Teshuvah* to *Shulhan Arukh*, *Yoreh Deah* 147n2. (The author of this commentary was Rabbi Avraham Zvi Eisenstadt [1813–1868], rabbi of Grodno and, later, of Kovno.)

24. Cf. Katz, *Exclusiveness and Tolerance*, 125, 168, and 191–94, esp. 191n6.

25. For an elaboration of the argument for Christian spiritual value on the basis of these texts, see especially the comments of Rabbi Marcus Horovitz, *Shu"t Mateh Levi* (Jerusalem: n. p., 1979), *Yoreh Deah* no. 28, who argues, on the basis on Rema's ruling, that pious Christians are "pillars of the world." Horovitz's views are examined in this book's chapter 10.

26. Yonah Emanuel, "In the Footsteps of Torah Giants in Germany," in *Rabbi Samson Raphael Hirsch: His Teaching and Method*, ed. Yonah Emmanuel (Jerusalem: Feldheim, 1962), 144–79 (in Hebrew).

27. See also Azriel Shohat, *In Changing Times: Beginnings of the Haskalah among German Jewry* (Jerusalem: Mosad Bialik, 1960), 67–71 (in Hebrew), for additional citations of German rabbis of the first half of the eighteenth century who espoused a tolerant view of Christianity and who viewed their Christian neighbors as among the "righteous of the nations." Hirsch was undoubtedly familiar with the statements of these rabbis as well.

28. See, for example, the sources cited in Yuval, *Two Nations*. See also Elliot Horowitz, *Reckless Rites: Purim and the Legacy of Jewish Violence* (Princeton, NJ: Princeton University Press, 2006), 157–81.

29. Jacob Katz has termed the period from the sixteenth century to the mid-eighteenth century the "Late Middle Ages" of Jewish history. More recent scholarship, especially David Ruderman's *Early Modern Jewry* (Princeton, NJ: Princeton University Press, 2010), has argued for a reevaluation of this period, which is now commonly regarded as the early modern period in Jewish history. A central thesis of this book is that the mindset of rabbis living during this period with respect to gentiles evinced a mentality that was more modern than medieval. However, it was not until the Jewish Enlightenment of the eighteenth century that the rabbinic view of non-Jews changed dramatically, even among traditionalist rabbis who opposed that movement.

30. See Moshe Miller, "R. Jacob Emden's Attitude toward Christianity," in *Turim: Studies in Jewish History and Literature Presented to Dr. Bernard Lander*, vol. 2 (New York: Touro College Press, 2008), 105–36; and Jacob J. Schacter, "Rabbi Jacob Emden, Sabbatianism, and Frankism: Attitudes toward Christianity in the Eighteenth Century," in Carlebach and Schacter, *New Perspectives*, 393–96.

31. Jacob Emden, *Megilat Sefer* (Kolome, 1886), 185–86.

32. Jonathan Eyebeschutz, *Kereti u-Peleti* (Jerusalem: n. p., 2004), introduction by Eyebeschutz's son.

33. Menahem Meiri, *Beit ha-Behirah al Masekhet Avodah Zarah*, ed. Avraham Sofer

(Jerusalem: Kedem, 1964), 4, 9. For a possible historical precedent for Meiri's seemingly farfetched interpretation, see Lawrence Zalcman, "Christians, Noserim, and Nebuchadnezzar's Daughter," *Jewish Quarterly Review*, n. s., 81, nos. 3–4 (January–April 1991): 411–26.

34. Yosef ben Yaakov Yitzhak, *Sefer Mishnat Hakhamim*, *Hilkhot Yesodei ha-Torah*, end of Prohibition no. 1 (Lemberg, 1827), no pagination.

35. These citations from Berlin are quoted by Emanuel, "In the Footsteps," 148–49.

36. Wolf Boskowitz, *Seder Mishnah*, Hil. Yesodei ha-Torah 1:7 (2b–3b) (Prague, 1820); Boskowitz, *Sefer Shoshan Edut* (Pax, 1903), 188a–189a.

37. "Who forbid Trinitarian worship:" Rabbi Kolin does not merely state that shittuf as an act of worship is forbidden for gentiles but explicitly refers to the "believers in the Trinity [*ma'aminei ha-shilush*] or even those who believe in two deities and say that one is above the other" as engaged in a forbidden act, thereby rejecting the view of *Olat Tamid*. By contrast, his son explicitly refers to "the nations of our time who recognize God's divinity but they [also] associate [other beings with God], and this is not forbidden for them." Boskowitz, *Sefer Shoshan Edut*, 188a. "In cases of making an oath": *Mahazit ha-Shekel* to *Shulhan Arukh* Orah Hayyim 156, note beginning with "*yithayev*."

38. Jacob Zvi Mecklenburg, *Ha-Ketav ve-Hakabbalah*, vol. 2, Deuteronomy (Berlin, 1880), 7–9 (commenting on Deuteronomy 4:19).

39. Mecklenburg, *Ha-Ketav ve-Hakabbalah*, 9.

40. *Hesronot ha-Shas* (Cracow, n.d.), unpaginated section s.v. *haskamat*.

41. Edward Breuer, "Between Haskalah and Orthodoxy: The Writings of R. Jacob Zvi Mecklenburg," *Hebrew Union College Annual* 66 (1995): 259–87, has argued that Mecklenburg ought to be considered a traditionalist rabbi who was influenced by the Haskalah. Breuer wishes to refocus attention on the connection between the Haskalah of the eighteenth century and the Neo-Orthodox movement of the nineteenth century, and he sees Mecklenburg as a connecting figure. My assessment of Mecklenburg as a figure who cannot be accounted among the Neo-Orthodox but who nevertheless incorporated an enlightened approach toward gentiles into his worldview is therefore, fundamentally, in agreement with Breuer's. It would have been highly unlikely for S. R. Hirsch to have written such an endorsement of *Hesronot ha-Shas*, a book containing texts that would have offended the sensibilities of his Christian contemporaries. It is due to the absence of these concerns on the part of Mecklenburg that I have classified him this way.

42. Moses Mendelssohn, *Gesammelte Schriften Jubiläumsausgabe* Band 16, *Biur* to Exodus 20:2 (Stuttgart: n. p., 1971), 186–87. Part of this passage is cited in Zvi Kaplan, "Mendelssohn's Religious Perspective of Non-Jews," *Journal of Ecumenical Studies* 41, nos. 3–4 (Summer–Fall 2004): 363. Thus, Kaplan's assertion in that same article, that Mendelssohn "twisted the Tosafot so as to make it conform to his own rationalistic and universalistic ideology," is questionable. In fact, the seventeenth-century author of *Olat Tamid* had already asserted that the correct meaning of Tosafot was that non-Jews are permitted to worship beings beside God so long as they recognize that such beings are under God's dominion. Mendelssohn thus had ample halachic precedent for this particular argument, if not for the rationalistic tone that underlies it. His rabbinic contemporary, Rabbi Jacob Emden (whom Mendelssohn characterized as his *rebbi* [rabbinic mentor]), concurred with *Olat Tamid* and, thus, with Mendelssohn's basic position.

43. Mecklenburg, *Ha-Ketav ve-HaKabbalah* to Leviticus 19:18. This view was also expressed by Rabbi Phineas Elijah of Vilna (d. 1821) in his *Sefer ha-Berit* (Jerusalem, 1990), 2:13, 13:5; apparently by Malbim (to be examined later) in his commentary to Leviticus 19:18; Rabbi David Zvi Hoffmann, *Das Buch Leviticus, übersetzt und erklärt von D. Hoffmann* (Berlin: n. p., 1905–6), 19:18 (footnote); and by Rabbi Barukh Halevi Epstein, *Barukh She'amar Pirkei Avot* (Tel Aviv: Am Olam, 1969), 121–23. These were not the only rabbis to express this view. Rabbi Naphtali Herz Wessely expressed the same view, both in his commentary to the verse in Leviticus (in Mendelssohn's *Biur*, Leviticus 19:18) and in his commentary to Tractate Avot, *Yeyn Levanon* (Berlin, 1755), 48b–49b. See this book's chapter 8, for Wessely's reputation among rabbinic scholars.

44. Bruriah Hutner-David, "The Dual Role of Rabbi Zvi Hirsch Chajes: Traditionalist and *Maskil*" (PhD diss., Columbia University, 1971). Most of the evidence that Hutner-David marshals in support of her thesis actually serves to prove that Chajes sided with the leaders of rabbinic Judaism on most major points of contention and only adopted maskilic positions in a very limited sense.

45. Ephraim Chamiel, *The Middle Way: The Emergence of Modern Religious Trends: Responses to Modernity in the Thought of Maharatz Chayot, Rabbi S. R. Hirsch, and S. D. Luzzatto* (Boston: Academic Studies Press, 2014), vol. 1, 34–40.

46. Zvi Hirsch Chajes, *Glosses to the Talmud, Yevamot* 61a. This passage as well as others relating to non-Jews is discussed in Hutner-David, "Dual Role," 64–71.

47. "To be classified as *gerei toshav*": A *Ger Toshav* is a non-Jew who has formally accepted to observe Noahide Law. (See Talmud *Avodah Zarah* 64b–65a). Such an individual is not subject to most of the legal discrimination to which other non-Jews are subject. For excellent analysis, see Yaakov Blidstein, *Studies in Halakhic and Aggadic Thought* (Beer-Sheva: Ben Gurion University Press, 2004), 155–63, 365–78 (in Hebrew). "Observe the other six Noahide Commandments": Zvi Hirsch Chajes, *Kol Sifrei Maharatz Chayot*, vol. 1 (Jerusalem: Divrei Chachamim, 1958), 489–90.

48. Chajes, *Kol Sifrei Maharatz Chayot*, vol. 2, 1032–36.

49. This did not stop the contemporary halachist Rabbi Nahum Rabinovitch (1928–2020) from arguing, based on Chajes's earlier statement (though making reference to the later statement), that Christians today have the halachic status of *gerei toshav*. See his *Melummedei Milhamah* (Ma'aleh Adumim: Maaliyot, 1993), 145. For a somewhat modified later formulation, see his *Shu"t Siah Nahum* (Ma'aleh Adumim: Maaliyot, 2008), 319–20. (Even the later formulation cites Chajes's earlier statement, among several other rabbinic sources, as a basis for the ruling he issues.)

50. Chajes, *Kol Sifrei Maharatz Chayos*, vol. 2, 607–8. Chajes asserts that the view that he propounded was shared by the "masters of Torah" (*sarei ha-Torah*) (in the same volume, 608).

51. Israel Lipschutz, *Tiferet Yisrael* to *Avot* 3:14, *Boaz*, note 1.

52. Lipschutz's Mishnah commentary was first printed in 1839.

53. Note that even Chajes, Lipschutz's contemporary, did not draw the conclusion that non-Jews are in any respect superior to Jews on the basis of this passage; he merely denied that any inference that they are inferior could legitimately be deduced from it.

54. Noteworthy is the fact that Lipschutz mentions four such individuals by name and that three of them—Jenner, Drake, and Gutenberg—are cited due to their contributions

to the welfare of the world at large and not necessarily Jews. This was noted by Rabbi Yitzchak Blau. See David Shatz, "Morality, Liberalism, and Interfaith Dialogue," in Carlebach and Schacter, *New Perspectives*, 496n17.

55. For Mendelssohn's views, see his letter to Jacob Emden in *Moses Mendelssohn: Writings on Judaism, Christianity, and the Bible*, ed. Michah Gottlieb (Waltham, MA: Brandeis University Press, 2011), 31–35. Mendelssohn reiterated his position in various contexts. For this assertion made to Lavater, who had effectively challenged Mendelssohn to convert to Christianity in order to save his soul, see Gottlieb, *Moses Mendelssohn*, 6–15.

56. Israel Lipschutz, *Tiferet Yisrael* to Avot 3:17, *Yakhin*, note 114.

57. Brill, *Judaism and Other Religions*, 114, extends Lipschutz's religious tolerance to Hinduism. I am not so sure that there is a basis for Lipschutz's words to be extended to polytheistic non-Abrahamic faiths such as Hinduism (although there are varying views as to the degree to which Hinduism does affirm a form of monotheism), since he makes it clear that "every nation" must believe the Torah is divine and may disagree only over the details (e.g., the Qur'an is also divine or the New Testament annulled the legal portions of the Torah). The monotheistic, but non-Abrahamitic, Sikh faith might also qualify for inclusion in Lipschutz's schema since it affirms that there are different paths to salvation for different peoples but neither affirms nor denies the authenticity of the Jewish claim that the Torah was divinely revealed. Ultimately, since Lipschutz was not familiar with the Sikh faith, it is difficult to determine what he would have thought of it, though his overall approach to other religions suggests that he would have been quite approving of Sikhism.

58. Haym Soloveitchik, "The 'Beit ha-Behirah' of R. Menahem ha-Meiri and Its Fate," in *Asufah le-Yosef*, ed. Y. Ben-Naehet al. (Jerusalem: Zalman Shazar Center, 2014), 253–59 (in Hebrew), suggests several possible reasons for the relative obscurity of Meiri's Talmud commentary prior to the twentieth century.

59. Jacob Katz, "Three Apologetic Statements and Their Development," *Zion* 23–24, nos. 3–4 (1958–9): 189–90 (notes 92 and 96) (in Hebrew); A. M. Habermann, "Declarations of Authors or Publishers in Their Books to Legitimize Them in the Eyes of Gentiles," in *Essays and Studies in Librarianship Presented to Curt David Wormann on His Seventy-Fifth Birthday* (Jerusalem: Magnes Press, 1975), 60–71 (in Hebrew). Habermann states that the first book with such a disclaimer was *Or E'nayim*, published in 1557 in Cremona, Italy.

60. The term *kutim*, which literally refers to the Samaritans, was sometimes used as a smokescreen when discussing gentiles in rabbinic writings, including in some editions of the Talmud.

61. Maimonides, *The Guide of the Perplexed*, trans. Michael Friedlander (New York: Hebrew Publishing, 1904), 3:29, 3:45, 3:46. The question of the historicity of the Sabians is a subject of scholarly debate. See Jonathan M. Elukin, "Maimonides and the Rise and Fall of the Sabians: Explaining Mosaic Laws and the Limits of Scholarship," *Journal of the History of Ideas* 63, no. 4 (2002): 619–37.

62. Ezekiel Landau, *Shu"t Noda bi-Yehudah* (Prague, 1776), unpaginated introduction titled "*hitnazlut*." Salmon, "Christians and Christianity in Halachic Literature," 129, concludes based on these comments that Rabbi Yehezkel Landau did not consider

Christianity to be AZ, a contention contested previously (note 11 of this chapter). On 143n30, referring to another passage in Landau's writings that refers favorably to Christians, Salmon states that "it should be pointed out that these statements were published under the supervision of the censor who requested that the publisher emphasize that the intent of the text," when referring to non-Jews, was not to Christians. Salmon does not draw any conclusions about the sincerity of Landau's remarks given the context in which they were written. (Yet, perplexingly, Salmon later refers to a different rabbi who had written positively about Christianity and notes that "his statements relating to Christianity . . . are not designed to satisfy the censor," but with the caveat that although "the text was prepared with the oversight of the censor," the comments exceeded the censor's demands. Salmon, "Christians and Christianity in Halachic Literature," 130, 143n40.) My purpose here is precisely to assess the sincerity of these types of comments.

63. Mordechai Breuer was certain of their sincerity, as he writes in "The Jewish Minority in the Enlightened Absolutist State," *German-Jewish History in Modern Times*, vol. 1, ed. Michael A. Meyer (New York: Columbia University Press, 1996), 161, that the policy of writing these prefaces "was not only a stratagem to preempt interference by state and Church censors but was often the result of honest conviction." Still, the insertion of "was often" suggests that Breuer believed there may have been at least some cases in which such disclaimers were not the result of sincere conviction.

64. I could only find Rabbi Landau's "disclaimer" preface in earlier printings of his *Shu"t Noda B'Yehudah*. Newer editions have simply removed those remarks without even noting that anything has been removed. In my view, whatever these publishers think of these remarks, it is not proper to simply remove entire passages written by the revered rabbinic luminaries who wrote them merely based on a suspicion of their insincerity. At the absolute most, the editors can insert a footnote pointing out the context for the remarks. Better yet, they can leave the disclaimers as they were printed over the centuries without the need for any editorial emendations. I consider these remarks just as sincere as, say, anti-gentile remarks written by rabbis who survived the Holocaust. When books with such remarks are published today, the editors do not feel the need to write footnotes placing the anti-gentile animus into context—and they certainly do not simply expunge these remarks.

65. Eleazar Fleckeles, *Teshuvah me-Ahavah*, 3 vols. (Prague, 1809–21).

66. Eleazar Fleckeles, essay titled "Kesut Enayim" printed at the beginning of *Teshuvah me-Ahavah* (no pagination).

67. Fleckeles, "Kesut Enayim" (last page).

68. Habermann, "Declarations," cites several such pro forma disclaimers, such as one printed at the beginning of the book *Ma'aseh Rokeah*, printed in Venice in 1742, which states, "Know my son that in any place in this book where the term *akum* appears, the reference is to those who worship stars and constellations." The beginning of the book *Maginei Eretz*, published in Amsterdam in 1754, featured the following statement: "[To] the reader: if you find in this book the words *goy*, *nokhri*, or *akum*, it does not refer to the Christian nation amongst whom we dwell and by whose shade we are protected, perish the thought. Rather it refers to the ancient nation of *Notserim* which bowed to the sun, stars and constellations, and the terms *goy*, *nokhri*, and *akum* refer to them."

69. See arguments for Fleckles's sincerity in Shmuel Lesher, "Rabbi Elazar Fleckles: An Early Rabbinic Humanist," *Tradition* 54, no. 2 (Spring 2022): 133–49.

70. Samson Raphael Hirsch, *The Collected Writings of Rabbi Samson Raphael Hirsch*, ed. and trans. Paul Forcheimer and Gertrude Hirschler, vol. 7 (New York: Feldheim, 1992), 226–28; Hirsch, *Judaism Eternal: Selected Essays from the Writings of Rabbi Samson Raphael Hirsch*, ed. and trans. I. Grunfeld (London: Soncino Press, 1956), vol. 2, 169–70. (The latter is a more truncated translation of Hirsch's essay, originally published as *Über die Beziehung des Talmuds zum Judenthum und zu der sozialen Stellung seiner Bekenner* [Frankfurt am Main, 1884]. The passage in question is on 19–21.) To be sure, Hirsch wrote this essay for the purpose of combating anti-Semitism, specifically anti-Talmudic sentiments that surfaced in Russia in the 1880s, which threatened to lead to the cessation of the printing of the Talmud and the closing down of Talmudic academies. Hirsch was enlisted to write this essay at the behest of Rabbi Isaac E. Spektor (1817–96), the leading authority of East European non-Hasidic Jewry. Despite this fact, as with everything else that Hirsch wrote, there can be little doubt as to its sincerity. I intend to explore this important essay by Hirsch in a future monograph that contextualizes it within the framework of late nineteenth-century attacks on the Talmud and Jewish responses.

71. Wessely, *Yeyn Levanon*, final page (unpaginated), last paragraph.

72. Indeed, there are certain passages in *Yeyn Levanon* where Wessely cites rabbinic passages that comment unfavorably on *Akum* when compared to the Jewish people (see, e.g., pp. 6a–b). Since Wessely elaborates on those comments, but neither repudiates them nor states that they are inapplicable in contemporary times, he may have felt it necessary to clarify for the record that these comments do, in fact, refer solely to ancient pagans but not to Christians.

73. One conspicuous example of this approach comes from Rabbi Jacob Joshua Falk, at the end of his book *P'nei Yehoshua al Masekhet Bava Metzia* (Frankfurt, 1756), 70b, where he states, "It is known the world over that all books and publications, such as the books of the Talmud and Codes and other similar books, where the term *akum* or the like is used, in all cases the sole intention is to those nations which used to worship stars and constellations, but those nations under whose shade we dwell, are not in this category." Rabbi Falk then goes on to discuss the severity of the prohibition of dishonesty toward gentiles and the obligation to pray for the welfare of the government. He notes that he has consistently emphasized these points in his public sermons. His formulation appears to go out of its way not to state anything positive about Christians or their religious beliefs but merely to exclude them from derogatory statements about gentiles and to forbid misconduct toward them. Thus, no conclusions about Falk's halachic evaluation of Christianity may be derived from here. This evaluation of Falk's position is rendered all the more compelling when one notes that the title page of his book expressly states that it was printed with "the permission of the great scholar, the master, Prof. Megarlin," presumably a government censor. (See this book's chapter 10 for Rabbi Marcus Horovitz's assessment of these comments of Rabbi Falk.)

Chapter 3

1. The views of nineteenth-century Italian rabbinic leaders and scholars, such as Samuel David Luzzatto, Rabbi Elijah Benamozegh, and Rabbi Yisrael Moshe Hazzan,

are significant. They treated the issues examined in this book in their writings. (See, especially, Rabbi Hazzan's responsum concerning church music, which treats the place of Christianity in the Jewish schema, in his *Krakh shel Romi* [Livorno, 1876], no. 1, 1a–6a.) Since the intellectual history of Italian Jewry differs so markedly from the rest of European Jewry, it is more properly treated separately, which I hope to do in the future.

2. See Michael K. Silber, "The Emergence of Ultra-Orthodoxy: The Invention of a Tradition," in *The Uses of Tradition*, ed. Jack Wertheimer (New York: Jewish Theological Seminary, 1992), 23–84, for a presentation of this view. More recent scholarship has not significantly challenged Silber's position. See, however, Moshe Y. Miller, "Between Frankfurt and Satmar: A Study of Two Schools of Orthodox Jewish Anti-Zionism" (MA thesis, Touro College, 2006), for several problems with this supposed dichotomy between the Orthodoxy of Hirsch and that of the Hungarian followers of Sofer.

3. Jacob Katz, "Towards a Biography of the Hatam Sofer," trans. David Ellenson, in *Profiles in Diversity: Jews in a Changing Europe, 1750–1870*, ed. Frances Malino and David Sorkin (Detroit: Wayne State University Press, 1998), 223–66; Meir Hildesheimer, "The German Language and Secular Studies: Attitudes towards Them in the Thought of the Hatam Sofer and His Disciples," *Proceedings of the American Academy for Jewish Research* 62 (1996): 129–63; Aaron M. Schreiber, "The Hatam Sofer's Nuanced Attitude towards Secular Learning, *Maskilim* and Reformers," *Torah U-Madda Journal* 11 (2002–3), 123–73; Marc B. Shapiro, "Aspects of Rabbi Moses Sofer's Intellectual Profile," in *Be'erot Yitzhak: Studies in Memory of Isadore Twersky*, ed. Jay M. Harris (Cambridge, MA: Harvard University Press, 2005), 285–310. Schreiber's essay, which is a revisionist attempt to soften Sofer's reputation as a hardliner on the issues mentioned in the article's title, does not attempt to soften Sofer's attitude toward non-Jews; indeed, that issue is not discussed at all.

4. Jacob Katz, *Exclusiveness and Tolerance* (New York: Behrman House, 1961), 193–94.

5. Moses Sofer, *Sefer Hatam Sofer: Derashot u-Ma'amarim*, vol. 2, 500 (Jerusalem: n. P., 1959); the same work, vol. 1, 334.

6. The Talmud, *Avodah Zarah* 26a, records a view that one does not save the lives of worshippers of AZ, for doing so will lead to the proliferation of AZ. Meiri (*Beit ha-Bechirah*) maintains that this is not a prohibition but merely an assertion that Jews are not *required* to save the lives of worshippers of AZ. Other medieval authorities assumed it was a prohibition, and this is Sofer's view as well. This Talmudic statement refers to any day of the week, not specifically the Sabbath.

7. Moses Sofer, *Shu"t Hatam Sofer, Yoreh Deah* (Bratislava, 1851), no. 131. Rabbi Sofer is at pains to emphasize that the primary issue is not the violation of Sabbath per se but rather the very act of saving the life of a worshipper of AZ. "To multiply the seed of Amalek": This last clause was not invented by Sofer. It is recorded that Rabbenu Yonah (d. 1263) employed this expression as a criticism of Nahmanides (1194–1270) for serving as a doctor for gentile women and helping them with infertility issues. This "dialogue" is cited by *Bet Yosef* to *Tur*, *Yoreh Deah*, no. 154. What is relevant here is that Sofer applied this expression to his Christian contemporaries. A later Hungarian halachist (Rabbi Yehuda Aszod) objected to this assertion on humanitarian grounds. See also Sofer's astonishing remarks regarding slavery in Judaism (whose perpetuation

he supports) and how it relates to the propagation of gentiles in the world, in his *Torat Moshe*, vol. 3 (Pressburg, 1879), commentary to Leviticus 25:46, 61a. (It is interesting that many contemporary halachists cite only a statement found later in the previously cited responsum allowing the violation of the Sabbath to save a gentile life if refraining from doing so would lead to anti-Jewish animosity that could breed violence. See, for example, Rabbi Moses Feinstein, *Igrot Moshe Orah Hayyim*, vol. 4 [New York: Noble Book Press, 1982], no. 79, 158.)

8. *Haggahot Hatam Sofer* to *Shulhan Arukh*, *Orah Hayyim* 156.

9. Moses Sofer, *Kovets Teshuvot Hatam Sofer* (Jerusalem: n. p. 1973), no. 90.

10. Sofer, *Shu"t Hatam Sofer*, *Yoreh Deah*, no. 336. For a critique of these comments of Hatam Sofer, see Avi Sagi, *Judaism: Between Religion and Morality* (Tel Aviv: Hakibbutz Hameuchad, 1998), 173–75 (in Hebrew). It is worth noting here that Rabbi Jacob Emden, whom Katz considers a "tolerant traditionalist," explicitly forbids performing autopsies on gentile corpses, arguing that they are no different from Jewish corpses. For a translation of a portion of this responsum, see Moshe Miller, "R. Jacob Emden's Attitude toward Christianity," in *Turim: Studies in Jewish History and Literature Presented to Dr. Bernard Lander*, vol. 2 (New York: Touro College Press 2008), 118–19.

11. It must be emphasized that this attitude is expressed solely in terms of ideology and in refraining from positive action on behalf of non-Jews. No hostile behavior toward non-Jews is called for or defended by Sofer.

12. Samson Raphael Hirsch, *The Collected Writings of Rabbi Samuel Raphael Hirsch*, ed. and trans. Paul Forcheimer and Gertrude Hirschler, vol. 7 (New York: Feldheim, 1992), 311–13. Hirsch expressed his veneration of Hatam Sofer by calling him "the greatest among all the luminaries still in living memory today. This man was endowed with a clear view and a spirit of moderation (*mit dem milden Sinn*), a sharp mind, all-encompassing knowledge and straightforward judgment, a man before whose name . . . I . . . along with all other living rabbis, willingly bow their heads and whom we all recognize as an authority." Hirsch also calls Sofer the "*rabban shel kol bnei ha-golah*" (the teacher of all the Jews in the Diaspora) and "the greatest of all rabbinic authorities." These comments come after a lengthy discussion by Hirsch of how the standard salutations employed in rabbinic correspondence bear no relation to reality. Hirsch, *The Collected Writings of Rabbi Samson Raphael Hirsch*, ed. and trans. Paul Forcheimer and Gertrude Hirschler, vol. 6 (New York: Feldheim, 1990), 262–64. This essay had previously appeared in Hirsch, *Gesammelte Schriften*, vol. 4 (Frankfurt: n. p., 1912), citation at 401–3 (from Hirsch's second open letter to S. B. Bamberger of May 1877).

13. See Judith Bleich, "Rabbi Akiva Eger and the Nascent Reform Movement," *World Congress of Jewish Studies* 9, B3 (1986): 1–8. There are also several reverential biographies of Eger.

14. Akiva Eger, *Shu"t Rabbi Akiva Eger he-Hadash*, vol. 4 (Jerusalem: Vagshal, 1998), *Yoreh Deah*, no. 43.

15. Eger, *Shu"t Rabbi Akiva Eger he-Hadash*, 210.

16. It may appear ironic that the more "Eastern" Warsaw Jews who wished to issue the pro-Christian proclamation were more tolerant of Christianity than the "Western" Rabbi Eger. However, Warsaw was a large cosmopolitan city, whereas Posen, where Eger resided, was in the eastern section of Prussia and was more typical of an East European

shtetl than the German cities in which resided the rabbis whose views are the subject of the present book.

17. On Netziv, see Henry Adler Sosland, "Discovering the Netziv and His 'Ha'amaik Davar," *Judaism* 51, no. 3 (2002): 315–27; Gil S. Perl, "Emek ha-Neziv: A Window into the Intellectual Universe of Rabbi Naftali Zvi Yehudah Berlin" (PhD diss., Harvard University, 2006); Perl, *The Pillar of Volozhin: Rabbi Naftali Zvi Yehuda Berlin and the World of Nineteenth-Century Lithuanian Torah Scholarship* (Boston: Academic Studies Press, 2012).

18. Naphtali Zvi Yehuda Berlin, *Ha'amek Davar* (Jerusalem: n. p., 1974), Exodus 12:51. My use of this term here is indebted to J. David Bleich, "*Tikkun Olam*: Jewish Obligations to Non-Jewish Society," in *Tikkun Olam: Social Responsibility in Jewish Thought and Law*, ed. David Shatz, Chaim I. Waxman, and Nathan J. Diament (Brooklyn: Ktav, 1997).

19. "On account of Israel [the Jewish people]": Midrash, made famous by Rashi's citation of it in his commentary to Genesis 1:1; "is to be understood as connoting, etc.": Berlin, *Ha'amek Davar*, preface to Exodus.

20. Berlin, *Ha'amek Davar*, introduction (*Kidmat ha-Emek*) to the book of Genesis, 1–4.

21. Berlin, *Ha'amek Davar*, preface (*Pesihah*) to the book of Genesis.

22. Berlin, *Ha'amek Davar*, commentary to Genesis 15:5 and Deuteronomy 7:7.

23. Berlin, *Ha'amek Davar*, commentary to Genesis 33:4.

24. Netziv, "She'ar Yisrael," printed at the conclusion of *Rina shel Torah*, his commentary to the Song of Songs (Jerusalem: n. p., 1999). This essay has been translated and annotated by Howard S. Joseph in Berlin, *Why Antisemitism? A Translation of "The Remnant of Israel" by Rabbi Naphtali Zvi Yehuda Berlin* (Northvale, NJ: Jason Aaronson, 1996).

25. For background on Soloveitchik, see Hayyim Karlinski, *The First in the Brisker Succession: The History of the Life and Work of the Gaon Rabbi Yosef Dov ha-Levi Soloveitchik, ZT"L, Head of the Volozhin Yeshiva and of the Courts of Slutsk and Brisk* (Jerusalem: n. p., 1984) (in Hebrew), whose account is reverential.

26. Joseph Baer Soloveitchik, *Beit ha-Levi al ha-Torah* (Warsaw, 1884), 33–34.

27. Soloveitchik, *Beit ha-Levi al ha-Torah*, 33.

28. For an example of his grandson Rabbi Velvel's views of non-Jews, see Yitzhak Zev Soloveitchik, *Hiddushei Rabbenu ha-Griz Soloveitchik Mi'pi Shemuah al ha-Torah* (Jerusalem: n. p., 5747 [1987]), 15. [Note that Rabbi Velvel did not write this book; its text reflects the formulation of his disciples.] See also Moshe Mordechai Shulzinger, *Sefer Peninei Rabbenu ha-Griz* (n. p.: Zichron Meir, 1991), 107, for another example of this harsh attitude. (The personal life of Rabbi Velvel, which included the murder of his wife and several children by the Nazis, ought not to be discounted when encountering these types of remarks in his writings.)

29. See Michael Stanislawski, *Tsar Nicholas I and the Jews: The Transformation of Jewish Society in Russia, 1825–1855* (Philadelphia: Jewish Publication Society of America, 1983); and the more recent studies of Olga Litvak, *Conscription and the Search for Modern Russian Jewry* (Bloomington: Indiana University Press, 2006) and Yohanan Petrovsky-Shtern, *Jews in the Russian Army, 1827–1917: Drafted into Modernity* (New York: Cambridge University Press, 2009).

30. Joseph Dov Soloveitchik, *Shu"t Beit ha-Levi* (Jerusalem: n. p., 1996), vol. 2, *Derush* 17.

31. Soloveitchik, *Shu"t Beit ha-Levi*. Rabbi Soloveitchik is not referring to theft from non-Jews, which is, of course, forbidden even according to the most exclusivist rabbis; he is dealing with the unique case discussed in *Baba Kamma* 38a.

32. A 2019 monograph provides historical context as well as an annotated English translation of Soloveitchik's commentary to Mathew and Mark. See Shaul Magid, ed., *The Bible, the Talmud, and the New Testament: Elijah Zvi Soloveitchik's Commentary to the Gospels* (Philadelphia: University of Pennsylvania Press, 2019). S. R. Hirsch clearly had a positive appraisal of E. Z. Soloveitchik's work, as Hirsch specifically encouraged Jewish readers to financially support the–then blind and elderly Soloveitchik (who had met Hirsch in Frankfurt) on the basis not only of his condition but also based on his writings on the New Testament. I thank Professor Shnayer Leiman for sharing Hirsch's December 9, 1880, letter in support of Soloveitchik with me. See also Dov Hyman, *Elijah Zvi Soloveitchik: The Man and His Writings* (Jerusalem: n. p., 1995), 95–96 (in Hebrew), regarding Hirsch's letter. It is unsurprising that it was Hirsch, and not Soloveitchik's East European rabbinic colleagues, who was the only strictly Orthodox rabbi known to have been supportive of Soloveitchik's iconoclastic project. (Rabbi Lazar Wogue, who taught at the École Centrale Rabbinique in Metz and who translated Soloveitchik's Hebrew commentary to Mark into French, would have been regarded by Hirsch and other like-minded Orthodox leaders as more of a Conservative than an Orthodox rabbi.)

33. See Svante Lundgren, *Particularism and Universalism in Modern Jewish Thought* (New York: SUNY Press, 2001), 181–84, for a general overview of attitudes toward non-Jews in Hasidic thought. To be sure, there are some exceptions to the general pattern of Hasidic attitudes toward gentiles. Most of these exceptions are cited in David Sears, *Compassion for Humanity in the Jewish Tradition* (Northvale, NJ: Jason Aronson, 1998), and many of those emerge from the Breslov Hasidim. A recent essay argues that the founder of Hasidism, the Ba'al Shem Tov (1698–1760), had a more benign attitude toward gentiles that his successors in later generations. See Menachem Kallus, "From Enmity to Unity: Recovering the Ba'al Shem Tov's Teachings on Non-Jews," in *Judaism's Challenge: Election, Divine Love, and Human Enmity*, ed. Alon Goshen-Gottstein (Boston: Academic Studies Press, 2020), 174–88.

34. This view was explicitly formulated by the founder of Habad Hasidism, Rabbi Shnayer Zalman of Liadi, in his *Sefer ha-Tanya* (Zelkova, 1805), end of chapter 1. See Elliot Wolfson, *Venturing Beyond: Law and Morality in Kabbalistic Mysticism* (New York: Oxford University Press, 2006), 5n15. However, Rabbi Shnayer Zalman appears to have softened his anti-gentile posture in later writings. See Naftali Loewenthal, *Hasidism beyond Modernity: Essays in Habad Thought and History* (Oxford: Littman Library, 2020), 87–107.

35. The regnant scholarly view is that the Kabbalah paints a very negative picture of gentiles, positing an ontological difference between Jews and non-Jews and a sometimes-demonic conception of the latter. See Wolfson, *Venturing Beyond*, 17–128. See, for example, at 89: "So noxious is the impurity of the non-Jew that in several passages the zoharic authorship insists that the Jew must avoid all contact with living non-Jews." Hirsch does not treat the Kabbalah's perception of non-Jews, but he does suggest that the masses of

Jews have misunderstood the meaning of the Zohar. See Hirsch's *Nineteen Letters*, letters 10 and 18. (This is not the forum in which to discuss Gershom Scholem's view of Hirsch's attitude toward Kabbalah. It should suffice to note that Hirsch never opposed Kabbalah per se but instead argued that it has all too often been misunderstood. For sources where Scholem makes this critique, and for an insightful discussion of the issue, see Hirsch, *Horeb*, ed. and trans. I. Grunfeld (London: Soncino Press, 1962), cxx–cxxix; and Mordechai Breuer, *Modernity within Tradition*, trans. E. Petuchowski (New York: Columbia University Press, 1992), 64–69. It should also be noted here that there were some outstanding Kabbalists who had a favorable view of non-Jews. Most outstanding among these is Rabbi Elijah Benamozegh. See Marc Gopin, "An Orthodox Embrace of Gentiles? Interfaith Tolerance in the Thought of S. D. Luzzatto and E. Benamozegh," *Modern Judaism* 18 (1998): 173–95. Clearly, Benamozegh and those like him had developed an understanding of the Zohar's comments about non-Jews that decidedly differs from the conventional understanding, whose approach is encapsulated in Wolfson's comments.

36. "Some did have a more benign image": Rabbi Yehuda Aryeh Leib Alter (1847–1905), known as the Sefat Emet, who was the second Rebbe of Gur, regarded non-Jews as worthy of receiving divine beneficence, though not truly suited to tap into spirituality, certainly not as Jews can. See Yehuda Aryeh Leib, *Sefat Emet, le-Sukkot*, vol. 2 (Jerusalem: n. p., 1953), 16. "There were none, etc.": The case of Rabbi Gershon Henoch Leiner (1839–90), of the Izhbitz dynasty, is illustrative. Unusual for a Hasidic Rebbe, Rabbi Leiner was primarily a talmudist and is most known for his Talmudic works, which received praise from leading rabbinic scholars throughout Europe (including S. R. Hirsch). In his *Sidrei Taharot* to Ohalot (Pietrakov: n. p. 1903), 4a s.v. *kivreihen*, Rabbi Leiner asserts that the corpse of a non-Jew does not radiate certain forms of ritual impurity—according to a particular opinion in the Talmud—because non-Jews are already "low and impure while they are alive," so their death does not bring about a ritual change (unlike with Jews who are holy while alive and thus radiate impurity after their souls depart their bodies).

37. An in-depth academic study of Rabbi Schick's life is a desideratum.

38. See Moshe Schick, *Shu"t Maharam Schick, Orah Hayyim* (Jerusalem: n. p., 1971), no. 306.

39. However, in one responsum, *Shu"t Maharam Schick, Yoreh Deah* (Jerusalem: n. p., 1971), no. 152, Schick does concur with Hatam Sofer's previously cited view that Christianity is considered to be AZ even for non-Jews. (However, Schick does not draw the conclusion that Christians have the same halachic status as pagans. Since he does not directly address that question at all, there are no grounds for making any deductions regarding this matter.)

40. Schick, *Shu"t Maharam Schick, Yoreh Deah*, no. 381.

41. Deuteronomy 7:1–2; cf. Exodus 23:32.

42. Schick's own view is that there are two separate prohibitions, one that applies specifically to the Seven Nations and one that applies to any idolatrous nation; "who, according to rabbinic tradition": Babylonian Talmud, *Yoma* 28a; "described in the book of Genesis": Genesis chapters 20–21.

43. Rabbi Schick served as a rabbi in several cities, and this responsum is undated, so it is difficult to determine which city was being discussed.

44. Even the signatories to the 1866 rabbinical decision at Michalowitz, the so-called Manifesto of Ultra-Orthodoxy, expressed strongly patriotic sentiments. They state that the obligation of gratefulness toward one's host country applies even to states that persecute Jews and all the more so to "these nations among whom we dwell . . . [whose] inhabitants . . . are upstanding, kind and just people, and they are at peace with us and do not . . . cause us to neglect the observance of our Torah and our religion." This text has been reproduced in *The Jew in the Modern World*, ed. Paul Mendes-Flohr and Jehuda Reihnarz, 3rd ed. (New York: Oxford University Press, 2011), 224–29. The Michalowitz ruling contained provisions that were so extreme that even Schick and Hatam Sofer's son, Rabbi Abraham Samuel Benjamin Sofer (known as Ketav Sofer), refused to sign it. For background on this ruling, see Jacob Katz, *A House Divided: Orthodoxy and Schism in Nineteenth-Century Central European Jewry*, trans. Ziporah Brody (Hanover, NH: University Press of New England, 1998), 77–85.

45. Yosef Salmon has argued that Hatam Sofer's views regarding gentiles incorporated elements of the "enlightened" attitude of eighteenth-century halachists such as Emden and Landau while at the same time according Christians the legal status of worshippers of AZ. By contrast, argues Salmon, Sofer's disciples, such as Schick, developed an even more negative posture toward gentiles and Christianity than their teacher's. This assertion is problematic, as Salmon does not cite most of the anti-Christian passages of Hatam Sofer discussed here. Furthermore, he deduces more than is warranted from the fact that Schick waged a battle against Hungarian Neologs (Reformers) in which he classified their synagogues as akin to the "idolatrous temples" of Christians. Salmon's thesis is that the battle waged by the emerging Orthodox camp in Central Europe against the non-Orthodox embittered their attitude toward Christians as well, especially since the former were often compared with the latter in Orthodox polemics. From the evidence we have cited here, it appears that it was precisely because the main enemy became the non-Orthodox that the Orthodox were able to soften their attitude toward non-Jews as well as emphasize their patriotic sentiments. There is no evidence for Salmon's assertion that Hatam Sofer had a more liberal attitude toward Christianity and gentiles than his disciples. See Yosef Salmon, "Christians and Christianity in Halachic Literature from the End of the Eighteenth Century to the Middle of the Nineteenth Century," *Modern Judaism* 33, no. 2 (May 2013): 125–47.

46. Schick, *Shu"t Maharam Schick*, *Orah Hayyim* and Schick, *Even ha-Ezer* (Munkacs, 1880), introduction by Schick's son (unpaginated).

47. Talmud *Avodah Zarah* 2b, and various other places in the Midrash.

48. On the Michalowitz ruling, see Nethanel Katzburg, "The Rabbinical Decision of Michalowitz in 1865," in *Studies in the History of Jewish Society in the Middle Ages and in the Modern Period*, ed. Immanuel Etkes and Yosef Salmon (Jerusalem: Magnes Press, 1980), 273–86 (in Hebrew); Silber, "Emergence of Ultra-Orthodoxy," 23–84; Katz, *House Divided*, 77–85. Biographical information on Rabbi Hayyim Sofer can be found in Adam S. Ferziger, "Religious Zealotry and Religious Law: Rethinking Conflict and Coexistence," *Journal of Religion* 84, no 1 (January 2004): 48–77, and the sources cited on 52n16. (See also the introduction to the Pressburg, 1897, printing of Hayyim Sofer, *Sha'arei Hayyim* to Psalms, pp. 6–9. Strangely, the 2012 [New York] edition does not contain a biographical sketch of Rabbi Hayyim Sofer.) See also Herman Dicker,

Piety and Perseverance: Jews from the Carpathian Mountains (New York: Sepher-Hermon Press, 1981), 12.

49. Sofer, *Sha'arei Hayyim* (Pressburg, 1897), commentary to Psalms 67:3 (pp. 113a–b; pp. 322–23 in the New York, 2012, edition).

50. Sofer, *Sha'arei Hayyim* (2012 edition), commentary to Psalms 97:6–8 (493–94). However, Sofer does state that the Jewish people will still retain their status as especially beloved by God due to their millennial dedication to Him and, as a result, the other nations will pay tribute to them. Sofer, *Sha'arei Hayyim*, commentary to Psalms 47:4–5 (227).

51. For elaboration on Sofer's position as a religious hardliner, see Ferziger, "Religious Zealotry," 55. ("In short, both R. Sofer's public behavior throughout his rabbinical career, as well as his literary efforts, attest to his stature as one of the most prominent and outspoken ideologues and practitioners of religious zealotry within mid-nineteenth-century Hungarian Jewish Orthodoxy.")

52. Hayyim Sofer is at pains to emphasize that even though the betterment of the Jews' lot is the result of a divine decree, Jews are nevertheless duty-bound to be grateful to those non-Jews who treat them well. Sofer, *Sha'arei Hayyim*, commentary to Psalms 117:1 (588–89). The 1866 Michalowitz ruling (translated in Mendes-Flohr and Reinharz, *Jew in the Modern World*, 224–29) also expresses strongly patriotic sentiments that, in light of what Sofer has written in his exegetical works, one is inclined to accept as sincere and not as a pro forma declaration made to appease those non-Jews who might read the ruling.

53. On Aszod, see Sigmund Büchler's admiring biography, *Die Lebensgeschichte des Rabbi Juda Aszod, 5556–5626* (Dunajská Streda: A. Weisz, 1933). For an even more reverential account, see the introduction to Yehuda Aszod, *Sefer Divrei Mahary"a* (Michalowitz: Mor Grünfeld, 1931), 6–41.

54. Yehuda Aszod, *Shu"t Yehudah Ya'aleh, Yoreh Deah* (Lemberg, 1880), no. 170. Aszod cites Shakh, *Yoreh Deah* 151:7, discussed previously, in support of his contention that Christianity is not considered AZ. Aszod was criticized by Rabbi Hayyim Elazar Shapira, the Rebbe of Munkacs, for his assertion that Christians do not worship AZ. See Hayyim Elazar Shapira, *Shu"t Minhat Elazar*, vol. 1 (Jerusalem: n. p., 1995), no. 53, section 3.

55. Talmud *Gittin* 57b; *Sanhedrin* 96b.

56. Aszod, *Shu"t Yehudah Ya'aleh, Yoreh Deah*, no. 230, section 2. The concern with Jews dining at non-Jewish festivities is formulated in *Shulhan Arukh, Yoreh Deah* 152:1.

57. Alexander Kohut, who championed a European version of Conservative Judaism, was positively ecstatic about the Hungarian fighters for emancipation, calling them "Magyar Maccabeans." See Howard N. Lupovitch, "Navigating Rough Waters: Alexander Kohut and the Hungarian Roots of Conservative Judaism," *AJS Review* 32 (2008): 70. Although Aszod held different views concerning the possibility for adjustments to Judaism in the modern era, he may well have shared Kohut's staunch patriotism.

58. On Malbim, see David Berger, "Malbim's Secular Knowledge and His Relationship to the Spirit of the Haskalah," *Yavneh Review* 5 (1966): 24–46; Noah H. Rosenbloom, *Malbim: Exegesis, Philosophy, Science, and Mysticism in the Writings of Rabbi Meir Leibush Malbim* (Jerusalem: Mossad Harav Kook, 1988) (in Hebrew); Yaakov Geller,

The Malbim: His Struggle with Haskalah and Reform in Bucharest 1858–1864 (Lod: Orot Yahadut haMegrav, 2000) (in Hebrew); as well as several essays by Geller.

59. Malbim, commentary to Exodus 22:19, Joshua 24:23, and Kings II 17:34, 41.

60. See Ernst Simon, "The Neighbor (Re'a) Whom We Shall Love," in *Modern Jewish Ethics: Theory and Practice*, ed. Marvin Fox (Columbus: Ohio State University Press, 1975), 50–51. Since Malbim does not say this explicitly, it must be conceded that he may not, after all, have intended to break with popular interpretations of this verse, in which case his universalism may not have been all that significant. See also Francis Nataf, "Malbim's Paean to (Ben Azzai's) Kantian Ethics," the *Lehrhaus* website, February 2, 2021, accessed January 4, 2023.

61. See Simon, "Neighbor"; see also Kenneth Reinhard, "The Ethics of the Neighbor: Universalism, Particularism, Exceptionalism," *Journal of Textual Reasoning* 4, no. 1 (2005): 4–7.

62. Meir Leibush Malbim, commentary to Numbers 14:21, section marked *Torah Or* (Bene Berak: Mosdot Alexander, 2000, 205–7). Further analysis of the ubiquity of the mission theory among nineteenth-century Jews of all stripes is presented later in this book.

63. Malbim, commentary to Jonah 1:2.

64. It should be noted that Malbim does follow Abravanel's views quite often in his biblical commentary, so his adoption of Abravanel's views here is not as remarkable as it would be had that not been the case. Furthermore, Malbim accepts the efficacy of the repentance (*teshuvah*) undertaken by the inhabitants of Ninveh. He is not in sympathy with the particularistic assertion of the Midrash Tanchumah (*Ha'azinu* 4)—one that is so at odds with the plain meaning of both the book of Jonah and its interpretation in no less authoritative a rabbinic text as the Mishnah (*Ta'anit* 2:1)—that non-Jews, unlike Jews, are not capable of receiving divine grace for performing acts of repentance for past misdeeds. (To be sure, this Midrash may not actually mean what it appears to be asserting at face value, particularly since the rabbis of the Mishnah [Ta'anit 2:1] clearly accepted the efficacy of non-Jewish repentance and went so far as to hold it up as an example worthy of emulation by Jews. Yet, several rabbis in recent centuries have interpreted this passage in the exclusivist fashion. See, for example, Rabbi Tzadok of Lublin, *Takanat ha-Shavin* [Petrikow: n. p., 1926] and Rabbi Zvi Elimelekh Spira of Dinov, *Bnei Yissaschar* [Petrikow: n. p., 1883]). Thus, Malbim's relation to universalism, though not of the same type as Hirsch's, nevertheless ran pretty deep.

65. David Berger, "Malbim's Secular Knowledge," 38. Berger also mentions Malbim's interpretation of the Book of Jonah as an illustration of how "Malbim's [proto-Zionist] nationalistic feelings left little room for universalism" and was also responsible for Malbim interpreting these two biblical passages "in a manner not at all complimentary toward Gentiles." Still, Malbim did express universalist sentiments elsewhere, as previously noted.

66. Even Hatam Sofer, whose views on non-Jews and Christianity have previously been characterized here as exclusionary, expressed his gratitude toward the ruling Austro-Hungarian authorities. See Sofer, *Derashot Hatam Sofer* (Jerusalem: n. p., 1959), 52–55, for his 1832 speech in honor of the fortieth year of the reign of Emperor Francis I.

Chapter 4

1. See Shmuel Feiner, *The Jewish Enlightenment*, trans. Chaya Naor (Philadelphia: University of Pennsylvania Press, 2004), 119–27. The first of Joseph's edicts of toleration (October 1781) was actually issued several months after von Dohm published his treatise about Jewish emancipation, so the edict can hardly be considered the basis for the public debate. Rather, a convergence of several factors in the final quarter of the eighteenth century engendered a public debate on Jewish emancipation in Central Europe as well as the first legal steps toward it. In general on this topic, see Jacob Katz, *Out of the Ghetto: The Social Background of Jewish Emancipation, 1770–1870* (Cambridge, MA: Harvard University Press, 1973), 57–79; Joseph Karniel, *Der Toleranzpolitik Kaiser Josephs II* (Stuttgart: Bleicher, 1986), esp. 378–99; Robert S. Wistrich, *The Jews of Vienna in the Age of Franz Joseph* (Oxford: Littman Library, 2006), 16–22; and Michael L. Miller, *Rabbis and Revolution: The Jews of Moravia in the Age of Emancipation* (Stanford, CA: Stanford University Press, 2011), 46–52.

2. Peter R. Erspamer, *The Elusiveness of Tolerance: The "Jewish Question" from Lessing to the Napoleonic Wars* (Chapel Hill: University of North Carolina Press, 1997), 3–4; Miller, *Rabbis and Revolution*, 46.

3. Wessely offered a unique interpretation of a Midrashic passage that asserted that a Torah scholar who did not pursue *Torat ha-Adam* was inferior to the carcass of an animal. Naphtali Herz Wessely, *Divrei Shalom ve-Emet* (Berlin, 1782), 3b, (my pagination; end of chapter 1). The rabbis who responded to Wessely turned this interpretation on its head, employing vituperative language to denounce Wessely. See Katz, *Out of the Ghetto*, 66–69; 145–51; Alexander Altmann, *Moses Mendelssohn: A Biographical Study* (Tuscaloosa: University of Alabama Press, 1973), 474–89. The most comprehensive treatment of the Wessely affair is Feiner, *Jewish Enlightenment*, 87–104. For a revisionist reading of the Wessely affair, see Olga Litvak, *Haskalah: The Romantic Movement in Judaism* (New Brunswick, NJ: Rutgers University Press, 2012), 91–112. It should be stressed that Wessely was horrified by the furious rabbinic reaction to his ideas, and he sought support from leading Italian rabbis, whom he (correctly) thought would be more in sympathy with his educational ideas. An excellent treatment of his sense of alienation after this controversy is Edward Breuer, "Naphtali Herz Wessely and the Cultural Dislocations of an Eighteenth-Century Maskil," in *New Perspectives on the Haskalah*, ed. Shmuel Feiner and David Sorkin (Oxford: Littman Library, 2001), 27–47. For the reactions of the Italian rabbis, see Lois C. Dubin, "Trieste and Berlin: The Italian Role in the Cultural Politics of the Haskalah," in *Toward Modernity: The European Jewish Model*, ed. Jacob Katz (Brunswick, NJ: Transaction Books, 1987), 189–224.

4. Jacob Katz has argued that a better rendering would be *Concerning the Civic Betterment of the Jews*, as Dohm's main goal was to reform Jewish culture to make Jews worthy of emancipation. See Katz, *Out of the Ghetto*, 68, 71; Katz, "The Term 'Jewish Emancipation': Its Origin and Historical Impact," in *Studies in Nineteenth-Century Jewish Intellectual History*, ed. Alexander Altmann (Cambridge, MA: Harvard University Press, 1964), 13–14. See also Edward Breuer, "Politics, Tradition, History: Rabbinic Judaism and the Eighteenth-Century Struggle for Civil Equality," *Harvard Theological Review* 85, no. 3 (1992), 368n34.

5. Dohm referred specifically to Eisenmenger's *Entdecktes Judentum*. On this work, see this book's chapter 9.

6. A translated excerpt from Dohm's pamphlet is found in *The Jew in the Modern World*, ed. Paul Mendes-Flohr and Jehuda Reihnarz, 3rd ed. (New York: Oxford University Press, 2011), 27–34. The classic discussion of Dohm's views is found in Katz, *Out of the Ghetto*, 57–64.

7. Johann David Michaelis, "Herr Ritter Michaelis Beurtheilung," in Christian Wilhelm von Dohm, *Über die bürgerliche Verbesserung der Juden*, vol. 2 (Berlin, 1783), 33–51, a condensed translation of which is found in Mendes-Flohr and Reinharz, *Jew in the Modern World*, 34–36.

8. Babylonian Talmud, *Ketubot* 111a. For an incisive evaluation of the impact that this passage has made on Jewish life and thought over the centuries, see Aviezer Ravitzky, *Messianism, Zionism, and Jewish Religious Radicalism*, trans. M. Swirsky and J. Chipman (Chicago: University of Chicago Press, 1996), 211–34.

9. Moses Mendelssohn, *Gesammelte Schriften*, ed. G. B. Mendelssohn, vol. 3 (Leipzig, 1843), 365–67, translated in Mendes-Flohr and Reinharz, *Jew in the Modern World*, 40–41.

10. One of the most recent, and one of the best, examinations of the Dohm-Michaelis debate is Paolo L. Bernardini and Diego Lucci, *The Jews, Instructions for Use: Four Eighteenth-Century Projects for the Emancipation of European Jews* (Boston: Academic Studies Press, 2012), 89–139. See the comprehensive list of literature on this subject cited in that volume, 89–90n2.

11. Anton Büsching, *Geschichte der jüdische Religion* (Berlin, 1779), 204, as cited in Robert Liberles, "From Toleration to *Verbesserung*: German and English Debates on the Jews in the Eighteenth Century," *Central European History* 22 (1989): 12–13.

12. Jacob Katz, *From Prejudice to Destruction: Anti-Semitism, 1700–1933* (Cambridge, MA: Harvard University Press, 1980), 13–22. See also "Eisenmenger's Method of Prooftexts from Talmudic Sources," in *Proceedings of the Fifth World Congress of Jewish Studies*, vol. 2 (Jerusalem: n. p., 1972), 210–16 (in Hebrew). For a more recent examination of one aspect of the impact of Eisenmenger's book, see Elisheva Carlebach, *Divided Souls: Converts from Judaism in Germany, 1500–1750* (New Haven, CT: Yale University Press, 2001), 212–21.

13. Bernardini and Lucci, *Jews, Instructions for Use*, 94–95.

14. See Michael A. Hoffman II's introductory essay, "Eisenmenger: Father of the European Enlightenment," to the 2006 reprinting of the English translation of Eisenmenger's book, *Traditions of the Jews* (Coeur d'Alene, ID: Independent History and Research, 2006). (Hoffman has made a career of authoring conspiratorial and anti-Semitic treatises and is a Holocaust denier.)

15. See Arthur Hertzberg, *The French Enlightenment and the Jews* (New York: Columbia University Press, 1968), 280–313; Katz, *From Prejudice to Destruction*, 34–47. For a contrary view, see Harvey Chisick, "Ethics and History in Voltaire's Attitudes towards the Jews," *Eighteenth-Century Studies* 35, no. 4 (June 2002): 577–600. For a broader reassessment of Voltaire's relationship to Judaism, see Harvey Mitchell, *Voltaire's Jews and Modern Jewish Identity: Rethinking the Enlightenment* (Abingdon, UK: Routledge, 2008).

16. German attitudes toward Jews had been saturated with anti-Semitism at least

since the dawn of the early modern period. The sixteenth century and the Protestant Reformation did not usher in an enlightened approach toward Jews in Germanic lands. Even Polish Jews who lived during this period wrote of the greater hatred for Jews in Germany when compared to other lands. See Michael Meyer, *German-Jewish History in Modern Times*, vol. 1 (New York: Columbia University Press, 1996), 57–70. Thus, there was nothing novel about the anti-Jewish views of nineteenth-century German intellectuals.

17. The most egregious example of this tendency is Daniel Jonah Goldhagen's *Hitler's Willing Executioners* (New York: Vintage, 1996). Goldhagen argues that what he terms "eliminationist antisemitism"—the ideology that bred Nazism—was part of the mainstream discourse in nineteenth-century German society. While Goldhagen's work has been the subject of several trenchant critiques, much of the criticism centers on his interpretation of twentieth-century events and their causes. An example of a critique of Goldhagen's reading of nineteenth-century trends is Hans Mommsen, *An Interview with Prof. Hans Mommsen* (Jerusalem: Yad Vashem, 1997), 5–6. Two studies that essentially adopt Goldhagen's reading of German history prior to the Nazi period are Michael Mack, *German Idealism and the Jew* (Chicago: University of Chicago Press, 2003) and David Aberbach, *The European Jews, Patriotism, and the Liberal State* (Abingdon, UK: Routledge, 2013). The latter work in particular is impressive in its scope and erudition. However, Aberbach does appear to repeat Goldhagen's reductionist approach to anti-Semitism. Additionally, John Weiss, *Ideology of Death: Why the Holocaust Happened in Germany* (Chicago: Ivan R. Dee, 1996), presents a view quite similar, though not identical, to that of Goldhagen. The key point that I am underlining here is that nineteenth-century German anti-Semitism *differed not only in intensity but also in kind* from its twentieth-century offshoot; the humanity of Jews was not in doubt in the earlier period. For a cogent statement about the need to avoid reading all pre-Holocaust German-Jewish history as "a mere prehistory of the Holocaust, which may give the impression that all developments inexorably lead to the 'Final Solution,' as if there were neither alternatives nor counter-developments," see Christian Wiese, *Challenging Colonial Discourse: Jewish Studies and Protestant Theology in Wilhelmine Germany*, trans. B. Harshav and C. Wiese (Leiden: Brill, 2005), 2–3.

18. One must take as hyperbole Mordechai Breuer's statement that "in statements made by high-ranking officials in scholarly circles, one could sometimes hear and read that the Jews too, like the Christians, were human beings." Mordechai Breuer, "The Jewish Minority in the Enlightened Absolutist State," in Meyer, *German-Jewish History in Modern Times*, vol. 1, 163. What Breuer no doubt means is that it was sometimes admitted in those circles that Jews were entitled to full human rights.

19. There were exceptions to this rule, such as Friedrich Traugott Hartmann, who regarded the Jews as incapable of "civic betterment" due to their inherently corrupt and parasitic nature. Hartmann specifically criticized Dohm's ideas, and his views are discussed in Bernardini and Lucci, *Jews, Instructions for Use*, 124–25.

20. Johann Gottlieb Fichte, *Beitrag zur Berichtigung der Urteile des Publikums über die französische Revolution* (1793), 115, note.

21. On Fichte's use of this terminology, see Sven-Erik Rose, "Lazarus Bendavid's and J. G. Fichte's Kantian Fantasies of Jewish Decapitation in 1793," *Jewish Social Studies* 13, no. 3 (Spring/Summer 2007): 73–102.

22. Fichte, *Beitrag zur Berichtigung*, 115, note.

23. Cited from Dohm's *Über die burgerliche Verbessurung der Juden* (Berlin, 1781), 28, in Ritchie Robertson, *The "Jewish Question" in German Literature 1749–1939* (New York: Oxford University Press, 1999), 48. See also David Nirenberg, *Anti-Judaism: The Western Tradition* (New York: W. W. Norton, 2013), 350–51. Goldhagen, *Hitler's Willing Executioners*, 56–57, advances a reading of Dohm's comment that is not compelling.

24. See Leora Batnitzky, *How Judaism Became a Religion* (Princeton, NJ: Princeton University Press, 2011), 18, who presents a contrary view.

25. See Mommsen, *An Interview*, for further elucidation of this point. See also David J. Fine, *Jewish Integration in the German Army in the First World War* (Berlin: De Gruyter, 2012), 1–10, for a cogent argument in favor of contextualizing pre-Holocaust manifestations of anti-Semitism in Germany and against conflating any and all German anti-Semitism with the Nazi variety. This relates to the controversial *Sonderweg* thesis of Germany's unique resistance to modernity. See the literature cited by Fine in *Jewish Integration*, 1n2. A less anachronistic reading of eighteenth-century German intellectual history that sees Michaelis as an early advocate of racial anti-Semitism was offered by Jonathan M. Hess, "Johann David Michaelis and the Colonial Imaginary: Orientalism and the Emergence of Racial Antisemitism in Eighteenth-Century Germany," *Jewish Social Studies* New Series 6, no. 2 (Winter 2000): 56–101. Hess does not draw any line of continuity between the variety of racial anti-Semitism he believes Michaelis propagated and that of the Nazi regime in the twentieth century. Hess is concerned with demonstrating that racial conceptions of Jews did exist in that earlier period, but he sees no direct link with Nazi ideology. By contrast, Bernardini and Lucci, *Jews, Instructions for Use*, 137–38, argue for a link between Jewish otherness in the debates over emancipation in the eighteenth century and the most violent culmination of notions of Jewish otherness, the Holocaust, in the twentieth.

26. Paul Mendes-Flohr, *German Jews: A Dual Identity* (New Haven: Yale University Press, 1999), 18–19. Albert S. Lindemann, *Esau's Tears: Modern Anti-Semitism and the Rise of the Jews* (Cambridge, UK: Cambridge University Press, 1997), 131–42, has also drawn attention to some of the peculiarities of Treitschke's anti-Jewish views. ("Many of Treitschke's positions seem strange ones for a man who has often been described as a proto-Nazi." Lindemann, *Esau's Tears*, 132.) However, Lindemann's attempt to portray Treitschke's positions as relatively reasonable is unconvincing, as are his similar attempts throughout the book to mitigate the perniciousness of other anti-Semites.

27. See Heinrich von Treitschke, "A Word about Our Jewry," in Mendes-Flohr and Reinharz, *Jew in the Modern World*, 319–22.

28. Irving Massey, *Philo-Semitism in Nineteenth-Century German Literature* (Tübingen: Max Niemeyer Verlag, 2000), 78–83.

29. Massey, *Philo-Semitism*, 171–78. "One cannot say that nineteenth-century German literature is actually haunted by Jews and Judaism, but I am struck by the way guilt towards Jews achieves a formulaic, almost a legendary status, in this body of literature." Massey, *Philo-Semitism*, 175. Note that a later study has painted a different picture of modern German literature with respect to its relationship to Jews. See Martha B. Helfer, *The Word Unheard: Legacies of Anti-Semitism in German Literature and Culture*

(Evanston, IL: Northwestern University Press, 2011). Massey's reading of the sources is more straightforward and, thus (in my view), more persuasive.

30. See Stanley Zucker, "Theodore Mommsen and Antisemitism," *Leo Baeck Institute Yearbook* 17, no. 1 (1972): 237–41. An excerpt from Mommsen's response to von Treitschke can be found in Mendes-Flohr and Reinharz, *Jew in the Modern World*, 322–25.

31. The impact that charges of particularism made on the rabbis examined in the present work are discussed in this book's chapter 9.

32. Massey, *Philo-Semitism*, 79n4: "The religious authorities in Westphalia explicitly forbade insults to Jews, on pain of fine or imprisonment."

33. Christhard Hoffmann, Werner Bergmann, and Helmut Walser Smith, eds., *Exclusionary Violence: Antisemitic Riots in Modern Germany* (Ann Arbor: University of Michigan Press, 2002), 2.

34. Hoffmann, Bergmann, and Smith, *Exclusionary Violence*, 23–24, 58, 68, 89–90 (cf., however, 63, 76–79); Aberbach, *European Jews*, 248. The exception was the so-called Hep-Hep riots of 1819, in which there was complicity on the part of some government and military officials. See Hoffmann, Bergmann, and Smith, 23–42.

35. There is substantial literature on this subject. For an excellent, thorough study, see John Doyle Klier, *Russians, Jews, and the Pogroms of 1881–1882* (New York: Cambridge University Press, 2011).

36. For introductory remarks concerning the place occupied by Kant in modern philosophy, see Roland N. Stromberg, *European Intellectual History since 1789*, 6th ed. (Englewood Cliffs, NJ: Prentice Hall, 1994), 23–29, and the literature cited on 343. For a unique perspective on Kant's role in modern philosophy by a twentieth-century philosopher, see Bertrand Russell, *A History of Western Philosophy* (New York: Simon and Schuster, 1972), 701–18.

37. Immanuel Kant, *Religion within the Limits of Reason Alone*, trans. T. M. Greene and H. H. Hudson (New York: Harper and Row, 1960), 116.

38. Kant, *Religion within the Limits of Reason Alone*, 117. Kant's critique of Judaism is quite deep and cannot be mitigated by any contingent factors. His entire philosophy of heteronomy presupposes Judaism's inferiority. For an excellent summary of Kant's critique, see Nathan Rotenstreich, *The Recurring Pattern: Studies in Anti-Judaism in Modern Thought* (New York: Horizon Press, 1964), 23–47. Rosenstreich goes so far as to assert that "one finds Kant to be highly extremist in his conception of the religious value of Judaism" (27). Cf. Rosenstreich, *Jews and German Philosophy: The Polemics of Emancipation* (New York: Schoken, 1982), 3–4. It should be noted that, according to Michael Meyer, Kant was, in many respects, following the approach charted by Spinoza a century earlier. Michael A. Meyer, "Reform Jewish Thinkers and Their German Intellectual Context," in *The Jewish Response to German Culture: From the Enlightenment to the Second World War*, ed. Jehuda Reinharz and Walter Schatzberg (Hanover, NH: University Press of New England, 1985), 65–67.

39. Kant, *Religion within the Limits of Reason Alone*, 117.

40. Immanuel Kant, *Gesammelte Schriften* (Berlin: n. p., 1902–38), vol. 6, 52–53, as cited in Nirenberg, *Anti-Judaism*, 359–60.

41. These quotes are cited from Kant's *Vermischte Schriften* (Halle, 1799–1807), in Léon Poliakov, *The Aryan Myth: A History of Racist and Nationalist Ideas in Europe*, trans.

Edmund Howard (New York: Basic Books, 1974), 172. Poliakov seems to overstate his case when he asserts that Kant "professed a belief in the unity of the human race for philosophic reasons," thereby "merely conforming to the predominant view of his time." Poliakov, *Aryan Myth*, 173. There does not appear to be support for the assertion that Kant was insincere in his acceptance of the unity of the human race. Despite his genuine acceptance of that premise, he perceived pervasive flaws in the Jews of his time, which he connected to the alleged deficiencies in their religion. See also Léon Poliakov, *Histoire de l'antisémitisme: De Voltaire à Wagner* (Paris: Calmann-Lévy, 1968), 196.

42. Michael Mack, *German Idealism and the Jew* (Chicago: University of Chicago Press, 2003), strives at great length to demonstrate the degree to which Kant's philosophy was saturated with anti-Semitism and notes the lack of a forceful Jewish response. See also the useful collection of essays in Horst Gronke, Thomas Meyer, and Barbara Neisser, eds., *Antisemitismus bei Kant und anderen Denkern der Aufklärung* (Würzberg: Königshausen und Neumann, 2001).

43. Cited in introduction to Hirsch, *Horeb*, ed. and trans. I. Grunfeld (London: Soncino Press, 1962), xxiv–xxv. Cf. David Ellenson, *After Emancipation: Jewish Religious Responses to Modernity* (Cincinnati: Hebrew Union College Press, 2004), 251–54.

44. Mendes-Flohr, *German Jews: A Dual Identity*, 29–30, discusses the veneration for Kant among German Jews.

45. Yirmiyahu Yovel, *Dark Riddle: Hegel, Nietzsche, and the Jews* (University Park: Penn State University Press, 1998), 74–82, 207n21. (Hegel uses the German spelling *Gojim.*)

46. G. W. F. Hegel, *Philosophy of Right*, trans. and with notes by T. M. Knox (New York: Oxford University Press, 1967), 169, note.

47. Yovel, *Dark Riddle*, 89–94. Yovel notes that Hegel did not merely support the Jews' political emancipation but also championed their "social integration and equal opportunities for them" (89).

48. Alfred D. Low, *Jews in the Eyes of Germans* (Philadelphia: Institute for the Study of Human Issues, 1979), 176–77.

49. Low, *Jews in the Eyes of Germans.*

50. Friedrich Schleiermacher, *On Religion*, trans. Richard Couter (New York: Cambridge University Press, 1996), 113–14. See Joseph W. Pickle, "Schleiermacher on Judaism," *Journal of Religion* 60, no. 2 (April 1980): 115–37.

51. Cited in Batnitzky, *How Judaism Became a Religion*, 26.

52. See Jerry F. Dawson, *Friedrich Schleiermacher: The Evolution of a Nationalist* (Austin: University of Texas Press, 1966).

53. Naturally, there were German-Jewish thinkers, such as Hermann Cohen, who regarded themselves as fully German, and who were deeply committed to the liberal tradition. What is crucial to the argument here is the dearth of non-Jewish German thinkers who regarded Jews as fully German. During the Enlightenment period, a few, such as Schiller and Lessing, stand out. From the turn of the nineteenth century on, these types of thinkers become more of a rarity, with Max Weber standing out as a possible exception. "Especially when compared to ... American culture": Cf. Alan T. Levenson, *Between Philosemitism and Antisemitism: Defenses of Jews and Judaism in Germany, 1871–1932* (Lincoln: University of Nebraska Press, 2004), vii: "The enthusiasm for Jews,

Judaism, or things Jewish that one finds in the Anglo-American tradition appears only rarely in German-speaking lands."

Chapter 5

1. George L. Mosse has stated, "The word *Bildung* combines the meaning carried by the English word 'education' with notions of character formation and moral education." Mosse, *German Jews beyond Judaism* (Cincinnati: Hebrew Union College Press, 1985), 3.

2. Sorkin discusses the origins of this idea, which were decidedly religious, and examines its permutation into a secular ideal of the Aufklärung in the last half of the eighteenth century. David Sorkin, *The Transformation of German Jewry 1780–1840* (Detroit: Wayne State University Press, 1999), 15–17. See also Hans Bach, *The German Jew: A Synthesis of Judaism and Western Civilization* (London: Littman Library, 1984).

3. David Sorkin, "The Genesis of the Ideology of Emancipation: 1806–1840," *Leo Baeck Institute Yearbook Annual* 32, no. 1 (1987): 19.

4. Jacob Katz, "German Culture and the Jews," in *The Jewish Response to German Culture*, ed. Jehuda Reinharz and Walter Schatzberg (Hanover, NH: University Press of New England, 1985), 86–87. Katz's assertion is not entirely verifiable and a re-examination of German Jews' relationship to German cultural pursuits remains a task for future scholarship. Nonetheless, it is hardly debatable that German Jews did avidly pursue these cultural activities, whether or not they exceeded German Christians in that endeavor.

5. Katz, "German Culture and the Jews," 88–89. This point is elaborated upon in Sorkin, *Transformation of German Jewry*.

6. Katz, "German Culture and the Jews," 90–92.

7. Cf. Mordechai Breuer, *Modernity within Tradition*, trans. E. Petuchowski (New York: Columbia University Press, 1992), 84.

8. Paul Mendes-Flohr, *German Jews: A Dual Identity* (New Haven: Yale University Press, 1999), 35–37.

9. Steven Lowenstein, *The Mechanics of Change: Essays in the Social History of German Jewry* (Atlanta: Scholars Press, 1992), 137.

10. David Ellenson, "German Jewish Orthodoxy: Tradition in the Context of Culture," in Wertheimer, *The Uses of Tradition*, 11; Benjamin M. Baader, *Gender, Judaism, and Bourgeois Culture in Germany, 1800–1870* (Bloomington: Indiana University Press, 2006), 12–13.

11. Cf. Breuer, *Modernity within Tradition*, 150, 248, 451n165; David Ellenson, *Rabbi Esriel Hildesheimer and the Creation of a Modern Jewish Orthodoxy* (Tuscaloosa: University of Alabama Press, 1990), 23–24.

12. Breuer, *Modernity within Tradition*, 312–13. I am using these terms with their most basic definitions. Acculturation refers to adapting to or borrowing traits from another culture (here: German Jews doing so with nineteenth-century bourgeois German culture). Integration refers to incorporation as equals into a society of individuals of different groups (here: German Jews being fully incorporated into nineteenth-century bourgeois German society). Assimilation refers to taking on the traits of the dominant culture to such a degree that the assimilating group becomes socially indistinguishable from other members of the society. As such, assimilation is the most extreme form of

acculturation. It should be evident here why German Orthodox Jews were clearly acculturated, were only somewhat integrated, and were not assimilated.

13. See Michah Gottlieb, *The Jewish Reformation: Bible Translation and Middle-Class German Judaism as Spiritual Enterprise* (New York: Oxford University Press, 2021), 96–124, who argues for the central role played by Mendelssohn in promoting Bildung as an essential feature of self-identity.

14. Abraham Berliner, *Ketavim nivḥarim* (Jerusalem: Mossad haRav Kook, 1969), vol. 1, 21–22.

15. Abraham Berliner, *Aus dem Leben der deutschen Juden im Mittealter* (Berlin: n. p., 1900), 105, as cited in Asaf Yedidya, "Abraham Berliner and the Making of Orthodox *Wissenschaft*," in *Jewish Historiography between Past and Future*, ed. P. Mendes-Flohr, R. Livneh-Freudenthal, and G. Miron (Berlin: De Gruyter, 2019), 83.

16. Von Dohm: "One finds perhaps in the Talmud places where . . . it is a minor misdemeanor to defraud a non-Jew. An example of such kind is the statement that expounds the law to 'love thy neighbor and not offend him' meaning only the Israelite" (cited in Paul Mendes-Flohr and Jehuda Reinharz, eds., *The Jew in the Modern World*, 3rd ed. [New York: Oxford University Press, 2011], 28, footnote). Berliner: "We are commanded not to differentiate between Jews and non-Jews as regards love of our fellow man and honest dealings" (cited in Yedidya, "Abraham Berliner," 83).

17. See the striking anecdote cited in Breuer, *Modernity within Tradition*, 313, where a Christian child approached an Orthodox rabbi, kissed his hand, and said, "Praised be Jesus Christ," to which the rabbi responded, "For ever and ever. Amen." When queried by a colleague, he responded, "But I could not disappoint the child!"

18. Chava Kruskal's assertion, *Mi Lashem Elai* (Jerusalem: Feldheim, 2009), 86–92, that Hirsch did not differ from Hatam Sofer on the issue of emancipation is quite puzzling, especially since her father, Mordechai Breuer, emphasized the difference of view between these two rabbis regarding this issue in his essays and books. See esp. *Modernity within Tradition*, 74–75. For Hirsch's programmatic statement in which he cautiously embraces emancipation, see *The Nineteen Letters*, letter 16 and the beginning of letter 17.

19. The Hebrew text is *le-or goyim*; likewise in the parallel passage in Isaiah 49:6. Rabbi Dr. Gil S. Perl has argued that the placement of the Hebrew letter *lamed* before *or* (light) rather than *goyim* (nations) changes the meaning to possession instead of direction: "God, through His prophet, is calling on the Jewish people to be a 'light of the nations,' not a 'light to the nations.'" Be that as it may, the core idea of the Jewish people serving as a centrifugal source of spiritual enlightenment to mankind, which is the rationale for their election as the Chosen People, remains. See Gil S. Perl, "A Modern Orthodox Hedgehog for a Postmodern World: Part 2," the *Lehrhaus* website, December 9, 2019, accessed January 4, 2023.

20. Michael L. Miller, *Rabbis and Revolution: The Jews of Moravia in the Age of Emancipation* (Stanford, CA: Stanford University Press, 2011), 60–98.

21. Noah Rosenbloom, *Tradition in an Age of Reform: The Religious Philosophy of Samson Raphael Hirsch* (Philadelphia: Jewish Publication Society, 1976), 92. This description by Rosenbloom is supposed to come from a work on Hirsch by Jekutiel Greenwald, but examination of that work, *The History of the Religious Reformation in Germany and in Hungary* (Columbus, OH, 1948), 54–58 (in Hebrew), reveals that Rosenbloom has

misrepresented what Greenwald wrote. Greenwald actually cites the testimony of a student of Hirsch from the Nikolsburg yeshiva who describes some of the tensions that arose after Hirsch was installed as the new rabbi of Nikolsburg. At no point is Hirsch characterized as having appeared to any of the local Jews as "not much different from a Reform rabbi."

22. Miller, *Rabbis and Revolution*, 72–73. Cf., however, Meir Hildesheimer, "The Attitude of the Hatam Sofer toward Moses Mendelssohn," *Proceedings of the American Academy for Jewish Research* 60 (1994): 174n82, according to which Rabbi Benet later "changed his approbation" to Homberg's book.

23. Miller, *Rabbis and Revolution*, 80. See also Meir Hildesheimer, "Moses Mendelssohn in Nineteenth-Century Rabbinical Literature," *Proceedings of the American Academy for Jewish Research* 55 (1988): 90–96, for ample evidence of Rabbi Benet's familiarity with and approval of Mendelssohn. Contrast Benet's indulgent attitude toward Mendelssohn with Hatam Sofer's more critical posture. See Hildesheimer, "Attitude of the Hatam Sofer towards Moses Mendelssohn."

24. By "the first generation of Orthodoxy," I mean the first decades of the nineteenth century when Orthodoxy emerged in opposition to the early Reform movement. Jacob Katz, "Orthodoxy in Historical Perspective," in *Studies in Contemporary Jewry*, ed. Peter H. Medding, vol. 2 (Bloomington: Indiana University Press, 1986), 3–17, and Moshe Samet, "The Beginnings of Orthodoxy," *Modern Judaism* 8 (1988): 249–69, have chronicled the emergence of Orthodoxy, but Adam Ferziger has devoted the most attention to the question of the "forerunners of Orthodoxy," rabbis of the latter part of the eighteenth century such as Jacob Emden and Ezekiel Landau whose approach to deviance from tradition served as a model for later Orthodox rabbis in their struggle with non-Orthodox movements. See Adam Ferziger, *Exclusion and Hierarchy: Orthodoxy, Nonobservance, and the Emergence of Modern Jewish Identity* (Philadelphia: University of Pennsylvania Press, 2005), 41–60. Here, I refer to rabbis like Mordechai Benet as a traditionalist rabbi of the first generation of Orthodoxy to indicate that he served in the rabbinate in the early decades of the nineteenth century when Orthodoxy as a movement emerged but before a specific Neo-Orthodox faction had developed. The most famous leader of early Orthodoxy (and a colleague of Benet), often considered the spiritual father of the later Ultra-Orthodox movement, was the Hatam Sofer. See Michael K. Silber, "The Emergence of Ultra-Orthodoxy: The Invention of a Tradition," in *The Uses of Tradition*, ed. Jack Wertheimer (New York: Jewish Theological Seminary, 1992).

25. See also Sharon Flatto, "A Tale of Three Generations: Shifting Attitudes toward Haskalah, Mendelssohn, and Acculturation," in *Jewish Culture in Early Modern Europe: Essays in Honor of David B. Ruderman*, ed. Richard I. Cohen et al. (Cincinnati: Hebrew Union College Press, 2014), 294–306.

26. Sorkin, *Transformation of German Jewry*, 107–55.

27. Ellenson, "German Jewish Orthodoxy," 11; Baader, *Gender, Judaism, and Bourgeois Culture*, 12–13.

28. Hirsch himself employed the term *Bildung* when describing his educational vision. As noted by Ephraim Chamiel, the English translation of one such essay by Hirsch omits the word *Bildung* altogether. See Chamiel, *The Dual Truth*, vol. 1 (Boston: Academic Studies Press, 2019), 34–35.

29. Simon Schwarzfuchs, *Napoleon, the Jews, and the Sanhedrin* (London: Littman Library, 1979); Franz Kobler, *Napoleon and the Jews* (Jerusalem: Schoken, 1976). Barukh Mevorakh, *Napoleon and His Era* (Jerusalem: Mosad Byalik, 1968) (in Hebrew) provides relevant documentary sources. Jay Berkovitz, *The Shaping of Jewish Identity in Nineteenth-Century France* (Detroit: Wayne State University Press, 1988), 57–84, focuses on the role of French maskilim in convening the Sanhedrin; Berkovitz, *Rites and Passages: The Beginnings of Modern Jewish Culture in France, 1650–1860* (Philadelphia: University of Pennsylvania Press, 2004), 115–43, offers additional insights on the intellectual currents that preceded the convening of the Assembly of Notables and the Sanhedrin. A valuable recent study that sheds light on one important aspect of the Sanhedrin is Simon Levis Sullam, "Prescribing Toleration at the Paris Sanhedrin (1806–1807)," in *Toleration within Judaism*, ed. Martin Goodman et al. (Oxford: Littman Library, 2013), 111–29.

30. Schwarzfuchs, *Napoleon, the Jews, and the Sanhedrin*, 22–63.

31. Cited in Mendes-Flohr and Reinharz, *Jew in the Modern World*, 152–56 (emphasis added). I have made slight modifications to the translation and punctuation.

32. See, for example, David Philipson, *The Reform Movement in Judaism* (New York: Macmillan, 1931), 149–63; Michael A. Meyer, *Response to Modernity: A History of the Reform Movement in Judaism* (New York: Oxford University Press, 1988), 134–35; Sorkin, *Transformation of German Jewry*, 138–39.

33. See *Derashot Hatam Sofer* (Jerusalem: n. p., 1959), I, 81a; and Jacob Katz, "Towards a Biography of the Hatam Sofer," trans. David Ellenson, in *Profiles in Diversity: Jews in a Changing Europe, 1750–1870*, ed. Frances Malino and David Sorkin (Detroit: Wayne State University Press, 1998), 258. For information about Sinzheim, see Nathan Raphael Auerbach, *The Guardians of the Sacred Trust: The Rabbis of the Auerbach Family in Germany*, vol. 1 (Jerusalem: Feldheim, 2009), 125–74 (in Hebrew); Alexis Blum, "Sinzheim Le Porte-Parole des Ashkenazim," in *Le Grand Sanhedrin de Napoleon*, ed. Bernhard Blumenkranz and Albert Soboul (Toulouse: E. Privat, 1979), 119–31; Joseph Sungolowsky, "Joseph Sinzheim, President of Napoleon's Sanhedrin and the First Chief Rabbi of France," *Midstream* 55, no. 1 (Winter 2009): 16–18, and the sources cited on 18, notes 1 and 15.

34. Babylonian Talmud, *Sanhedrin* 98a.

35. Berkovitz, *Rites and Passage*, 125–26 draws attention to the fact the Sanhedrin's response to the question of intermarriage was carefully worded so as to avoid any statements that could be regarded as a departure from halacha, as it was interpreted by authorities up to that time. For the rabbinic sources pertaining to intermarriage, see Babylonian Talmud *Avodah Zarah* 36b, *Kiddushin* 68b, *Yevamot* 23a; Maimonides, *Mishneh Torah*, *Hil. Issurei Biah* 12:1, and *Kesef Mishnah*, ad. loc. (and the medieval authorities cited there); *Shulhan Arukh*, *Even ha-Ezer* 16:1. Cf. Schwarzfuchs, *Napoleon, the Jews, and the Sanhedrin*, 69–71.

36. Schwarzfuchs, *Napoleon, the Jews, and the Sanhedrin*, 95–96. The fact that Sinzheim spoke under the watchful gaze of Napoleon ought not to negate the significance of his speech since Sinzheim was not compelled with regard to the content of his statements. A traditionalist rabbi of an earlier generation, or an anti-universalist contemporary such as Hatam Sofer, may not have singled out the brotherhood of mankind as an ideal to be lauded but more likely would instead have resorted to traditional terms, such as "a

kingdom of kindness," when referring to Napoleon's regime. Still, given the context, Sinzheim's speech is not revolutionary and cannot be regarded with as much significance as the later universalistic writings of rabbis like S. R. Hirsch, who were expressing their sincere convictions, rather than applauding a government's benevolence in the presence of its leader, as was the case with Sinzheim.

37. Schwarzfuchs, *Napoleon, the Jews, and the Sanhedrin*, 72.

38. Schwarzfuchs, *Napoleon, the Jews, and the Sanhedrin*, 71–72, seems to miss this point when he states: "Here again the answer [of the assembly] meant that Christianity would no more be considered a form of idolatry." As the assembly never actually said this in so many words—saying that Christians are not pagans is not the same as absolving Christianity of any avodah zarah—it appears to be a conclusion that cannot be substantiated.

39. Jacob Haberman, "Kaufmann Kohler and His Teacher Samson Raphael Hirsch," *Leo Baeck Institute Yearbook* 43 (1998): 73–103, has argued that Kohler (1843–1926), one of the more radical of Reform ideologues, was influenced by Hirsch's conception of the mission theory. (Hirsch had been his childhood teacher.) Even if this was true, the mission theory did not originate with Hirsch, but with Mendelssohn in the previous century; and even if Kohler heard about the idea from Hirsch, he may have heard a more robust formulation from Reform ideologues, such as Abraham Geiger (whom he knew well), after leaving Hirsch's school (and Orthodoxy). The mission theory is based on ideas in medieval texts but in modern times it emerges in Mendelssohn's writings. It is also found in *Moreh Nevukhei ha-Zeman* of Nachman Krochmal, who was associated with Positive-Historical Judaism (the precursor to Conservative Judaism). Krochmal died in 1840, though the book was first published in 1851. The mission theory is also found in the writings of Reformers such as Heimann Jolowicz. See his short *Israel's Beruf* (1846), referred to in Meyer, *Response to Modernity*, 429n144. See also Salomon Formstecher, *Die Religion des Geistes: Eine wissenschaftliche Darstellung des Judentums* (Frankfurt, 1841), esp. 365–423. There is little doubt that while it was a central creed of Reform Judaism, it did not achieve that degree of centrality in Orthodox thought. Hirsch did repeat the mission theory many times in his writings, as Haberman correctly notes, but Hirsch did not make this a central credo of his philosophy. Cf. Sorkin, *Transformation of German Jewry*, 170: "Hirsch's rehabilitation of the commandments allowed him to make use of the reformers' best ideas—mission, confessionalization—even while attacking them."

40. "Hirsch's classmate": Hirsch and Geiger attended the University of Bonn together in 1829–30 and jointly established a speaking society for Jewish students. They also studied passages from the Talmud together during their time in Bonn. Eliyahu Meir Klugman, *Rabbi Samson Raphael Hirsch* (New York: Mesorah, 1996), 43–44. "And later ideological … anyone else": See Michael A. Meyer, "Universalism and Jewish Unity in the Thought of Abraham Geiger," in *The Role of Religion in Modern Jewish History*, ed. Jacob Katz (Cambridge, MA: Association for Jewish Studies, 1975), 91–104. More generally, see Max Wiener, *Abraham Geiger and Liberal Judaism: The Challenge of the Nineteenth Century*, trans. Ernst J. Schlochauer (Philadelphia: Jewish Publication Society, 1962).

41. For recent analysis of this issue, see Michah Gottlieb, "Does Judaism Have Dogma? Moses Mendelssohn and a Pivotal Nineteenth-Century Debate," *Yearbook of the Maimonides Centre for Advanced Studies 2019* (Berlin: De Gruyter, 2020), 219–42.

42. Moses Mendelssohn, *Jerusalem*, trans. Allan Arkush (Hanover, NH: University Press of New England, 1983), 95–96. Cf., however, Elias Sacks, *Moses Mendelssohn's Living Script: Philosophy, Practice, History, Judaism* (Bloomington: Indiana University Press, 2016).

43. Mendelssohn, *Jerusalem*, 118 (emphasis in original). Cf. Shmuel Feiner, *Moses Mendelssohn: Sage of Modernity*, trans. Anthony Berris (New Haven, CT: Yale University Press, 2010), 171.

44. Robert Gale, "Samson Raphael Hirsch and Moses Mendelssohn" (BA thesis, Brandeis University, 1985), 64–77, argues that it was specifically Hirsch who borrowed the mission idea from Mendelssohn. Presumably, Reform ideologues also got the idea from Mendelssohn, rather than from Hirsch. (If Reformers co-opted the mission theory from Hirsch, that would be sui generis!) David Sorkin argues that Hirsch borrowed the mission theory from Mendelssohn but that "he expanded the scope of the idea . . . by understanding it through the very *Aufklärung* notion of a progressive education of mankind which Mendelssohn had rejected." Sorkin, *Transformation of German Jewry*, 169. See note 39 to this chapter.

45. Ismar Schorsch, *From Text to Context: The Turn to History in Modern Judaism* (Hanover, NH: University Press of New England, 1994), 161–70, 177–86, 345–52; Nils H. Roemer, *Jewish Scholarship and Culture in Nineteenth-Century Germany: Between History and Faith* (Madison: University of Wisconsin Press, 2005), 15–46.

46. Meyer, *Response to Modernity*, 28–30.

47. Email correspondence with Dr. Michael A. Meyer, May 2012.

48. *Protokolle der ersten Rabbiner-Versammlung abgehalten zu Braunschweig* (Brunswick, 1844), 74–76, in Mendes-Flohr and Reinharz, *Jew in the Modern World*, 201–2.

49. See W. Gunther Plaut, *The Rise of Reform Judaism: A Sourcebook of Its European Origins* (New York: World Union for Progressive Judaism, 1963), 133–42. Plaut attributes Reform Judaism's universalism to the twin influences of Enlightenment and "nineteenth century idealism" (at 133).

50. Cf. Nathan Rotenstreich, "For and Against Emancipation: The Bruno Bauer Controversy," *Leo Baeck Institute Yearbook* 4 (1959): 12: "[Bruno] Bauer's anti-Jewish arguments regarding Jewish exclusiveness and their negative attitude towards the Gentile nations are essentially the same as those of the Reformers."

51. Nathan Rotenstreich, *The Recurring Pattern: Studies in Anti-Judaism in Modern Thought* (New York: Horizon Press, 1964), 41–42; Michael A. Meyer, "Reform Jewish Thinkers and their German Intellectual Context," in Reinharz and Schatzberg), *Jewish Response to German Culture: From the Enlightenment to the Second World War*, 64–84.

52. Meyer, "Reform Jewish Thinkers," 69.

53. Meyer, "Reform Jewish Thinkers," 72, 75.

54. Noteworthy in this regard is the two-volume *Der Biblische Orient*, published anonymously in Munich in 1821. Although the work has sometimes been attributed to Isaac Bernays, this has never been satisfactorily demonstrated (see this book's chapter 6). This work contains an original exposition of the mission theory and a universalist conception of classical Judaism. See Baruch Mevorakh, "The Belief in the Messiah in Early Reform Polemics," *Zion* 34 (1969): 217n92 (in Hebrew).

55. Samuel Holdheim, *Gemischte Ehen zwischen Juden und Christen* (Berlin, 1850), 64, as cited in Meyer, *Response to Modernity*, 82.

56. Samuel Holdheim, *Die religiöse Stellung des weiblichen Geschlechts im talmudischen Judenthum* (Schwerin, 1846), cited in Meyer, *Response to Modernity*, 429n148.

57. Samuel Holdheim, *Das Ceremonialgesetz im Messiasreich* (Schwerin, 1845), 122–23.

58. To be sure, Holdheim, in an 1853 sermon, "This Is Our Task" (translated by W. Gunther Plaut, in Plaut, *The Rise of Reform Judaism*, 138) concedes that the Talmud contained germs of a theory of religious tolerance. In the sermon, Holdheim credits the rabbis of the Talmud with espousing a modicum of tolerance through their conception of the Seven Noahide Laws but qualified himself by noting that the rabbinic formulation needs to be translated into "our more purified expression" and broadened in its scope and meaning. However, the charge that Jewish law, as formulated in the Talmud, contained anti-gentile discrimination and thereby excluded non-Jews from the duties of brotherly love, was not challenged by Holdheim.

59. It should be noted that by no means did Holdheim represent the dominant position of nineteenth-century Reform Judaism. On the contrary, he was known as a radical. See Meyer, *Response to Modernity*, 80–84; Meyer, "'Most of My Brethren Find Me Unacceptable': The Controversial Career of Rabbi Samuel Holdheim," in *Redefining Judaism in an Age of Emancipation: Comparative Perspectives on Samuel Holdheim (1806–1860)*, ed. Christian Wiese (Leiden: Brill, 2007), 3–22. What is key to my argument here is that the critique of Judaism as tribalistic was accepted, in one way or another, by various German Reform Jewish thinkers. To the best of my knowledge, none of them offered a defense of Rabbinic or Talmudic Judaism from charges of tribalism. Their nonacceptance of Talmudic authority no doubt played a role in the lack of any such defense, which contrasts with Hirsch's position.

60. Moshe Y. Miller, "Rabbi Samson Raphael Hirsch's *Nineteen Letters on Judaism*: Orthodoxy Confronts Modernity," in *Books of the People*, ed. Stuart W. Halpern (New Milford, CT: Maggid Books, 2017), 202–3.

61. See Ismar Schorsch, *Jewish Reactions to German Anti-Semitism, 1870–1914* (New York: Columbia University Press, 1972), 10; Meyer, *Response to Modernity*, 78, and others.

62. Michael A. Meyer, "Jewish Self-Understanding," in Meyer, ed., *German-Jewish History in Modern Times*, vol. 2, *Emancipation and Acculturation 1780–1871*, 146.

63. Ephraim Chamiel, *The Middle Way: The Emergence of Modern Religious Trends: Responses to Modernity in the Thought of Maharatz Chayot, Rabbi S. R. Hirsch, and S. D. Luzzatto* (Boston: Academic Studies Press, 2014), vol. 2, 15–38, 224–38, has gathered the relevant quotes from Chajes concerning Israel's election and the value of non-Judaic religions. For this and the next note, see chapter 3 of this book.

64. Moshe Schick, *Shu"t Maharam Schick*, volume on *Orah Hayyim* and *Even ha-Ezer* (Munkacs, 1880), introduction by Schick's son (unpaginated).

65. Meyer, *Response to Modernity*, 95–97, 319–20, 388–91; Jonathan Sarna, *American Judaism: A History* (New Haven: Yale University Press, 2004), 253–54; Robert S. Wistrich, "Zionism and Its Jewish 'Assimilationist' Critics (1897–1948)," *Jewish Social Studies*, n. s., 4, no. 2 (Winter 1998): 60, 70–71.

66. A premise here is that a general overview will suffice because none of the rabbis surveyed were serious theologians and they thus did not formulate their views of Christianity based on meticulous research into the precise contours of Christian theology.

Rather, they were aware of the general currents of Christian thought (and Hirsch may have been familiar with Schleiermacher's conception of the Trinity) and used these as a basis on which to critique Christianity as well as to promulgate a theory of religious tolerance, according to which Christianity is (at least) a legitimate religion for non-Jews.

67. Claude Welch, ed., *God and Incarnation in Mid-Nineteenth Century German Theology* (New York: Oxford University Press, 1965).

68. Michael Wyschogrod, "A Jewish Perspective on Incarnation," *Modern Theology* 12, no. 2 (April 1996): 195–209.

69. See Rabbi Yehuda Herzl Henkin, *Shu"t Benei Banim*, vol. 3 (Jerusalem: n. p., 1997), 116: "[Christianity is considered AZ due to] the belief in the Trinity [consisting] of the Father, the Holy Spirit, and the Son—[the fact that Christians] consider Jesus to be divine. If not for this, the mere division of the unity of the Creator between the Father and the Holy Spirit would not be considered AZ for them [non-Jews] so long as they do not affirm the incarnation—even though such belief would constitute heresy for us [Jews]. And even if they considered Jesus to be the son of God [in some sense], perish the thought, but not actually God, and they did not worship him, this would constitute heresy but not AZ."

70. Karl Barth, *Protestant Theology in the Nineteenth Century: Its Background and History*, trans. Brian Cozens and John Bowden (London: SCM Press, 1972). See 306–54 for Barth's analysis of Schleiermacher, including his critiques of the latter's conception of the Trinity. "Criticized Schleiermacher's conception": Francis Schüssler Fiorenza, "Schleiermacher's Understanding of God as Triune," in *The Cambridge Companion to Friedrich Schleiermacher*, ed. Jacqueline Marina (New York: Cambridge University Press, 2005), 171–88.

71. Schleiermacher's views on the Trinity can be found in his *The Christian Faith*, trans. H. R. Mackintosh and J. S. Stewart (London: T&T Clark, 1928) (a translation of the second German edition of Schleiermacher's work [Berlin, 1830]), 391–424 and 738–47.

72. Rabbi Samuel, author of *Olat Tamid*, had stated that if gentiles believe that "one is above the other and do not detract from the unity of God" that is acceptable, but if they believe that there are two deities, it is forbidden. Although no Christians ever espoused the belief in two deities, Samuel's formulation of the acceptable belief for non-Jews dovetails with Schleiermacher's conception of the Trinity, although these two scholars were separated by nearly two centuries. See chapter 2 of the present volume.

73. I. Grunfeld, introduction to Hirsch, *Horeb*, lxxxvi–lxxxix

74. Printed from manuscript in Hirsch, *Shemesh Marpeh*, ed. Eliahu Meyer Klugman (New York: Mesorah, 1992), 171.

75. There is one passage in which Hirsch calls upon Christians to reject the need for an intermediary in a nonhalachic context (see this book's chapter 9). Hirsch also alludes to the issue of shittuf with respect to non-Jews in his protest against the Brunswick Reform synod that had taken place in June 1844. Hirsch does not take a firm position on the matter, just noting sarcastically that the Reform rabbis who permitted Jews to marry monotheistic gentiles, such as Christians, had put aside "the concern over shittuf" (*da'agat ha-shittuf*), which Hirsch felt in any case paled in comparison to the more egregious misrepresentations of Jewish law, and the overall impression that monotheism

was their sole concern, that emerged from the Brunswick synod. This Hebrew-language protest is printed in full in Hirsch, *Shemesh Marpeh*, 188–96 (citation at 196).

76. Moses of Coucy, *Sefer Mitzvot Gadol* (Jerusalem, 1991), First Prohibition, p. 1.

77. Hirsch, commentary to Exodus 20:3 (259–60 in Levy ed.).

78. Hirsch accepts as normative Jewish law the view of Rabbi Shimon ben Yohai, who stated in that Talmudic passage that "whoever associates the name of Heaven with something else will be uprooted from the world." On this basis, Hirsch terms shittuf an even graver offense than standard AZ. (The rationale for this view is that it is degrading to God to acknowledge and worship Him while simultaneously worshiping nondeities as though they were on a par with the one true God!) Ironically, Hirsch's ideological nemesis on the secession issue, Rabbi Marcus Horovitz, argues for a diametrically opposed interpretation of *Sanhedrin* 63a in his responsum on Christianity. See this book's chapter 10.

79. Hirsch, *Shemesh Marpeh*, *Yoreh Deah*, no. 58, p. 74. This responsum is also discussed in Ellenson and Gordis, *Pledges of Jewish Allegiance: Conversion, Law, and Policymaking in Nineteenth- and Twentieth-Century Orthodox Responsa* (Stanford, CA: Stanford University Press, 2012), 44–45.

80. Maimonides, *Guide of the Perplexed*, trans. Michael Friedlander 3:54 (302–5). Hirsch famously launched a scathing attack on Maimonides's views on this matter in letter 18 of *The Nineteen Letters*. So sharp was Hirsch's critique that one of the foremost twentieth-century Haredi leaders, the Hazon Ish (1878–1953), directed a Haredi translator of this book to omit the passage discussing Maimonides. See Hirsch, *The Nineteen Letters*, ed. and trans. Joseph Elias, 291 (editor's notes). See also Michah Gottlieb, "Counter-Enlightenment in a Jewish Key: Anti-Maimonideanism in Nineteenth-Century Orthodoxy," in *The Cultures of Maimonideanism: New Approaches to the History of Jewish Thought*, ed. James T. Robinson (Leiden: Brill, 2009), 259–87; George Y. Kohler, *Reading Maimonides' Philosophy in 19th Century Germany: The Guide to Religious Reform* (Heidelberg: Springer, 2012), 50; Moshe Halbertal, *Maimonides: Life and Thought*, trans. Joel Linsider (Princeton, NJ: Princeton University Press, 2014), 139.

Chapter 6

1. There is a controversy over the anonymously published *Der Biblische Orient*, which some believe was authored by Bernays. See Shnayer Z. Leiman, *Rabbinic Responses to Modernity* (Kew Gardens Hills, NY: S. Z. Leiman, 2007), 35–37n41. See also Heinz Moshe Graupe, *The Rise of Modern Judaism*, trans. John Robinson (New York: Robert E. Krieger, 1979), 172n187. Since there are strong grounds on which to contest Bernays's authorship of this work, it will not be examined in this book. Rivka Horwitz concluded that "von Kalb [Bernays's Christian colleague] is most likely the author and Bernays assisted him." Rivka Horwitz, "On Kabbala and Myth in 19th Century Germany: Isaac Bernays," *Proceedings of the American Academy for Jewish Research* 59 (1993): 156. Horwitz comes to this conclusion based on a thorough analysis of the book as well as an extensive investigation into the intellectual legacy of both Bernays and von Kalb.

2. Cited in Grunfeld, introduction to Hirsch, *Judaism Eternal: Selected Essays from the Writings of Rabbi Samson Raphael Hirsch*, ed. and trans. I. Grunfeld (London: Soncino

Press, 1956), vol. 1, xxiv. (This is Grunfeld's translation of Heinrich Graetz, *Geschichte der Juden*, ed. M. Brann, second edition [Leipzig, 1900], vol. 11, 388.)

3. Cited in Eliyahu Meir Klugman, *Rabbi Samson Raphael Hirsch* (New York: Mesorah, 1996), 31–32.

4. For the impact of Schelling's philosophy on Bernays, see Werner J. Cahnman, "Friedrich Wilhelm Schelling and the New Thinking of Judaism," in *German Jewry: Its History and Sociology*, ed. Joseph B. Maier, Judith Marcus, and Zoltan Tarr (Brunswick, NJ: Transaction Books, 1989), 209–48.

5. I. Bernays, "Kritik des kleinen hebräischen Handworterbuchs von Gesenius," in *Neue Theologische Annalen (Jahrbücher der Theologie und theologischen Nachrichten)* 1 (Frankfurt, 1817): 180–95, as cited in Leiman, *Rabbinic Responses*, 38.

6. Leiman, *Rabbinic Responses*, 38. Kalb was born into a Protestant family but later switched his religious allegiances to Catholicism.

7. Eduard Duckesz, "Zur Biographie des Chacham Isaak Bernays," *Jahrbuch der jüdischen-literarischen Gesellschaft* 5 (1907): 300.

8. Bernays even went so far as to state, upon hearing of a possible post for a Jewish Talmudist or theologian at a university, that he would consider it his duty as a Jew to resign his post as the rabbi of Hamburg and to accept the academic post instead. (The position never materialized.) Leiman, *Rabbinic Responses*, 47.

9. Hirsch refers to Bernays as "my unforgettable teacher." See Hirsch's commentary to Genesis 4:26. See also his commentary to Numbers 20:8 and Psalms 16:1. In the nineteenth letter of his *Nineteen Letters*, Hirsch characterizes Bernays as "a star" that shone before him and guided him. Hirsch is also quoted as saying, "What I gained from him [Bernays] was stimulation, in general, and the thriving to enter the halls of Torah thirsting for enlightenment, for which he showed me the way." Cited in Hirsch, *The Nineteen Letters*, trans. Paritzky, with a commentary by Joseph Elias (New York: Feldheim, 1995), 339 (hereafter cited as *Nineteen Letters*, ed. Elias). Although Rosenbloom (*Tradition in an Age of Reform: The Religious Philosophy of Samson Raphael Hirsch* [Philadelphia: Jewish Publication Society, 1976], 58) argues that Bernays's influence on Hirsch "has been overrated and exaggerated," Roland Tasch has argued that this influence was in fact decisive. See Roland Tasch, *Samson Raphael Hirsch: Jüdische Erfahrungswelten im Historischen Kontext* (Berlin: De Gruyter, 2011), 47n101, and 103–5. For the classic presentation of Hirsch's relationship to Bernays, see Isaac Heinemann, "The Relationship between S. R. Hirsch and His Teacher Isaac Bernays," *Zion* 16 (1951): 44–90 (in Hebrew).

10. Rosenbloom, *Tradition in an Age of Reform*, 56–57, 415–16n78.

11. The regnant position among historians is that Orthodoxy was born in 1819, the year that the Hamburg rabbinical court issued a manifesto denouncing the newly established Reform temple in Hamburg. Jacob Katz and his disciples consistently upheld this position. For pertinent sources and evaluations of this view, see *Orthodox Judaism: New Perspectives*, ed. Y. Salmon, A. Ravitzky, and A. Ferziger (Jerusalem: Magnes Press, 2006) (in Hebrew). Note that this volume presents views that suggest that Orthodoxy may have emerged *prior* to 1819; however, *no* scholars maintain that Orthodoxy was born *later than* 1819. See also Jeffrey Blutinger, "'So-Called Orthodoxy': The History of an Unwanted Label," *Modern Judaism* 27, no. 3 (2007): 310–28. (Blutinger distinguishes between eighteenth- and nineteenth-century usage of the term.)

12. Duckesz, "Zur Biographie," 319. That eulogy was first published in *Shomer Zion ha-Ne'eman* 5, no. 21 (May 25, 1849) and has been translated into Hebrew and published in *Yerushateinu* 1 (5767): 96–103, and in Jacob Ettlinger, *Minhah Arukhah: Kitvei Ba'al ha-Arukh La-Ner*, ed. Yehuda Horovitz (Jerusalem: Yeshivat Dvar Yerushalayim, 2008), 178–86.

13. Meir Hildesheimer, "The Rabbi and His Student: Rabbi Jacob Ettlinger and Rabbi Esriel Hildesheimer," *Ha-Ma'ayan* 12, no. 3 (Nissan 5732), 40 (in Hebrew).

14. Judith Bleich, "Rabbi Jacob Ettlinger, His Life and Works: The Emergence of Modern Orthodoxy in Germany" (PhD diss., New York University, 1974), 2–3.

15. Akiva Posner and Ernest Freiman, "Rabbi Jacob Ettlinger," in *Guardians of Our Heritage*, ed. Leo Jung (New York: Bloch, 1958), 233.

16. Kaufmann Kohler, "Personal Reminiscences of My Early Life," in Kohler, *Studies, Addresses and Personal Papers* (New York: Alumni Association of the Hebrew Union College, 1931), 474.

17. See Jacob Ettlinger, *Minhat Ani* (Bene Berak: n. p., 2012), commentary to *parshat Tazria* (192–93), *parshat Naso* (304–5), and *parshat Hukat* (356–57). I have noted the parshah to which Ettlinger commented because this book has been through several editions that change the pagination of the original 1873 Altona edition. The page numbers cited here are from the 2012 Bene Berak edition.

18. Posner and Freiman, "Rabbi Jacob Ettlinger," 233.

19. Bleich, "Rabbi Jacob Ettlinger," 262–65, 267–70. Bleich extensively treats Ettlinger's relationship to the creation of rabbinic seminaries.

20. Jacob Ettlinger, *Predigten, gehalten in den Synagogen zu Karlsruhe und Brül* (Carlsruhe, 1824), 37, as cited in Mordechai Breuer, *Modernity within Tradition*, trans. E. Petuchowski (New York: Columbia University Press, 1992), 304 (and in Breuer's original German text, *Jüdische Orthodoxie im Deutschen Reich, 1871–1918: Sozialgeschichte einer religiösen Minderheit*, Frankfurt am Main: Athenäum, 1986, 273). The sentence beginning with "Regard them" was excised from the Hebrew translation of this essay, presumably because it presents Ettlinger as more "liberal" than the Haredi editors of the volume wish for him to be seen. See Ettlinger, *Minhah Arukhah*, 211.

21. Ettlinger's last will has been published in *Rabbi Jacob Ettlinger of Blessed Memory* (Jerusalem, 1972), 19–22 (in Hebrew); also published in *HaMa'ayan* 12, no. 2 (Tevet 5732): 37–40.

22. Jacob Ettlinger, *Das Gotteshaus als Vorhalle zur Ewigkeit* (Altona, 1845), 12, as cited by Bleich, "Jacob Ettlinger," 257.

23. It is worth noting that the most patriotic sentiments that Hirsch expressed in writing are in his *Horeb*, which he wrote when he was twenty-seven years old. His youth must be considered a not insubstantial factor in generating that type of rhetoric. By contrast, his later writings reflect a more critical posture toward German nationalism. See Breuer, *Modernity within Tradition*, 304–8. Further, it is interesting that Ettlinger and the editor of the German-language journal he founded, Dr. Samuel Enoch, followed Hirsch's activities throughout his career, as evidenced in the material from *Der true Zionswachter* gathered in Meir Hildesheimer and Matthias Morgenstern, *Rabbiner Samson Raphael Hirsch in der deutschsprachigen jüdischen Presse: Materialien zu einer bibliographischen Übersicht* (Berlin: Lit Verlag, 2013), 93–101.

24. The first edition was published in Altona in 1873. The individual sermons are not dated.

25. Ettlinger, *Minhat Ani*, parshat Noah, 10–11.

26. Hirsch, *The Collected Writings of Rabbi Samson Raphael Hirsch*, ed. and trans. Paul Forcheimer and Gertrude Hirschler, vol. 1 (New York: Feldheim), 117–18, originally in *Gesammelte Schriften*, vol. 1, 75–77 (from *Jeschurun* 1. Jahrgang, Iyar 5615).

27. Ettlinger, *Minhat Ani*, parshat Bamidbar, 295.

28. Jacob Ettlinger, *Shu"t Binyan Zion*, vol. 1, ed. Yehuda A. Horovitz (Jerusalem: Yeshivat Dvar Yerushalayim, 2002), no. 63.

29. Babylonian Talmud *Yevamot* 47b, commenting on the book of Ruth, chapter 1.

30. Yaakov Ettlinger, *Arukh la-Ner al ha-Shas* to Yevamot (Bene Berak: Sifrei Ohr haChaim, 2004), 220.

31. Ettlinger, *Arukh la-Ner* to Sanhedrin, 63b (128).

32. Ettlinger, *Aruck la-Ner* to Sukkah (Bene Berak, 2004), 45b (291).

Chapter 7

1. David Ellenson, *Rabbi Esriel Hildesheimer and the Creation of a Modern Jewish Orthodoxy* (Tuscaloosa: University of Alabama Press, 1990), 14.

2. Jacob Ettlinger, *Shu"t Binyan Zion*, vol. 1, ed. Yehuda A. Horovitz (Jerusalem: Yeshivat Dvar Yerushalayim, 2002), no. 50.

3. This is not meant to suggest that Hirsch was less gifted in his Talmudic acumen than Hildesheimer but merely that advanced Talmudic studies were not the main focus of Hirsch's scholarly endeavors, unlike the case with Hildesheimer, as evidenced by the corpus of the two men's writings. See Yaakov Perlow, "Rav S. R. Hirsch: The Gaon in Talmud and Mikra," in *The Living Hirschian Legacy*, ed. Eliyahu Glucksman et al. (New York: Feldheim, 1988), 75–89, for examples of Hirsch's Talmudic virtuosity. See also Jacob Katz, *A House Divided: Orthodoxy and Schism in Nineteenth-Century Central European Jewry*, trans. Ziporah Brody (Hanover, NH: University Press of New England, 1998), 328n27, and the text on 263, for testaments to Hirsch's halachic prowess.

4. Hildesheimer was born in Halberstadt, in Saxony, a province of Prussia. He was later a rabbi in Eisenstadt, then part of Hungary, before assuming a rabbinical position in Berlin in 1869.

5. Ellenson, *Rabbi Esriel Hildesheimer*, 31–32.

6. Ellenson, *Rabbi Esriel Hildesheimer*, 24.

7. Ellenson, *Rabbi Esriel Hildesheimer*, 109.

8. "In the here and now ... residence": Ellenson, *Rabbi Esriel Hildesheimer*, 109; "and must not ... Redemption": Israel Hildesheimer, *Rabbiner Dr. I. Hildesheimer: Gesammelte Aufsatze*, ed. Meir Hildesheimer (Frankfurt am Main: Verlag Hermon A. G., 1923), 216.

9. Esriel Hildesheimer, *Shu"t Rabbi Esriel*, *Yoreh Deah* (Tel Aviv: Lipa Friedman, 1969), no. 180.

10. *Hagahot Maimuni* to Maimonides, Laws of Idolatry 5:10n3. (The reference to Jesus is not found in all editions. Deutsch cites from the Kushta edition.)

11. This contrasts with Hirsch, who in his single reference to the rabbinic discussion of shittuf, mentions *only* the permissive view, which he endorses (while clarifying its parameters).

12. Indeed, in a different responsum, *Shu"t Rabbi Esriel*, *Orah Hayyim* no. 34, Hildesheimer affirms that the accepted view among latter-day authorities is to be lenient regarding partnerships with non-Jews, particularly since Christians do not worship avodah zarah but instead engage in shittuf-worship (although he stops short of stating explicitly that he considers shittuf to be nonidolatrous for gentiles). In yet another responsum, *Yoreh Deah*, no. 182, Hildesheimer relies upon a simple reading of Rema (to *Shulhan Arukh*, *Orah Hayyim* 156) to generate a permissive ruling regarding an act that will likely involve causing Christians to engage in Trinitarian worship, on the grounds that this does not constitute avodah zarah for them. The consensus that emerges from reading these responsa in conjunction with each other is that Hildesheimer did not consider Christianity to run afoul of the prohibition against avodah zarah as far as non-Jews are concerned.

13. Maimonides, *Mishneh Torah*, Laws of Kings 10:9.

14. Maimonides, *Mishneh Torah*, Laws of Kings 10:10.

15. The most cogent discussion of this is Gerald Blidstein, "Maimonides and Meiri on the Legitimacy of Non-Judaic Religion," in *Scholars and Scholarship: The Interaction between Judaism and Other Cultures*, ed. Leo Landman (New York: Ktav, 1990), 27–35.

16. Maimonides himself notes that his use of the term *goy* refers to a gentile who is engaged in avodah zarah. *Mishneh Torah*, Laws of Forbidden Foods 11:8.

17. Hildesheimer, *Shu"t Rabbi Esriel*, *Yoreh Deah*, no. 230, 277.

18. Hildesheimer's assertion at the beginning of the paragraph ("Maimonides has satisfactorily resolved") supports this interpretation of Hildesheimer's words.

19. Hildesheimer, *Shu"t Rabbi Esriel*, *Yoreh Deah*, no. 229, page 270 (column 1).

20. Kalischer had furthermore, in the context of the aforementioned discussion, cited the verse from Malachi (2:10) that states, "Have we not all one father?" and employed it specifically in the context of a Jewish embrace of gentiles and a concern for their spiritual well-being. Hildesheimer was unmoved by Kalischer's appeal to this text in the limited context of the case they were discussing; naturally, he agreed with the sentiments expressed by the prophet Malachi.

21. Mordechai Breuer, *Modernity within Tradition*, trans. E. Petuchowski (New York: Columbia University Press, 1992), 255, 453n206.

22. Breuer, *Modernity within Tradition*, 254.

23. See, for example, Michael A. Meyer, *Response to Modernity: A History of the Reform Movement in Judaism* (New York: Oxford University Press, 1988), 42–43, regarding the dedication of Israel Jacobson's temple in Seesen, Westphalia; and Robert Liberles, *Religious Conflict in Social Context: The Resurgence of Orthodox Judaism in Frankfurt am Main, 1838–1877* (Westport, CT: Greenwood Press, 1985), 140, and Eliyahu Meir Klugman, *Rabbi Samson Raphael Hirsch* (New York: Mesorah, 1996), 125, regarding the dedication of Hirsch's synagogue in Frankfurt.

24. Israel Hildesheimer, *Gesammelte Aufsätze*, 1–23 (and a Hebrew summary of this position on 24–26).

25. At this point, it should be mentioned that I have examined, in addition to Hildesheimer's halachic writings, the three volumes of his Talmudic novellae that were first published in Jerusalem in the 1980s and 1990s. I could not find instances where Hildesheimer interprets Talmudic passages that could be seen as pejorative to gentiles

(e.g., *Yevamot* 61a) in a more liberal fashion. He simply does not address these concerns at all in his comments to those passages. That is why these books are not cited in the present work.

26. Moshe Mendelsohn-Frankfurter of Hamburg is not to be confused with Moses Mendelssohn of Berlin (1729–1786), after whom Moses Frankfurter amended his last name. Mendelsohn-Frankfurter authored *P'nei Tevel* (Amsterdam, 1872), among other works. His father, who was Hirsch's grandfather, was Rabbi Mendel Frankfurter, the rabbinic judge of Altona from 1805 until his death in 1823. "Hildesheimer decries . . .": Esriel Hildescheimer, *Rabbiner Esriel Hildesheimer Briefe*, ed. Mordechai Eliav (Jerusalem: Verlag Rubin Mass, 1965), 18 (Hebrew section). The letter is dated November 20, 1847.

27. Babylonian Talmud, *Sanhedrin* 105a; Tosefta, *Sanhedrin* 13:2. Maimonides (Laws of Kings 8:11) famously endorsed the view of Rabbi Joshua and therefore ruled that "the pious of [all] nations have a share in the world to come." Maimonides's formulation of his ruling concerning the righteous among the nations and the necessity for them to accept Mosaic revelation had been the subject of contention for centuries, with figures such as Spinoza and Mendelssohn having been troubled by its exclusivist implications. It seems likely—though this has not been proven decisively—that Maimonides based his ruling on a passage in the Midrashic compilation *Mishnat Rabbi Eliezer* (New York: Bloch, 1934), chapter 6, 121. See Nahum E. Rabinovitch, *Yad Peshutah Sefer Shoftim*, vol. 3 (Maale Adumim, 2011), 595–98 (on Hilkhot Melakhim 8:11). It should be stressed that if Rabbi Kook's interpretation of this passage is correct, then Maimonides did *not* base his formulation on *Mishnat Rabbi Eliezer*. See Avraham Yitzhak Kook, *Iggerot ha-Raaya"h*, vol. 1 (Jerusalem: Mossad haRav Kook, 1962), 99–100. Menachem Kellner has argued that the exclusivist reading of Maimonides is untenable. See his *Maimonides' Confrontation with Mysticism* (Oxford: Littman Library, 2006), 241–50. See also Michael Z. Nehorai, "A Portion in the World to Come for the Righteous/Sages of the Nations," *Da'at* 50–52 (2003): 97–105 (in Hebrew), who likewise argues for the untenability of the exclusivist reading.

28. See Hirsch, *Horeb*, paragraph 503 (379 in Grunfeld ed.).

29. Hildesheimer, *Rabbiner Esriel Hildesheimer Briefe*, letter 66 (German section), 195–97.

30. The non-Orthodox declaration can be found in *Allgemeine Zeitung des Judentums* 20 (May 13, 1884): 321–22; *Allgemeine Zeitung des Judentums* 23 (June 3, 1884): 360–64. The statement concerning religious tolerance referred to several passages from the writings of medieval and early modern rabbinic authorities, including, notably, ha-Meiri (as cited by *Shittah me-Kubetset*) and Rabbi Jacob Emden.

31. Hildesheimer, in a private letter that introduced his counterstatement to a colleague, noted sarcastically that one of the Reform rabbis who was a signatory to the declaration was himself a partner in a marriage that was in violation of Jewish law. Hildesheimer implied that it is perhaps for this reason that the non-Orthodox did not wish to speak of forbidden sexual relations when referring to non-Jewish obligations. Hildesheimer, *Rabbiner Hildesheimer Briefe*, 195.

32. Hildesheimer, *Rabbiner Hildesheimer Briefe*, 197. As noted by the editor Eliav, the final draft of Hildesheimer's statement makes it very clear that Christianity is to

be distinguished from paganism, a matter that was left a bit vaguer in an earlier version of his statement (same volume, 260n90). The legal issues concerning which non-Jews might qualify for the title *ger toshav* are not discussed in this letter, presumably because of the legal hurdles that would have to be overcome to employ that term in the present-day and which, in any case, was not necessary in order for Jews to be required to treat those non-Jews who observed the Noahide Laws with the highest level of brotherly love. Hildesheimer did discuss the theoretical legal aspects of *ger toshav* in his responsa, *Shu"t Rabbi Esriel, Yoreh Deah*, no. 229, 272–73. There he states that formal acceptance of the Noahide laws would be required for a non-Jew to be considered a *ger toshav*.

33. Thus, one must qualify Adam Ferziger's assertion, *Exclusion and Hierarchy: Orthodoxy, Nonobservance, and the Emergence of Modern Jewish Identity* (Philadelphia: University of Pennsylvania Press, 2005), 153–54, that Hildesheimer was willing "to join with non-Orthodox rabbis . . . in order to fight anti-Semitism" as well as other matters that affected the entire Jewish community. This was only true when the non-Orthodox were not thereby legitimated in their declarations of a religious nature. See the following note.

34. Ellenson, *Rabbi Esriel Hildesheimer*, 84–85. Ellenson further states, "Clearly, Hildesheimer was a religious sectarian on matters he deemed to be of an exclusively religious nature; he refused to acknowledge the validity of Jewish religious pluralism, counseling noncooperation with the non-Orthodox religious bodies on matters of religious import" (the same volume, 85–86).

35. There is some irony here since one of the signatories to Hildesheimer's counterstatement was Rabbi Marcus Horovitz, the rabbi of the Communal Orthodox synagogue in Frankfurt. Horovitz was one of two Orthodox rabbis who joined with three Reform rabbis in protesting against Theodore Herzl's planned Zionist Congress in Munich. These five rabbis were dubbed the *Protestrabbiner* by Herzl. See the text of this protest in Paul Mendes-Flohr and Jehuda Reinharz, eds., *The Jew in the Modern World*, 3rd ed. (New York: Oxford University Press, 2011), 603–4.

36. In fact, although the proposed German rabbinic organization that would include both Orthodox and non-Orthodox rabbis did not materialize during Hirsch's lifetime, largely as a result of Hildesheimer's protest, matters took a different course after Hirsch's death. In 1898 an organization of Orthodox rabbis who were willing to work together with non-Orthodox rabbis on matters pertaining to all of German Jewry, such as anti-Semitism, was created. It was called Vereinigung traditionell gesetzestreuer Rabbiner Deutschlands, and it cooperated with the non-Orthodox Allgemeiner Rabbiner Verband in Deutschland, originally created in 1884 and reorganized in 1896. The leaders of the Vereinigung were Rabbis Marcus Horovitz and Aviezri Auerbach, and Rabbi Esriel Hildesheimer's signature was affixed at the head of those Orthodox rabbis who supported the creation of this organization. Hildesheimer's hardline stance on this very issue in 1884, combined with his advanced age and ill health in 1898, caused Rabbi Salomon Breuer, Hirsch's son-in-law, to assert that Hildesheimer's 1898 signature had been forged, or at least obtained under duress. The matter is thoroughly documented in Yaakov Zur, "German-Jewish Orthodoxy and Its Attitude toward Internal Organization and Zionism (1896–1911)" (PhD diss., Tel-Aviv University, 1982), vol. 1, 92–138 (in Hebrew).

37. This correspondence is cited by Hildesheimer, *Rabbiner Esriel Hildesheimer*,

260n91. In further correspondence (found in the same volume), letter 67, 198–99, Hildesheimer took umbrage at Hirsch's sharp attacks, which he considered very hurtful. Hildesheimer assured Hirsch that he had no intention of forming a union between Orthodox and non-Orthodox rabbis, but that common courtesy (Hildesheimer employed the Hebrew term *derekh eretz*) demanded that he not decline Ungerleider's request for a meeting. Cf. Ellenson, *Rabbi Esriel Hildesheimer*, 100–101.

38. The full text of Hirsch's response to Hildesheimer's counterstatement, from which the editor Eliav cited select passages, does not appear in the Sänger Collection. (This has been verified by Mrs. Chaya-Bathya Markovits, curator of the collection, in an email correspondence from February 2014.) Since Eliav's notes to the Hildesheimer letters that he edited and published are very thorough, it would seem safe to say that Hirsch's letters do not address this issue at all.

39. Hildesheimer, *Rabbiner Esriel Hildesheimer*, 71 (Hebrew section). The letter is dated March 17, 1885.

40. See Gordon R. Mork, "German Nationalism and Jewish Assimilation: The Bismarck Period," *Leo Baeck Institute Yearbook* 22 (1977): 81–90; Fritz Stern, *Gold and Iron: Bismarck, Bleichröder, and the Building of the German Empire* (New York: Vintage, 1979), 3–6.

41. Hildesheimer, *Rabbiner Esriel Hildesheimer*, 106n232 (Hebrew section), identifies this organization as the Deutsche Gesellschaft für die Kolonisation, which was established in 1884 under the auspices of Bismarck's government.

42. Hildesheimer expressed other causes for concern, such as, for example, the inhospitable conditions for the furtherance of traditional Judaism that would likely meet the Kishinev Jews when they arrived in any of the countries that were suggested as destinations for immigration.

43. In another letter, dated December 1890, Hildesheimer is very frank about the prevalence of German anti-Semitism, noting that even assimilated Jews are not immune to the Jew-baiting of the anti-Semites. See *Rabbiner Esriel Hildesheimer*, 78–79 (Hebrew section).

44. Their views were discussed in chapter 5 of this book.

45. Sources of information on Lehmann, though dated, are *Gedenk-blätter an Rabbiner Dr. Marcus Lehmann* (Mainz, 1890) (a collection of eulogies said at Lehmann's funeral), Jon Lehmann, *Dr. Markus Lehmann* (Frankfurt am Main: Kauffmann, 1910), and Moche Catane, *La Vie et l'oeuvre du Rabbin M. Lehmann (1831–1890)* (Jerusalem: Université de Jérusalem, 1971). A reverential treatment can be found in Meir Lehmann, *Masekhet Avot im Perush Meir Nativ*, vol. 1 (Bene Berak, 1968), 7–17, "History of the Author" by Aharon Sorski (in Hebrew). See also Dror Edar, "Meir Lehmann: Jewish Orthodoxy Tested," *Mi-kan* 10 (5771): 19–51 (in Hebrew). Sebastian Bauer's "Ludwig Philippson und Marcus Lehmann: Jüdische Kontroversen zwischen Reform und Orthodoxie als identitätsstiftende Momente im neunzehnten Jahrhundert" (PhD diss., Ludwig Maximilian University of Munich, 2016) is an excellent resource on Lehmann. Bauer's analysis of Lehmann's Neo-Orthodox perspective on Jewish universalism (on 133–40) complements that of the present work, and on 135 he cites passages from Lehmann's sermons and a novel that further demonstrate his universalist outlook.

46. Mishnah, Sanhedrin 10:1.

47. Tosefta, *Sanhedrin* 13:2; Babylonian Talmud, *Sanhedrin* 105a.

48. Lehmann, *Sprüche der Väter von Dr. M. Lehmann* (Frankfurt am Main: n. p., 1921), 7–8. There is an English edition of this commentary, *The Lehmann-Prins Pirkei Avoth*, trans. C. H. Moore (New York: Feldheim, 1992), which is a somewhat truncated translation of the German original but is still faithful to the spirit of the original text. Some sentences have been simplified and some details have been omitted, but Lehmann's comments have not been censored.

49. Lehmann, *Sprüche der Väter*, 89. ("*Die allgemeine Menschenliebe ist die edelste Frucht des glaubigen Lebens*"). Further in this passage, in discussing Hillel's maxim of not doing unto others what we would not have done to us, Lehmann makes it clear that Judaism's conception of love of fellow is not a tribalistic notion and is not limited to "*unser Glaubensgenosse, unser Stammesgenosse*" (same volume, 89–90).

50. Rabbi Ahron Soloveichik, *Logic of the Heart, Logic of the Mind* (Jerusalem: Genesis Jerusalem Press, 1991), 70–78.

51. Lehmann, *Sprüche der Väter*, 224–25.

52. Lehmann, *Sprüche der Väter*, 134–43. Lehmann makes a point of singling out different racial groups when he says, with respect to the "man" (*Adam*) referred to in the Mishnah, "*jeder gemeint ist, der den Namen Mensch tragt, ohne Ruecksicht auf die Verschiedenheiten in bezug auf Farbe, Gestalt, Rasse, Nationalitat, Religion, Bildung, oder andere Varietaeten. Jeder Mensch, sei er ein Neger oder die Weisser, sei er in Malaie oder ein Kaukasier*" (*Sprüche der Väter*, 135).

53. Lehmann, *Sprüche der Väter*, 135–36; Naphtali Herz Wessely, *Yeyn Levanon* (Berlin, 1755), 48b–49b.

54. Lehmann, *Sprüche der Väter*, 144–45. To be sure, Lehmann notes that the Jews' status as God's "children" can never be forfeited, just as an actual child's relationship to his parent is unconditional ("*Der Sohn bleibt immer der Sohn, under allen Verhaltnissen, bedingungslos*" (*Sprüche der Väter*, 145).

55. Jacob Katz, *Exclusiveness and Tolerance* (New York: Behrman House, 1961), 165–66.

56. Marcus Lehmann, *Lehmann's Passover Haggadah: With the Commentary of Rabbi Dr. Marcus Lehmann of Mainz* (London: n. p., 1969), 272–74. (Unlike the Avot commentary, this is a literal translation of Lehmann's Haggadah commentary.) The original can be found in Marcus Lehmann, *Hagadah schel Pesach mit Erläuterungen von Dr. M. Lehmann* (Frankfurt am Main, 1918), 162–64. This entire passage has been excised from the Hebrew edition of the Lehmann Haggadah, *Haggadah shel Pesach im peirush "Meir Nativ" me-et HaRav Meir Lehmann A"BD Mainz* (Bene Berak: n. p., 1967), 252–53. In its place is the following sentence: "In our circles, and throughout the entire world, there are no longer nations and kingdoms which do not recognize God." (No indication is given that anything has been left out, added, or edited.) Presumably, the editors of this edition felt that Ashkenazi's words have no relevance to the contemporary world of Haredi Jews in Israel, or perhaps that they were written apologetically.

57. Lehmann, *Hagadah schel Pesach* (German original), 164.

58. It is worth noting that Rabbi Moshe Mainz was Hirsch's primary opponent in Frankfurt when it came to Hirsch's struggle for *Austritt*, a cause that Marcus Lehmann championed together with Hirsch.

59. See the title page of Tevele Bondi, *Haggadah shel Pesach* (Jerusalem: Feldheim, 2002, facsimile).

60. *Lehmann Haggadah*, 355–56; German edition, 208. The editors of the English edition added in the following footnote to Bondi's comments: "Written in the latter half of the 19th century, when no one dreamt that the veneer of 'civilization' would one day fall away, and produce the Nazi holocaust which devoured 6,000,000 of our brethren." The editors of the Hebrew edition have added in an even longer note bemoaning the transformation of "civilized" Germans into mass murderers, and their wording suggests that the genocidal intent of the Nazis was not entirely absent from ordinary Germans even when this commentary was written.

61. To be sure, in an already-referred-to responsum (*Yoreh Deah*, no. 229) Hildesheimer affirmed that the normative halacha does not recognize a distinction between contemporary gentiles and the ones in Talmudic times with respect to whether they are suspect regarding killing Jews. The only distinction that normative halacha made that rendered contemporary gentiles unlike their pagan predecessors from Talmudic times was regarding the suspicion that they may engage in bestiality: while ancient pagans were so suspect, contemporary Christians are not. It was Kalischer, who is generally not regarded as an advocate of Neo-Orthodoxy, who argued that contemporary Christians are not suspect concerning bloodshed. It seems, however, that Hildesheimer may well have agreed with the sentiment expressed by Bondi here. He merely affirmed that the Talmudic suspicion of bloodshed on the part of pagans was not formally removed from later nonpagan gentiles, arguing that mainstream rabbinic sources made no such distinction, but he may have considered his Christian contemporaries in Germany to be too civilized to suggest the mass murder of Jews, just as Bondi wrote in the passage examined here.

62. Lehmann, *Sprüche der Väter*, 256. Later in his commentary to the same Mishnah (Avot 2:18, 257–58), Lehmann notes that Judaism rejects Christianity's doctrine of original sin ("*nach der Lehre des Judentums gibt es keine Erbsünde*"), as well as the notion that Jesus is needed as an intermediary between man and God ("*nicht bedarf sie der Vermittelung zwischen sich und ihrem Schöpfer*").

63. "When written for a public audience": See, for example, Moses Mendelssohn, "Letter to Lavater" (written in response to Lavater's challenge to Mendelssohn to convert), discussed in Alexander Altmann, *Moses Mendelssohn: A Biographical Study* (Tuscaloosa: University of Alabama Press, 1973), 211–23. Mendelssohn wrote a far more scathing attack on Christianity in an essay not initially intended for publication. See Michah Gottlieb, *Moses Mendelssohn: Writings on Judaism, Christianity, and the Bible* (Waltham, MA: Brandeis University Press, 2011), 16–30. "The legacy of not insignificant Jewish conversion to Christianity": See Meyer, *Response to Modernity*, 43–44; and Steven Lowenstein, *The Berlin Jewish Community: Enlightenment, Family, and Crisis (1770–1830)* (New York: Oxford University Press), 120–33.

64. Breuer, *Modernity within Tradition*, 41–42, 74.

65. Yitzhak Dov Bamberger, *Shu"t Yad HaLevy* (Jerusalem: n. p. 1965), vol. 1, no. 1 (p. 1).

66. This point is arguably sharpened by the fact that the proof text was not from the Pentateuch but from a later biblical book. In this regard, see the Talmudic principle *divre Torah mi-divre Kabbalah lo yalfinan* (biblical laws are not derived from tradition

[i.e., non-Mosaic biblical passages]) in, for example, Babylonian Talmud, Tractate *Bava Kamma* 2b.

67. Simhah ha-Levi Bamberger, *Sefer Zekher Simhah* (Frankfurt am Main, 1925), no. 109.

68. Babylonian Talmud, Tractate *Hullin* 13b.

69. Leviticus 19:14; Babylonian Talmud, Tractate *Pesahim* 22b.

70. *Pithei Teshuvah* to *Shulhan Arukh*, *Yoreh Deah* 147, no. 2.

71. Abraham ben Isaac of Narbonne, *Sefer ha-Eshkol im be'ur Nahal Eshkol*, ed. Zvi Binyamin Auerbach (Halberstadt, 1867–69).

72. Shalom Albeck, *Kofer ha-Eshkol* (Warsaw: haTzefirah, 1910), which followed Albeck's 1909 "Open Letter" accusing Auerbach of forgery and a 1910 defense of Auerbach by several prominent rabbis and scholars. See *Encyclopedia Judaica*, vol. 3 (New York: Macmillan, 1971), 843. A useful recent study of the Auerbach rabbinical family, written from a reverential perspective, is Nathan Raphael Auerbach, *The Guardians of the Sacred Trust: The Rabbis of the Auerbach Family in Germany* (Jerusalem: Feldheim, 2009) (in Hebrew). For a biography of Rabbi Benjamin Zvi Auerbach, see volume 1 of that same work, 225–392.

73. Auerbach, *Sefer ha-Eshkol*, vol. 3, 119–20n16. The permissive view regarding shittuf Auerbach rejects is that of Rabbi Zvi Hirsch Chajes, already discussed, though Auerbach does not mention Chajes by name.

74. Rabbi Auerbach was awarded a doctorate in philosophy from the University of Giessen in 1834, although even during the period of his university studies he devoted as much spare time as possible to Torah study. Auerbach, *Guardians of the Sacred Trust*, vol. 1, 230n23.

75. Auerbach, *Guardians of the Sacred Trust*, vol. 1, 230–33, 238–46. It is worth noting here that Auerbach was a friend of S. R. Hirsch from the period when they studied together at Jacob Ettlinger's yeshiva in Mannheim. Klugman, *Rabbi Samson Raphael Hirsch*, 41–42, 256 note e.

76. See Ellenson, *Rabbi Esriel Hildesheimer*, 90–92.

Chapter 8

1. A list of this literature can be found in Shlomo Spitzer and Chaya-Bathya Markowits, eds., *Rabbi Samson Raphael Hirsch: Bibliography* (Ramat-Gan: Bar-Ilan, 2003), 38–69. Since 2003, the literature has grown substantially and is amply cited in this book. (An unscientific survey would place Rabbi Abraham Isaac Kook close to Hirsch in terms of amount of secondary literature devoted to his biography and thought.)

2. This book does not seek to trace the influence of various German thinkers and philosophers on Hirsch's thought, a task that has already been done by others, most notably Pinhas Paul Grünewald, *Pedagogie, esthetique et ticoun olam—Redressement du monde: Samson Raphael Hirsch* (Berne: Peter Lang International Academic, 1986) and, more recently, by Roland Tasch, *Samson Raphael Hirsch: Jüdische Erfahrungswelten im Historischen Kontext* (Berlin: De Gruyter, 2011). This book situates Hirsch as a thoroughly rabbinic Jew who utilized the idiom of many contemporary and earlier German writers in his explication of Judaism, which he intended for an audience of Jews who were familiar with those German thinkers. This reading of Hirsch is based on his declared principle

of the autarchy of Judaism (cf. Hirsch, *Nineteen Letters*, letter 18; Mordechai Breuer, *Modernity within Tradition*, trans. E. Petuchowski (New York: Columbia University Press, 1992), 68; and I. Grunfeld, introduction to Hirsch, *Horeb*, xli), which is also the basis for the dilemma addressed later in this chapter.

3. Cf. Grunfeld, introduction to Hirsch, *Horeb*, xciv–xcv. For an insightful analysis of Hirsch's views concerning the value of science, see Lawrence Kaplan, "*Torah U-Madda* in the Thought of Rabbi Samson Raphael Hirsch," *B.D.D.* 5 (Summer 1997): 5–31.

4. Jacob Katz has argued that Hirsch's later views on secession are to be regarded as a break with his outlook prior to the late 1860s. See Katz, *A House Divided: Orthodoxy and Schism in Nineteenth-Century Central European Jewry*, trans. Ziporah Brody (Hanover, NH: University Press of New England, 1998), 26–28; Katz, "R. Samson Raphael Hirsch: The Right- and Left-Winger," in Katz, *Halakhah in Straits* (Jerusalem: Magnes Press, 1992), 230–31 (in Hebrew). (Immanuel Jakobovits has argued that Hirsch's sectarian communal policies contradict his broad outlook on worldly culture. See I. Jakobovits, *The Timely and the Timeless: Jews, Judaism, and Society in a Storm-Tossed Decade* (London: Vallentine Mitchell, 1977), 255. A close reading of Hirsch's protest against the 1844 Brunswick synod, *Shemesh Marpeh* (ed. Eliahu Meyer Klugman [New York: Mesorah, 1992]), 188–96, leads one to the conclusion that Hirsch could not envision any communal ties whatsoever with Reform Judaism as early as 1844.

5. See Moshe Pelli, *The Age of Haskalah: Studies in Hebrew Literature of the Enlightenment in Germany* (Leiden: n. p., 1979), 113–30; Jacob Katz, *Out of the Ghetto: The Social Background of Jewish Emancipation, 1770–1870* (Cambridge, MA: Harvard University Press, 1973), 66–69; and Shmuel Feiner, *The Jewish Enlightenment*, trans. Chaya Naor (Philadelphia: University of Pennsylvania Press, 2004), 90–99.

6. Noah Rosenbloom, *Tradition in an Age of Reform: The Religious Philosophy of Samson Raphael Hirsch* (Philadelphia: Jewish Publication Society, 1976), 52.

7. Tasch, *Samson Raphael Hirsch*, 36–48.

8. Moses Mendelsohn of Hamburg (Hirsch's uncle), *P'nei Tevel* (Amsterdam, 1872), 241. For Hirsch's grandfather's connection to Moses Mendelssohn, see 234.

9. Rosenbloom, *Tradition in an Age of Reform*, 44–53, 56–57, 348.

10. Rosenbloom, *Tradition in an Age of Reform*, 72–73.

11. Just as there was no Haskalah in nineteenth-century Germany, so too there was no Haskalah in twentieth-century America. I once heard an ultra-Orthodox rabbi attack Rabbi Joseph B. Soloveitchik (1903–93) for his "maskilic" tendencies. Given his context, the very charge is specious.

12. Breuer, *Modernity within Tradition*, 72. A similar evaluation of Hirsch is found in Shnayer Leiman, *Rabbinic Responses to Modernity* (Kew Gardens Hills, NY: S. Z. Leiman, 2007), 57–96. Leiman cites and rejects Rosenbloom's approach on 63n91.

13. Naphtali Herz Wessely, *Divrei Shalom ve-Emet* (Berlin, 1782), 3–4.

14. Wessely's educational program was written as a response to the Edict of Toleration of the Austro-Hungarian Emperor Joseph II, which pertained to Jewish education in his empire. Cf. Olga Litvak, *Haskalah: The Romantic Movement in Judaism* (New Brunswick, NJ: Rutgers University Press, 2012), 90–91.

15. Hirsch, *Horeb*, trans. I Grunfeld, 408–12. Details of the curriculum in Hirsch's school in Frankfurt can be found in Hans Thiel, *Die Samson-Raphael-Hirsch-Schule in*

Frankfurt am Main: Dokumente, Erinnerungen, Analysen (Frankfurt: Verlag Waldemar Kramer, 2001).

16. Hirsch, *Horeb*, 409.

17. Wessely, *Divrei Shalom ve-Emet*, 3.

18. Rosenbloom, *Tradition in an Age of Reform*, 48–49, 52–53. For an example of one of Hirsch's greatest admirers acknowledging the Hirsch family's "enlightened" side, see "Samson Raphael Hirsch—The Man and His Mission" in Hirsch, *Judaism Eternal: Selected Essays from the Writings of Rabbi Samson Raphael Hirsch*, ed. and trans. I. Grunfeld (London: Soncino Press, 1956), vol. 1, xxii–xxiii. There, Grunfeld concedes that "in those days" it was "an extraordinary thing for pious Jewish parents" to send their son to a non-Jewish grammar school. But the unconventionality of the decision does not turn Hirsch's parents into "maskilim" any more than Jacob Ettlinger's decision to attend university at around the same time rendered him a "maskil." The openness to non-Jewish culture exhibited in both cases was a harbinger of the Neo-Orthodoxy fashioned by these rabbis in the years that followed. Mordechai Breuer, who is repeatedly criticized by Rosenbloom for his alleged overveneration of Hirsch, wrote that Wessely was "a figure much admired by Hirsch's family." Breuer further notes that Wessely's educational program "bears a certain similarity to the doctrine of S. R. Hirsch, yet the two are far from being identical." Mordechai Breuer, *The "Torah-im-Derekh-Eretz of Samson Raphael Hirsch"* (New York: Feldheim, 1970), 11 and 54n20.

19. This is all the more important given that Mordechai Breuer, in his scathing critique of Rosenbloom's book (published in the journal *Tradition* 16, no. 4 [Summer 1977]: 140–49), does not even mention Rosenbloom's treatment of Hirsch's relationship to Mendelssohn and Wessely, though he notes that "the space of a review essay does not allow for enumeration of all errors, omissions, and misjudgments encountered [in one chapter of the book]."

20. Rosenbloom, *Tradition in an Age of Reform*, 415n76.

21. Meir Hildesheimer, "Moses Mendelssohn in Nineteenth-Century Rabbinical Literature," *Proceedings of the American Academy for Jewish Research* 55 (1988): 79–133. Further sources can be found in Hildesheimer, "The Attitude of the Hatam Sofer toward Moses Mendelssohn," *Proceedings of the American Academy for Jewish Research* 60 (1994): 141–87, esp. 159–62n59. It should perhaps go without saying that German Orthodox colleagues of Hirsch also cited Wessely by name. See Meir Hildesheimer, "Moses Mendelssohn," for examples of Esriel Hildesheimer citing Wessely. To those can be added Marcus Lehmann's citations of Wessely in his *Avot* commentary, such as where he refers to "Rabbi Wessely" and his "highly ingenious explanation" in *The Lehmann-Prins Pirkei Avoth*, 61, 69, 135, 160, 179, 180, 200, 212, et al.

22. Jacob Ettlinger, approbation to Naphtali Herz Wessely, *Olelot Naphtali* (Hamburg, 1842). (The language employed by Ettlinger does differ from that found in standard approbations for Talmudic works because Wessely did not achieve renown in that field and the book for which Ettlinger was writing an approbation was a Bible commentary.) This approbation has been reprinted in its entirety in Naphtali Herz Weisel [Wessely], *Yeyn Levanon*, 5–6. Noteworthy is the fact that Rosenbloom cited another approbation to this work, by Isaac Bernays (another of Hirsch's teachers), as evidence of Bernays's departure from traditionalism. Nowhere does Rosenbloom inform the reader

that Ettlinger had written an even more laudatory approbation (approximately three times the length of Bernays's), presumably because Rosenbloom was aware that Ettlinger's Orthodoxy was unimpeachable and his thesis about Hirsch would then have been undermined. See Rosenbloom, *Tradition in an Age of Reform*, 416n82.

23. Tractate Avot, chapter 3 Mishnah 11, commentary of Tiferet Yisrael, no. 76.

24. Jacob Katz, "Tzevi Hirsch Kalischer," in *Jewish Leaders*, ed. Leo Jung (New York: Bloch Publishing, 1953), 209–27. For a challenge to this characterization, see Moshe Y. Miller, "Between Frankfurt and Satmar: A Study of Two Schools of Orthodox Jewish Anti-Zionism" (MA thesis, Touro College, 2006)," 144n66.

25. See Jacob Zvi Mecklenberg, *Ha-Ketav ve-Ha'Kabbalah*, Exodus 3:15, 7:18, 8:17, et al. For his approbation, see *Humash Mekor Hayyim*, ed. J. Heinemann (Berlin, 1832), s.v. Haskamah, unpaginated section at the beginning. I am indebted to the editors of the 2003 edition of Wessely's *Yeyn Levanon* for many of the citations I have enumerated here (edited by Y. Segal and S. Levy, published in Rishon le-Tziyon: Yeshivat haHesder, 2003).

26. Yitzhak Dov Bamberger, *Koreh be-Emet*, 4; *Nahalei Devash*, 68.

27. Moshe Schick, *Derashot Maharam Schick* (Cluj: n. p., 1936), 30b. Cf. Meir Hildesheimer, "The Attitude of the Hatam Sofer," 181, who refers to Schick citing Wessely's "works" in his "speeches."

28. Hildesheimer, "Attitude of the Hatam Sofer," 184n106. Cf. the series of articles by Yisrael Natan Heschel, "The View of the Torah Giants in Their War against the Maskil Naphtali Herz Weisel," in *Kovets Beis Aharon* 43 (1993) (in Hebrew). These articles paint a malevolent picture of Wessely but, based as they are on a tendentious and ideology-driven reading of the sources, they are largely unreliable (except as a source for the perception that many contemporary Haredi Jews have of Wessely). (An example of this tendentiousness is the final footnote, which poses the "question" of how could many prominent rabbis and Torah scholars cite from Wessely's works, and even praise him, given that he was a well-known heretic and evil man? The author cannot think of a satisfying answer to this question. This kind of circular reasoning is a hallmark of these articles.)

29. Wessely apparently incorporated elements of that commentary into his commentary on Leviticus for Mendelssohn's *Biur* project, since Wessely makes frequent reference to the *Torat Kohanim* in the latter work.

30. Moses Mendelsohn of Hamburg, *Pnei Tevel* (Amsterdam, 1872), 240. Noah Rosenbloom's conjecture, in "Critical Evaluations in Mendelsohn of Hamburg's 'Penei Tevel'," in *Migvan: Studies in Hebrew Literature in Honor of Jacob Kabakoff*, ed. Stanley Nash (Lod: Habermann Institute for Literary Research, 1988), 388–89 (in Hebrew), that Eyebeschutz was not really praising Wessely at all with these remarks but was instead alluding to his concern that Wessely may have been a heretic (a fear allayed by "forcing" Wessely to read portions of his commentary, which did not contain heretical ideas) is highly speculative and not in the least compelling. It also assumes that Wessely, who proudly recounted this story, was totally oblivious to Eyebeschutz's suspicions regarding him, which would have been highly unlikely had such suspicions existed. In all probability, they did not exist, and this anecdote is to be taken at face value.

31. Even if Hirsch's uncle had not discussed this anecdote with him, Hirsch likely read it in *Pnei Tevel*, which was published during his lifetime. Hirsch's citations of Wessely occur in his Pentateuch commentary, part of which was published after *Pnei Tevel*—Hirsch's commentary to Leviticus, where most of the Wessely citations are found, was first published in 1873—and in his commentary to the Siddur, which was written during the 1880s and published posthumously.

32. In Mendel Frankfurter's last will and testament, he exhorts his family members to study the works of Wessely, which he characterizes as "unimpeachable" (*unantastbar*). The will has been reprinted in Eduard Duckesz, "Zur Genealogie Samson Raphael Hirsch," *Jahrbuch der jüdisch-literarischen Gesellschaft* 17 (Frankfurt am Main, 1926), 120–22, citation at 122. (At the same time, Frankfurter warns his family to stay away from the works of the radical maskilim, whom he characterizes as "innovators" [*Neuerern*] ("Zur Genealogie," 120). He obviously did not consider Wessely to be an innovator! As we have shown, many other leading Orthodox rabbis likewise did not regard Wessely this way.)

33. In fact, East European Orthodox rabbis occasionally cited Wessely's works as well. See, for example, Malbim's commentary to Isaiah 17:14; Netziv, *Emek ha-Netziv*, vol. 3, 79; Rabbi Joseph Saul Nathanson, *Divrei Sha'ul*, commentary to Talmud Berakhot 34a.

34. Rosenbloom, *Tradition in an Age of Reform*, 415n76. Cf. Katz, *House Divided*, 239: "[Hirsch was Mendelssohn's] spiritual descendent." Katz made this remark in the context of discussing Hirsch's views regarding religious coercion and Mendelssohn's views on the same subject.

35. Hirsch writes that Mendelssohn "had not drawn his mental development from Judaism [and] was great chiefly in philosophical disciplines, in metaphysics, and aesthetics. [He] treated the Bible only philologically and aesthetically, and did not build up Judaism as a science from itself, but merely defended it against political stupidity and pietistic Christian audacity, and who was personally an observant Jew." S. R. Hirsch, *The Nineteen Letters*, letter 18 (quote from Drachman translation, 189). Thus, Hirsch issued a harsher indictment of Mendelssohn than many of his rabbinic contemporaries elsewhere in Europe.

36. See Hildesheimer, "Moses Mendelssohn," and Hildesheimer, "Attitude of the Hatam Sofer."

37. Breuer, *Modernity within Tradition*, 80.

38. Michah Gottlieb, *The Jewish Reformation: Bible Translation and Middle-Class German Judaism as Spiritual Enterprise* (New York: Oxford University Press, 2021).

39. If, on the other hand, Hirsch was not a maskil, there is nothing remotely surprising about a young aspiring rabbi choosing to study in an institution in which Talmud and Jewish law were taught on a high level. Hirsch was ultimately ordained as an Orthodox rabbi by Ettlinger after studying for fifteen months in this yeshiva. Hirsch, *Shemesh Marpeh*, 278. Gottlieb also does not cite Hirsch's letter to L. P. Prins of Amsterdam, in which Hirsch demarcates an ambitious program of advanced Talmud study that Hirsch hoped Jewish boys would acquire at his school in Frankfurt. See Mayer Herskovics, ed., *Liepman Philip Prins: His Scholarly Correspondence* (Hoboken, NJ: Ktav, 1992), 37.

40. Gottlieb, *Jewish Reformation*, 257; previous citation from 239.

41. Hirsch, *Judaism Eternal*, vol. 2, 239–44. For the tendency among Orthodox writers, see Breuer, *Modernity within Tradition*, 80.

42. Gottlieb, *Jewish Reformation*, 240.

43. See chapter 6, note 11. For a concise summary of this regnant view, see Michael K. Silber, "Orthodoxy," in *The YIVO Encyclopedia of Jews in Eastern Europe*, available at the YIVO encyclopedia's website, accessed January 4, 2023. Cf. G. Bendheim, M. Butler, J. M. Harris, and U. Katz, eds., *Jacob Katz on the Origins of Orthodoxy* (Cambridge, MA: Shikey Press, 2022).

44. See the excellent recent study of Adler by Derek Taylor, *Chief Rabbi Nathan Marcus Adler: The Forgotten Founder* (London: Vallentine Mitchell, 2020).

45. Mordechai Breuer, Review of Noah Rosenbloom, *Tradition in an Age of Reform*, 141.

46. Leo Trepp, *Die Oldenburger Judenschaft: Bild und Vorbild jüdischen Seins und Werdens in Deutschland* (Oldenburg: Heinz Holzberg Verlag, 1973), 122–24. Only the questions posed to Hirsch have been preserved, not Hirsch's replies. Hirsch was also interviewed by a Christian superintendent.

47. *Sefer Torat ha-Kena'ot* (Amsterdam, 1845), 3a–5a. See Aaltje E. Kooij-Bas, "Nothing but Heretics: Torat ha-Qena'ot: A Study and Translation of Nineteenth Century Responsa against Religious Reform" (PhD diss., Tilburg University, 2006), 53n102, for a contemporaneous assessment of this book as representative of extreme Orthodoxy. On the book's primary editor, Zvi Hirsch Lehren, as a champion of ultra-Orthodoxy, see Chaya Brasz, "Dutch Jewry and Its Undesired German Rabbinate," *Leo Baeck Institute Yearbook* 57, no. 1 (2012): 73–86. Nevertheless, Hirsch's 1844 essay included his first explicit reference to "Torah and Derek Eretz" as a cure to the religious troubles of the times. Cf. Gottlieb, *Jewish Reformation*, 308–10.

48. See the beginning of Letter Two, where Naphtali reproaches Benjamin for the latter's assertion, at the end of Letter One, that he hoped Naphtali would tell Benjamin what he *really thinks*, not what he is required to say as a rabbi. Gottlieb, *Jewish Reformation*, 247–53, advances the speculative thesis that Hirsch's maskilic sensibilities engendered his independent approach to investigating Judaism. As shown here, the more compelling explanation is far more straightforward.

49. For Frankel's position, see his 1845 essay labeled "On Changes in Judaism," in *The Jew in the Modern World*, ed. Paul Mendes-Flohr and Jehuda Reinharz, *The Jew in the Modern World*, 3rd ed. (New York: Oxford University Press, 2011), 217–19.

50. Hirsch first posits this in *The Nineteen Letters*, letters 2, 17, 18, and 19. See I. Grunfeld, introduction to Hirsch, *Horeb*, trans. Grunfeld, xli; and Yizhak Ahren, "Samson Raphael Hirsch (1808–1888)," in *Judentum verstehen: Die Aktualität jüdischen Denkens von Maimonides bis Hannah Arendt*, ed. Hans Erler and Ernst Ludwig Ehrlich (Frankfurt am Main: Campus Verlag, 2002), 109–20.

51. Hirsch, *Nineteen Letters*, letter 18.

52. Hirsch, *Nineteen Letters*, letter 3 (29–30 in Drachman translation).

53. Hirsch, *Nineteen Letters*, letter 15 (156–57 in Drachman translation).

54. Hirsch, *Nineteen Letters*, letter 19 (cited from pp. 333–34 in Elias ed.; p. 215 in Drachman translation).

55. Ra'avad, glosses to Maimonides, *Mishneh Torah, Hil. Avot ha-Tume'ot* 2:10.

56. Hirsch, commentary to Genesis 6:6 (*The Pentateuch Translated and Explained by Samson Raphael Hirsch*, trans. Isaac Levy [Gateshead: Judaica Press, 1976], 133; *Der Pentateuch, übersetzt und erläutert von Samson Raphael Hirsch* [Frankfurt am Main, 1911], 110). The context is Hirsch's agreement with Ra'avad that Maimonides was mistaken for asserting that ascribing any corporeality to God is heresy. Hirsch argues that the Bible intentionally describes God as having human emotions, such as grief, so as to give humans a sense of God's personality.

57. "Jerusalem Talmud": see Jerusalem Talmud, *Berakhot* 9:1; "Midrash": see Midrash *Shir ha-Shirim Rabbah* 7:8; Midrash *Tanhuma*, Bemidbar 20.

58. Aharon Lichtenstein, *Leaves of Faith: The World of Jewish Living* (Jersey City: Ktav, 2004), 304.

59. "Sometimes referred to as a leader of Italian Neo-Orthodoxy": See, for example, David Rudavsky, "Samuel David Luzzatto and Neo-Orthodoxy," *Tradition* 7, no. 3 (Fall 1965): 21–44. Cf. Daniel Klein, ed., *The Book of Genesis: A Commentary by Shadal* (Northvale, NJ: Jason Aronson, 1998), xiv–xv, for discussion regarding Luzzatto's relationship to Orthodoxy, including references to how he has been characterized by different sources. See also the excellent study of Luzzatto by Shmuel Vargon, *Shmuel David Luzzatto: Moderate Criticism in Biblical Exegesis* (Ramat-Gan: Bar-Ilan, 2013) (in Hebrew), and Moshe Y. Miller, Review Essay of Ephraim Chamiel, *The Middle Way*, *Tradition* 49, no. 3 (Fall 2016): 37–40. "Argued that, etc.": Marc Gopin, "An Orthodox Embrace of Gentiles? Interfaith Tolerance in the Thought of S. D. Luzzatto and E. Benamozegh," *Modern Judaism* 18 (1998): 174–75. According to Isaac Heinemann, *The Reasons for the Commandments in Jewish Literature*, vol. 2 (Jerusalem: Jewish Agency, 1956), 266n64 (in Hebrew), Luzzatto and Hirsch were in complete agreement on the value of humanism, but apparently not on the precise value they each attributed to universalism, as demonstrated here.

60. Luzzatto, as cited in Gopin, "An Orthodox Embrace of Gentiles?" 176. Gopin notes that the Hebrew translation of this passage, published in Jerusalem in 1976 (ed. M. E. Arton), substitutes "all Jews" for "all human beings" in an obvious case of anti-universalist censorship. (Luzzatto wrote this passage in 1848.)

61. Luzzatto, as cited in Gopin, "Orthodox Embrace of Gentiles?" 180. (Luzzatto wrote this passage in 1862.)

62. For a thorough recent discussion of Luzzatto's views on the Oral Law, see Ephraim Chamiel, *The Middle Way: The Emergence of Modern Religious Trends: Responses to Modernity in the Thought of Maharatz Chayot, Rabbi S. R. Hirsch, and S. D. Luzzatto* (Boston: Academic Studies Press, 2014), vol. 1.

63. Michael Friedlander, *The History and Philosophy of the Jewish Religion* (New York: Pardes, 1946), 313.

64. It is for this reason that not much attention has been devoted here to Zechariah Frankel even though he, like Hirsch, believed that Judaism must be understood *aus such selbst* (out of itself). Since Frankel, unlike Hirsch, did not accept the notion that the Oral Torah was divinely revealed simultaneously with the Written Torah, his reaction to statements found in rabbinic literature that appear to conflict with modern sensibilities about universal human rights is not pertinent to the present study. Frankel, unlike

Hirsch, would have the freedom to dismiss those texts as the products of their human authors, living in ancient times.

65. Katell Berthelot, *Le monothéisme peut-il être humaniste?* (Paris: Fayard, 2006), 113–21.

66. Berthelot, *Le monothéisme peut-il être humaniste?* 122–23; 130–31.

67. Hirsch, commentary to Leviticus 19:33/34 (563–64 in Levy translation), possibly based on Sifra to Leviticus 19:33. An essay published in 2009 was developed on the presumption that Hirsch interpreted "love thy neighbor" as inclusive of non-Jews. On this basis, together with its reading of a passage in the commentary to the *Haftarot* by Hirsch's son Mendel as though Hirsch himself authored it, the author argues that Hirsch's universalism "is at times almost [*sic*] complete contradiction with Jewish legal literature," just as Hermann Cohen's universalism was. Hirsch is also charged with other departures from Jewish tradition regarding Jewish chosenness. However, a closer reading of the totality of Hirsch's writings—this essay limits its analysis to citations from Hirsch's Pentateuch commentary—would have painted a different picture. See Meir Soloveichik, "To Be German and Jewish: Hermann Cohen and Rabbi Samson Raphael Hirsch," in *Rav Chesed: Essays in Honor of Rabbi Dr. Haskel Lookstein*, ed. Rafael Medoff, vol. 2 (Jersey City: Ktav, 2009), 211–34 (citation from 214). For another recent portrayal of Hermann Cohen's conception of "neighbor-love," which discusses how he grappled with the Talmudic tradition relating to this issue, see Dana Hollander, "Love-of-Neighbor and Ethics Out of Law in the Philosophy of Hermann Cohen," in *German-Jewish Thought between Politics and Religion*, ed. C. Wiese and M. Urban (Berlin: De Gruyter, 2012), 83–113.

68. Shlomo Chertok, *An Old Flask of New Wine: Innovation and Conservatism in Rabbi Samson Raphael Hirsch's Biblical Commentary* (Tel Aviv: ha-Kibutz ha-me'uhad, 2010), 36–37 (in Hebrew), referring to Hirsch's commentary to Exodus 23:9 and Numbers 10:19. See also Isaac Heinemann, *The Reasons for the Commandments in Jewish Literature*, vol. 2 (Jerusalem: Jewish Agency, 1956), 127–30.

69. Chertok, *Old Flask*, 67; Hirsch, commentary to Exodus 21:1 (287–88); Hirsch, *Shemesh Marpeh*, 167.

70. See, for example, Hirsch's commentary to Leviticus 19:33/34.

71. Hirsch, commentary to Exodus 22:20.

72. *Jüdische Anmerkungen zu den Bemerkungen eines Protestanten über die Confession der 22 bremischen Pastoren* (Gerhard Stalling, 1841), published anonymously. Translated in Hirsch, *The Collected Writings*, vol. 9, *Timeless Hashkafah* (New York: Feldheim, 2012), 103–28. The matter is documented in Trepp, *Die Oldenburger Judenschaft*, 143–66, who also includes the original German text of Hirsch's essay.

73. For insightful background on aspects of the Kulturkampf that underlay this controversy, see Marjorie Lamberti, "Lutheran Orthodoxy and the Beginning of Conservative Party Organization in Prussia," *Church History* 37, no. 4 (December 1968): 439–53.

74. Hirsch, *Collected Writings*, vol. 9, 110.

75. This is essentially Luzzatto's position, that is, the simple meaning of the term *ger* is a non-Jew who lives in the land of Israel, and the rabbinic interpretation is forced. This is in keeping with his position that when basic principles such as of love of humanity, which he believed was one of the core teachings of the Torah, conflict with rabbinic

statements, the rabbinic view should be rejected. See Gopin, "Orthodox Embrace of Gentiles," 179–81.

76. The publication of Hirsch's responsa and Talmudic novellae in 1992 (Hirsch, *Shemesh Marpeh*) demonstrated, if such demonstration was needed, that Hirsch was not unlearned in the Talmud. Hirsch's polemics with Graetz over volume 4 of the latter's *Geschichte der Juden*, published in Hirsch's *Gesammelte Schriften* (and translated in *Collected Writings of Rabbi Samson Raphael Hirsch*, ed. and trans. Paul Forcheimer and Gertrude Hirschler, 8 vols. [New York: Feldheim, 1983–95], vol. 5) demonstrate Hirsch's Talmudic virtuosity, as he cites numerous passages from throughout the Babylonian and Jerusalem Talmuds, as well as the Tosefta and the various Midrashim. Since this volume of Hirsch's *Gesammelte Schriften* was available at the time of the publication of Rosenbloom's book, it renders all the more problematic Rosenbloom's assertions about Hirsch's ignorance of the Talmud and rabbinic literature and raises doubts about Rosenbloom's scholarly objectivity when it comes to S. R. Hirsch.

77. This interpretation of Hirsch is indebted to the analysis of Rabbi Dr. Mordechai Z. Cohen in his *The Rule of Peshat* (Philadelphia: University of Pennsylvania Press, 2020), chapter 4. See esp. 143, 146. (I thank Professor Cohen for graciously sharing his book with me.) That chapter treats the views of Rashbam and Rabbi Joseph Qara, and their approach appears to constitute ample precedent for Hirsch's, at least in this particular case. As a general rule, however, Hirsch considered the rabbinic exegesis of biblical verses, particularly exegesis that pertains to halacha, to be the only legitimate way of interpreting the text. See, for example, Hirsch's commentary to Exodus 21:2. Thus, it should be stressed here that Hirsch's own approach to biblical exegesis departs considerably from Rashbam's, particularly in terms of how each understands the relationship of rabbinic legal exegesis to the "simple" meaning of the biblical text. Further elucidation of Hirsch's approach to biblical exegesis is beyond the scope of the present work.

78. See Nahmanides to Exodus 22:20. Ibn Ezra, in his comments to that verse, explicitly endorses the view that the *ger* in question is a monotheistic non-Jew. Given Ibn Ezra's tendency to follow the straightforward meaning of biblical verses, this could have buttressed Hirsch's inclination to understand that verse as an exhortation pertaining to any stranger, Jew or non-Jew. (Even Rashi appears to understand that verse as referring to any stranger, whatever his nationality or religion. However, the supercommentaries to Rashi on that verse generally interpret Rashi's comments as pertaining only to fellow Jews.) On Ibn Ezra's approach to the Biblical "*ger*," see Yaakov Blidstein, "Ethics and Exegesis: The Biblical 'Stranger' according to Ibn Ezra," in Blidsten, *Studies in Halakhic and Aggadic Thought* (Beer-Sheva: Ben Gurion University Press, 2004), 365–78 (in Hebrew). Blidstein stresses the importance of the treatment of the biblical *ger* to the ethic of Judaism, particularly with respect to the "Other," which is why the meaning of the "*ger*" is central to understanding how Jewish thinkers like Ibn Ezra and Hirsch treated the status of non-Jews in Judaism. "Particularly given Hirsch's veneration of Nahmanides": See Hirsch's *Nineteen Letters*, letter 18.

79. Exodus 22:20; Leviticus 19:33–34; Leviticus 25:35; as well as Exodus 23:9, already noted by Chertok with respect to Hirsch's commentary to that verse in his Pentateuch translation.

80. Professors Mara Benjamin and Abigail Gillman suggested to me at an academic

seminar in December of 2013 that, in some sense, there were "two Hirsches": the polemicist and defender of Judaism to the outside world, on the one hand, and the rabbinic scholar dedicated to explicating the dense Talmudic material pertaining to the biblical verses he wrote a commentary to, on the other. These two personas, they suggested, were not necessarily always consistent with one another. Although I do not endorse that suggestion in my reading of Hirsch in this book, it is clear that Hirsch did face enormous pressures from both within and outside the Jewish community, and he chose to highlight those texts that were most suitable for each situation. I thank them for their suggestion, which has helped me to better formulate my ideas here. See also Abigail Gillman, *A History of German Jewish Bible Translation* (Chicago: University of Chicago Press, 2018), 144–96.

81. Another already discussed relevant factor is the Napoleonic Sanhedrin, whose supreme halachic authority was David Sinzheim (a figure who was revered even by the architect of Ultra-Orthodoxy, Hatam Sofer). Sinzheim allowed the citation of biblical verses admonishing Jews to treat the "stranger" with "the most tender care" and to "consider strangers as their brethren" as proof that Judaism considered French Christians to be their brethren, even though the verses cited were interpreted by rabbinic tradition as referring either to *gerei toshav* or to converts. (See Mendes-Flohr and Reinharz, *Jew in the Modern World*, 153, for this passage.) Hirsch was aware of the transactions of the Sanhedrin and likely regarded it as offering precedent for his own use of some of these verses in a similarly delicate situation where demonstrating Judaism's universalism was a pressing mandate.

82. See Chamiel, *Middle Way*, vol. 2, 319–26, for analysis of the biblical meaning of *ger* in the commentaries of Hirsch and Samuel David Luzzatto. Chamiel argues that Hirsch accorded primacy to the rabbinic interpretation of the term, which allows for some exceptions to the general rule that *ger* refers to a convert: "Hirsch tries to make coherent sense out of the matter, but with only slight success, with inner contradictions" (319). This book has argued that Hirsch's views are not contradictory.

83. Rosenbloom's book was subject to withering criticism by reviewers at the time of the book's publication. See Mordechai Breuer, Review of Noah H. Rosenbloom, *Tradition in an Age of Reform*, *Tradition*, 16 (Summer 1977): 140–47; Ismar Schorsch, "On the Father of Neo-Orthodoxy," *Judaism* 26, no. 3 (Summer 1977): 381–83. See also Robert Liberles, *Religious Conflict in Social Context: The Resurgence of Orthodox Judaism in Frankfurt am Main, 1838–1877* (Westport, CT: Greenwood Press, 1985), 263n32: "Rosenbloom has fabricated a scandalous falsehood out of this material."

84. Rosenbloom, *Tradition in an Age of Reform*, 60.

85. Rosenbloom, *Tradition in an Age of Reform*, 419n109.

86. "Earlier writiers": see, for example, Saemy Japhet, "The Secession from the Frankfurt Jewish Community under Samson Raphael Hirsch," *Historia Judaica* 10 (1948): 99–122. "Later scholars": See for example, David Sorkin, *The Transformation of German Jewry 1780–1840* (Detroit: Wayne State University Press, 1999), 156–71 and David Aberbach, *The European Jews, Patriotism, and the Liberal State* (Abingdon, UK: Routledge, 2013), 43: Hirsch "broke with traditionalists in his deep emotional attachment to the German people and culture and was fully identified with Schiller's German nationalism." Following this analysis, Aberbach cites Noah Rosenbloom's book. On p. 145,

Aberbach makes the unsubstantiated assertion that Hirsch (among other German-Orthodox rabbis) "regarded German *Kultur*, especially the German classics, as virtually equal in importance to the Hebrew Bible and Talmud."

87. See also Yaakov Perlow, "Rav S. R. Hirsch: The Gaon in Talmud and Mikra," in *The Living Hirschian Legacy*, ed. Eliyahu Glucksman et al. (New York: Feldheim, 1988), 75–89, who demonstrates Hirsch's Talmudic prowess based on material that predates the publication of Hirsch's responsa in 1992. See note 76, above.

88. Hirsch, commentary to Exodus 6:7 (Levy ed., 67–69; German original, 53–54). Cf. Hirsch's commentary to Genesis 11:7 (213–14 in Levy ed.). It is thus clear that Hirsch conceived of Judaism in national terms, but not in a sense that would require a common territory to generate that nationhood. See the text that follows this quote.

89. Hirsch, *Horeb*, paragraphs 551, 553.

90. This issue has been treated at length in Miller, "Between Frankfurt and Satmar."

91. Breuer, *Modernity within Tradition*, 295–96, has noted that when relations with the state were at issue, Hirsch did present Judaism in denominational, rather than national, terms. Thus, when he was a rabbi in Moravia he refused a request to lead a Jewish delegation before Franz Joseph II on the occasion of his ascension to the throne, stating, "Only as a religion are we a fellowship like all other religions in the fatherland, but in any connection pertaining to the state we should not and will not appear as a distinct body." This was based, argues Breuer, on Hirsch's "tendency to refrain from any political action that did not imply a specifically religious Jewish aspect" since the proposed delegation was not seeking to achieve any religious goals. This approach, in turn, is an outgrowth of Hirsch's view that Jews ought to contribute, without reservations, to the well-being of the nations in which they resided, but it has no bearing whatsoever, according to Breuer, on Hirsch's conception of Jewish nationhood.

92. Hirsch, *Horeb*, trans. I. Grunfeld, 462 (*Horev* [Altona, 1837], 617).

93. Hirsch's demand for internalization of the duty to the state is echoed in a medieval rabbinic source. Rabbi Bahya ben Asher, in his commentary to *parshat Matot* (Numbers ch. 29) (ed. C. D. Chavel, Jerusalem, 1994), 211–12, writes, on the basis of Proverbs 24:21, that just as one must *always* fear God since He is always present, so too must one *always* fear and respect the king, whether he is nearby or far away—one must always have the mindset that it is as though the king was present. Rabbi Bahya describes this as a religious duty imposed by God. It is clear from his comments that Rabbi Bahya was discussing a non-Jewish king, since he invokes Avot 3:2 (which describes the requirement to pray for the welfare of non-Jewish governing authorities). Hirsch (who read Bahya's Torah commentary) may have considered these remarks as a precedent for his own (though this is obviously speculative).

94. Hirsch, *Horeb*, 462 (*Horev* [Altona, 1837], 618).

95. Howard I. Levine, "Enduring and Transitory Elements in the Philosophy of Samson Raphael Hirsch," *Tradition* 5 (Fall 1962): 278–97. For more recent echoes of Levine's criticism, see Moshe Aberbach, *Jewish Education and History: Continuity, Crisis and Change*, trans. D. Aberbach (London: Routledge, 2009), 89–90, as cited in Aberbach, *European Jews*, xxxi–xxxii. For a reply to Levine, see Shelomoh E. Danziger, "Clarification of R. Hirsch's Concepts—A Rejoinder," *Tradition* 6 (Spring–Summer 1964): 141–58.

96. Judith Bleich, *Defenders of the Faith: Studies in Nineteenth- and Twentieth-Century Orthodoxy and Reform* (New York: Touro University Press, 2020), 186–87. Bleich, 187, cites the position of Rabbi Moshe Shmuel Glasner (1856–1924), who regarded it as a religious imperative of Judaism to sacrifice one's life, if need be, for king and country. Glasner, who was the leading Religious Zionist in Hungary (he founded the Hungarian branch of the Mizrachi), and who made aliyah when he moved to Jerusalem in 1923—at his farewell speech he implored his followers to follow his lead in abandoning Europe for the Holy Land—cannot be charged with overinfatuation with his country of residence. That he ruled as he did with respect to military service and sacrifice of one's life indicates that there may be no correlation between Hirsch's alleged adoration of the German Fatherland and his comments regarding army service. In any case, the context in which the *Horeb* was written was decisive, as will be shown.

97. Trepp, *Die Oldenburger Judenschaft*, 119–207; Trepp, "A Reappraisal of Samson Raphael Hirsch," *CCAR Journal* (Winter 1987): 29–40.

98. Adler vacated the position to assist his ailing father, the rabbi of Hanover.

99. Trepp, "Reappraisal," 30.

100. This is contra Liberles, *Religious Conflict in Social Context*, 113 (among others), who states that early in his career, Hirsch was regarded as "the most progressive leader of German Orthodoxy." Although he became even more militant in his Frankfurt years, he was regarded as rigid in his Orthodoxy even in his younger years.

101. This is the only modicum of truth to the Haredi legend that Hirsch was compelled to attend university in order to attain a rabbinical position.

102. Babylonian Talmud, *Baba Kamma* 113a; *Shulhan Arukh, Hoshen Mishpat* 369:6. Rabbi Moses Isserles, here, goes so far as to rule that even if discriminatory taxes are imposed upon Jews, they are required to pay them. This may have been a precedent for Hirsch's assertion that the duty of loyalty to one's host country is not dependent on how well-disposed the government is toward its Jewish subjects, although Isserles was codifying the laws of ethical conduct with respect to monetary affairs while Hirsch was expressing exhortatory patriotic sentiments.

103. In fact, affirmations of German patriotism were sometimes made for obviously political reasons, such as when, in 1846, the Orthodox party in Breslau petitioned the government on behalf of its desire to appoint Gedaliah Tiktin as its rabbi after the passing of his father and asked that Abraham Geiger's request for the post be denied. The Orthodox claimed that only those who were most faithful to their ancestral religion could be considered to be true patriots. See Liberles, *Religious Conflict in Social Context*, 83.

104. In his Pentateuch commentary, composed in Frankfurt between 1867 and 1878 (with the section on Leviticus appearing in 1873), Hirsch states that the biblical injunction to "Love thy neighbor as thyself" (Leviticus 19:18) applies only to fellow Jews (Levy ed., Leviticus, 563–64). He did, however, advocate love of all humanity on different grounds, as discussed.

105. Another German rabbi, Rabbi Israel Lipschutz (1782–1860; see this book's chapter 2), living in Danzig, authored a commentary to the Mishnah in which he refers to non-Jews as "our brethren from the [other] nations" (*aheinu me'ha-umot*). See *Tiferet Yisrael* to Mishna *Bava Kamma* 4:3, Boaz, note 1. Lipschutz wrote in Hebrew and there is no reason to believe that he was concerned with government oversight of his rabbinic

oeuvre. According to the *Jewish Encyclopedia*, in its website entry on Lipschutz, he led the life of an ascetic, often fasting for three days in a row. His relationship to German Bildung was quite limited.

106. These are found in the Sänger Collection at Bar-Ilan University. I thank Professor Gershon Bacon for putting me in contact with the director of the collection, Chaya-Bathya Markovits, who graciously provided me with copies of the letters I requested. I will refer to letters by their catalogue numbers as found in Shlomo Spitzer and Chaya-Bathya Markovits, eds., *The "Sänger Collection:" The Catalogue of the German and Hebrew Manuscripts* (Ramat-Gan: Bar-Ilan University, 2004).

107. Sänger Collection: Die deutschen Handschriften, no. 13 (dated May 28, 1847). It is interesting that Hirsch specifically refers to his children's knowledge of Latin grammar in this letter, which is a revealing glimpse into Hirsch's views on education, particularly as it concerned his own sons.

108. Naphtali Zvi Yehuda Berlin, *Why Antisemitism? A Translation of "The Remnant of Israel" by Rabbi Naphtali Zvi Yehuda Berlin*, ed. and trans. Howard S. Joseph (Northvale, NJ: Jason Aronson, 1996), 5–41. Hirsch's views about the equality of Jews and Christians with respect to his children's treatment in Moravia is consistent with his speeches in the Moravian Diet, in which he expressed the same view regarding the emancipation of the Jewish community.

109. Sänger Collection: Die deutschen Handschriften, no. 210 (dated 1870; no month or day is given).

110. At this point, one other aspect of Hirsch's personal relations with non-Jews should briefly be noted. Hirsch appears to have had little or no social contact with non-Jews. One possible exception may be the philosopher Arthur Schopenhauer (1788–1860). After he moved to Frankfurt, he lived in the same building as Schopenhauer (Eliyahu Meir Klugman, *Rabbi Samson Raphael Hirsch* [New York: Mesorah, 1996], 185). Certainly Hirsch's idealistic philosophy, often couched in Leibnizean terms, bears no traces of Schopenhauer's pessimism. Schopenhauer's daring—for a German writer of the period—adoption of atheism stands in stark contrast to Hirsch's consistently reverential adoration of God. But did Hirsch and Schopenhauer ever meet and discuss philosophical or religious questions? Schopenhauer's avowed anti-Judaism would have made such a meeting unlikely, though by no means impossible. I am not aware of any evidence of such a meeting.

111. Hirsch, commentary to Exodus 1:8–9 (5–6 in Levy translation).

112. Hirsch, *Horeb* trans. I. Grunfeld, 443 (*Horev* [Altona, 1837], p. 591) (emphasis added). Hirsch's interpretation of the biblical text pertaining to despising the Egyptian is based on the Babylonian Talmud, Tractate *Bava Kamma* 92b, and Rashi's commentary to Deuteronomy 23:8.

113. As late as 1865, the hardline Orthodox rabbis who have been characterized as the founders of Hungarian Ultra-Orthodoxy cited the biblical text and the Talmudic interpretation of the prohibition against despising the Egyptian and applied it to contemporary Hungarian gentiles. See the so-called Manifesto of Ultra-Orthodoxy in Mendes-Flohr and Reinharz, *Jew in the Modern World*, 227.

114. *Eleh Divrei ha-Berit* (Altona, 1819), 95–96.

115. *Eleh Divrei ha-Berit*, 95–96.

116. Mordechai Breuer, "Samson Raphael Hirsch and Modern Orthodoxy," *Niv Midrashia* 24–25 (1993): 32. Cf., however, Matthias Morgenstern, "Rabbi S. R. Hirsch and His Perception of Germany and German Jewry," in Steven Aschheim and Vivian Liska, eds., *Perspectives on Jewish Texts and Contexts: The German-Jewish Experience Revisited* (Berlin: De Gruyter, 2015), 220–21.

117. Gertrude Hirschler, "Rabbi and Statesman: Samson Raphael Hirsch, Landesrabbiner of Moravia (1847–1851)," *Review of the Society for the History of Czechoslovak Jews* 1 (1987): 121–49; Michael L. Miller, "Samson Raphael Hirsch and the Revolution of 1848," *Jewish Studies at the Central European University* 2 (2002): 223–38; Michael L. Miller, *Rabbis and Revolution: The Jews of Moravia in the Age of Emancipation* (Stanford, CA: Stanford University Press, 2011), 177–218. See also the pioneering study of Salo Baron, "The Revolution of 1848 and Jewish Scholarship: Part II: Austria," *Proceedings of the American Academy for Jewish Research* 20 (1951): 1–100.

118. For concise overviews of the trajectory of Jewish emancipation in Germany and the setbacks that German Jews faced, see Reinhard Rürup, "The Tortuous and Thorny Path to Legal Equality: 'Jew Laws' and Emancipatory Legislation in Germany from the Late Eighteenth Century," *Leo Baeck Institute Yearbook* 31 (1986): 3–33; Werner E. Mosse, "From '*Schutzjuden*' to '*Deutsche Staatsbürger Jüdischen Glaubens*': The Long and Bumpy Road of Jewish Emancipation in Germany," in *Paths of Emancipation: Jews, States, and Citizenship*, ed. Pierre Birnbaum and Ira Katznelson (Princeton, NJ: Princeton University Press, 1995), 59–93. For an excellent study with somewhat later periodization, see Peter Pulzer, *Jews and the German State: The Political History of a Minority, 1848–1933* (Detroit: Wayne State University Press, 2003). For a different—somewhat revisionist—perspective, see David Vital, *A People Apart: The Jews in Europe, 1789–1939* (New York: Oxford University Press, 1999), 63–69.

119. Miller, *Rabbis and Revolution*, 190–91, draws attention to Hirsch's statement in this petition of March 20, 1848, that "German princes have already sealed their justice by granting the Jewish children of their empire equal rights; will Austria's noble sons be the last?" Hirsch was anything but naive, and he was well aware that Jewish emancipation had hardly been fulfilled in all of the German states as of 1848, as noted by Christian Wiese, *Challenging Colonial Discourse: Jewish Studies and Protestant Theology in Wilhelmine Germany*, trans. B. Harshav and C. Wiese (Leiden: Brill, 2005), 43n14. Hirsch's point here was to draw attention to the fact that the emancipatory process had already begun in the German states (the first such edict dated March 11, 1812), whereas in the Hapsburg empire, the process had been much more belated, and Hirsch, who took an active role in championing emancipation during the period of the 1848 revolutions used this exhortatory rhetoric to draw attention to this fact. Thus, Miller's claim (193) that Hirsch's call to hold the burghers responsible for any outbreaks of anti-Jewish violence was "more wishful thinking than anything else" may be overstated. Furthermore, although Hirsch chose his language carefully to suit the situation at hand, there can be little doubt that Hirsch was genuinely optimistic about the prospects for Jewish emancipation to come about as a result of God-fearing, justice-seeking Christians. This is in keeping with Hirsch's overall view of the genuineness of Christian piety, discussed further in the next chapter.

120. Hirsch, *Nineteen Letters*, letter 10 (146 in Elias ed.). Cf. the end of letter 2 (17

in Elias ed.). See also I. Grunfeld's discussion of this term in Hirsch, *Horeb*, trans. Grunfeld, 269–70; and Grünewald, *Pedagogie, Esthetique et Ticoun Olam*, 57–59. The most concise explication that Hirsch himself gave to this term appears in his commentary to Genesis 17:1, where he writes that "to be a Jew presupposes that nothing of the purely human qualities is lacking in you" (291 in Levy ed.). Cf. Hirsch's commentary to Genesis 1:11–13 (18–19 in Levy ed.).

121. For example, Rosenbloom, *Tradition in an Age of Reform*, 168. According to Tasch, *Samson Raphael Hirsch*, 105n206, "Mensch-Yisroel" is Hirsch's version of Schleiermacher's "Neuem Menschen." Tasch cites a passage in Hirsch's *Gesammelte Schriften*, vol. 2 (330), where Hirsch comments on the Book of Isaiah and employs terminology that appears to be virtually identical to Schleiermacher's and, even more striking, to that of the Reformer Salomon Ludwig Steinheim. The present analysis confirms Tasch's: Hirsch did utilize terminology that he found in the writings of ideological opponents, both Jewish and non-Jewish. However, when Hirsch co-opted these terms, he did so carefully, placing his own unique imprint on them and channeling them to serve his own pedagogic ends. For Hirsch's intellectual debt to German philosophers and writers for his formulation of his religious philosophy, see Grünewald, *Pedagogie*, 107–26. (It should be noted that Grünewald, in the same volume at 127–77, painstakingly demonstrates that all key aspects of Hirsch's religious philosophy have precedent in traditional rabbinic sources, including the Zohar and the writings of Rabbis Isaac Luria and Hayyim Vital.) The following programmatic statement by Grünewald should be cited in this context: "Hirsch introduit la terminologie de la philosophie allemande dans son système, mais souvent les termes prennent chez lui un autre sens" (*Pedagogie*, 14).

122. Mordechai Breuer, Review of Noah H. Rosenbloom, *Tradition* 16, no. 4 (Summer 1977): 146–47. Cf. the view of Ignaz Maybaum, cited by Breuer, *Modernity within Tradition*, 420n78: "Be a 'Mensch,' preached Geiger, that is the mission of the Jew. . . . Be a Jew, preached S. R. Hirsch, that is your mission as a man."

123. Heinemann, *Reasons*, vol. 2, 154–56; Breuer, *Modernity within Tradition*, 294–307; Matthias Morgenstern, *From Frankfurt to Jerusalem: Isaac Breuer and the History of the Secession Dispute in Modern Jewish Orthodoxy* (Leiden: Brill, 2002), 109n25 and 183n77; Morgenstern, "Rabbi S. R. Hirsch." Cf. Michael K. Silber, "The Emergence of Ultra-Orthodoxy: The Invention of a Tradition," in *The Uses of Tradition*, ed. Jack Wertheimer (New York: Jewish Theological Seminary, 1992) 32n15.

124. Hirsch, commentary to Exodus 6:7.

125. Hirsch, *Horeb*, 409.

126. Hirsch, *The Collected Writings of Rabbi Samuel Raphael Hirsch*, ed. and trans. Paul Forcheimer and Gertrude Hirschler, vol. 7 (New York: Feldheim, 1992), 63–64. The essay was first written after the opening of Hirsch's school in Frankfurt (the Realschule) in 1853 and was intended as an explication of the school's principles for a general audience. It first appeared in *Einladungsschrift zu der öffentlichen Prüfung* ... (Frankfurt am Main, 1866) and was later reprinted in *Gesammelte Schriften*, vol. 2 (Frankfurt, 1904), 433–48. As this was a time of revival of German nationalism, Hirsch is quite bold in asserting that there is a *Jewish nation* that is independent of the German nation. It is unlikely that German Reform ideologues would have concurred with Hirsch.

127. Hirsch, *Collected Writings of Rabbi Samson Raphael Hirsch*, ed. and trans. Paul Forcheimer and Gertrude Hirschler, 8 vols. (New York: Feldheim, 1983–95), vol. 8, 21–60, from *Gesammelte Schriften*, vol. 5 (Frankfurt, 1910), 143–99. This originally appeared in eight installments of *Jeschurun* 8. Jahrgang: Kislev 5622 (1861)-Elul 5622 (1862).

128. Zionism, as a political movement, emerged in the decade following Hirsch's death in 1888, but there were developments in his lifetime related to the Zionist ideology, to which he reacted. The fullest treatment of the issue is Miller, "Between Frankfurt and Satmar."

129. This view has been advanced by Benjamin Brown, "Breuer, Hirsch and Jewish Nationalism: Change and Continuity—Principle versus Supra-Principle," *Journal of Jewish Studies* 64, no. 2 (Autumn 2013): 383–402. Brown concedes that it would be incorrect "to say that Hirsch regarded the Jews as nothing but a religious entity"; however, in his view, Hirsch considered the national identity of the Jews to be "purely a function of their religion, defined exclusively by the Torah" (387). Brown further alleges that "Hirsch was at one with the reformist 'innovators' calling for the Jews' total integration with their host countries," and he cites Rosenbloom's study of Hirsch as a basis for this interpretation (389).

130. This view is argued most cogently by Zev Levy, "The Land of Israel in Jewish Thought in Germany from Hirsch to Rosenzweig," *Kivunim* 4 (1979): 54–66 (in Hebrew). Levy cites only from Hirsch's *Nineteen Letters* in support of his interpretation of Hirsch's views on Jewish nationalism. It would have been helpful for Levy to cite more than just one work out of Hirsch's prolific writings. Rosenbloom, *Tradition in an Age of Reform*, espouses essentially the same position as Levy, and it is likely that Levy read Rosenbloom's 1976 book when writing his essay. Although Rosenbloom periodically cites Hirsch's later writings, he relies heavily on Hirsch's first two books even in cases where Hirsch clarifies ideas expressed in those books in his later writings. The view of Levy and Rosenbloom has been repeated in later studies (e.g., Victor Karady, *The Jews of Europe in the Modern Era: A Socio-historical Outline*, trans. Tim Wilkinson [Budapest: Central European University, 2004], 213). Cf. Rivka Horwitz, "The Relationship of Rabbi Samson Raphael Hirsch to the Land of Israel," in Rivka Horwitz, *Multiple Faceted Judaism* (Beer-Sheva: Ben Gurion University, 2003), 387–407 (in Hebrew).

131. Michael A. Meyer, *Response to Modernity: A History of the Reform Movement in Judaism* (New York: Oxford University Press, 1988), 78. The evidence Meyer cites for this assertion has largely to do with Hirsch's approach toward minhag (customary practices). A distinction should be made here between the authority of the written text of the Torah and the oral traditions of the Rabbis, on the one hand, and various customs that are not based on explicit Talmudic texts, on the other. With respect to the former, Hirsch was as rigid a traditionalist as any rabbi in Germany at any time. With respect to the latter, Hirsch simply felt that certain practices were erroneous and not grounded in any authoritative rabbinic sources and should be discontinued. Mention may be made here of the Gaon of Vilna (1720–97), whose approach toward practices that he believed were not sanctioned by the Talmud—even when there was ample precedent for them among medieval authorities and whose practice was widely accepted—was quite bold. Yet, it would be inconceivable to characterize the Gaon as "not a traditionalist by principle." See Immanuel Etkes, *The Gaon of Vilna: Image and Reality* (Berkeley: University of

California Press, 2003). Compare, however, the study of Eliyahu Stern, *The Genius: Elijah of Vilna and the Making of Modern Judaism* (New Haven, CT: Yale University Press, 2013), which challenges this interpretation of the Gaon. Stern's interpretation of the Gaon has been the subject of substantial criticism. See, for example, Lawrence Kaplan's November 9, 2013, review, found online: Review of Eliyahu Stern, *The Genius: Elijah of Vilna and the Making of Modern Judaism*, *Seforim Blog* (blog), November 19, 2013.

132. "No future ingathering of Jews": Meyer, *Response to Modernity*, 89–99. "Jerusalem no longer holds any significance": Abraham Geiger, *Das Judenthum und seine Geschichte*, vol. 3 (Breslau, 1871), 121, as cited in Isaac Barzilay, *Shlomo Yehuda Rapoport and His Contemporaries: Some Aspects of Jewish Scholarship of the Nineteenth Century* (Ramat-Gan: Massada Press, 1969), 17. See also Jacob J. Petuchowski, *Prayerbook Reform in Europe* (New York: World Union for Progressive Judaism, 1968), 278–81, for further references to primary sources where Geiger expresses his views on this subject. (Jerusalem "is for us an entirely indifferent city. It is nothing more than a venerable ruin, a decayed knight's castle." Geiger, as cited in Petuchowski, 280.)

133. Abraham Geiger, *Protokolle und Aktenstücke der zweiten Rabbinerversammlung abgehalten zu Frankfurt am Main* (Frankfurt am Main, 1845), 32–33, as cited by Barzilay, *Shlomo Yehuda Rapoport*, 17.

134. Hirsch, *Horeb*, paragraph 719 (the last paragraph in the book), 575–76 in Grunfeld translation.

135. The most famous source for this proscription, the so-called "Three Oaths," is the Babylonian Talmud, Tractate *Ketubot*, 111a. Hirsch's understanding of this as actual halacha (including references to the places in his writings where this is cited) is examined in Miller, "Between Frankfurt and Satmar."

136. Hirsch, *Neunzehn Briefe über Judentum* (Zurich: Verlag Morascha, 2013), letter 16, pp. 87–88.

137. Japhet, "Secession from the Frankfurt Jewish Community," 105–6.

138. Rosenbloom, *Tradition in an Age of Reform*, 110; Meyer, *Response to Modernity*, 78; Ismar Schorsch, *Jewish Reactions to German Anti-Semitism, 1870–1914* (New York: Columbia University Press, 1972), 10. See other sources cited earlier.

139. For example, Hirsch, *The Hirsch Siddur*, trans. Gertrude Hirschler (New York: Feldheim, 1969), 139: "As long as the Jewish national organism is dispersed in exile, it is sick." Cf. *Horeb*, 576.

140. Hirsch, *Neunzehn Briefe über Judentum*, letter 16, (87 in Zurich, 2013 ed.). This is my own translation, which includes portions of the translations of Drachman (New York: Funk and Wagnalls, 1899), 161–62, and Paritzky/Elias (New York: Feldheim, 1995), 224. The parentheses are in the original.

141. See Hirsch, *Horeb*, paragraph 608 (460–61 in Grunfeld ed.): "alone among all the peoples of the earth, the possession of the land and the ensuing organization of the State was for Israel not an end but a means to the better fulfillment of their Jewish duties"; Hirsch, commentary to Genesis 11:7 (214 in Levy ed.); Commentary to Exodus 22:24 (376); Hirsch, *The Hirsch Psalms*, trans. Gertrude Hirschler (New York: Feldheim, 1978), 313–14 (commenting on 117:1–2) (Hirsch, *Die Psalmen, übersetzt und erläutert von Rabbiner Samson Raphael Hirsch* [Frankfurt: Hermon Verlags-Aktiengesellschaft, 1924, 230), where Hirsch says that the "tribes of mankind" (*ha-umim*) refers to "a uniting of men in accordance

with their descent" ("*eine Vereinigung von Menschen nach ihrer Abstammung*"). Hirsch considers the Jewish people also to bear this characteristic.

142. See Hirsch, *The Collected Writings of Rabbi Samson Raphael Hirsch*, ed. and trans. Paul Forcheimer and Gertrude Hirschler, vol. 6 (New York: Feldheim, 1990).

143. See, for example, Hirsch, *Collected Writings*, vol. 6, 158–59.

144. Hirsch, *Collected Writings*, vol. 6, 61–106.

145. Hirsch, *Collected Writings*, vol. 6, 170–86.

146. Cf. Hirsch, *Collected Writings*, vol. 6, 206–7: "We no longer have *minim* or *apikorsim* [varieties of heretics] as defined in our legal codes . . . [Just as idolatry no longer exists in the strict sense], the same is true of our present-day fellow Jews who subscribe to *minut* and *apikorsut* in theory and practice . . . [Orthodox Jews must retain social contacts with Reform Jews], hoping that by such contacts we will be able to win their hearts and minds for all that is genuinely Jewish." Clearly, Hirsch regarded all who were Jewish by birth (i.e., born of Jewish mothers, in keeping with Orthodox law) to be members of the same nation. The task of the faithful was to return the unfaithful to the fold of the faithful (as Hirsch understood this concept).

Chapter 9

1. See Moshe Miller, "R. Jacob Emden's Attitude toward Christianity," in *Turim: Studies in Jewish History and Literature Presented to Dr. Bernard Lander*, vol. 2 (New York: Touro College Press 2008), 128–31.

2. Avraham Ben Moshe, *Perush Rabbenu Avraham ben ha-Rambam al Bereshit u-Shemot*, ed. Ephraim Y. Weisenberg (London: S. D. Sassoon, 1958), 302.

3. Ovadia Seforno, commentary to Exodus 19:5–6. Cf. Max Wiener, "The Conception of Mission in Traditional Judaism," *YIVO Annual of Jewish Social Science* 2–3 (1947–48): 9–24.

4. Jacob Haberman, "Kaufmann Kohler and His Teacher Samson Raphael Hirsch," *Leo Baeck Institute Yearbook* 43 (1998): 78.

5. Judith Bleich, "Rabbi Jacob Ettlinger, His Life and Works: The Emergence of Modern Orthodoxy in Germany" (PhD diss., New York University, 1974), 261n1.

6. Hirsch, *The Collected Writings of Rabbi Samson Raphael Hirsch*, ed. and trans. Paul Forcheimer and Gertrude Hirschler, vol. 7 (New York: Feldheim, 1992), 12–13, 19–25, 83–87; compare vol. 8, 321–25.

7. This analysis is indebted to Michael Meyer, *Response to Modernity: A History of the Reform Movement in Judaism* (New York: Oxford University Press, 1988) 67–99, 112–42.

8. Aaron F. Kleinberger, "Nationalist Ferment in German Jewry in the First Half of the 19th Century," in *Studies in the History of Jewish Society in the Middle Ages and in the Modern Period*, ed. E. Etkes and Y. Salmon (Jerusalem: Magnes Press, 1980), 230 (in Hebrew). Cf. Mordechai Breuer, *The "Torah-im-Derekh-Eretz of Samson Raphael Hirsch"* (New York: Feldheim, 1970), 35–36: "The universal mission of Israel does not postulate an active engagement in moulding the spiritual images of other nations. The participation of Israel in the spiritual life of the nations of the world bears an essentially passive and receptive character, reflected in knowledge, understanding, observance and expectation."

9. Isaac Heinemann, *The Reasons for the Commandments in Jewish Literature*, vol. 2 (Jerusalem: Jewish Agency, 1956), 96–97, 265n34; Heinemann, "Samson Raphael Hirsch:

The Formative Years of the Leader of Modern Orthodoxy," *Historia Judaica* 13 (1951): 43; Noah Rosenbloom, *Tradition in an Age of Reform: The Religious Philosophy of Samson Raphael Hirsch* (Philadelphia: Jewish Publication Society, 1976), 68–70; Meyer, *Response to Modernity*, 77. See also Jacob J. Petuchowski, *Prayerbook Reform in Europe* (New York: World Union for Progressive Judaism, 1968), 337–38.

10. See Mordechai Breuer, "Perakim Mitokh Biographiah: Al Bitul Kol Nidre be-Oldenburg," *HaMa'ayan* 4, no. 2 (5624), 7–12; Immanuel Jackobovits (private letter), as cited in Petuchowski, *Prayerbook Reform in Europe*, 337; Shalom Meir Wallach, *Penine Ha-Rashar Hirsch* (Bene Berak: Tevunah, 5769), 312–13. Ironically, one of Hirsch's detractors, Saemy Japhet, offers an apologia for Hirsch's actions: "Only once did he yield to outside pressure, when—in Oldenburg—he allowed *Kol Nidre* to be abolished." Saemy Japhet, "The Secession from the Frankfurt Jewish Community under Samson Raphael Hirsch," *Historia Judaica* 10 (1948): 105. Note Japhet's characterization of Hirsch's action as something he "allowed" due to [unspecified] "outside pressure."

11. David Charles Smith, "Protestant Anti-Judaism in the German Emancipation Era," *Jewish Social Studies* 36, nos. 3–4 (July–October 1974): 206–7.

12. Roland Tasch, *Samson Raphael Hirsch: Jüdische Erfahrungswelten im Historischen Kontext* (Berlin: De Gruyter, 2011), 136–51.

13. See Heinemann, *Reasons*, 96–97, 146–47.

14. Tasch, *Samson Raphael Hirsch*, 146–48.

15. Tasch, *Samson Raphael Hirsch*, 151.

16. See the analysis in Leo Trepp, *Die Oldenburger Judenschaft: Bild und Vorbild jüdischen Seins und Werdens in Deutschland* (Oldenburg: Heinz Holzberg Verlag, 1973).

17. *Allgemeine Zeitung des Judentums* 6, no. 12 (March 19, 1842): 170. (The report about Hirsch is dated February 28, 1842, and it cites an earlier essay by Holdheim.) The reporter for this paper made reference to Hirsch's abolition of the prayer three years prior (1839) and cited a letter that Hirsch wrote to him explaining his decision to annul *Kol Nidre*. In it, Hirsch refers to the abolishment being justifiable on legal grounds, with *al pi ha-din* [lit., in accordance with the law] written in Hebrew characters in his German letter. Hirsch adds that the prayer was abolished only once and was then reinstituted for the reasons already outlined.

18. This interpretation echoes one that was earlier suggested by Leo Trepp, namely, that Hirsch was concerned (like many of his Reform rivals) about the special "Jewish Oath" administered to Jews due to concerns of untrustworthiness on their part. Cited in Petuchowski, *Prayerbook Reform*, 337–38. In another place, Trepp suggests the influence of Hirsch's predecessor in the Oldenburg rabbinate, Nathan Marcus Adler. Adler had been concerned about anti-Jewish sentiment festering as a result of the *Kol Nidre* prayer and was convinced that its abolishment would not violate Jewish law. See Trepp, *Die Oldenburger Judenschaft*, 97n86.

19. Hirsch, commentary to Numbers 22:8 (394 in Levy translation).

20. Hirsch, commentary to Numbers 22:8 (394 in Levy translation).

21. Hirsch, commentary to Numbers 22:8 (394 in Levy translation). Hirsch paraphrases Bamidbar Rabbah 20:1. On this Midrash, see Ephraim E. Urbach, "Homilies of the Rabbis on the Prophets of the Nations and the Balaam Narrative," *Tarbiz* 25, no. 3 (April 1956): 272–89 (in Hebrew).

22. Menachem Kellner, *Maimonides on Judaism and the Jewish People* (Albany: SUNY Press, 1991); Kellner, *Maimonides' Confrontation with Mysticism* (Oxford: Littman Library, 2006), 216–64. The most expansive treatment of this issue is in Kellner's book *They Too Are Called Human: Gentiles in the Eyes of Maimonides* (Ramat-Gan: Bar-Ilan, 2016) (in Hebrew). See also Kellner, *Maimonides the Universalist: The Ethical Horizons of the Mishneh Torah* (Oxford: Littman Library, 2020). Kellner's own Maimonidean-inspired universalism is formulated in his *We Are Not Alone: A Mamonidean Theology of the Other* (Boston: Academic Studies Press, 2021).

23. Hirsch, commentary to Genesis 34:25 (523–24 in Levy ed.; 430–32 in German original).

24. Babylonian Talmud *Yevamot*, 79a.

25. Hirsch *Pentateuch*, commentary to Numbers 16:4, 272–73 in Levy edition (emphasis added). In the original, Hirsch quotes the biblical verses in Hebrew; I used his own translations in this quotation.

26. Yeshayahu Leibowitz, *Judaism, Human Values, and the Jewish State*, ed. and trans. Eliezer Goldman (Cambridge, MA: Harvard University Press, 1995), 78, makes the same point about the falsehood of Korah's premises. However, classical Jewish commentaries to the Pentateuch (at least those I have seen) do not make this assertion.

27. Kellner discusses this at length in multiple publications, including *Maimonides on Judaism and the Jewish People*, *Maimonides' Confrontation with Mysticism*, *They Too Are Called Human*, *Maimonides the Universalist*, and *We Are Not Alone*.

28. For a classic presentation of Maharal's views on Israel and the nations, see Jacob Katz, *Exclusiveness and Tolerance* (New York: Behrman House, 1961), 135–42. A study that attributes much significance to Maharal's exclusivism in the development of Orthodoxy is David Sorotzkin, "Kehillat ha-al Zeman be-Idan ha-Temurot" (PhD diss., Hebrew University, 2007), cited in David B. Ruderman, *Early Modern Jewry* (Princeton, NJ: Princeton University Press, 2010), 147–48. See also Sorotzkin's book, *Orthodoxy and Modern Disciplination* (Tel Aviv: Kibbutz ha-me'uhad, 2011) (in Hebrew). Jacob Katz's view has been challenged by Hayyim Hillel Ben-Sasson and David B. Ruderman. See Ruderman, *Jewish Thought and Scientific Discovery in Early Modern Europe* (Detroit, Wayne State University Press, 1995), 60–66 (which includes the Ben-Sasson citations). More recently, Joanna Weinberg, "A Humanist in the Kloyz: New Perspectives on the Maharal of Prague and Jacques Bongars," *Journal of the History of Ideas* 77, no. 4 (October 2016): 521–37, challenged this critique and effectively reaffirmed Katz's position. Several highly exclusionary passages from Maharal are cited there. It would seem that this debate does not call into question Maharal's exclusivism at all. The point of contention is to what extent Katz's assertion that Maharal's exclusivism was generated by isolation from the Christian world is tenable. There can be no question, however, that Maharal's essentialist typology of Jewish and gentile proclivities, where the gentile is ontologically incapable of spirituality while the Jew by nature is a spiritual being, is the most extreme formulation of exclusivism toward gentiles that had ever been expressed by a Jewish thinker prior to Maharal, with the exception of certain Kabbalistic texts and works based upon them, as noted.

29. Babylonian Talmud, *Avodah Zarah*, 3a, and in several other Midrashic passages.

30. Maharal, *Gevurot Hashem* (London: n. p., 1964), chapter 72, 327–28.

31. Moses Hayyim Luzzatto, *Derekh Hashem* (Jerusalem: A. M. Lunz, 1914), part 2, chapter 4, par. 7 (35–36).

32. Hirsch *Pentateuch*, commentary to Genesis 12:7 (233 in Levy translation). Noteworthy is the context in which Hirsch makes this assertion. Hirsch notes that the land of Israel had been the home of the debauched Canaanites whom the land "spewed out," and yet the same land was chosen for the Jewish people. This demonstrates, according to Hirsch, that the entry of Israel into its land was meant to demonstrate that "there can be no race of mankind in any land whatsoever who cannot be won" to the truths of Torah.

33. Cf. Eliyahu Meir Klugman, *Rabbi Samson Raphael Hirsch* (New York: Mesorah, 1996), 284: "[Hirsch's views were] a far cry from the attitude prevalent in Eastern Europe in his day, which saw Judaism as concerned only with Jews and uninterested in the '*treifene*, anti-Semitic outside world.' Although easily understood in light of centuries of ghetto life and unremitting persecution, this view, he held, is nevertheless a distortion of Judaism."

34. Hirsch, *Collected Writings*, vol. 7, 85–87. A slightly different translation appears in Hirsch, *Judaism Eternal: Selected Essays from the Writings of Rabbi Samson Raphael Hirsch*, ed. and trans. I. Grunfeld (London: Soncino Press, 1956), vol. 1, 207–9.

35. Described in the Book of Exodus, chaps. 19–20.

36. Hirsch, *The Hirsch Siddur*, trans. Gertrude Hirschler (New York: Feldheim, 1969), 605 (emphasis added).

37. Hirsch, *The Nineteen Letters* (ed. Joseph Elias), commentary to letter 7, 111.

38. Moses Hayyim Luzzatto, *Derekh Hashem*, part 2, chapter 4, par. 5.

39. See Moses Hayyim Luzzatto, *The Way of God*, trans. Aryeh Kaplan (New York: Feldheim, 1997), 141: "At this time [Sinai] God also gave the nations a last chance . . . If any nation would have then accepted the Torah, it would have elevated itself from its lower state. As it was, none of them desired the Torah, and their judgment was therefore sealed completely. The gate was permanently closed, never again to be opened." Any reconciliation of these words with Hirsch's views is impossible.

40. Hirsch, *Hirsch Siddur*, 13. Hirsch hereby affirms that despite uttering the words that thank God for not having made a Jew a non-Jew (text: "who has not made me a gentile"), Jews are really contemplating their unique roles as Jews. No earlier commentator reacted this way to the issues engendered by the negative formulation in this text.

41. See Petuchowski, *Prayerbook Reform in Europe*, 298–306.

42. The charge, first made in the year 1400, that this text referred to Jesus was refuted by Menasseh ben Israel in the seventeenth century, although it is far from clear that the accusation was without basis. See Yaakov Elbaum, "Concerning Two Textual Emendations in the *Aleinu* Prayer," *Tarbiz* 42, no. 1–2 (October 1972–March 1973): 204–8 (in Hebrew), and the literature cited there, esp. 206n16; and the excellent study by Ruth Langer, "The Censorship of Aleinu in Ashkenaz and Its Aftermath," in *The Experience of Jewish Liturgy*, ed. Debra Reed Blank (Leiden: Brill, 2011), 147–66; Ruth Langer, *Cursing the Christians? A History of the Birkat HaMinim* (New York: Oxford University Press, 2012), 123–24. See also Israel Jacob Yuval, *Two Nations in Your Womb: Perceptions of Jews and Christians in Late Antiquity and the Middle Ages*, trans. Barbara Harshav and Jonathan Chipman (Berkeley: University of California Press, 2008), 192–204, and Yoel

H. Kahn, *The Three Blessings: Boundaries, Censorship, and Identity in Jewish Liturgy* (New York: Oxford University Press, 2011), 48–49, 154n25.

43. Indeed, the spiritual successor to Hirsch's Frankfurt *kehillah*, K'hal Adath Jeshurun of New York, has likewise chosen to omit that sentence. See *Mahzor Shivhei Yeshurun*, ed. David Hayyim Roth (Washington Heights, NY, 2016), 63n1.

44. Hirsch, *Hirsch Siddur*, 209.

45. See David Berger, *Persecution, Polemic, and Dialogue: Essays in Jewish-Christian Relations* (Boston: Academic Studies Press, 2010), 109–38, esp. 121–27. For an overview of more modern approaches to the question, see David Shatz, "A Jewish Perspective," in *The Oxford Handbook of Religious Diversity*, ed. Chad V. Meister (New York: Oxford University Press, 2011), 365–80, esp. 370–71.

46. Hirsch, *Hirsch Siddur*, 208–9.

47. Hirsch, *Hirsch Siddur*, 427.

48. Hirsch, *Hirsch Siddur*, 446.

49. Jerusalem Talmud, Tractate Nedarim 9:4; Sifra (to Leviticus) 19:18. Tanna Ben Azzai was a Mishnaic Sage from the early second century CE.

50. Hirsch, commentary to Genesis 5:1 (118 in Levy translation) (emphasis in original).

51. Interestingly, it was Rabbi David Frankel, Mendelssohn's teacher in rabbinics, who first brought out the universalistic implications of Ben Azzai's statement. In his commentary, *Korban ha-Edah*, to the Jerusalem Talmud (Nedarim 9:4 s. v. *zeh sefer*), Frankel suggests as one of the two possible meanings of Ben Azzai's seemingly enigmatic assertion that, "This book is of the developments of man" is an even greater principle than "Love Thy Neighbor as Thyself," the connection between Genesis 5:1 and the genealogy of Adam's descendants that follows. This genealogy demonstrates the brotherhood of mankind—the idea that all human beings descend from one common ancestor, a radical supposition in the ancient world—and it is that notion that encompasses a far broader principle than the injunction for Jews to love fellow Jews as themselves. It is possible that Hirsch alludes to this when he says the verse indicates a "much higher union of all men."

52. Maimonides, *Mishneh Torah*, Laws of Kings 9:14.

53. Nahmanides, commentary to Genesis 34:13.

54. Hirsch, Pentateuch commentary, to Genesis 34:25 (523 in Levy ed.).

55. Hirsch, Pentateuch commentary, to Genesis 12:10–13 (236–37 in Levy ed.).

56. Noteworthy also is Hirsch's reading of Jacob's censure of his sons' conduct as a reproach of their moral failings, and of its impact on the reputation of Jacob as a beacon of justice to the world. Jacob's remarks are usually understood as pragmatic chastisement of behavior that could endanger his family.

57. Hirsch, commentary to Deuteronomy 7:16 (133 in Levy ed.). In his commentary to Deuteronomy 20:10–14 (391–93 in Levy ed.), Hirsch adopts the view of Maimonides and Nahmanides that the offer of peace referred to in the biblical text was a halachic requirement regardless of whether the war the Jews were engaged in was a voluntary war or a mandatory one, even that which was waged against the pagan inhabitants of the land of Israel at the explicit behest of God. This would mean (as Hirsch notes) that the command to extirpate these pagans found in verses 16–17 ("thou shall not leave any soul alive") was not an absolute imperative and was only to be carried out if the pagans refused

to accept the terms of the peace offer. However, this was not the unanimous view among rabbinic authorities. Rashi, in his commentary to verse 10, citing the Rabbinic Midrash to Deuteronomy, the Sifre, adopts the view that no offer of peace was to be made when it came to mandatory wars. (See also Ra'avad's glosses to Maimonides [*Hil. Melakhim* 6:1] and the commentary of the *Lehem Mishneh* thereon.) Hirsch does not mention this alternative position but merely refers to the view that peace must be offered in *all* cases as the correct one, which he characterizes as "the most general views expressed in Sifre and Yerushalmi, and upheld also by Rambam and Ramban." Despite Hirsch's harsh censure of Maimonides in *The Nineteen Letters* (letter 18), here his humanitarian instincts led him to adopt the view of Maimonides (which Nahmanides shared).

58. See Matthias Morgenstern, "The Embarrassment of Joshua: Strategies for Interpreting the Biblical Account of the Conquest of Canaan in German-Jewish Neo-Orthodoxy in the Late Nineteenth and Early Twentieth Centuries," in *The Gift of the Land and the Fate of the Canaanites in Jewish Thought*, ed. Katell Berthelot, Joseph E. David, and Marc Hirshman (New York: Oxford University Press, 2014), 230–50, who draws attention to Hirsch's humanistic reading of the Biblical texts pertaining to the conquer of the land of Israel.

59. Hirsch, *The Hirsch Psalms*, trans. Gertrude Hirschler (New York: Feldheim, 1978), introduction, xi (Hirsch, *Die Psalmen* [Frankfurt am Main: Hermon Verlags-Aktiengesellschaft, 1924], i).

60. Hirsch, *Hirsch Psalms*, xv (Hirsch, *Die Psalmen*, iv).

61. For an example of a contemporary of Hirsch who took a diametrically opposed position, see Rabbi Yosef Hayyim of Baghdad, *Shu"t Rav Pe'alim*, *Yoreh Deah*, vol. 4 (Jerusalem: n. p., 1912), no. 29, 44. Rabbi Yosef Hayyim (1834–1909) was asked if it might be permissible to sell a copy of the Book of Psalms in Hebrew to a non-Jew (the English consul in Baghdad) who requested it. The rabbi forbade such a sale on the grounds that a non-Jew may only study the Seven Noahide Laws, none of which are discussed in the Book of Psalms.

62. See, for example, Jacob Zvi Mecklenburg, *Ha-Ketav ve-Hakabalah*, to Deuteronomy 4:19, for an elaboration of this point based on rabbinic sources.

63. Cf. Ephraim Chamiel, *The Middle Way: The Emergence of Modern Religious Trends: Responses to Modernity in the Thought of Maharatz Chayot, Rabbi S. R. Hirsch, and S. D. Luzzatto* (Boston: Academic Studies Press, 2014), vol. 2, 78–81.

64. At this juncture, one must address the following question: how did Hirsch deal with the well-known view of Rabbi Judah Halevy in his Kuzari regarding Jewish chosenness and the inherent superiority of the Jewish people over all other nations (see esp. Kuzari I, 27)? Hirsch specifically singles out Halevy in the eighteenth letter of his *Nineteen Letters* as one of the most faithful bearers of Jewish tradition over the ages. Did Hirsch simply reject Halevy's views on this matter? It is quite possible that he did, regarding Halevy's approach as having been generated by the medieval context in which he wrote. But there is another possibility: a rereading of Halevy that negates the apparent Jewish chauvinism that Halevy is supposed to have expressed. A recent argument for this type of reading is Micah Goodman, *The Dream of the Kuzari* (Or Yehuda: Dvir, 2012) (in Hebrew). Although Goodman's interpretation of Halevy relies on an unconventional approach to the text, Hirsch may nevertheless have understood Halevy in a similar fashion—that is to say that the views expressed by the Jewish sage in

the Kuzari do not represent the sole authentic Jewish view on the issues he discusses. Rather, a more holistic understanding of these issues emerges from reading the book as a dialogue where the king of the Khazars expresses equally valid viewpoints. If this is how Hirsch understood the Kuzari, then there would be no conflict between his own views on Jewish chosenness and those he imputed to Judah Halevy, whom he revered so greatly. See also Lippman Bodoff, "Was Yehudah Halevi Racist?" *Judaism* 38 (Spring 1989): 176–84. Chamiel, *Middle Way*, vol. 2, 81, asserts that Hirsch rejected Halevy's position concerning the nature of Jewish chosenness. Mordechai Breuer, *Modernity within Tradition*, trans. E. Petuchowski (New York: Columbia University Press, 1992), 59, asserts that "the spell of the Enlightenment made him [Hirsch] balk at Halevi's quasi-biological interpretation of Jewish peoplehood." "Whom Hirsch has characterized as 'one of our most thoughtful commentators': Hirsch, commentary to Genesis 37:11–12 (544 in Levy translation). "Expressed a similar viewpoint": See commentary of Ovadia Seforno to Exodus 19:5 and 6 (ed. Zev Gottlieb, [Jerusalem, 1992], 169); introduction of Seforno to his Genesis commentary (Gottlieb ed., 4–6).

65. See the commentaries of Hezekiah ben Manoah [Hizkuni], *Perush al ha-Torah*, ed. C. D. Chavel (Jerusalem: Mossad haRav Kook, 1981) and Rabbi Joseph Bekhor Shor, *Perush al ha-Torah* (Jerusalem: Mossad haRav Kook, 1994) to Exodus 4:22.

66. Hirsch, commentary to Exodus 4:22–23 (48–49 in Levy translation). Emphasis added.

67. Hirsch, commentary to Leviticus 20:26 (584–85 in Levy translation). Note that Hirsch characterizes this as a "great saying," a characterization he does not employ whenever he cites a Midrash. Clearly, this particular passage was of singular significance for Hirsch's conception of Jewish chosenness.

68. Hirsch, commentary to Genesis 18:1 (311–12 in the Levy translation; 256–57 in original German). Emphasis in the original.

69. See Tova Ganzel, "Explicit and Implicit Polemic in Rabbi Samson Raphael Hirsch's Bible Commentary," *Hebrew Union College Annual* 81 (2012): 171–91.

70. Friedrich Schleiermacher, *The Christian Faith*, trans. H. R. Mackintosh and J. S. Stewart (London: T&T Clark, 1928), 37.

71. The foregoing discussion of Bauer's views is based on Nathan Rotenstreich, "For and Against Emancipation: The Bruno Bauer Controversy," *Leo Baeck Institute Yearbook* 4 (1959): 3–36. For a recent treatment, see George Y. Kohler, "The Birth of Modern Theology: Reactions to Bruno Bauer's Secular Supersessionism," *Journal for the History of Modern Theology* 28 (2021): 1–20. See also Yoav Peled, "From Theology to Sociology: Bruno Bauer and Karl Marx on the Question of Jewish Emancipation," *History of Political Thought* 13, no. 3 (1992): 463–85.

72. Rotenstreich, "For and Against Emancipation," 10.

73. Rotenstreich, "For and Against Emancipation," 10. Samuel Hirsch, Reform rabbi and disciple of Samuel Holdheim, accepted Bauer's claim that Talmudic Judaism—unlike certain forms of Biblical Judaism—was intolerant of non-Jews. For analysis of Hirsch's views, see Judith Frishman, "Good Enough for the Goyim? Samuel Hirsch and Samuel Holdheim on Christianity," in *Interaction between Judaism and Christianity in History, Religion, Art and Literature*, ed. M. Poorthuis, J. J. Schwartz, and J. Turner (Leiden: Brill, 2009), 271–87.

74. Rotenstreich, "For and Against Emancipation," 11–12.

75. Ghillany's views were met with a response by the Reform thinker Abraham Jacob Adler, in which Adler conceded that even if Jewish prayers do contain calls for vengeance on "the goyim," most contemporary Jews simply did not understand these Hebrew prayers and they therefore do not shape their outlook. See Michael A. Meyer, "Religious Reform and Political Revolution in Mid-Nineteenth Century Germany: The Case of Abraham Jakob Adler," in *German-Jewish Thought between Politics and Religion*, ed. Christian Wiese and Martina Urban (Berlin: De Gruyter, 2012), 68.

76. See chapter 3 of this book.

77. See Eliyahu Stern, "Genius and Demographics in Modern Jewish History," *Jewish Quarterly Review* 101, no. 3 (Summer 2011): 347–82; Stern, *The Genius: Elijah of Vilna and the Making of Modern Judaism* (New Haven, CT: Yale University Press, 2013), 2, 32, 63–82, 166–71.

78. One, already cited, is Jerusalem Talmud, Tractate *Nedarim* 9:4 (the view of Ben Azzai).

79. The speech was first printed in *Jeschurun* (6. Jahrgang, Teveth 5619 [1859], 188–208), titled, "Worte, gesprochen bei der Schulfeier der Unterrichtsanstalt der Israelitischen. Religionsgesellschaft zu Frankfurt a.M., den 9 November 1859, am Vorabend der Schillerfeier"; reprinted in *Gesammelte Schriften*, vol. 6 (Frankfurt: n. p., 1912), 308–21. Two English translations exist. The first was by Gertrude Hirschler and was published in *The Collected Writings of Rabbi Samson Raphael Hirsch*, vol. 9 (New York: Feldheim, 2012), 137–52. The second is by Marc B. Shapiro, "Rabbi Samson Raphael Hirsch and Friedrich von Schiller," *Torah u-Madda Journal* 15 (2008–9): 172–87. (The Hirschler translation was a manuscript for many years before it was published in 2012.)

80. Hirsch, *Collected Writings*, vol. 9, 148, and *Jeschurun* (6. Jahrgang, Teveth 5619 [1859], 199).

81. Alexander Mathäs, "Faith and Reason: Schiller's 'Die Sending Moses,'" *German Quarterly* 81, no. 3 (2008): 283–301. See also the earlier sources cited there, at 298n3. Cf. Jeffrey L. High, "Clever Priests and the Missions of Moses and Schiller: From Monotheism to the Aesthetic Civilization of the Individual," in *Religion, Reason, and Culture in the Age of Goethe*, ed. Elisabeth Krimmer and Patricia Anne Simpson (New York: Camden House, 2013), 79–98.

82. I owe this formulation (of an insight that I first noted many years ago) to Zahava Ginsberg, a student in my course Readings in Rabbi S. R. Hirsch in the spring 2021 semester at Lander College for Women. Her persistence in challenging my presentation of Hirsch's tribute to Schiller compelled me to reconsider Hirsch's relationship to "heretical" views and thereby produce the formulation here.

83. Friedrich Schiller, "Die Sendung Moses," in his *Sämtliche Werke*, vol. 15 (Karlsruhe, 1822), 1–33. Hirsch did criticize Schiller elsewhere, though not by name. See his Pentateuch commentary, to Genesis 47:22 (640 in Levy ed.), and his *Collected Writings*, vol. 7, 97–98. Generally, see Michah Gottlieb, "Orthodoxy and the Orient: Samson Raphael Hirsch on the Location of Judaism," in *Wissenschaft des Judentums beyond Tradition*, ed. D. M. Salzer, C. Gafni, and H. Harif (Berlin: De Gruyter, 2019), 53–71.

84. Hirsch, *Neunzehn Briefe uber Judentum* (Zurich, 2013), 77.

85. Hirsch, *The Nineteen Letters of Ben Uziel*, trans. Bernard Drachman (New York,

1899), 142–43. The 1995 Elias edition translates this as "universal acceptance of the brotherhood of mankind," where "acceptance" appears to be an editorial insertion; Hirsch, *The Nineteen Letters on Judaism*, prepared by Jacob Breuer (New York: Feldheim, 1960), 97.

86. Hirsch expresses this view in a footnote to this text. He writes that the rabbinic statement that "the righteous of the nations of the world have a share in the next world [*olam ha-ba*]" can be understood to mean that the righteous of all nations have a share in attaining the historical goal of the development of humanity (i.e., the messianic era portended by the Prophets). Hirsch, *Neunzehn Briefe*, 77–78n2. The unconventionality of Hirsch's reading of this rabbinic statement did not go unnoticed by reviewers of Hirsch's book. Abraham Geiger pointed this out in his review. See Breuer, *Modernity within Tradition*, 419n62.

87. Yehuda Levi, *Ha-Ma'ayan* 48 (Nissan 5768), 35, asserts that Hirsch gave the Schiller speech out of a sense of compulsion. What I am suggesting is quite different: Hirsch could not ignore the occasion of Schiller's centenary, but he certainly sincerely believed in the ideas that he expressed in the speech.

88. On the other hand, Hirsch reserved his praise for a genuine universalist such as Schiller. By contrast, it is said that after reciting his speech in honor of Schiller, Hirsch stated that had Goethe's hundredth birth anniversary (1849) come while Hirsch was in Frankfurt, he would have left the city solely to avoid having to pay any respects to Goethe. Heinemann, *Reasons*, 267n75.

89. Hirsch, *Judaism Eternal*, vol. 2, 221.

90. The Sages of the Talmud make no such statement, but Maimonides does say this at the end of the introduction to his work *Shemonah Perakim* (Venice, 1539). That Hirsch cites this Maimonidean maxim as if it were of rabbinic origin is very telling, especially given that Hirsch vociferously opposed Maimonides's philosophical approach to Judaism. See Hirsch, *Nineteen Letters*, letter 18. Joseph H. Hertz, ed., *The Pentateuch and Haphtoroth* (London: Soncino Press, 1981), vii, also cites this Maimonidean adage as though it was of Rabbinic origin.

91. See *Mishnato shel ha-Rav Kook*, ed. Zvi Yaron (Jerusalem: n. p., 1974), 306–7.

92. Hirsch, commentary to Exodus 12:44 (156–57 in Levy translation).

93. For a succinct overview of traditionalist approaches to slavery, including Hirsch's, see Gamliel Shmalo, "Orthodox Approaches to Biblical Slavery," *Torah U-Madda Journal* 16 (2012–13): 1–20.

94. See, especially, the comments of Netziv in his *Ha'amek Davar* to Genesis 9:25 and Leviticus 25:45. Hirsch could not assert, as did Ephraim E. Urbach, that slavery in Judaism was an entrenched institution as it was in other ancient cultures. See Ephraim E. Urbach, "Humanistic Aspects of Jewish Law," in Urbach, *Collected Writings in Jewish Studies*, ed. R. Brody and M. D. Herr (Jerusalem: Magnes Press, 1999), 39. (Hirsch was opposed to the historicization of Judaism, and this lay at the heart of his struggles with the Wissenschaft des Judentums movement and two of its leading exponents, Heinrich Graetz and Zechariah Frankel.)

95. Moses Mielziner, *Die Verhältnisse der Sklaven bei den alten Hebräern, nach biblischen und talmudischen Quellen dargestellt: Ein Beitrag zur hebräisch-jüdischen Alterthumskunde* (Copenhagen, 1859).

96. Hirsch, commentary to Exodus 21:21 (311 in Levy translation).

97. Hirsch does not provide the definition of "reasons of general morality." In the original German, Hirsch gives as his source for this claim *daselbst* (meaning "there") (in parenthesis), which would mean the last source he cited, *Gittin* 38b. (Strangely, the English translation by Levy leaves out this word.) This idea is not found explicitly in either *Gittin* 38b or in the halachic codes. The source for Hirsch's claim about freeing slaves for the performance of mitzvot is the story cited in *Berakhot* 57b (and repeated in *Gittin* 38b), in which a great sage freed his non-Jewish slave (who, if previously circumcised, becomes Jewish upon release) to complete the quorum of ten men necessary for public prayer. Rabbenu Nissim (on Tractate *Gittin*, 20b in the pages of Rif, s.v. *kol ha-meshahrer*) notes that the "positive command" (*aseh*) for maintaining slaves mentioned by the Talmud must not involve an outright biblical violation when freeing the slave because completing a quorum would not justify such a violation. Hirsch may have inferred that if there is no outright prohibition violated when freeing slaves then perhaps reasons not involving the performance of clear-cut mitzvot—what Hirsch terms *Sittlichkeitsgründen*—would also justify freeing the slave. Hirsch's formulation, using the language of morality, nevertheless remains a bold claim, demonstrating his sensitivity to the issue of slavery in Judaism. A similar halachic analysis of the issue of the apparent command to perpetuate slavery that is guided by a strong ethical sense is that offered by Rabbi Nahum Rabinovitch (1928–2020). In his *Darkah shel Torah* (Jerusalem: Ma'aliyot,1998), 13–19, Rabinovitch attempts to demonstrate that not only is there no command to acquire non-Jewish slaves but that the ostensibly biblical prohibition on freeing them is actually only a rabbinic prohibition (based on a concern with compelling freed slaves to adopt Judaism out of compulsion) and that indeed the ultimate goal of the Torah was the abolition of slavery. He argues that the abolition of slavery that occurred in the Western world was a result of the knowledge of the Torah having spread far and wide, allowing for the recognition of the divine dignity of every human being. Rabinovitch bases this interpretation on, among other sources, his reading of select passages of Maimonides's *Guide of the Perplexed* and his *Mishneh Torah*. Rabinovitch's views are somewhat expanded in his *Mesilot Bilvavam* (Ma'aleh Adumim: Maaliyot, 2015). An English translation of his original formulation is his essay, "The Way of Torah," *Edah Journal* 3, no. 1 (Tevet 5763 [2003]): 1–34.

98. Hirsch, commentary to Leviticus 25:44–46 (774–75 in Levy translation).

99. Catherine Hezser, *Jewish Slavery in Antiquity* (New York: Oxford University Press, 2006), 5.

100. Michael A. Meyer, "Reform Jewish Thinkers and Their German Intellectual Context," in *The Jewish Response to German Culture: From the Enlightenment to the Second World War*, ed. Jehuda Reinharz and Walter Schatzberg (Hanover, NH: University Press of New England, 1985), 64–84.

101. Katz, *Exclusiveness and Tolerance*, 196. In note 1 to that page of this work, Katz explicitly cites Hirsch as one example of these "learned Jews."

102. On the relative obscurity of Meiri's work prior to the twentieth century, see Haym Soloveitchik, "The 'Beit ha-Behirah' of R. Menahem ha-Meiri and Its Fate," in *Asufah le-Yosef*, ed. Y. Ben-Naehet al. (Jerusalem: Zalman Shazar Center, 2014). In the first passage, Meiri states that the discrimination that the Talmud in Tractate *Bava*

Kamma (37b–38a) applies to gentiles, who are charged with nonobservance of the Seven Noahide Laws, applies only to such gentiles. However, those who *do* observe these laws, such as contemporary "nations restricted by the ways of religion," are exempt from such discrimination. Later in that tractate (113a), the Talmud makes several distinctions in ethical obligations Jews owe to fellow Jews but not to gentiles, such as returning lost objects. After noting that the examples given by the Talmud refer not to issues of outright theft but of "acts of piety," which Jews are not compelled to perform for those "who have no religion," Meiri emphatically states. "Thus, whoever is a member of the nations restricted by the ways of religion and the worship of God in any manner, even though their faith is distant from ours, is not included in this category [of being subject to discrimination] but rather they are like a full-fledged Jew regarding these matters, be it lost objects, errors [made by a gentile in giving more change than a customer deserved], and all other such matters, without any distinction whatsoever." Both of these passages from Meiri's commentary are cited in full by Ashkenazi.

103. See chapter 2 of this book.

104. Azriel Shohat, "The German Jews' Integration within Their Non-Jewish Environment in the First Half of the Eighteenth Century," *Zion* 21 (1956): 230–31 (in Hebrew).

105. Shlomo ben Moshe of Khelm, *Merkevet ha-Mishneh* (Frankfurt-on-the-Oder, 1761), commentary to Maimonides, Laws of Monetary Damages 8:5. In exempting Christians and Muslims from this discrimination, *Merkevet ha-Mishneh* states, "the nations of our time are upholders of religion and observe the Seven Noahide Laws."

106. Alexander Altmann, *Moses Mendelssohn: A Biographical Study* (Tuscaloosa: University of Alabama Press, 1973), 354. Although there is no direct evidence of Hirsch's parents' admiration for Dubno, they did admire Wessely and the conservative maskilim of the eighteenth century (see chapter 8 of this book). Dubno, who left Mendelsson's *Biur* project before completing his assigned tasks (see Altmann, *Moses Mendelssohn*, 382, 398–409), was perhaps the most conservative member of this circle and may have served as a model for the young Hirsch. It must be stated forthrightly that this conjecture is speculative.

107. It is possible that this is what Hirsch means when he writes in *The Nineteen Letters*, letter 19 (Elias ed., 333–34) that although Judaism, properly understood, "constitutes a bond of love and justice encompassing all creatures," there are "isolated passages [that have been] taken out of context, deliberately misinterpreted, not seen as an integral part of the whole structure, [and] have been misused by evil design, as pointed arrows or blunt cudgels, to oppress and injure helpless victims." These "isolated passages" may be the Talmudic remarks that he was convinced applied to ancient pagans only, but which German anti-Semites such as Eisenmenger claimed applied to *all* non-Jews. This claim was then used as a justification for anti-Jewish violence, even though the passages in question, in their original context, were "an integral part of the whole structure" of Judaism's opposition to paganism and idolatry. To be sure, this is speculative since Hirsch may have had other aspects of Judaism in mind when he wrote those comments.

108. Yair Hayyim Bacharach, *Havot Yair* (Frankfurt am Main, 1699), 5b. The clause "for all matters" suggests that for certain matters, Christians are indeed considered worshippers of AZ. Presumably, this would include certain ritual laws relating to AZ from

which even Meiri did not wish to exclude Christians. See Katz, *Exclusiveness and Tolerance*, 125–28.

109. See Hirsch's commentary to Exodus 22:13 (365 in Levy ed.).

110. Moshe Schwarz, "Jewish Religious Trends Emerging from the Confrontation with German Culture," in *Perspectives of German-Jewish History in the 19th and 20th Century*, ed. Meir Gilon and Hanna Schmorak (Jerusalem: Jerusalem Academic Press, 1971), 49–50.

111. See Susannah Heschel, *Abraham Geiger and the Jewish Jesus* (Chicago: University of Chicago Press, 1998). See also Matthew Hoffman, *From Rebel to Rabbi: Reclaiming Jesus and the Making of Modern Jewish Culture* (Stanford: Stanford University Press, 2007), 34–51. For the views of two other prominent nineteenth-century German Reform thinkers concerning Christianity, see Frishman, "Good Enough for the Goyim?"

112. Hirsch, *Horeb*, ed. Grunfeld, paragraph 503, 379–80 (*Horev* [Altona, 1837], 500).

113. Yonah Emanuel, "Israel Opposite Christianity: Rav Hirsch on Christianity and the Relationship between Christians and Jews," *Ha-Ma'ayan* 29, no. 2 (5749): 39–40 (in Hebrew), argues that Hirsch's comments on Christianity were written in a bold manner and fearlessly pointed out fundamental flaws in Christian doctrine. I do not disagree with this assessment insofar as similar attacks on Christianity by rabbinic contemporaries of Hirsch are concerned—they are quite rare and are less polemical in tone. However, when comparing Hirsch's comments to medieval Jewish polemics, it becomes quite clear that Hirsch evinced respect for the piety of Christian believers in a manner that cannot be found in the writings of his medieval predecessors. As noted, Hirsch's comments regarding Christianity are also moderate when compared with the critiques issued by his more liberal contemporaries.

114. *Jeschurun* 4. Jahrgang (May 1858), 399. For an English translation of this essay, see Marc B. Shapiro, "Rabbi Samson Raphael Hirsch on Jews in a Non-Jewish World," *Hakirah* 27 (Fall 2019): 167–73.

115. Marc B. Shapiro, "Torah Study on Christmas Eve," *Journal of Jewish Thought and Philosophy* 8 (1999): 346n100.

116. Hirsch, *Collected Writings of Rabbi Samson Raphael Hirsch*, ed. and trans. Paul Forcheimer and Gertrude Hirschler, 8 vols. (New York: Feldheim, 1983–95), vol. 2, 205: "Only the theory was revealed to mankind [by Christianity] while the 'Law' was omitted; the one factor was withheld on which the redemption and the harmonious organization of all mankind is based." (From: *Gesammelte Schriften*, vol. 2, 33–34.)

117. For a particularly sharp critique of Christianity by Hirsch along these lines, see *Collected Writings of Rabbi Samson Raphael Hirsch*, ed. and trans. Paul Forcheimer and Gertrude Hirschler, 8 vols. (New York: Feldheim, 1983–95), vol. 8, 242–43. See also Hirsch's commentary to Genesis 6:5 (130–31) for a similar critique of the doctrine of original sin.

118. See Hirsch, *Horeb*, ed. Grunfeld, xcv.

119. See Hirsch's essay "Jewish Joyfulness," in *Collected Writings*, vol. 8, 249–57; the identical essay in different translation in *Judaism Eternal*, vol. 2, 145–54. (Both are translations of the original "Die jüdische Heiterkeit" from *Gesammelte Schriften*, vol. 1 [Frankfurt, 1902], 471–80, originally in *Jeschurun* 2. Jahrgang Av 5616 [1856].) Incidentally,

Hirsch's views on the positive religious value of laughter and the experience of (permissible) pleasure—which he elaborates upon in the previously cited essay—were diametrically opposed to the views of his non-Hasidic East European contemporaries, particularly those associated with the Mussar movement. Cf. Immanuel Etkes, *Rabbi Israel Salanter and the Mussar Movement*, trans. Jonathan Chipman (Philadelphia: Jewish Publication Society, 1993), 159, 247. For an expressed denigration of physicality, and worldly matters in general, as antithetical to religiosity and a championing of the ideal of moderate asceticism—albeit from the next century—see Eliyahu E. Dessler, *Mikhtav me-Eliyahu*, vol. 3 (Bene Berak: n. p. 1964), 152–53.

120. Hirsch, *Shemesh Marpeh* (ed. Eliahu Meyer Klugman [New York: Mesorah, 1992]), 221–23 (quote at 223).

121. Jacob J. Schacter, "Rabbi Jacob Emden, Sabbatianism, and Frankism: Attitudes toward Christianity in the Eighteenth Century," in Elisheva Carlebach and Jacob J. Schacter, *New Perspectives on Christianity*, 393–96, has argued that Emden's positive statements about Christians were written from a theoretical perspective, whereas his day-to-day interactions with Christians confirmed his suspicions about their ill will toward Jews. By contrast, here Hirsch argues for optimism regarding the actual conduct, on a mundane level, of his Christian contemporaries.

122. Hirsch, *Nineteen Letters*, ed. Elias, 126 (*Die Neunzehn Briefe* [Zurich, 2013], 46).

123. Maimonides, *Mishneh Torah* Laws of Kings 11:4, uncensored texts. See Isadore Twersky, *A Maimonides Reader* (West Orange: Behrman House 1972), 226–27 for an English translation of this passage. For a similar idea expressed by the medieval rabbi whose views Hirsch said he preferred over those of Maimonides, see Judah Halevi, *Kitab Al Khazari*, trans. H. Hirschfeld (New York: Bernard G. Richards, 1927), 4:23, 226–27.

124. See Miller, "R. Jacob Emden's Attitude toward Christianity," for further discussion. Breuer, *Modernity within Tradition*, 88, speaking of Hirsch's views, writes, "It is unlikely that a conditionally positive evaluation of Christianity had ever before been expressed so eloquently in Orthodox Jewry."

125. Cited in Alan Brill, *Judaism and World Religions: Encountering Christianity, Islam, and Eastern Traditions* (New York: Palgrave Macmillan, 2012), 56–57.

126. Matthias Morgenstern, "Between the Noahide Laws and Israelite-Edomite Brotherhood: Paradigms of Humanity in Modern Jewish Orthodoxy," in *The Quest for a Common Humanity*, ed. Katell Berthelot and Matthias Morgenstern (Leiden: Brill, 2011), 101–21; Maimonides, *Mishneh Torah, Laws of Kings and Their Wars* 8:11.

127. Although much has been written about Hirsch's approach to philology, the best introduction to Hirsch's method is Matityahu Clark, *Etymological Dictionary of Biblical Hebrew Based on the Commentaries of Samson Raphael Hirsch* (Jerusalem: Feldheim, 1999), esp. ix–xiv. (For an example of criticism of Hirsch's approach, see the comments of Barry Levy cited in Hirsch, *Nineteen Letters*, ed. Elias, 23.)

128. Hirsch, commentary to Genesis 1:26 (30 in the Levy translation).

129. Morgenstern, "Between the Noahide Laws," 118–20. It should be noted that Morgenstern's interpretation of Hirsch's understanding of Edom, though persuasively argued, is speculative, as Hirsch does not express this idea explicitly in any of his writings.

130. Israel Zinberg, *A History of Jewish Literature*, vol. 10, trans. Bernard Martin (New York: Ktav, 1977), 180; Klugman, *Rabbi Samson Raphael Hirsch*, 56.

131. See Heschel, *Abraham Geiger and the Jewish Jesus*, esp. 194–97. For Geiger's failure, see also Heschel, "Abraham Geiger and the 19th-Century Failure of Christian-Jewish Relations," *Kirchliche Zeitgeschichte* 16 (2003): 17–36.

132. Heinrich von Treitschke, "A Word about Our Jewry," as translated in Paul Mendes-Flohr and Jehuda Reinharz, *The Jew in the Modern World*, 3rd ed. (New York: Oxford University Press, 2011), 320. Although he mentioned Graetz by name in this context and not Geiger, his remarks are clearly aimed at Geiger as well.

133. Franz Delitzsch, *Rohling's Talmudjude beleuchtet* (Leipzig, 1881), 9.

134. Delitzsch, *Rohling's Talmudjude beleuchtet*, 8.

135. Hirsch, *The Collected Writings of Rabbi Samson Raphael Hirsch*, ed. and trans. Paul Forcheimer and Gertrude Hirschler, vol. 1 (New York: Feldheim, 1983), 369.

136. See Miller, "R. Jacob Emden's Attitude," 112, where Emden is quoted as asserting that "not one of our Sages spoke more fervently [than Jesus] about the eternal duty to fulfill the Law."

137. Hirsch, commentary to Exodus 6:14 (72 in Levy ed.).

138. There are many versions of this work. The classic treatment of this subject is that of Samuel Krauss, *Das Leben Jesu nach jüdischen Quellen* (Berlin: S. Calvary, 1902). A valuable study is Philip S. Alexander, "Yeshu/Yeshua ben Yosef of Nazareth: Discerning the Jewish Face of Jesus," in *The Birth of Jesus: Biblical and Theological Reflections*, ed. George J. Brook (Edinburgh: Bloomsbury, 2000), 9–21. As of this writing, Peter Schäfer and others are preparing a critical edition, with translation and commentary, of the *Toledot Yeshu* text. See "Toledot Yeshu," project description, Program in Judaic Studies/the Ronald O. Perelman Institute for Judaic Studies, Princeton University (website), accessed December 19, 2022. "Suggesting that it was the lack of clear knowledge about the identity of Jesus's father": The remainder of the passage, where Hirsch contrasts Moses's family background with Jesus's, makes it clear that this is his intended meaning.

139. In one passage, Hirsch refers to the emergence of early Christian doctrine and the time when "the adherents of this creed even began to worship a son of these exiles [the Jews] as their divine savior, and to revere that book [the Bible] and that son as the foundation of all future civilizations and of the advancement of salvation on earth." Hirsch continues this essay by discussing the development of classical Christian anti-Semitism as a way of retaining the idea that the Jewish people's existence and its teachings are central to world history, while providing a religious imprimatur to hatred of this very people, who were considered to be rejected by God, who had revoked His covenant with them. Hirsch, *Collected Writings*, vol. 2, 424–25 (citation at 424).

140. See Breuer, *Modernity within Tradition*, 424n169, for references to Hirsch's writings where this view is expressed. See especially *Collected Writings*, vol. 2, 436–38.

141. Translation of essay in Hirsch, *Collected Writings*, vol. 1, 173–82 (citation at 180; emphasis added). Originally in *Gesammelte Schriften*, vol. 6, 88–98 (citation at 95), from *Jeschurun* 6. Jahrgang Iyar 5620 (1860).

142. Translation of essay in Hirsch, *Collected Writings*, vol. 8, 314. Originally from *Jeschurun* 10. Jahrgang, vol. 5 (Shevat 5624) (1864), 145–67 (citation at 166).

143. Marjorie Lamberti, *Jewish Activism in Imperial Germany: The Struggle for Civil Equality* (New Haven, CT: Yale University Press, 1978), 177. (Cf. the same volume, p. 4.)

144. Breuer, *Modernity within Tradition*, 84. David Sorkin has expressed a similar

idea: Hirsch's "self-appointed task" was "to convince the new bourgeoisie that the ideal of *Bildung* could be attained only through Orthodoxy." David Sorkin, *The Transformation of German Jewry 1780–1840* (Detroit: Wayne State University Press, 1999), 164.

145. To Exodus 1:14 (10 in Levy ed.).

146. Rabbi Michael Melchior (b. 1954), a leading Orthodox Zionist thinker and activist (and former member of the Israeli Knesset), who has done much to advance peace between Jews and Arabs, has been influenced by Hirsch's thought, as he told me when I met him in Jerusalem in the summer of 2018. Melchior's Scandinavian roots—Danish-born, he is a descendent of a long line of Danish rabbis, and he still retains the title of Chief Rabbi of Norway, where he lived during the 1980s—render him an heir to the legacy of Hirsch's humanistic West European Orthodoxy.

147. Cf. Breuer, *Modernity within Tradition*, 424n172, regarding Werner Sombart's use of Hirsch's *Horeb*.

148. A full treatment of this period is beyond the scope of this book. See, however, the next chapter.

Chapter 10

1. For an excellent treatment of the three different periods of Jewish emancipation in Germany, of which the 1871 unification was the last, see Robert Liberles, "Was There a Jewish Movement for Emancipation in Germany?" *Leo Baeck Institute Yearbook* 31, no. 1 (1986): 35–49. (See also Reinhard Rürup, "The Tortuous and Thorny Path to Legal Equality: 'Jew Laws' and Emancipatory Legislation in Germany from the Late Eighteenth Century," *Leo Baeck Institute Yearbook* 31 [1986]: 3–33).

2. The most concise presentation of the state of Jewish-Christian relations during this period, including the pressures that were exerted upon German Jews of all religious denominations, is Christian Wiese, *Challenging Colonial Discourse: Jewish Studies and Protestant Theology in Wilhelmine Germany*, trans. B. Harshav and C. Wiese (Leiden: Brill, 2005), 4–12. It is worth citing Wiese's assertion that this period was marked by "the tension between the desire to protect Jewish identity and the hope to integrate into a society that was increasingly defined by nationalist, exclusivist ideas" (10), and that "the anti-Semitic movement reached its temporary apogee" in the last two decades of the nineteenth century (11). This assessment serves as background to the discussion here. The classic presentation of the various forces that impacted Jewish-Christian relations in Germany during this period is Uriel Tal, *Christians and Jews in Germany: Religion, Politics, and Ideology in the Second Reich, 1870–1914*, trans. Noah Jonathan Jacobs (Ithaca, NY: Cornell University Press, 1975). See also Sanford Ragins, *Jewish Responses to Anti-Semitism in Germany, 1870–1914* (Cincinnati: Hebrew Union College Press, 1980). Chapter 6, "In the German Empire," pp. 283–354, of Mordechai Breuer's *Modernity within Tradition*, trans. E. Petuchowski (New York: Columbia University Press, 1992), is also an indispensable source for research about this period, particularly as it pertains to Orthodox Jewry. (Cf. Tal, *Christians and Jews in Germany*, 222n87, regarding the need for a special study of Orthodox Jewry and its efforts to integrate into German society during this period.) An exhaustive survey of the rather extensive literature treating the period of the Second Reich is beyond the limited scope of this chapter.

3. For an excellent study of Hoffmann's work in responding to anti-Talmudic charges,

see Alexander A. Dubrau, "A Jewish Orthodox Response to the Hostility towards the Morality of Jewish Law and the Jewish God at the Beginning of the Twentieth Century in Germany: Rabbi David Zvi Hoffmann on the Relationship between Jews and Gentiles," in *Religion and Transfer: Interactions between Judaism, Christianity, and Islam from the Middle Ages to the Twentieth Century*, ed. A. A. Dubrau, D. Scotto, and R. Vimercati (Tübingen: Mohr Siebeck, 2020), 273–304.

4. I intend to treat Hoffmann's book in a future study, where I hope to demonstrate the merits of this claim. For now, it will suffice to note that Hoffmann cites Hirsch's writings concerning non-Jews in his book. See, for example, David Zvi Hoffmann, *Der Schulchan Aruch und die Rabbinen über das Verhältnis der Juden zu Andersgläubigen*, 2nd ed. (Berlin, 1894), 144, 177–78.

5. During the same period, Hirsch's eldest son, Mendel (1833–1900), and his most famous son-in-law, Rabbi Salomon Breuer (1850–1926), who was the rabbi of Hirsch's *kehillah* in Frankfurt, expressed their own views concerning non-Jews, which were entirely in keeping with those of S. R. Hirsch, and in the case of Mendel, perhaps even exceeding his father's universalism. (Cf. Alan Brill, *Judaism and Other Religions: Models of Understanding* [New York: Palgrave Macmillan, 2010], 118–19).

6. Esriel Hildescheimer, *Rabbiner Esriel Hildesheimer Briefe*, ed. Mordechai Eliav (Jerusalem: Verlag Rubin Mass, 1965), 139. A zaddik is a righteous man. Note that this clause is written by Hildesheimer in rabbinic Hebrew, although the rest of this letter is in German.

7. This was the synagogue created by the official Frankfurt Jewish community, then dominated by supporters of Reform, as a result of the secession law passed on July 28, 1876. The Reform-controlled community, concerned that the secession of the Orthodox would weaken its financial stability, made concessions that allowed for the maintenance of strictly Orthodox institutions within the general communal framework. It was as a result of these concessions that S. B. Bamberger issued his famous ruling that secession was not mandatory (setting off a heated debate with Hirsch), and the new circumstances in Frankfurt allowed Marcus Horovitz to accept the position of Orthodox rabbi within the communal framework, a move that was in keeping with his views concerning Jewish unity.

8. The best source of biographical information on Horovitz is Joseph Unna, "Rabbi Dr. Mordechai HaLevi Horovitz—His Life and Works," in Mordechai Horovitz, "The Rabbis of Frankfurt," trans. Joshua Amir (Jerusalem: Mossad ha-Rav Kook, 1972), 329–50 (in Hebrew). For a recent study of Horovitz that utilizes his halachic views to provide insight into his worldview, see Joseph A. Skloot, "Halakhic Flexibility and Communal Unity: R. Marcus Horowitz and the Schächtfrage," *Modern Judaism* 40, no. 3 (October 2020): 355–75.

9. Marcus Horovitz, *Shu"t Matteh Levi* (Jerusalem, 1979), sec. 2, *Yoreh Deah* no. 28.

10. To *Bekhorot* 2b and *Megillah* 28a, though in the latter source the Tosafists do not actually make the entire claim about a gentile's oath being permitted nowadays on these specific grounds.

11. *Darkhei Moshe* to *Tur*, *Yoreh Deah* 151, as expanded by Shakh, *Yoreh Deah* 151:7, no. 7.

12. The views that Horovitz cites are those of the authors of *Me'il Tzedaah* and *Sha'ar*

Ephraim, who had argued that the Tosafists had not intended to permit Trinitarian worship to Christians.

13. Babylonian Talmud *Sanhedrin* 63a, one folio prior to the Tosafists' discussion of a gentile's oath.

14. Maimonides, *Mishneh Torah*, Laws of Idolatry 1:1. Maimonides does not employ the word *shittuf* here.

15. Horovitz's assertion that a key passage in Maimonides's halachic code did not, in fact, express any halachic view is characteristic of the Wissenschaft movement to which Horovitz was a not insubstantial contributor. The critical historical lens through which that movement viewed rabbinic texts was conducive to this type of reading of Maimonides's code. It would have been highly unlikely for an East European contemporary of Horovitz to have made such an assertion.

16. Horovitz, *Matteh Levi*, sec. 2, 82, column 1.

17. Horovitz, *Matteh Levi*, sec. 2, 83–84.

18. It is not the most remarkable responsum about Christianity ever penned by *any* halachist, as the responsum authored by Rabbi Yosef Messas (1892–1974), *Mayim Hayyim*, vol. 2 (Jerusalem: n. p., 1984), *Yoreh Deah* no. 108, is even more startling. Messas recalls that when he was a rabbi in Tlemcen, Algeria, he was asked about converting a church into a synagogue, and he proceeds to argue that the premise of the question, that the church is a house of AZ, is mistaken. Messas recounts a conversation he had with a priest (while standing in his church!), in which the latter affirmed that Christian monotheism is impeccable. Christians do not worship Jesus nor any of the images found in churches, and the term "Son of God" used with reference to Jesus is simply a hyperbolic form of poetry, such as the biblical references to angels as "sons of God," the priest told Messas. Therefore, Messas concludes, Christianity is devoid of any taint of AZ and Jews have wrongfully characterized Christian worship as shittuf, as though Christians actually believed in the Incarnation and worshipped a tripartite godhead! Messas was known as an iconoclastic scholar even among Moroccan rabbis and was sometimes referred to as "Yosef ha-Mattir," "Yosef who permits (that which is forbidden)." See Harvey E. Goldberg, "Sephardi Rabbinic 'Openness' in Nineteenth-Century Tripoli: Examining a Modern Myth in Context," in *Jewish Religious Leadership: Image and Reality*, ed. Jack Wertheimer, vol. 2 (New York: Jewish Theological Seminary, 2004), 699.

19. Jacob Katz, *Exclusiveness and Tolerance* (New York: Behrman House, 1961), 162. Cf. the same work at 44, 53n2, 98, 103n1. "But failed to allow this position to impact cases": Katz, *Exclusiveness and Tolerance*, 126. Katz was discussing the views of Meiri when he used this expression to describe Meiri's reluctance to grant blanket permission to sell Christian sacred objects.

20. Horovitz's son, Jacob, who edited his father's responsa collection, makes an even bolder comment in a note to this responsum. He states that Maimonides singles out Muslims as an example of a non-Jewish monotheistic religious group solely because they were the people he knew and dealt with on a daily basis. Maimonides would have agreed, writes Jacob Horovitz, with the view of Shakh that it is not forbidden to use Christian wine. See *Matteh Levi*, 83n1. Jacob Horovitz did not see the uncensored text of the passage from Maimonides that he cites, which states explicitly that while Muslim wine is permitted, the wine of those engaged in AZ, such as Christians, is forbidden.

21. David Ellenson, *Tradition in Transition: Orthodoxy, Halakhah and the Boundaries of Modern Jewish Identity* (Lanham, MD: University Press of America, 1989), 143–59. Cf. Louis Jacobs, *Theology in the Responsa* (London: Littman Library, 1975), 281.

22. David Zvi Hoffmann, *Shu"t Melamed LeHo'il* (Jerusalem: n. p., 2010), *Yoreh Deah* no. 148, section 2. Cf. Jacobs, *Theology in the Responsa*, 299–300, and Daniel Gordis, "Dialectics of Community, Continuity, and Compassion: The Legal Writings of Rabbi David Zvi Hoffmann and their Philosophic Foundations" (PhD diss., University of Southern California, 1992), 223.

23. Marc B. Shapiro, "Review Essay: Sociology and Halakha." *Tradition* 27, no. 1 (Fall 1992): 77.

24. Shapiro, in soliciting responses from several contemporary halachists about the permissibility of donating money to be used toward the building of a church, sent a copy of this responsum by Horovitz to Rabbi Shalom Messas (1909–2003) as a foundational source for leniency regarding this question. See Messas's responsa collection, *Shu"t Shemesh U-Magen*, vol. 3, *Orah Hayyim* (Jerusalem: n. p., 2000), nos. 30–31, where Messas concurs with Horovitz's ruling.

25. Marcus Horovitz, *Rabbanei Frankfurt*, trans. Joshua Amir (Jerusalem: Mossad ha-Rav Kook, 1972).

26. See chapter 2 of this book for an analysis of the sincerity of rabbinic disclaimers of this nature.

27. Marcus Horovitz, *Fünf Reden* (Frankfurt am Main: M. Lehrberger, 1925), 62–63.

28. The Hebrew quote employed by Horovitz is "Hasidei umot ha-olam yesh la-hem helek la-olam ha-ba," which is actually based on Maimonides's formulation in his *Mishneh Torah* Laws of Kings 8:11 rather than Talmud *Sanhedrin* 105a.

29. Unna, "Rabbi Dr. Mordechai HaLevi Horovitz," 331–32.

30. Jacob Katz, *A House Divided: Orthodoxy and Schism in Nineteenth-Century Central European Jewry*, trans. Ziporah Brody (Hanover, NH: University Press of New England, 1998), 271–72 and 330n64.

31. Isaac Breuer, *Darki* (Jerusalem: n. p., 1988), 10. The author is Salomon Breuer's son.

32. Unna, "Rabbi Dr. Mordechai ha-Levi Horovitz," 336. Cf. Horovitz, *Shu"t Matteh Levi*, vol. 2, *Yoreh Deah* no. 36, 92, where Horovitz expresses appreciation for Hirsch's work on behalf of revitalizing Orthodox Judaism in Frankfurt.

33. Naomi Seidler, *Sarah Schenirer and the Bais Yaakov Movement* (Oxford: Littman Library, 2019), 244n7 and 47n82. "Introduced Schenirer": Isaac Breuer, *Moriah* (Jerusalem: n. p., 1982), 148; Cf. Judith Grunfeld-Rosenbaum, "Sara Schenirer," in *Jewish Leaders, 1750–1940*, ed. Leo Jung (New York: Bloch, 1953), 407–32; and Pearl Benisch, *Carry Me in Your Heart: The Life and Legacy of Sarah Schenirer, Founder and Visionary of the Bais Yaakov Movement* (New York: Feldheim, 2004), 21–22, 27, 30, 109–14.

34. Cited from an autobiographical essay of Schenirer by Seidler, *Sarah Schenirer*, 148.

35. Schenirer does not mean to proselytize to them but simply to gain respect for Judaism among them.

36. *Em be-Yisrael: Kitvei Sarah Schenirer*, vol. 2 (Jerusalem: n. p. 1975), 75–76. This essay has recently been translated into English by Naomi Seidler, *Sarah Schenirer*, 347–49. (The translation used here is my own.)

37. Cf. the story recounted in Benisch, *Carry Me in Your Heart*, xvii–xviii, where Rabbi Yehezkel Sarna, then the Rosh Yeshiva of the Slabodka yeshiva in Israel, told a group of distinguished rabbis, all descendants of well-known Talmudists from the previous century, that the Jew who had done the greatest work on behalf of the Jewish people in the twentieth century was someone "who never learned a *blatt Gemara* [a page of the Talmud] their entire life." Pressed as to the identity of this "ignoramus," Sarna said he was referring to Sarah Schenirer, who saved Jewish women from assimilation.

38. Seidler, *Sarah Schenirer*, 163–65.

39. Schenirer did acquire some knowledge of Talmud on her own. See the eulogy for her cited in Seidler, *Sarah Schenirer*, 141–42.

40. Indeed, most editions of the Talmud in use during Schenirer's lifetime, as well as the lives of the rabbis discussed here, substituted the term *akum*, an acronym that stands for "worshippers of stars and constellations," for *goyim*. This issue is treated extensively in Hoffmann, *Der Schulchan Aruch*.

41. Informal anecdotal evidence suggests that, to this very day, strictly Orthodox young women who have been educated in the Bais Yaakov system or its equivalent are far less likely to hold anti-gentile views than their male counterparts who study in yeshivot. (I teach Judaic Studies at Lander College for Women; its student population is composed of Orthodox Jewish women, many of them products of the Bais Yaakov system.) No doubt the texts that these two groups are or are not exposed to play a role in the views they formulate concerning the value of gentiles in the view of Judaism. (Even religiously educated Bais Yaakov girls do not study the Talmud and its commentaries.) The gender of most of the teachers that these respective groups employ—men in boys' yeshivot, women in girls' schools—is another likely factor that may account for this difference in outlook.

42. The most thorough and meticulous biographical treatment of Weinberg is Marc B. Shapiro, *Between the Yeshiva World and Modern Orthodoxy* (Oxford: Littman Library, 1999). An excellent examination of his writings and thought can be found in Judith Bleich's *Defenders of the Faith: Studies in Nineteenth- and Twentieth-Century Orthodoxy and Reform* (New York: Touro University Press, 2020), 243–336. See the same work at 244–45n1 for an extensive listing of secondary literature concerning Weinberg.

43. "It has already been demonstrated by the earliest and latest authorities that these matters [discriminatory legislation] have no application to Christians, who accept the truth of divine faith and recognize the value of human rights." Yehiel Yaakov Weinberg, *Lifrakim*, 6th ed. (Jerusalem: A. A. Weingort, 2010), 275. Weinberg expressed sensitivity to the legal status of non-Jews in his responsa collection, Seridei Eish, as well. See Bleich, *Defenders of the Faith*, 294n137, for examples.

44. For astute analysis of this early essay by Weinberg, see Shapiro, *Between the Yeshiva World and Modern Orthodoxy*, 48–50.

45. Letter from Weinberg to his childhood friend Samuel Atlas, dated October 26, 1964, cited in Marc B. Shapiro, "Scholars and Friends: Rabbi Jehiel Jacob Weinberg and Professor Samuel Atlas," *Torah U-Madda Journal* 7 (1997): 118, and Shapiro, *Between the Yeshiva World and Modern Orthodoxy*, 183.

46. See chapter 3 of this book.

47. Shapiro, *Between the Yeshiva World and Modern Orthodoxy*, 183.

48. See Ephraim Chamiel, *The Dual Truth* (Boston: Academic Studies Press, 2019), vol. 2, 368–406, who demonstrates through extensive analysis of Weinberg's writings Hirsch's decisive influence upon him. Rabbi Isidore Grunfeld, the celebrated translator of Hirsch's writings, who knew Weinberg personally both from the prewar and postwar periods, wrote in his biographical sketch that Weinberg was deeply influenced by Hirsch's views. See I. Grunfeld, "The 'Ba'al Seride Esh,'" in *The Torah Personality*, ed. Nisson Wolpin (New York: Mesorah, 1980), 99–105.

49. Letter to Samuel Atlas, September 19, 1957, cited in Shapiro, "Scholars and Friends," 111–12; Shapiro, *Between the Yeshiva World and Modern Orthodoxy*, 182.

50. S. R. Hirsch, *Pentateuch*, commentary to Exodus 21:2: "the first matter to be dealt with, quite naturally deals with the rights of man . . . With these sentences [Exodus 21:2–11], the contents of which deny and limit the very holiest personal right of man, the right to personal freedom. . . . The language used in [the Pentateuch] is so skillfully chosen that . . . a whole train of ideas of justice and human rights is indicated." These lines could not have been penned by any of Hirsch's East European rabbinic contemporaries.

51. Chamiel, *Dual Truth*, vol. 2, 397, in summarizing Hirsch's views.

52. See the treatment of Weinberg's view of the Jewish people and non-Jews in Shmuel Lesher, "For the Love of Humanity: The Religious Humanism of Rabbi Samson Raphael Hirsch," *Hakirah* 32 (Fall 2022): 94–97. This excellent essay treats many of the themes in this book but was published when the book was already in press.

53. David Berger, "Jews, Gentiles, and the Modern Egalitarian Ethos: Some Tentative Thoughts," in *Formulating Responses in an Egalitarian Age*, ed. Marc D. Stern (Lanham, MD: Rowman and Littlefield, 2005), 83–108. One may now add, among others, Rabbi Yehuda Kelemer (1946–2021). See Matt Lubin, "Torat Hesed: My Rabbi, Rav Yehuda Kelemer," the *Lehrhaus* website, February 7, 2021.

54. An interesting question is the role of the Holocaust in Weinberg's attitude to non-Jews. Some rabbis and lay Jews believe that the Holocaust demonstrates the inherently anti-Semitic nature of all non-Jews, thereby undercutting any claims for non-Jews to be regarded by Jews as equals. But Rabbi Simcha Krauss (1937–2022) has argued the very opposite with respect to Weinberg. See Simcha Krauss, Review Essay, *Between the Yeshiva World and Modern Orthodoxy: The Life and Works of Rabbi Jehiel Jacob Weinberg* by Marc B. Shapiro, *Edah Journal* 1, no. 1 (2000/Marheshvan 5761): 3. Krauss writes that "as a survivor of the Holocaust, he [Weinberg] personally experienced the evil that results from intolerance and hatred." According to this view, Weinberg championed religious tolerance not *despite* his experiences in the Holocaust but *because* of them.

Conclusion

1. The exception is the work of David Zvi Hoffmann, discussed at the beginning of chapter 10.

2. See chapter 1 of this book.

3. On the relationship of these men to Jewish scholars of the period and their nuanced view of Judaism, see Alan Levenson, "Missionary Protestants as Defenders and Detractors of Judaism: Franz Delitzsch and Hermann Strack," *Jewish Quarterly Review* 92, no. 3–4 (January–April 2002): 383–420. Levenson demonstrates that Strack was

familiar with Hirsch's writings. On Wohlgemuth, see 386 in that same article. Further analysis can be found in Christian Wiese's *Challenging Colonial Discourse: Jewish Studies and Protestant Theology in Wilhelmine Germany*, trans. B. Harshav and C. Wiese (Leiden: Brill, 2005). See also Susannah Heschel, *Abraham Geiger and the Jewish Jesus* (Chicago: University of Chicago Press, 1998), 194–97.

4. For a tribute to the Kahles by Paul's student, see Lea Goldberg (trans. Tsipi Keller), "On a Man's Greatness," *Jewish Currents* (website), April 7, 2020.

Bibliography

Journals and Archival Material

Allgemeine Zeitung des Judentums. Leipzig and Berlin, 1837–1922.

Ha-Ma'ayan. Jerusalem, 1952–present.

Jeschurun. Frankfurt am Main, 1854–70.

Sänger Collection. Institute for the Study of Diaspora Jewry. Bar-Ilan University, Ramat-Gan.

Shomer Zion ha-Ne'eman. Altona, 1845–54.

Yerushateinu. Bene Berak, 5767–present.

Primary Sources

Albeck, Shalom. *Kofer ha-Eshkol*. Warsaw: haTzefirah, 1910.

Ashkenazi, Eliezer. *Ma'asei Hashem*. Warsaw, 1871.

Aszod, Yehuda. *Sefer Divrei Mahary"a*. Michalowitz: Mor Grünfeld, 1931.

———. *Shu"t Yehudah Ya'aleh*. Lemberg, 1880.

Auerbach, Benjamin Zvi, ed. *Sefer ha-Eshkol im be'ur Nahal Eshkol*. Halberstadt, 1867–69.

Bacharach, Yair Hayyim. *Havot Yair*. Frankfurt am Main, 1699.

Bamberger, Simhah. *Sefer Zekher Simhah*. Frankfurt am Main: n. p., 1925.

Bamberger, Yitzhak Dov. *Shu"t Yad HaLevy*. Vol. 1. Jerusalem: n. p., 1965.

ben Asher, Bahya. *Perush al ha-Torah*. Edited by C. D. Chavel. Jerusalem: Mossad HaRav Kook, 1994.

ben Joseph, Samuel. *Olat Tamid* (Jerusalem: n. p., 2003).

Ben Manoah, Hezekiah [Hizkuni]. *Perush al ha-Torah*. Edited by C. D. Chavel. Jerusalem: Mossad haRav Kook, 1981.

ben Meshulam, [Rabbenu] Yeruham. *Sefer Toldot Adam ve-Havvah*. Venice, 1553.

ben Moshe, Avraham. *Perush Rabbenu Avraham ben ha-Rambam al Bereshit u-Shemot*. Edited and translated by Ephraim Y. Weisenberg. London: S. D. Sassoon, 1958.

ben Moshe of Khelm, Shlomo. *Merkevet ha-Mishneh*. Frankfurt-on-the-Oder, 1761.

ben Yaakov Yitzhak, Yosef. *Sefer Mishnat Hakhamim*. Lemberg, 1827.

Berlin, Naphtali Zvi Yehuda. *Ha'amek Davar*. Jerusalem: n. p., 1974.

———. *Why Antisemitism? A Translation of "The Remnant of Israel" by Rabbi Naphtali Zvi Yehuda Berlin*. Edited and translated by Howard S. Joseph. Northvale, NJ: Jason Aronson, 1996.

Berliner, Abraham. *Ketavim nivharim*. Jerusalem: Mossad haRav Kook, 1969.

Bondi, Tevele. *Haggadah shel Pesach*. Jerusalem: Feldheim, 2002.
Boskowitz, Wolf. *Seder Mishnah*. Prague, 1820.
———. *Sefer Shoshan Edut*. Pax, 1903.
Breuer, Isaac. *Darki*. Translated by Michael Schwarz. Jerusalem: n. p., 1988.
———. *Moriah*. Jerusalem: n. p., 1982.
Chajes, Zvi Hirsch. *Kol Sifrei Maharatz Chayot*. 2 vols. Jerusalem: Divrei Chachamim, 1958.
Delitzsch, Franz. *Rohling's Talmudjude beleuchtet*. Leipzig, 1881.
Dessler, Eliyahu E. *Mikhtav me-Eliyahu*. Vol. 3. Bene Berak: n. p., 1964.
Eger, Akiva. *Shu"t Rabbi Akiva Eger he-Hadash*. 5 vols. Jerusalem: Vagshal, 1998.
Eleh Divrei ha-Berit. Altona, 1819.
Emden, Jacob. *Megilat Sefer*. Kolome, 1886.
Epstein, Barukh HaLevy. *Barukh She'amar Pirkei Avot*. Tel Aviv: Am Olam, 1969.
Ettlinger, Jacob. *Arukh La-Ner al ha-Shas*. Bene Berak: Sifrei Ohr haChaim, 2004.
———. *Minhah Arukhah: Kitvei Ba'al ha-Arukh La-Ner*. Edited by Yehuda A. Horovitz. Jerusalem: Yeshivat Dvar Yerushalayim, 2008.
———. *Minhat Ani*. Bene Berak: n. p., 2012.
———. *Shu"t Binyan Zion*. Edited by Yehuda A. Horovitz. 2 vols. Jerusalem: Yeshivat Dvar Yerushalayim, 2002.
Eyebeschutz, Jonathan. *Kereti u-Peleti*. Jerusalem: n. p., 2004.
Falk, Jacob Joshua. *P'nei Yehoshua al Masekhet Bava Metzia*. Frankfurt, 1756.
Feinstein, Moses. *Igrot Moshe Orah Hayyim*. Vol. 4. New York: Noble Book Press, 1982.
Fichte, Johann Gottlieb. *Beitrag zur Berichtigung der Urteile des Publikums über die französische Revolution*. n. p., 1793.
Fleckeles, Eleazar. *Teshuvah me-Ahavah*. 3 vols. Prague, 1809–21.
Formstecher, Salomon. *Die Religion des Geistes: Eine wissenschaftliche Darstellung des Judentums*. Frankfurt, 1841.
Friedlander, Michael. *The History and Philosophy of the Jewish Religion*. New York: Pardes, 1946.
Halevi, Judah. *Kitab Al Khazari*. Translated by Hartwig Hirschfeld. New York: Bernard G. Richards, 1927.
Hazzan, Israel Moses. *Krakh shel Romi*. Livorno, 1876.
Hegel, Georg Wilhelm Friedrich. *Philosophy of Right*. Edited and translated by T. M. Knox. New York: Oxford University Press, 1967.
Herskovics, Mayer, ed. *Liepman Philip Prins: His Scholarly Correspondence*. Hoboken, NJ: Ktav, 1992.
Hesronot ha-Shas. Cracow, n.d.
Hildesheimer, Esriel. *Rabbiner Dr. I. Hildesheimer: Gesammelte Aufsatze*. Edited by Meier Hildesheimer. Frankfurt am Main: Verlag Hermon A. G., 1923.
———. *Rabbiner Esriel Hildesheimer Briefe*. Edited by Mordechai Eliav. Jerusalem: Verlag Rubin Mass, 1965.
———. *Shu"t Rabbi Esriel*. 2 vols. Tel Aviv: Lipa Friedman, 1969 and 1976.
Hirsch, Samson Raphael. *The Collected Writings*. Vol. 9, *Timeless Hashkafah*. New York: Feldheim, 2012.
———. *The Collected Writings of Rabbi Samson Raphael Hirsch*. Edited and translated

by Paul Forcheimer and Gertrude Hirschler. 8 vols. New York: Feldheim, 1983–95.

———. *Einladungsschrift zu der öffentlichen Prüfung der Unterrichts-Anstalt der israelitischen Religions-Gesellschaft zu Frankfurt a. M., welche am 19., 20., 21. und 22. März im Schulgebäude (Ecke der Schützen- und Rechneigrabenstrasse) stattfindet.* Frankfurt am Main, 1866.

———. *Gesammelte Schriften [von Rabbiner Samson Raphael Hirsch].* 6 vols. Frankfurt am Main: J. Kauffmann, 1912.

———. *The Hirsch Psalms.* Translated by Gertrude Hirschler. New York: Feldheim, 1978.

———. *The Hirsch Siddur.* Translated by Gertrude Hirschler. New York: Feldheim, 1969.

———. *Horeb.* Edited and translated by I. Grunfeld. London: Soncino Press, 1962.

———. *Horev: Versuche über Jissroels Plichten in der Zerstreuung, zunachst für Jissroëls denkende Junglinge und Jungfrauen.* Altona, 1837.

———. *Judaism Eternal: Selected Essays from the Writings of Rabbi Samson Raphael Hirsch.* Translated and edited by I. Grunfeld. 2 vols. London: Soncino Press, 1956.

———. *Die Neunzehn Briefe über Judentum.* Zurich: Verlag Morascha, 2013.

———. *The Nineteen Letters.* Translated by Karin Paritzky, with a commentary by Joseph Elias. New York: Feldheim, 1995.

———. *The Nineteen Letters of Ben Uziel.* Translated by Bernard Drachman. New York: Funk and Wagnalls, 1899.

———. *Der Pentateuch, übersetzt und erläutert von Samson Raphael Hirsch.* Frankfurt am Main: J. Kauffmann, 1867–78.

———. *The Pentateuch Translated and Explained by Samson Raphael Hirsch.* Translated by Isaac Levy. Gateshead: Judaica Press, 1976.

———. *Die Psalmen, übersetzt und erläutert von Rabbiner Samson Raphael Hirsch.* Frankfurt am Main: Hermon Verlags-Aktiengesellschaft, 1924.

———. *Shemesh Marpeh.* Edited by Eliyahu Meir Klugman. New York: Mesorah, 1992.

———. *Über die Beziehung des Talmuds zum Judenthum und zu der sozialen Stellung seiner Bekenner.* Frankfurt am Main, 1884.

———. "Worte, gesprochen bei der Schulfeier der Unterrichtsanstalt der Israel . . ." Frankfurt am Main, 1859.

Hoffmann, David Zvi. *Das Buch Leviticus, übersetzt und erklärt von D. Hoffmann.* Berlin: n. p., 1905–6.

———. *Der Schulchan Aruch und die Rabbinen über das Verhältnis der Juden zu Andersgläubigen.* 2nd ed. Berlin, 1894.

———. *Shu"t Melamed LeHo'il.* Jerusalem: n. p., 2010.

Holdheim, Samuel. *Das Ceremonialgesetz im Messiasreich.* Schwerin, 1845.

Horovitz, Marcus. *Fünf Reden.* Frankfurt am Main: M. Lehrberger, 1925.

———. *Rabbanei Frankfurt.* Translated by Joshua Amir. Jerusalem: Mossad ha-Rav Kook, 1972.

———. *Shu"t Matteh Levi.* Jerusalem: n. p., 1979.

Humash Mekor Hayyim. Edited by J. Heinemann. Berlin, 1832.

Jüdische Anmerkungen zu den Bemerkungen eines Protestanten über die Confession der 22 bremischen Pastoren. Gerhard Stalling, 1841.

Kant, Immanuel. *Religion within the Limits of Reason Alone.* Translated by T. M. Greene and H. H. Hudson. New York: Harper and Row, 1960.

Kook, Avraham Yitzhak. *Iggerot ha-Raaya"h.* Vol. 1. Jerusalem: Mossad haRav Kook, 1962.

Landau, Ezekiel. *Shu"t Noda bi-Yehudah.* Prague, 1776.

Lehmann, Marcus. *Haggadah shel Pesach im Peirush "Meir Nativ"* . . . Bene Berak: n. p., 1967.

———. *Hagadah schel Pesach mit Erläuterungen von M. Lehmann.* Frankfurt am Main: n. p., 1918.

———. *Lehmann's Passover Haggadah: With the Commentary of Rabbi Dr. Marcus Lehmann of Mainz.* London: n. p., 1969.

———. *The Lehmann-Prins Pirkei Avoth.* Translated by C. H. Moore. New York: Feldheim, 1992.

———. *Masekhet Avot im Perush Meir Nativ.* Vol. 1. Bene Berak: n. p., 1968.

———. *Sprüche der Väter.* Frankfurt am Main: J. Kaufmann, 1921.

Leiner, Gershon Henoch. *Sidrei Taharot to Ohalot.* Pietrakov: n. p., 1903.

Lipschutz, Israel. *Tiferet Yisrael Yakhin u-Boaz, Seder Nezikin.* New York: Vagshal, 1999.

Luzzatto, Moses Hayyim. *Derekh Hashem.* Jerusalem: A. M. Lunz, 1914.

———. *The Way of God.* Translated by Aryeh Kaplan. New York: Feldheim, 1997.

Maharal. *Gevurot Hashem.* London: n. p., 1964.

Maimonides, Moses. *The Guide of the Perplexed.* Translated by Michael Friedlander. New York: Hebrew Publishing, 1904.

———. *Mishneh Torah.* Edited by Shabbetai Frankel. Jerusalem: n. p., 1975.

———. *Perush ha-Mishnayot.* Translated by Yosef Qafih. Jerusalem: Mossad haRav Kook, 1968.

Malbim, Meir Leibush. *Torah im Peirush ha-Malbim.* Bene Berak: Mosdot Alexander, 2000.

Mecklenberg, Jacob Zvi. *Ha-Ketav ve-HaKabbalah.* Berlin, 1880.

Meiri, Menahem. *Beit ha-Behirah al Masekhet Avodah Zarah.* Edited by Avraham Sofer. Jerusalem: Kedem, 1964.

Mendelsohn-Frankfurter, Moses. *Pnei Tevel.* Amsterdam, 1872.

Mendelssohn, Moses. *Gesammelte Schriften Jubiläumsausgabe.* Band 16. Stuttgart: n. p., 1971.

———. *Jerusalem.* Translated by Allan Arkush, with introduction and commentary by Alexander Altmann. Hanover, NH: University Press of New England 1983.

Messas, Shalom. *Shu"t Shemesh U-Magen.* Vol. 3. Jerusalem: n. p., 2000.

Messas, Yosef. *Mayim Hayyim.* Vol. 2. Jerusalem: n. p., 1984.

Mielziner, Moses. *Die Verhältnisse der Sklaven bei den alten Hebräern, nach biblischen und talmudischen Quellen dargestellt: Ein Beitrag zur hebräisch-jüdischen Alterthumskunde.* Copenhagen, 1859.

Mishnat Rabbi Eliezer. New York: Bloch, 1934.

Moses of Coucy. *Sefer Mitzvot Gadol.* Jerusalem: n. p., 1991.

Phineas Elijah of Vilna. *Sefer ha-Berit.* Jerusalem: n. p., 1990.

Sasportas, Jacob. *Kitzur Tzitzat Novel Tzvi.* Altona, 1757.

Schenirer, Sarah. *Em be-Yisrael: Kitvei Sarah Schenirer.* Vol. 2. Jerusalem: n. p., 1975.

Schick, Moshe. *Derashot Maharam Schick*. Cluj: n. p., 1936.
———. *Shu"t Maharam Schick*. Jerusalem: n. p., 1971.
Schiller, Friedrich. "Die Sendung Moses." In Schiller, *Sämtliche Werke*, vol. 15, 1–33. Karlsruhe, 1822.
Schleiermacher, Friedrich. *The Christian Faith*. Translated by H. R. Mackintosh and J. S. Stewart. London: T&T Clark, 1928.
———. *On Religion*. Translated by Richard Couter. New York: Cambridge University Press, 1996.
Sefer Torat ha-Kena'ot. Amsterdam, 1845.
Shnayer Zalman of Liadi. *Sefer ha-Tanya*. Zelkova, 1805.
Shor, Joseph Bekhor. *Perush al ha-Torah*. Jerusalem: Mossad haRav Kook, 1994.
Shulhan Arukh. [Rabbi Joseph Karo and Rabbi Moses Isserelis]. Jerusalem: Vagshal, 2007.
Simha, Meir, of Dvinsk. *Meshekh Hokhmah*. Riga: Even Yisrael, 1927.
Sofer, Hatam. *Derashot Hatam Sofer*. Jerusalem: n. p., 1959.
Sofer, Hayyim. *Sha'arei Hayyim*. New York: A. Iliovits, 2012. Previously published Pressburg, 1897.
Sofer, Moshe. *Kovets Teshuvot Hatam Sofer*. Jerusalem: n. p., 1973.
———. *Sefer Hatam Sofer: Derashot u-Ma'amarim*. Jerusalem: n. p., 1959.
———. *Shu"t Hatam Sofer*. Bratislava, 1851.
———. *Torat Moshe*. Pressburg, 1879.
Soloveichik, Ahron. *Logic of the Heart, Logic of the Mind*. Jerusalem: Genesis Jerusalem Press, 1991.
Soloveitchik, Yitzhak Zev. *Hiddushei Rabbenu ha-Griz Soloveitchik Mi'pi Shemuah al ha-Torah*. Jerusalem: n. p., 5747 (1987).
Soloveitchik, Yosef Dov. *Beit ha-Levi al ha-Torah*. Warsaw, 1884.
———. *Shu"t Beit ha-Levi*. Jerusalem: n. p., 1996.
Wechsler, M. P. E. *Ein Wort der Mahnung an Israel*. Edited by Rivka Horwitz. Jerusalem: Dinur Center, 1991.
Weinberg, Yehiel Yaakov. *Lifrakim*. 6th ed. Jerusalem: A. A. Weingort, 2010.
Weisel [Wessely], Naphtali Herz. *Divrei Shalom ve-Emet*. Berlin, 1782.
———. *Olelot Naphtali*. Hamburg, 1842.
———. *Yeyn Levanon*. Berlin, 1775.
———. *Yeyn Levanon*. Edited by Y. Segal and S. Levy. Rishon le-Tziyon: Yeshivat ha-Hesder, 2003.
Yosef Hayyim of Baghdad. *Shu"t Rav Pe'alim*. Jerusalem: n. p., 1912.

Secondary Sources

Aberbach, David. *The European Jews, Patriotism and the Liberal State 1789–1939*. Abingdon, UK: Routledge, 2013.
Ahren, Yizhak. "Samson Raphael Hirsch (1808–1888)." In *Judentum verstehen: Die Aktualität jüdischen Denkens von Maimonides bis Hannah Arendt*, edited by Hans Erler and Ernst Ludwig Ehrlich, 109–20. Frankfurt am Main: Campus Verlag, 2002.
Alexander, Philip S. "Yeshu/Yeshua ben Yosef of Nazareth: Discerning the Jewish Face of Jesus." In *The Birth of Jesus: Biblical and Theological Reflections*, edited by George J. Brook, 9–21. Edinburgh: Bloomsbury, 2000.

Altmann, Alexander. *Moses Mendelssohn: A Biographical Study*. Tuscaloosa: University of Alabama Press, 1973.

Auerbach, Nathan Raphael. *The Guardians of the Sacred Trust: The Rabbis of the Auerbach Family in Germany*. 2 Vols. Jerusalem: Feldheim, 2009. Hebrew.

Baader, Benjamin M. *Gender, Judaism, and Bourgeois Culture in Germany, 1800–1870*. Bloomington: Indiana University Press, 2006.

Bach, Hans. *The German Jew: A Synthesis of Judaism and Western Civilization*. London: Littman Library, 1984.

Baron, Salo W. "The Revolution of 1848 and Jewish Scholarship: Part II: Austria." *Proceedings of the American Academy for Jewish Research* 20 (1951): 1–100.

Barth, Karl. *Protestant Theology in the Nineteenth Century: Its Background and History*. Translated by Brian Cozens and John Bowden. London: SCM Press, 1959.

Barzilay, Isaac. *Shlomo Yehuda Rapoport and His Contemporaries: Some Aspects of Jewish Scholarship of the Nineteenth Century*. Ramat-Gan: Massada Press, 1969.

Batnitzky, Leora. *How Judaism Became a Religion*. Princeton, NJ: Princeton University Press, 2011.

Bauer, Sebastian. "Ludwig Philippson und Marcus Lehmann: Jüdische Kontroversen zwischen Reform und Orthodoxie als identitätsstiftende Momente im neunzehnten Jahrhundert." PhD diss., Ludwig Maximilian University of Munich, 2016.

Bendheim, Giti, Menachem Butler, Jay M. Harris, and Uriel Katz, eds. *Jacob Katz on the Origins of Orthodoxy*. Cambridge, MA: Shikey Press, 2022.

Benisch, Pearl. *Carry Me in Your Heart: The Life and Legacy of Sarah Schenirer, Founder and Visionary of the Bais Yaakov Movement*. New York: Feldheim, 2004.

Berger, David. "Jews, Gentiles, and the Modern Egalitarian Ethos: Some Tentative Thoughts." In *Formulating Responses in an Egalitarian Age*, edited by Marc D. Stern, 83–108. Lanham, MD: Rowman and Littlefield, 2005.

———. "Malbim's Secular Knowledge and His Relationship to the Spirit of the Haskalah." *Yavneh Review* 5 (1966): 24–46.

———. *Persecution, Polemic, and Dialogue: Essays in Jewish-Christian Relations*. Boston: Academic Studies Press, 2010.

Berkovitz, Jay R. *The Shaping of Jewish Identity in Nineteenth-Century France*. Detroit: Wayne State University Press, 1988.

———. *Rites and Passages: The Beginnings of Modern Jewish Culture in France, 1650–1860*. Philadelphia: University of Pennsylvania Press 2004.

Bernardini, Paolo L., and Diego, Lucci. *The Jews, Instructions for Use: Four Eighteenth-Century Projects for the Emancipation of European Jews*. Boston: Academic Studies Press, 2012.

Berthelot, Katell. *Le monothéisme peut-il être humaniste?* Paris: Fayard, 2006.

Biale, David. *Gershom Scholem: Master of the Kabbalah*. New Haven, CT: Yale University Press, 2018.

Bleich, J. David. *The Philosophical Quest: Of Philosophy, Ethics, Law and Halakhah*. Jerusalem: Koren, 2013.

———. "*Tikkun Olam*: Jewish Obligations to Non-Jewish Society." In *Tikkun Olam: Social Responsibility in Jewish Thought and Law*, edited by David Shatz, Chaim I. Waxman, and Nathan J. Diament, 61–102. Brooklyn: Ktav, 1997.

Bleich, Judith. *Defenders of the Faith: Studies in Nineteenth- and Twentieth-Century Orthodoxy and Reform.* New York: Touro University Press, 2020.

———. "Rabbi Akiva Eger and the Nascent Reform Movement." *World Congress of Jewish Studies* 9, B3 (1986): 1–8.

———. "Rabbi Jacob Ettlinger, His Life and Works: The Emergence of Modern Orthodoxy in Germany." PhD diss., New York University, 1974.

Blidstein, Gerald [Yaakov]. "Menahem Meiri's Attitude toward Gentiles—Apologetics or Worldview?" In *Binah 3: Jewish Intellectual History in the Middle Ages*, edited by Joseph Dan, 119–33. Westport, CT: Praeger, 1994.

———. "Maimonides and Meiri on the Legitimacy of Non-Judaic Religion." In *Scholars and Scholarship: The Interaction between Judaism and Other Cultures*, edited by Leo Landman, 27–35. New York: Ktav, 1990.

———. *Studies in Halakhic and Aggadic Thought.* Beer-Sheva: Ben-Gurion University of the Negev Press, 2004. Hebrew.

Blum, Alexis. "Sinzheim Le Porte-Parole des Ashkenazim." In *Le Grand Sanhedrin de Napoleon*, edited by Bernhard Blumenkranz and Albert Soboul, 119–31. Toulouse: E. Privat, 1979.

Blutinger, Jeffrey. "'So-Called Orthodoxy': The History of an Unwanted Label." *Modern Judaism* 27, no. 3 (2007): 310–28.

Bodoff, Lipmann. "Was Yehudah Halevi Racist?" *Judaism* 38 (Spring 1989): 176–84.

Boulouque, Clemence. *Another Modernity: Elia Benamozegh's Jewish Universalism.* Stanford, CA: Stanford University Press, 2020.

Brämer, Andreas. *Rabbiner Zacharias Frankel: Wissenschaft des Judentums und konservative Reform im 19. Jahrhundert.* Hildesheim: G. Olms, 2000.

Brasz, Chaya. "Dutch Jewry and Its Undesired German Rabbinate." *Leo Baeck Institute Yearbook* 57, no. 1 (2012): 73–86.

Breuer, Edward. "Between Haskalah and Orthodoxy: The Writings of R. Jacob Zvi Mecklenburg." *Hebrew Union College Annual* 66 (1995): 259–87.

———. "Naphtali Herz Wessely and the Cultural Dislocations of an Eighteenth-Century Maskil." In *New Perspectives on the Haskalah*, edited by Shmuel Feiner and David Sorkin, 27–47. Oxford: Littman Library, 2001.

———. "Politics, Tradition, History: Rabbinic Judaism and the Eighteenth-Century Struggle for Civil Equality." *Harvard Theological Review* 85, no. 3 (1992): 357–83.

Breuer, Mordechai. "The Jewish Minority in the Enlightened Absolutist State." In Meyer, *German-Jewish History in Modern Times*, vol. 1.

———. *Modernity within Tradition: The Social History of Orthodox Jewry in Imperial Germany.* Translated by E. Petuchowski. New York: Columbia University Press, 1992.

———. "Perakim Mitokh Biographiah: Al Bitul Kol Nidre be-Oldenburg." *Ha-Ma'ayan* 4, no. 2 (5624): 7–12.

———. Review of Noah H. Rosenbloom, *Tradition in an Age of Reform. Tradition* 16, no. 4 (Summer 1977): 140–49.

———. "Samson Raphael Hirsch and Modern Orthodoxy." *Niv ha-Midrashiyah* 24/25 (1993): 32–34.

———. *The "Torah-im-Derekh-Eretz of Samson Raphael Hirsch".* New York: Feldheim, 1970.

Brill, Alan. *Judaism and Other Religions: Models of Understanding*. New York: Palgrave Macmillan, 2010.

———. *Judaism and World Religions: Encountering Christianity, Islam, and Eastern Traditions*. New York: Palgrave Macmillan, 2012.

Brill, Alan, and Rori Picker Neiss. "Jewish Views of World Religions: Four Models." In Goshen-Gottstein and Korn, *Jewish Theology and World Religions*, 41–60.

Brown, Benjamin. "Breuer, Hirsch and Jewish Nationalism: Change and Continuity—Principle versus Supra-Principle." *Journal of Jewish Studies* 64, no. 2 (Autumn 2013): 383–402.

Büchler, Sigmund. *Die Lebensgeschichte des Rabbi Juda Aszod, 5556–5626*. Dunajská Streda: A. Weisz, 1933.

Cahnman, Werner J. "Friedrich Wilhelm Schelling and the New Thinking of Judaism." In *German Jewry: Its History and Sociology*, edited by Joseph B. Maier, Judith Marcus, and Zoltan Tarr, 209–48. Brunswick, NJ: Transaction Books, 1989.

Carlebach, Elisheva. *Divided Souls: Converts from Judaism in Germany, 1500–1750*. New Haven, CT: Yale University Press, 2001.

Carlebach, Elisheva, and Jacob J. Schacter, eds. *New Perspectives on Jewish-Christian Relations in Honor of David Berger*. Leiden: Brill, 2012.

Catane, Moche. *La Vie et l'oeuvre du Rabbin M. Lehmann (1831–1890)*. Jerusalem: Université de Jérusalem, 1971.

Chamiel, Ephraim. *The Dual Truth: Studies on Nineteenth-Century Modern Religious Thought and Its Influence on Twentieth-Century Jewish Philosophy*. 2 vols. Boston: Academic Studies Press, 2019.

———. *The Middle Way: The Emergence of Modern Religious Trends: Responses to Modernity in the Thought of Maharatz Chayot, Rabbi S. R. Hirsch, and S. D. Luzzatto*. 2 vols. Boston: Academic Studies Press, 2014.

Chertok, Shlomo. *An Old Flask of New Wine: Innovation and Conservatism in Rabbi Samson Raphael Hirsch's Biblical Commentary*. Tel Aviv: ha-Kibutz ha-me'uhad, 2010. Hebrew.

Chisick, Harvey. "Ethics and History in Voltaire's Attitudes towards the Jews." *Eighteenth-Century Studies* 35, no. 4 (June 2002): 577–600.

Clark, Matityahu. *Etymological Dictionary of Biblical Hebrew Based on the Commentaries of Samson Raphael Hirsch*. New York: Feldheim, 1999.

Cohen, Mordechai Z. *The Rule of Peshat*. Philadelphia: University of Pennsylvania Press, 2020.

Danziger, Shelomoh E. "Clarification of R. Hirsch's Concepts—A Rejoinder." *Tradition* 6 (Spring–Summer 1964): 141–58.

Dawson, Jerry F. *Friedrich Schleiermacher: The Evolution of a Nationalist*. Austin: University of Texas Press, 1966.

Dubin, Lois C. "Trieste and Berlin: The Italian Role in the Cultural Politics of the Haskalah." In *Toward Modernity: The European Jewish Model*, edited by Jacob Katz, 189–224. Brunswick, NJ: Transaction Books, 1987.

Dubrau, Alexander A. "A Jewish Orthodox Response to the Hostility towards the Morality of Jewish Law and the Jewish God at the Beginning of the Twentieth Century in Germany: Rabbi David Zvi Hoffmann on the Relationship between Jews and Gentiles." In *Religion and Transfer: Interactions between Judaism, Christianity, and Islam from the Middle Ages to the Twentieth Century*, edited by A. A. Dubrau, D. Scotto, and R. Vimercati Sanseverino, 273–304. Tübingen: Mohr Siebeck, 2020.

Duckesz, Eduard. "Zur Biographie des Chacham Isaak Bernays." *Jahrbuch der jüdischen-literarischen Gesellschaft* 5 (1907): 297–322.

———. "Zur Genealogie Samson Raphael Hirsch." *Jahrbuch der jüdisch-literarischen Gesellschaft* 17 (1926): 103–31.

Edar, Dror. "Meir Lehmann: Jewish Orthodoxy Tested." *Mi-kan* 10 (5771): 19–51. Hebrew.

Elbaum, Yaakov. "Concerning Two Textual Emendations in the *Aleinu* Prayer." *Tarbiz* 42, no. 1–2 (October 1972–March 1973): 204–8. Hebrew.

Ellenson, David. *After Emancipation: Jewish Religious Responses to Modernity*. Cincinnati: Hebrew Union College Press, 2004.

———. "German Jewish Orthodoxy: Tradition in the Context of Culture." In Wertheimer, *Uses of Tradition*, 5–22.

———. *Rabbi Esriel Hildesheimer and the Creation of a Modern Jewish Orthodoxy*. Tuscaloosa: University of Alabama Press, 1990.

———. *Tradition in Transition*. Lanham, MD: University Press of America, 1989.

Ellenson, David, and Daniel Gordis. *Pledges of Jewish Allegiance: Conversion, Law, and Policymaking in Nineteenth- and Twentieth-Century Orthodox Responsa*. Stanford, CA: Stanford University Press, 2012.

Elman, Yaakov. "Meiri and the Non-Jew: A Comparative Investigation." In Carlebach and Schacter, *New Perspectives*, 265–96.

Elukin, Jonathan M. "Maimonides and the Rise and Fall of the Sabians: Explaining Mosaic Laws and the Limits of Scholarship." *Journal of the History of Ideas* 63, no. 4 (2002): 619–37.

Emanuel, Yonah. "Israel Opposite Christianity: Rav Hirsch on Christianity and the Relationship of Christians to Jews." *Ha-Ma'ayan* 29, no. 2 (5749): 38–49. Hebrew.

Emanuel, Yonah, ed. *Rabbi Samson Raphael Hirsch: His Teaching and Method*. Jerusalem: Feldheim, 1962. Hebrew.

Encyclopedia Judaica. New York: Macmillan, 1971.

Erspamer, Peter R. *The Elusiveness of Tolerance: The "Jewish Question" from Lessing to the Napoleonic Wars*. Chapel Hill: University of North Carolina Press, 1997.

Etkes, E., and Y. Salmon, eds. *Studies in the History of Jewish Society in the Middle Ages and in the Modern Period*. Jerusalem: Magnes Press, 1980. Hebrew.

Etkes, Immanuel. *The Gaon of Vilna: Image and Reality*. Berkeley: University of California Press, 2003.

———. *Rabbi Israel Salanter and the Mussar Movement: Seeking the Torah of Truth*. Translated by Jonathan Chipman. Philadelphia: Jewish Publication Society, 1993.

Feiner, Shmuel. *The Jewish Enlightenment*. Translated by Chaya Naor. Philadelphia: University of Pennsylvania Press, 2004.

———. *Moses Mendelssohn: Sage of Modernity*. Translated by Anthony Berris. New Haven, CT: Yale University Press, 2010.

Ferziger, Adam S. *Exclusion and Hierarchy: Orthodoxy, Nonobservance, and the Emergence of Modern Jewish Identity*. Philadelphia: University of Pennsylvania Press, 2005.

———. "Religious Zealotry and Religious Law: Rethinking Conflict and Coexistence." *Journal of Religion* 84, no. 1 (January 2004): 48–77.

Fine, David J. *Jewish Integration in the German Army in the First World War*. Berlin: De Gruyter, 2012.

Fixler, Dror, and Gil Nadel. "Are Contemporary Christians Worshippers of Avodah Zarah?" *Tehumin* 22 (2002): 68–78. Hebrew.

Flatto, Sharon. "A Tale of Three Generations: Shifting Attitudes toward Haskalah, Mendelssohn, and Acculturation." In *Jewish Culture in Early Modern Europe: Essays in Honor of David B. Ruderman*, edited by Richard I. Cohen et al., 294–306. Cincinnati: Hebrew Union College Press, 2014.

Frishman, Judith. "Good Enough for the Goyim? Samuel Hirsch and Samuel Holdheim on Christianity." In *Interaction between Judaism and Christianity in History, Religion, Art and Literature*, edited by M. Poorthuis, J. J. Schwartz, and J. Turner, 271–87. Leiden: Brill, 2009.

Ganzel, Tova. "Explicit and Implicit Polemic in Rabbi Samson Raphael Hirsch's Bible Commentary." *Hebrew Union College Annual* 81 (2012): 171–91.

Geller, Yaakov. *The Malbim: His Struggle with Haskalah and Reform in Bucharest 1858–1864*. Lod: Orot Yahadut haMegrav, 2000. Hebrew.

Gedenk-blätter an Rabbiner Dr. Marcus Lehmann. Mainz, 1890.

Gillman, Abigail. *A History of German Jewish Bible Translation*. Chicago: University of Chicago Press, 2018.

Goldberg, Harvey E. "Sephardi Rabbinic 'Openness' in Nineteenth-Century Tripoli: Examining a Modern Myth in Context." In *Jewish Religious Leadership: Image and Reality*, edited by Jack Wertheimer, vol. 2, 695–714. New York: Jewish Theological Seminary, 2004.

Goldhagen, Daniel Jonah. *Hitler's Willing Executioners*. New York: Vintage, 1996.

Goldstein, Moshe, ed. *Hiddushe ha-Ritva al Massekhet Avodah Zarah*. Jerusalem: Mossad haRav Kook, 1978.

Goodman, Micah. *The Dream of the Kuzari*. Or Yehuda: Dvir, 2012. Hebrew.

Gopin, Marc. "An Orthodox Embrace of Gentiles? Interfaith Tolerance in the Thought of S. D. Luzzatto and E. Benamozegh." *Modern Judaism* 18 (1998): 173–95.

Goshen-Gottstein, Alon, and Eugene Korn, eds. *Jewish Theology and World Religions*. Oxford: Littman Library, 2012.

Gottlieb, Michah. "Counter-Enlightenment in a Jewish Key: Anti-Maimonideanism in Nineteenth-Century Orthodoxy." In *The Cultures of Maimonideanism: New Approaches to the History of Jewish Thought*, edited by James T. Robinson, 259–87. Leiden: Brill, 2009.

———. "Does Judaism Have Dogma? Moses Mendelssohn and a Pivotal Nineteenth-Century Debate." *Yearbook of the Maimonides Centre for Advanced Studies 2019*, 219–42. Berlin: De Gruyter, 2020.

———. *The Jewish Reformation: Bible Translation and Middle-Class German Judaism as Spiritual Enterprise*. New York: Oxford University Press, 2021.

———. *Moses Mendelssohn: Writings on Judaism, Christianity, and the Bible*. Waltham, MA: Brandeis University Press, 2011.

———. "Orthodoxy and the Orient: Samson Raphael Hirsch on the Location of Judaism." In *Wissenschaft des Judentums beyond Tradition*, edited by D. M. Salzer, C. Gafni, and H. Harif, 53–71. Berlin: De Gruyter, 2019.

Graetz, Heinrich. *Geschichte der Juden*. Edited by M. Brann. 2nd ed. Vol. 11. Leipzig, 1900.

Graupe, Heinz Moshe. *The Rise of Modern Judaism: An Intellectual History of German Jewry 1650–1942*. Translated by John Robinson. New York: Robert E. Krieger, 1979.

Greenwald, Jekuthiel Judah. *The History of the Religious Reformation in Germany and in Hungary*. Columbus, OH: n. p., 1948. Hebrew.

Gronke, Horst, Thomas Meyer, and Barbara Neisser, eds. *Antisemitismus bei Kant und anderen Denkern der Aufklärung*. Würzberg: Königshausen und Neumann, 2001.

Grunewald, Pinhas Paul. *Pedagogie, esthetique et ticoun olam—Redressement du monde: Samson Raphael Hirsch*. Berne: Peter Lang International Academic, 1986.

Grunfeld, I. "The 'Ba'al Seride Esh.'" In *The Torah Personality*, edited by Nisson Wolpin, 99–105. New York: Mesorah, 1980.

Grunfeld-Rosenbaum, Judith. "Sara Schenirer." In Jung, *Jewish Leaders*, 407–32.

Haberman, Jacob. "Kaufmann Kohler and His Teacher Samson Raphael Hirsch." *Leo Baeck Institute Yearbook* 43 (1998): 73–103.

Habermann, A. M. "Declarations of Authors or Publishers in Their Books to Legitimize Them in the Eyes of Gentiles." In *Essays and Studies in Librarianship Presented to Curt David Wormann on His Seventy-Fifth Birthday*, 60– 71. Jerusalem: Magnes Press, 1975. Hebrew.

Halbertal, Moshe. *Between Torah and Wisdom: Rabbi Menahem ha-Meiri and the Maimonidean Halakhists in Provence*. Jerusalem: Magnes Press, 2000. Hebrew.

———. *Maimonides: Life and Thought*. Translated by Joel Linsider. Princeton, NJ: Princeton University Press, 2014.

Halbertal, Moshe, and Margalit, Avishai. *Idolatry*. Translated by Naomi Goldblum. Cambridge, MA: Harvard University Press, 1992.

Heinemann, Isaac. *The Reasons for the Commandments in Jewish Literature*. Vol. 2. Jerusalem: Jewish Agency, 1956. Hebrew.

———. "The Relationship between S. R. Hirsch and His Teacher Isaac Bernays." *Zion* 16 (1951): 44–90. Hebrew.

———. "Samson Raphael Hirsch: The Formative Years of the Leader of Modern Orthodoxy." *Historia Judaica* 13 (1951): 29–54.

Helfer, Martha B. *The Word Unheard: Legacies of Anti-Semitism in German Literature and Culture*. Evanston, IL: Northwestern University Press, 2011.

Henkin, Yehuda Herzl. *Shu"t Bnei Banim*. Vol. 3. Jerusalem: n. p., 1997.

Hertz, Joseph H., ed. *The Pentateuch and Haphtoroth*. London: Soncino Press, 1981.

Hertzberg, Arthur. *The French Enlightenment and the Jews*. New York: Columbia University Press, 1968.

Heschel, Susannah. *Abraham Geiger and the Jewish Jesus*. Chicago: University of Chicago Press, 1998.

———. "Abraham Geiger and the 19th-Century Failure of Christian-Jewish Relations." *Kirchliche Zeitgeschichte* 16 (2003): 17–36.

Heschel, Yisrael Natan. "The View of the Torah Giants in Their War against the Maskil Naphtali Herz Weisel." *Kovets Beis Aharon* 43 (1993). Hebrew.

Hess, Jonathan M. "Johann David Michaelis and the Colonial Imagery: Orientalism and the Emergence of Racial Antisemitism in Eighteenth-Century Germany." *Jewish Social Studies*, n.s., 6, no. 2 (Winter 2000): 56–101.

Hezser, Catherine. *Jewish Slavery in Antiquity*. New York: Oxford University Press, 2006.

Hildesheimer, Meir. "The Attitude of the Hatam Sofer toward Moses Mendelssohn." *Proceedings for the American Academy for Jewish Research* 60 (1994): 141–87.

———. "The German Language and Secular Studies: Attitudes towards Them in the Thought of the Hatam Sofer and His Disciples." *Proceedings of the American Academy for Jewish Research* 62 (1996): 129–63.

———. "Moses Mendelssohn in Nineteenth-Century Rabbinical Literature." *Proceedings of the American Academy for Jewish Research* 55 (1988): 79–133.

———. "The Rabbi and His Student: Rabbi Jacob Ettlinger and Rabbi Esriel Hildesheimer." *HaMa'ayan* 12, no. 3 (Nissan 5732): 40–48. Hebrew.

Hildesheimer, Meir, and Matthias Morgenstern. *Rabbiner Samson Raphael Hirsch in der deutschsprachigen jüdischen Presse: Materialien zu einer bibliographischen Übersicht*. Berlin: Lit Verlag, 2013.

Hirschler, Gertrude. "Rabbi and Statesman: Samson Raphael Hirsch, *Landesrabbiner* of Moravia (1847–1851)." *Review of the Society for the History of Czechoslovak Jews* 1 (1987): 121–49.

Hoffman, Matthew. *From Rebel to Rabbi: Reclaiming Jesus and the Making of Modern Jewish Culture*. Stanford, CA: Stanford University Press, 2007.

Hoffmann, Christhard, Werner Bergmann, and Helmut Walser Smith, eds. *Exclusionary Violence: Antisemitic Riots in Modern Germany*. Ann Arbor: University of Michigan Press, 2002.

Hollander, Dana. "Love-of-Neighbor and Ethics Out of Law in the Philosophy of Hermann Cohen." In Wiese and Urban, *German-Jewish Thought*, 83–113.

Horowitz, Elliot. *Reckless Rites: Purim and the Legacy of Jewish Violence*. Princeton, NJ: Princeton University Press, 2006.

Horwitz, Rivka. "On Kabbala and Myth in 19th Century Germany: Isaac Bernays." *Proceedings of the American Academy for Jewish Research* 59 (1993): 137–83.

———. "The Relationship of Rabbi Samson Raphael Hirsch to the Land of Israel." In *Multiple Faceted Judaism*, 387–407. Beer-Sheva: Ben Gurion University, 2002. Hebrew.

Hutner-David, Bruriah. "The Dual Role of Rabbi Zvi Hirsch Chajes: Traditionalist and *Maskil*." PhD diss., Columbia University, 1971.

Jacobs, Louis. *Theology in the Responsa*. London: Littman Library, 1975.

Japhet, Saemy. "The Secession from the Frankfurt Jewish Community under Samson Raphael Hirsch." *Historia Judaica* 10 (1948): 99–122.

Jung, Leo, ed. *Jewish Leaders, 1750–1940*. New York: Bloch, 1953.

Kahn, Yoel H. *The Three Blessings: Boundaries, Censorship, and Identity in Jewish Liturgy*. New York: Oxford University Press, 2011.

Kallus, Menachem. "From Enmity to Unity: Recovering the Ba'al Shem Tov's Teachings on Non-Jews." In *Judaism's Challenge: Election, Divine Love, and Human Enmity*, edited by Alon Goshen-Gottstein, 174–88. Boston: Academic Studies Press, 2020.

Kaplan, Lawrence. Review of Eliyahu Stern, *The Genius: Elijah of Vilna and the Making of Modern Judaism*. *Seforim Blog* (blog), November 19, 2013.

———. "*Torah U-Madda* in the Thought of Rabbi Samson Raphael Hirsch." *B.D.D.* 5 (Summer 1997): 5–31.

Kaplan, Zvi Jonathan. "Mendelssohn's Religious Perspective of Non-Jews." *Journal of Ecumenical Studies* 41, nos. 3–4 (Summer–Fall 2004): 355–66.

Karady, Victor. *The Jews of Europe in the Modern Era: A Socio-Historical Outline*. Translated by Tim Wilkinson. Budapest: Central European University, 2004.

Karniel, Joseph. *Der Toleranzpolitik Kaiser Josephs II*. Stuttgart: Bleicher, 1986.

Katz, Jacob. "Eisenmenger's Method of Prooftexts from Talmudic Sources." In *Proceedings of the World Congress of Jewish Studies*. Vol. 2, 210–16. Jerusalem, 1972. Hebrew.

———. *Exclusiveness and Tolerance*. New York: Behrman House, 1961.

———. *From Prejudice to Destruction: Anti-Semitism, 1700–1933*. Cambridge, MA: Harvard University Press, 1980.

———. "German Culture and the Jews." In Reinharz and Schatzberg, *Jewish Response to German Culture*, 86–87.

———. *Halakhah in Straits*. Jerusalem: Magnes Press, 1992. Hebrew.

———. *A House Divided: Orthodoxy and Schism in Nineteenth-Century Central European Jewry*. Translated by Ziporah Brody. Hanover, NH: University Press of New England, 1998.

———. "Orthodoxy in Historical Perspective." In *Studies in Contemporary Jewry*, edited by Peter H. Medding, vol. 2, 3–17. Bloomington: Indiana University Press, 1986.

———. *Out of the Ghetto: The Social Background of Jewish Emancipation, 1770–1870*. Cambridge, MA: Harvard University Press, 1973.

———. "The Term 'Jewish Emancipation': Its Origins and Historical Impact." In *Studies in Nineteenth-Century Jewish Intellectual History*, edited by Alexander Altmann, 1–25. Cambridge, MA: Harvard University Press, 1964.

———. "Three Apologetic Statements and Their Development." *Zion* 23–24, nos. 3–4 (1958–9): 174–93.

———. "Towards a Biography of the Hatam Sofer." Translated by David Ellenson. In *Profiles in Diversity: Jews in a Changing Europe, 1750–1870*, edited by Frances Malino and David Sorkin, 223–66. Detroit: Wayne State University Press, 1998.

———. "Tzevi Hirsch Kalischer." In Jung, *Jewish Leaders*, 209–27.

———. "The Vicissitude of Three Apologetic Passages." *Zion* 23–24, nos. 3–4 (1958–9): 174–93. Hebrew.

Katzburg, Nethanel. "The Rabbinical Decision of Michalowitz in 1865." In Etkes and Salmon, *Studies in the History of Jewish Society*, 273–86. Hebrew.

Kellner, Menachem. *Maimonides' Confrontation with Mysticism*. Oxford: Littman Library, 2006.

———. *Maimonides on Judaism and the Jewish People*. Albany: SUNY Press, 1991.

———. *Maimonides the Universalist: The Ethical Horizons of the Mishneh Torah*. Oxford: Littman Library, 2020.

———. *They Too Are Called Human: Gentiles in the Eyes of Maimonides*. Ramat-Gan: Bar-Ilan, 2016. Hebrew.

———. *We Are Not Alone: A Mamonidean Theology of the Other*. Boston: Academic Studies Press, 2021.

Klein, Daniel, ed. *The Book of Genesis: A Commentary by Shadal*. Northvale, NJ: Jason Aronson, 1998.

Kleinberger, Aaron F. "Nationalist Ferment in German Jewry in the First Half of the 19th Century." In Etkes and Salmon, *Studies in the History of Jewish Society*. Hebrew.

Klier, John Doyle. *Russians, Jews, and the Pogroms of 1881–1882*. New York: Cambridge University Press, 2011.

Klugman, Eliyahu Meir. *Rabbi Samson Raphael Hirsch*. New York: Mesorah, 1996.

Kobler, Franz. *Napoleon and the Jews*. Jerusalem: Schoken, 1976.

Kocka, Jürgen. "German History before Hitler: The Debate about the German *Sonderweg*." *Journal of Contemporary History* 23, no. 1 (January 1988): 3–16.

Kohler, George Y. "The Birth of Modern Theology: Reactions to Bruno Bauer's Secular Supersessionism." *Journal for the History of Modern Theology* 28 (2021): 1–20.

———. "Manuel Joel in Defense of the Talmud: Liberal Responses to Religious Antisemitism in Nineteenth-Century Germany." *Hebrew Union College Annual* 79 (2008): 141–63.

———. *Reading Maimonides' Philosophy in 19th Century Germany: The Guide to Religious Reform* (Heidelberg: Springer, 2012).

Kohler, Kaufmann. "Personal Reminiscences of My Early Life." In Kohler, *Studies, Addresses and Personal Papers*. New York: Alumni Association of the Hebrew Union College, 1931.

Kolbrener, William. *The Last Rabbi: Joseph Soloveitchik and Talmudic Tradition*. Bloomington: Indiana University Press, 2016.

Kooij-Bas, Aaltje E. "Nothing but Heretics: Torat ha-Qena'ot: A Study and Translation of Nineteenth Century Responsa against Religious Reform." PhD diss., Tilburg University, 2006.

Korn, Eugene. "Gentiles, the World to Come, and Judaism: The Odyssey of a Rabbinic Text." *Modern Judaism* 14 (1994): 265–87.

———. "Rethinking Christianity: Rabbinic Positions and Possibilities." In Goshen-Gottstein and Korn, *Jewish Theology and World Religions*, 189–216.

———. *To Be a Holy People: Jewish Tradition and Ethical Values*. Jerusalem: Urim, 2021.

Krauss, Samuel. *Das Leben Jesu nach jüdischen Quellen*. Berlin: S. Calvary, 1902.

Krauss, Simcha. Review Essay, *Between the Yeshiva World and Modern Orthodoxy: The Life and Works of Rabbi Jehiel Jacob Weinberg* by Marc B. Shapiro, *Edah Journal* 1, no. 1 (2000/Marheshvan 5761): 1–6.

Kruskal, Chava. *Mi Lashem Elai*. Jerusalem: Feldheim, 2009.

Lamberti, Marjorie. *Jewish Activism in Imperial Germany: The Struggle for Civil Equality*. New Haven, CT: Yale University Press, 1978.

———. "Lutheran Orthodoxy and the Beginning of Conservative Party Organization in Prussia." *Church History* 37, no. 4 (December 1968): 439–53.

Langer, Ruth. "The Censorship of Aleinu in Ashkenaz and Its Aftermath." In *The Experience of Jewish Liturgy: Studies Dedicated to Menahem Schmelzer*, edited by Debra Reed Blank, 147–66. Leiden: Brill, 2011.

———. *Cursing the Christians?: A History of the Birkat haminim*. New York: Oxford University Press, 2012.

Lehmann, Jon. *Dr. Markus Lehmann*. Frankfurt am Main: Kauffmann, 1910.

Leibowitz, Yeshayahu. *Judaism, Human Values, and the Jewish State*. Edited and translated by Eliezer Goldman. Cambridge, MA: Harvard University Press, 1995.

Leiman, Shnayer Z. *Rabbinic Responses to Modernity*. Kew Gardens Hills, NY: S. Z. Leiman, 2007.

Lesher, Shmuel. "For the Love of Humanity: The Religious Humanism of Rabbi Samson Raphael Hirsch." *Hakirah* 32 (Fall 2022): 65–98.

———. "Rabbi Elazar Fleckles: An Early Rabbinic Humanist." *Tradition* 54, no. 2 (Spring 2022): 133–49.

Levenson, Alan T. *Between Philosemitism and Antisemitism: Defenses of Jews and Judaism in Germany, 1871–1932*. Lincoln: University of Nebraska Press, 2004.

———. "Missionary Protestants as Defenders and Detractors of Judaism: Franz Delitzsch and Hermann Strack." *Jewish Quarterly Review* 92, no. 3–4 (January–April 2002): 383–420.

Levine, Howard I. "Enduring and Transitory Elements in the Philosophy of Samson Raphael Hirsch." *Tradition* 5 (Fall 1962): 278–97.

Levy, Zev. "The Land of Israel in Jewish Thought in Germany from Hirsch to Rosenzweig." *Kivunim* 4 (1979): 54–66. Hebrew.

Liberles, Robert. "Champion of Orthodoxy: The Emergence of Samson Raphael Hirsch as Religious Leader." *AJS Review* 6 (1981): 43–60.

———. "From Toleration to *Verbesserung*: German and English Debates on the Jews in the Eighteenth Century." *Central European History* 22 (1989): 3–32.

———. *Religious Conflict in Social Context: The Resurgence of Orthodox Judaism in Frankfurt am Main, 1838–1877*. Westport, CT: Greenwood Press, 1985.

———. "Was There a Jewish Movement for Emancipation in Germany?" *Leo Baeck Institute Yearbook* 31, no. 1 (1986): 35–49.

Lichtenstein, Aharon. *Leaves of Faith: The World of Jewish Living*. Jersey City: Ktav, 2004.

Lindemann, Albert S. *Esau's Tears: Modern Anti-Semitism and the Rise of the Jews*. Cambridge, UK: Cambridge University Press, 1997.

Litvak, Olga. *Conscription and the Search for Modern Russian Jewry*. Bloomington: Indiana University Press, 2006.

———. *Haskalah: The Romantic Movement in Judaism*. New Brunswick, NJ: Rutgers University Press, 2012.

Loewenthal, Naftali. *Hasidism beyond Modernity: Essays in Habad Thought and History*. Oxford: Littman Library, 2020.

Low, Alfred D. *Jews in the Eyes of Germans*. Philadelphia: Institute for the Study of Human Issues, 1979.

Lowenstein, Steven. *The Berlin Jewish Community: Enlightenment, Family, and Crisis (1770–1830)*. New York: Oxford University Press, 1994.

———. *The Mechanics of Change: Essays in the Social History of German Jewry*. Atlanta: Scholars Press, 1992.

Lundgren, Svante. *Particularism and Universalism in Modern Jewish Thought*. New York: SUNY Press, 2001.

Lupovitch, Howard N. "Navigating Rough Waters: Alexander Kohut and the Hungarian Roots of Conservative Judaism." *AJS Review* 32 (2008): 49–78.

Mack, Michael. *German Idealism and the Jew*. Chicago: University of Chicago Press, 2003.

Magid, Shaul. *The Bible, the Talmud, and the New Testament: Elijah Zvi Soloveitchik's Commentary to the Gospels*. Philadelphia: University of Pennsylvania Press, 2019.

Massey, Irving. *Philo-Semitism in Nineteenth-Century German Literature*. Tübingen: Max Niemeyer Verlag, 2000.

Mathäs, Alexander. "Faith and Reason: Schiller's 'Die Sendung Moses.'" *German Quarterly* 81, no. 3 (2008): 283–301.

Mendes-Flohr, Paul. *German Jews: A Dual Identity*. New Haven: Yale University Press, 1999.

Mendes-Flohr, Paul, and Jehuda Reinharz, eds. *The Jew in the Modern World: A Documentary History*. 3rd ed. New York: Oxford University Press, 2011.

Mevorakh, Barukh. "The Belief in the Messiah in Early Reform Polemics." *Zion* 34 (1969): 189–218. Hebrew.

———. *Napoleon and His Era*. Jerusalem: Mosad Byalik, 1968. Hebrew.

Michael A. Meyer, "Jewish Self-Understanding." In Meyer, *German-Jewish History in Modern Times*, vol. 2.

———. "'Most of My Brethren Find Me Unacceptable': The Controversial Career of Rabbi Samuel Holdheim." In *Redefining Judaism in an Age of Emancipation: Comparative Perspectives on Samuel Holdheim (1806–1860)*, edited by Christian Wiese, 3–22. Leiden: Brill, 2007.

———. "Reform Jewish Thinkers and Their German Intellectual Context." In Reinharz and Schatzberg, *Jewish Response to German Culture*, 64–84.

———. "Religious Reform and Political Revolution in Mid-Nineteenth Century Germany: The Case of Abraham Jakob Adler." In Wiese and Urban, *German-Jewish Thought between Religion and Politics*, 59–81.

———. *Response to Modernity: A History of the Reform Movement in Judaism*. New York: Oxford University Press, 1988.

———. "Universalism and Jewish Unity in the Thought of Abraham Geiger." In *The Role of Religion in Modern Jewish History*, edited by Jacob Katz, 91–104. Cambridge, MA: Association for Jewish Studies, 1975.

Meyer, Michael A., ed. *German-Jewish History in Modern Times*. Vols. 1 and 2. New York: Columbia University Press, 1996–97.

Miller, Michael L. *Rabbis and Revolution: The Jews of Moravia in the Age of Emancipation*. Stanford, CA: Stanford University Press, 2011.

———. "Samson Raphael Hirsch and the Revolution of 1848." *Jewish Studies at the Central European University* 2 (2002): 223–38.

Miller, Moshe Y. "Between Frankfurt and Satmar: A Study of Two Schools of Orthodox Jewish Anti-Zionism." MA Thesis, Touro College, 2006.

———. "R. Jacob Emden's Attitude toward Christianity." In *Turim: Studies in Jewish History and Literature Presented to Dr. Bernard Lander*, vol. 2, 105–36. New York: Touro College Press, 2008.

———. "Rabbi Samson Raphael Hirsch's *Nineteen Letters on Judaism*: Orthodoxy Confronts Modernity." In *Books of the People*, edited by Stuart W. Halpern, 177–208. New Milford: Maggid Books, 2017.

———. Review Essay, Ephraim Chamiel, *The Middle Way*, *Tradition* 49, no. 3 (Fall 2016): 37–53.

Mitchell, Harvey. *Voltaire's Jews and Modern Jewish Identity: Rethinking the Enlightenment*. Abingdon, UK: Routledge, 2008.

Mommsen, Hans. *An Interview with Prof. Hans Mommsen*. Jerusalem: Yad Vashem, 1997.

Morgenstern, Matthias. "Between the Noahide Laws and Israelite-Edomite Brotherhood: Paradigms of Humanity in Modern Jewish Orthodoxy." In *The Quest for a Common Humanity*, edited by Katell Berthelot and Matthias Morgenstern, 101–21. Leiden: Brill, 2011.

———. "The Embarrassment of Joshua: Strategies for Interpreting the Biblical Account of the Conquest of Canaan in German-Jewish Neo-Orthodoxy in the Late Nineteenth and Early Twentieth Centuries." In *The Gift of the Land and the Fate of the Canaanites in Jewish Thought*, edited by Katell Berthelot, Joseph E. David, and Marc Hirshman, 230–50. New York: Oxford University Press, 2014.

———. *From Frankfurt to Jerusalem: Isaac Breuer and the History of the Secession Dispute in Modern Jewish Orthodoxy*. Leiden: Brill, 2002.

———. "Rabbi S. R. Hirsch and His Perception of Germany and German Jewry." In *The German-Jewish Experience Revisited*, edited by Steven E. Aschheim and Vivian Liska 207–30. Berlin: De Gruyter, 2015.

Mork, Gordon R. "German Nationalism and Jewish Assimilation: The Bismarck Period." *Leo Baeck Institute Yearbook* 22 (1977): 81–90.

Mosse, George L. *German Jews beyond Judaism*. Cincinnati: Hebrew Union College Press, 1985.

Mosse, Werner E. "From '*Schutzjuden*' to '*Deutsche Staatsbürger Jüdischen Glaubens*': The Long and Bumpy Road of Jewish Emancipation in Germany." In *Paths of Emancipation: Jews, States, and Citizenship*, edited by Pierre Birnbaum and Ira Katznelson, 59–93. Princeton, NJ: Princeton University Press, 1995.

Mosse, Werner E., Arnold Paucker, and Reinhard Rürup, eds. *Revolution and Evolution: 1848 in German-Jewish History*. Tübingen: Mohr Siebeck, 1981.

Nehorai, Michael Z. "A Portion in the World to Come for the Righteous/Sages of the Nations." *Da'at* 50–52 (2003): 97–105. Hebrew.

Nirenberg, David. *Anti-Judaism: The Western Tradition*. New York: W. W. Norton, 2013.

Novak, David. *The Image of the Non-Jew in Judaism*. 2nd ed. Oxford: Littman Library, 2011.

———. "Maimonides' Treatment of Christianity and Its Normative Implications." In Goshen-Gottstein and Korn, *Jewish Theology and World Religions*, 217–33.

Ophir, Adi, and Rosen-Zvi, Ishay. *Goy: Israel's Multiple Others and the Birth of the Gentile*. Oxford University Press, 2018.

Peled, Yoav. "From Theology to Sociology: Bruno Bauer and Karl Marx on the Question of Jewish Emancipation." *History of Political Thought* 13, no. 3 (1992): 463–85.

Pelli, Moshe. *The Age of Haskalah: Studies in Hebrew Literature of the Enlightenment in Germany*. Leiden: Brill, 1979.

Perl, Gil. "Emek ha-Neziv: A Window into the Intellectual Universe of Rabbi Naftali Zvi Yehudah Berlin." PhD diss., Harvard University, 2006.

———. *The Pillar of Volozhin: Rabbi Naftali Zvi Yehuda Berlin and the World of Nineteenth-Century Lithuanian Torah Scholarship*. Boston: Academic Studies Press, 2012.

Perlow, Yaakov. "Rav S. R. Hirsch: The Gaon in Talmud and Mikra." In *The Living Hirschian Legacy*, edited by Eliyahu Glucksman et al., 75–89. New York: Feldheim, 1988.

Petrovsky-Shtern, Yohanan. *Jews in the Russian Army, 1827–1917: Drafted into Modernity*. New York: Cambridge University Press, 2009.

Petuchowski, Jacob J. *Prayerbook Reform in Europe*. New York: World Union for Progressive Judaism, 1968.

Philipson, David. *The Reform Movement in Judaism*. New York: Macmillan, 1931.

Pickle, Joseph W. "Schleiermacher on Judaism." *Journal of Religion* 60, no. 2 (April 1980): 115–37.

Plaut, W. Gunther. *The Rise of Reform Judaism: A Sourcebook of Its European Origins*. New York: World Union for Progressive Judaism, 1963.

Poliakov, Léon. *The Aryan Myth: A History of Racist and Nationalist Ideas in Europe*. Translated by Edmund Howard. New York: Basic Books, 1974.

———. *Histoire de l'antisémitisme: De Voltaire à Wagner*. Paris: Calmann-Lévy, 1968.

Posner, Akiva, and Ernest Freiman. "Rabbi Jacob Ettlinger." In *Guardians of Our Heritage*, edited by Leo Jung, 229–43. New York: Bloch, 1958.

Pulzer, Peter. *Jews and the German State: The Political History of a Minority, 1848–1933*. Detroit: Wayne State University Press, 2003.

Rabbi Jacob Ettlinger of Blessed Memory. Jerusalem, 1972. Hebrew.

Rabinovitch, Nahum. *Darkah shel Torah*. Ma'aleh Adumim: Maaliyot, 1998.

———. *Melummedei Milhamah*. Ma'aleh Adumim: Maaliyot, 1993.

———. *Mesilot Bilvavam*. Ma'aleh Adumim: Maaliyot, 2015.

———. *Shu"t Siah Nahum*. Ma'aleh Adumim: Maaliyot, 2008.

———. "The Way of Torah." *Edah Journal* 3, no. 1 (Tevet 5763 [2003]): 1–34.

Ragins, Sanford. *Jewish Responses to Anti-Semitism in Germany, 1870–1914*. Cincinnati: Hebrew Union College Press, 1980.

Ravitzky, Aviezer. *Messianism, Zionism, and Jewish Religious Radicalism*. Translated by M. Swirsky and J. Chipman. Chicago: University of Chicago Press, 1996.

Reinhard, Kenneth. "The Ethics of the Neighbor: Universalism, Particularism, Exceptionalism." *Journal of Textual Reasoning* 4, no. 1 (2005): 4–7.

Reinharz, Jehuda and Schatzberg, Walter, eds. *The Jewish Response to German Culture: From the Enlightenment to the Second World War*. Hanover, NH: University Press of New England, 1985.

Remer, Gary. "Ha-Me'iri's Theory of Religious Toleration." In *Beyond the Persecuting Society: Religious Toleration before the Enlightenment*, edited by Christian Laursen and Cary J. Nederman, 71–91. Philadelphia: University of Pennsylvania Press, 1998.

Robertson, Ritchie. *The "Jewish Question" in German Literature 1749–1939: Emancipation and Its Discontents.* New York: Oxford University Press, 1999.

Roemer, Nils H. *Jewish Scholarship and Culture in Nineteenth-Century Germany: Between History and Faith.* Madison: University of Wisconsin Press, 2005.

Rose, Sven-Erik. "Lazarus Bendavid's and J. G. Fichte's Kantian Fantasies of Jewish Decapitation in 1793." *Jewish Social Studies* 13, no. 3 (Spring/Summer 2007): 73–102.

Rosenbloom, Noah H. "Critical Evaluations in Mendelsohn of Hamburg's 'Penei Tevel'." In *Migvan: Studies in Hebrew Literature in Honor of Jacob Kabakoff*, edited by Stanley Nash, 367–93. Lod: Habermann Institute for Literary Research, 1988. Hebrew.

———. *Malbim: Exegesis, Philosophy, Science, and Mysticism in the Writings of Rabbi Meir Leibush Malbim.* Jerusalem: Mossad Ha-Rav Kook, 1988. Hebrew.

———. *Tradition in an Age of Reform: The Religious Philosophy of Samson Raphael Hirsch.* Philadelphia: Jewish Publication Society, 1976.

Rotenstreich, Nathan. "For and Against Emancipation: The Bruno Bauer Controversy." *Leo Baeck Institute Yearbook* 4 (1959): 3–36.

———. *Jews and German Philosophy: The Polemics of Emancipation.* New York: Schoken, 1982.

———. *The Recurring Pattern: Studies in Anti-Judaism in Modern Thought.* New York: Horizon Press, 1964.

Rudavsky, David. "Samuel David Luzzatto and Neo-Orthodoxy." *Tradition* 7, no. 3 (Fall 1965): 21–44.

Ruderman, David B. *Early Modern Jewry: A New Cultural History.* Princeton, NJ: Princeton University Press, 2010.

———. *Jewish Thought and Scientific Discovery in Early Modern Europe.* Detroit, MI: Wayne State University Press, 1995.

Rürup, Reinhard. "The Tortuous and Thorny Path to Legal Equality: 'Jew Laws' and Emancipatory Legislation in Germany from the Late Eighteenth Century." *Leo Baeck Institute Yearbook* 31 (1986): 3–33.

Russell, Bertrand. *A History of Western Philosophy.* New York: Simon and Schuster, 1972.

Sacks, Elias. *Moses Mendelssohn's Living Script: Philosophy, Practice, History, Judaism.* Bloomington: Indiana University Press, 2016.

Sagi, Avi. *Jewish Religion after Theology.* Translated by Batya Stein. Boston: Academic Studies Press, 2009.

———. *Judaism: Between Religion and Morality.* Tel Aviv: Hakibbutz Hameuchad, 1998. Hebrew.

Salmon, Yosef. "Christians and Christianity in Halachic Literature from the End of the Eighteenth Century to the Middle of the Nineteenth Century." *Modern Judaism* 33, no. 2 (May 2013): 125–47.

Salmon, Y., A. Ravitzky, and A. Ferziger, eds. *Orthodox Judaism: New Perspectives*. Jerusalem: Magnes Press, 2006. Hebrew.

Samet, Moshe. "The Beginnings of Orthodoxy." *Modern Judaism* 8 (1988): 249–69.

Sarna, Jonathan. *American Judaism: A History*. New Haven, CT: Yale University Press, 2004.

Schacter, Jacob J. "Rabbi Jacob Emden, Sabbatianism, and Frankism: Attitudes toward Christianity in the Eighteenth Century." In Carlebach and Schacter, *New Perspectives*, 393–96.

Schochet, Elijah Judah. *Rabbi Joel Sirkes: His Life, Works and Times*. New York: Feldheim, 1971.

Scholem, Gershom. "Jews and Germans." *Commentary Magazine*, November 1966. Available at the *Commentary* website.

Schorsch, Ismar. *From Text to Context: The Turn to History in Modern Judaism*. Hanover, NH: University Press of New England, 1994.

———. *Jewish Reactions to German Anti-Semitism, 1870–1914*. New York: Columbia University Press, 1972.

———. "On the Father of Neo-Orthodoxy." *Judaism* 26, no. 3 (Summer 1977): 381–83.

Schreiber, Aaron M. "The Hatam Sofer's Nuanced Attitude towards Secular Learning, *Maskilim* and Reformers." *Torah U-Madda Journal* 11 (2002–3): 123–73.

Schüssler Fiorenza, Francis. "Schleiermacher's Understanding of God as Triune." In *The Cambridge Companion to Friedrich Schleiermacher*, edited by Jacqueline Marina, 171–88. New York: Cambridge University Press, 2005.

Schwarz, Moshe. "Jewish Religious Trends Emerging from the Confrontation with German Culture." In *Perspectives of German-Jewish History in the 19th and 20th Century*, edited by Meir Gilon and Hanna Schmorak. Jerusalem: Jerusalem Academic Press, 1971.

Schwarzfuchs, Simon. *Napoleon, the Jews, and the Sanhedrin*. London: Littman Library, 1979.

Sears, David. *Compassion for Humanity in the Jewish Tradition*. Northvale, NJ: Jason Aronson, 1998.

Seidler, Naomi. *Sarah Schenirer and the Bais Yaakov Movement*. Oxford: Littman Library, 2019.

Shapiro, Marc. B. "Aspects of Rabbi Moses Sofer's Intellectual Profile." In *Be'erot Yitzhak: Studies in Memory of Isadore Twersky*, edited by Jay M. Harris, 285–310 Cambridge, MA: Harvard University Press, 2005.

———. *Between the Yeshiva World and Modern Orthodoxy: The Life and Works of Rabbi Jehiel Jacob Weinberg, 1884–1966*. Oxford: Littman Library, 1999.

———. "Rabbi Samson Raphael Hirsch and Friedrich von Schiller." *Torah u-Madda Journal* 15 (2008–9): 172–87.

———. "Rabbi Samson Raphael Hirsch on Jews in a Non-Jewish World." *Hakirah* 27 (Fall 2019): 167–73.

———. "Review Essay: Sociology and Halakha." *Tradition* 27, no. 1 (Fall 1992): 75–85.

———. "Scholars and Friends: Rabbi Jehiel Jacob Weinberg and Professor Samuel Atlas." *Torah U-Madda Journal* 7 (1997): 105–21.

———. "Torah Study on Christmas Eve." *Journal of Jewish Thought and Philosophy* 8 (1999): 319–53.

Shatz, David. "A Jewish Perspective." In *The Oxford Handbook of Religious Diversity*, edited by Chad V. Meister, 365–80. New York: Oxford University Press, 2011.

———. "Morality, Liberalism, and Interfaith Dialogue." In Carlebach and Schacter, *New Perspectives*.

Shmalo, Gamliel. "Orthodox Approaches to Biblical Slavery." *Torah U-Madda Journal* 16 (2012–13): 1–20.

Shohat, Azriel. "The German Jews' Integration within Their Non-Jewish Environment in the First Half of the Eighteenth Century." *Zion* 21 (1956): 207–35. Hebrew.

———. *In Changing Times: Beginnings of the Haskalah among German Jewry*. Jerusalem: Mosad Bialik, 1960. Hebrew.

Silber, Michael K. "Orthodoxy." *The YIVO Encyclopedia of Jews in Eastern Europe*. Available at the YIVO Encyclopedia website, accessed January 4, 2023.

———. "The Emergence of Ultra-Orthodoxy: The Invention of a Tradition." In Wertheim, *Uses of Tradition*, 23–84.

Simon, Ernst. "The Neighbor (Re'a) Whom We Shall Love." In *Modern Jewish Ethics: Theory and Practice*, edited by Marvin Fox, 29–56. Columbus: Ohio State University Press, 1975.

Skloot, Joseph A., "Halakhic Flexibility and Communal Unity: R. Marcus Horowitz and the Schächtfrage." *Modern Judaism* 40, no. 3 (October 2020): 355–75.

Smith, David Charles. "Protestant Anti-Judaism in the German Emancipation Era." *Jewish Social Studies* 36, nos. 3–4 (July–October 1974): 203–19.

Soloveichik, Meir. "To Be German and Jewish: Hermann Cohen and Rabbi Samson Raphael Hirsch." In *Rav Chesed: Essays in Honor of Rabbi Dr. Haskel Lookstein*, edited by Raphael Medoff, vol. 2, 211–34. Jersey City: Ktav, 2009.

Soloveitchik, Haym. "The 'Beit ha-Behirah' of R. Menahem ha-Meiri and Its Fate." In *Asufah le-Yosef*, edited by Y. Ben-Naeh, M. Idel, J. Cohen, and Y. Kaplan, 253–59. Jerusalem: Zalman Shazar Center, 2014. Hebrew.

Sorkin, David. "The Genesis of the Ideology of Emancipation: 1806–1840." *Leo Baeck Institute Yearbook Annual* 32, no. 1 (January 1987): 11–40.

———. "Jews, the Enlightenment and Religious Toleration—Some Reflections." *Leo Baeck Institute Yearbook* 37 (1992): 3–16.

———. *The Religious Enlightenment: Protestants, Jews and Catholics from London to Vienna*. Princeton, NJ: Princeton University Press, 2008.

———. *The Transformation of German Jewry 1780–1840*. Detroit: Wayne State University Press, 1999.

Sorotzkin, David. *Orthodoxy and Modern Disciplination*. Tel Aviv: Kibbutz ha-me'uhad, 2011. Hebrew.

Spitzer, Shlomo, and Chaya-Batya Markovitz, eds. *Rabbi Samson Raphael Hirsch: Bibliography*. Ramat-Gan: Bar-Ilan University, 2003.

———. *The "Sänger Collection": The Catalogue of the German and Hebrew Manuscripts*. Ramat-Gan: Bar-Ilan University, 2004.

Stanislawski, Michael. *Tsar Nicholas I and the Jews: The Transformation of Jewish Society in Russia, 1825–1855*. Philadelphia: Jewish Publication Society of America, 1983.

Stern, Eliyahu. "Genius and Demographics in Modern Jewish History." *Jewish Quarterly Review* 101, no. 3 (Summer 2011): 347–82.

———. *The Genius: Elijah of Vilna and the Making of Modern Judaism*. New Haven, CT: Yale University Press, 2013.

Stern, Fritz. *Gold and Iron: Bismarck, Bleichröder, and the Building of the German Empire*. New York: Vintage, 1979.

Stern, Gregg. *Philosophy and Rabbinic Culture: Jewish Interpretation and Controversy in Medieval Languedoc*. Abingdon, UK: Routledge, 2009.

Stone, Suzanne Last. "Sinaitic and Noahide Law: Legal Pluralism in Jewish Law." *Cardozo Law Review* 12 (1990–91): 1157–71.

———. "Tolerance versus Pluralism in Judaism." *Journal of Human Rights* 2, no. 1 (March 2003): 105–17.

Stromberg, Roland N. *European Intellectual History since 1789*. 6th ed. Englewood Cliffs, NJ: Prentice Hall, 1994.

Sullam, Simon Levis. "Prescribing Toleration at the Paris Sanhedrin (1806–1807)." In *Toleration within Judaism*, edited by Martin Goodman et al., 111–29. Oxford: Littman Library, 2013.

Sungolowsky, Joseph. "Joseph Sinzheim, President of Napoleon's Sanhedrin and the First Chief Rabbi of France." *Midstream* 55, no. 1 (Winter 2009): 16–18.

Tal, Uriel. *Christians and Jews in Germany: Religion, Politics, and Ideology in the Second Reich, 1870–1914*. Translated by Noah J. Jacobs. Ithaca, NY: Cornell University Press, 1975.

Tasch, Roland. *Samson Raphael Hirsch: Jüdische Erfahrungswelten im Historischen Kontext*. Berlin: De Gruyter, 2011.

Thiel, Hans, ed. *Die Samson-Raphael-Hirsch-Schule in Frankfurt am Main: Dokumente, Erinnerungen, Analysen*. Frankfurt: Verlag Waldemar Kramer, 2001.

Traverso, Enzo, *The Jews and Germany: From the "Judeo-German Symbiosis" to the Memory of Auschwitz*. Lincoln: University of Nebraska Press, 1995.

Trepp, Leo. *Die Oldenberger Judenschaft: Bild und Vorbild judischen Seins und Werdens in Deutschland*. Oldenberg: Heinz Holzberg Verlag, 1973.

———. "A Reappraisal of Samson Raphael Hirsch." *CCAR Journal* (Winter 1987): 29–40.

Twersky, Isadore. *A Maimonides Reader*. West Orange: Behrman House, 1972.

Urbach, Ephraim E. "Homilies of the Rabbis on the Prophets of the Nations and the Balaam Narrative." *Tarbiz* 25, no. 3 (April 1956): 272–89. Hebrew.

———. "Humanistic Aspects of Jewish Law." In Urbach, *Collected Writings in Jewish Studies*, edited by R. Brody and M. D. Herr. Jerusalem: Magnes Press, 1999.

Vargon, Shmuel. *Shmuel David Luzzatto: Moderate Criticism in Biblical Exegesis*. Ramat-Gan: Bar-Ilan, 2013. Hebrew.

Vital, David. *A People Apart: The Jews in Europe, 1789–1939*. New York: Oxford University Press, 1999.

Von Treitschke, Heinrich. "A Word about Our Jewry." In Mendes-Flohr and Reinharz, *Jew in the Modern World*, 319–22.

Wallach, Shalom Meir. *Penine Ha-Rashar Hirsch*. Bene Berak: Tevunah, 5769.

Weinberg, Joanna. "A Humanist in the Kloyz: New Perspectives on the Maharal of

Prague and Jacques Bongars." *Journal of the History of Ideas* 77, no. 4 (October 2016): 521–37.

Weiss, John. *Ideology of Death: Why the Holocaust Happened in Germany*. Chicago: Ivan R. Dee, 1996.

Welch, Claude, ed. *God and Incarnation in Mid-Nineteenth Century German Theology*. New York: Oxford University Press, 1965.

Wertheimer, Jack. *The Uses of Tradition*. New York: Jewish Theological Seminary, 1992.

Wiener, Max. *Abraham Geiger and Liberal Judaism: The Challenge of the Nineteenth Century*. Translated by Ernst J. Schlochauer. Philadelphia: Jewish Publication Society, 1962.

———. "The Conception of Mission in Traditional Judaism." *YIVO Annual of Jewish Social Science* 2–3 (1947–48): 9–24.

Wiese, Christian. *Challenging Colonial Discourse: Jewish Studies and Protestant Theology in Wilhelmine Germany*. Translated by Barbara Harshav and Christian Wiese. Leiden: Brill, 2005.

Wiese, Christian, and M. Urban. *German-Jewish Thought between Politics and Religion*. Berlin: De Gruyter, 2012.

Wistrich, Robert S. *The Jews of Vienna in the Age of Franz Joseph*. Oxford: Littman Library, 2006.

———. "Zionism and Its Jewish 'Assimilationist' Critics (1897–1948)." *Jewish Social Studies* New Series 4, no. 2 (Winter 1998): 59–111.

Wolfson, Elliot R. *Venturing Beyond: Law and Morality in Kabbalistic Mysticism*. New York: Oxford University Press, 2006,

Wyschogrod, Michael. "A Jewish Perspective on Incarnation." *Modern Theology* 12, no. 2 (April 1996): 195–209.

Yaron, Zvi, ed. *Mishnato shel ha-Rav Kook*. Jerusalem: n. p., 1974.

Yedidya, Asaf. "Abraham Berliner and the Making of Orthodox *Wissenschaft*." In *Jewish Historiography between Past and Future*, edited by P. Mendes-Flohr, R. Livneh-Freudenthal, and G. Miron, 77–90. Berlin: De Gruyter, 2019.

———. "Orthodox Reactions to *'Wissenschaft des Judentums'*," *Modern Judaism* 30, no. 1 (February 2010): 69–94.

Yovel, Yirmiyahu. *Dark Riddle: Hegel, Nietzsche, and the Jews*. University Park: Penn State University Press, 1998.

Yuval, Israel J. *Two Nations in Your Womb: Perceptions of Jews and Christians in Late Antiquity and the Middle Ages*. Translated by Barbara Harshav and Jonathan Chipman. Berkeley: University of California Press, 2006.

Zalcman, Lawrence. "Christians, Noserim, and Nebuchadnezzar's Daughter." *Jewish Quarterly Review*, n. s., 81, nos. 3–4 (January–April 1991): 411–26.

Zinberg, Israel. *A History of Jewish Literature*. Vol. 10. Translated by Bernard Martin. New York: Ktav, 1977.

Zucker, Stanley. "Theodore Mommsen and Antisemitism." *Leo Baeck Institute Yearbook* 17, no. 1 (1972): 237–41.

Zur, Yaakov. "German-Jewish Orthodoxy and Its Attitude toward Internal Organization and Zionism (1896–1911)." PhD diss., Tel-Aviv University, 1982. Hebrew.

Index